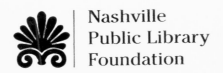

The Cambridge Companion to Shakespearean Tragedy

The *Companion* acquaints the student reader with the forms, contexts, and critical and theatrical lives of the ten plays considered to be Shakespeare's tragedies. Shakespearean tragedy is a highly complex and demanding theatre genre, but the thirteen essays, written by leading scholars in Britain and North America, are clear, concise, and informative. They address the ways in which Shakespearean tragedy originated, developed, and diversified, as well as how it has fared on stage, as text, and in criticism. Topics covered include the literary precursors of Shakespearean tragedies (medieval, classical, and contemporary), cultural backgrounds (political, religious, social, and psychological), and the sub-genres of Shakespeare's tragedy (love tragedy, revenge tragedy, and classical tragedy), as well as the critical and theatrical receptions of the plays. The book examines the four major tragedies and, in addition, *Titus Andronicus, Romeo and Juliet, Julius Caesar, Antony and Cleopatra, Coriolanus,* and *Timon of Athens.*

Claire McEachern is Associate Professor at the Department of English, University of California, Los Angeles. She is the author of *The Poetics of English Nationhood, 1512–1612* (Cambridge, 1996), and co-editor (with Debora Shuger) of *Religion and Culture in the English Renaissance* (Cambridge, 1997).

THE CAMBRIDGE
COMPANION TO
SHAKESPEAREAN
TRAGEDY

EDITED BY

CLAIRE McEACHERN

CAMBRIDGE
UNIVERSITY PRESS

PUBLISHED BY THE PRESS SYNDICATE OF THE UNIVERSITY OF CAMBRIDGE
The Pitt Building, Trumpington Street, Cambridge CB2 IRP, United Kingdom

CAMBRIDGE UNIVERSITY PRESS
The Edinburgh Building, Cambridge, CB2 2RU, UK
40 West 20th Street, New York, NY 10011-4211, USA
477 Williamstown Road, Port Melbourne, VIC 3207, Australia
Ruiz de Alarcón 13, 28014 Madrid, Spain
Dock House, The Waterfront, Cape Town 8001, South Africa

http://www.cambridge.org

© Cambridge University Press 2002

First published 2002

Printed in the United Kingdom at the University Press, Cambridge

Typeface Sabon 10/13 pt   *System* LATEX 2$_\varepsilon$ [TB]

A catalogue record for this book is available from the British Library

Library of Congress Cataloguing in Publication data

The Cambridge Companion to Shakespearean Tragedy / edited by Claire McEachern.
p.   cm. – (Cambridge Companions to Literature)
Includes bibliographical references and index.
ISBN 0 521 79009 3 – ISBN 0 521 79359 9 (pb.)
1. Shakespeare, William, 1564–1616 – Tragedies – Handbooks, manuals, etc.
2. Tragedy – Handbooks, manuals, etc.
1. McEachern, Claire Elizabeth, 1963– II. Series.
PR2983.C28   2002
822.3″3 – dc21   2002067262

ISBN 0 521 79009 3 hardback
ISBN 0 521 79359 9 paperback

CONTENTS

CONTENTS

ILLUSTRATIONS

CONTRIBUTORS

CATHERINE BATES, University of Warwick

CATHERINE BELSEY, University of Cardiff

DAVID BEVINGTON, University of Chicago

HUSTON DIEHL, University of Iowa

R. A. FOAKES, University of California, Los Angeles

MICHAEL HATTAWAY, University of Sheffield

BARBARA HODGDON, Drake University

COPPÉLIA KAHN, Brown University

TOM MCALINDON, University of Hull

RUSS MCDONALD, University of North Carolina, Greensboro

GAIL PASTER, George Washington University

MICHAEL WARREN, University of California, Santa Cruz

R. N. WATSON, University of California, Los Angeles

The Cambridge Companion to Shakespearean Tragedy seeks to acquaint the undergraduate reader with the forms, contexts, kinds, and critical and theatrical lives of the ten plays we consider Shakespeare's tragedies: *Titus Andronicus, Romeo and Juliet, Hamlet, Othello, King Lear, Macbeth, Julius Caesar, Antony and Cleopatra, Coriolanus,* and *Timon of Athens.* The following thirteen essays address the ways in which Shakespearean tragedy originated, developed, and diversified, as well as how it has fared on stage, on the page, and in critical history.

The first four essays take up the forms and definitions of the genre which Shakespeare inherits and develops. Tom McAlindon introduces the models of tragedy that Shakespeare had to work with, and by which he has been evaluated; Russ McDonald reviews the rhetorical resources which fuel Shakespeare's tragic voice; David Bevington undertakes a holistic account of Shakespeare's repeated revisitations of the form throughout his career (often in plays not considered tragedies), and Michael Warren provides an account of the curious nature of the material texts on which critical castles are built. The four essays which follow treat the Tudor–Stuart political and social identities which inform these plays. Huston Diehl considers the religious cultures of Shakespeare's moment, and Michael Hattaway, the political. Catherine Belsey introduces us to the early modern family, and Gail Paster to the mysterious realm of the early modern body. The next three essays, on 'themes', address traditional sub-genres of Shakespearean tragedy – the plays of revenge and ambition, love, and classical history – albeit from new perspectives. R. N. Watson re-evaluates the contemporary historical and philosophical understandings of the revenge form; Catherine Bates explores the paradoxes of love and loss that tragedy forces, and Coppélia Kahn renders the way in which early modern understandings of classical civilization inform the texture of the five Greco-Roman plays. The final two pieces, on critical and theatrical fortunes, treat the ways in which reading and playing have shaped our experience of these plays. R. A. Foakes traces the critical categories which Shakespearean tragedy helped to engender, as well as its fortunes therein, and, finally, Barbara Hodgdon demonstrates, in her study of the multiple theatrical lives of *Antony and Cleopatra*, just how much performance identities should and do shape our experience of any given play.

While this book will profit from being read sequentially, each essay is designed to be a self-contained study of its object. With the exception of the last essay, I have avoided a chapter-per-play approach; thus the reader will encounter different plays in different lights and from different perspectives (*Titus Andronicus*, for instance, receives consideration in terms of the family, revenge tragedy, and classical models). At the same time, care has been taken to provide sustained coverage of each tragedy somewhere in the volume (the index reveals these concentrations). This prismatic design, in which a given play appears from multiple vantage points, is intended to avoid the restriction of the identity of any one play to any particular critical category or meaning, and urge the reader to the juxtapositions of an organic and cross-referenced critical appreciation.

I wish to thank the research staffs of the Huntington Library and the Shakespeare Centre Library for their assistance in procuring illustrations, and their institutions for permission to reproduce the photographs which accompany chapters 4 and 13. I also wish to thank Sarah Stanton of Cambridge University Press for her guidance in producing this volume.

Act, scene, and line references to Shakespeare's plays are to the volumes of the New Cambridge series.

Claire McEachern
University of California, Los Angeles

CHRONOLOGY

Dates given for plays are of first performance unless otherwise specified; most of these dates are approximate and those cited in individual chapters of the *Companion* may differ. For a fuller record of plays in the period, see the *Cambridge Companion to Renaissance Drama*, ed. Braunmuller and Hattaway.

1564	Shakespeare born in Stratford-upon-Avon
1566	Red Lion playhouse opens
1576	The Theatre opens
1577	Curtain playhouse opens; Blackfriars Theatre opens
1581	*Seneca His Tenne Tragedies* (trans. Newton) published
1582	Shakespeare marries Anne Hathaway; the licence is issued on November 27 and the first child (Susanna) is born six months later
1585	Shakespeare's twin son and daughter, Hamnet and Judith, born
c. 1586	Shakespeare leaves Stratford; nothing is known for certain of his life between this date and 1592, by which time he is in London
1587	Rose playhouse opens. Kyd, *The Spanish Tragedy*; Marlowe, *Tamburlaine* 1 and 2
1590	Anon., *King Leir*
c. 1591	Shakespeare, *Titus Andronicus*
c. 1592	Marlowe, *Doctor Faustus, Edward II*
1593	Marlowe, *The Massacre at Paris*
c. 1594	Around this time Shakespeare becomes a sharer in the Chamberlain's Men. Swan Theatre built
c. 1595	Shakespeare, *Romeo and Juliet*
c. 1599	Globe Theatre opens; Shakespeare's principal clown, Will Kempe, leaves the company; his successor is Robert Armin. Shakespeare, *Julius Caesar*
1600	Fortune Theatre built. Shakespeare, *Hamlet*

1603   Queen Elizabeth dies and is succeeded by James I, who takes the acting companies under royal patronage; Shakespeare's company, the Chamberlain's Men, becomes the King's Men. Jonson, *Sejanus*

1605   Shakespeare, *King Lear, Timon of Athens, Othello*

1606   Marston, *The Revenger's Tragedy*; Shakespeare, *Macbeth, Antony and Cleopatra*

c. 1608   Shakespeare, *Coriolanus*

c. 1610   Beaumont and Fletcher, *The Maid's Tragedy*

1611   Jonson, *Catiline*; Tourneur, *The Atheist's Tragedy*

1612   Webster, *The White Devil*

1614   Webster, *The Duchess of Malfi*

1616   Shakespeare dies in Stratford

1623   Publication of the First Folio, the first collected edition of Shakespeare's plays

ABBREVIATIONS

Shakespeare's works

Cor.	*Coriolanus*	*Mac.*	*Macbeth*
Ham.	*Hamlet*	*Oth.*	*Othello*
H5	*King Henry the Fifth*	*R3*	*King Richard the Third*
JC	*Julius Caesar*	*Rom.*	*Romeo and Juliet*
Lear	*King Lear*	*Tim.*	*Timon of Athens*
Luc.	*The Rape of Lucrece*	*Tit.*	*Titus Andronicus*

General

F	Folio	Q2	Second quarto
Q1	First quarto	s.d.	stage direction

I

TOM McALINDON

What is a Shakespearean tragedy?

'Double, double toil and trouble . . .'
(*Mac.* 4.1.10)

I

An eminent Shakespearean scholar famously remarked that there is no such thing as Shakespearean Tragedy: there are only Shakespearean tragedies. Attempts (he added) to find a formula which fits every one of Shakespeare's tragedies and distinguishes them collectively from those of other dramatists invariably meet with little success. Yet when challenging one such attempt he noted its failure to observe what he termed 'an essential part of the [Shakespearean] tragic pattern';[1] which would seem to imply that these plays do have some shared characteristics peculiar to them.

Nevertheless, objections to comprehensive definitions of 'Shakespearean Tragedy' are well founded. Such definitions tend to ignore the uniqueness of each play and the way it has been structured and styled to fit the particular source-narrative. More generally, they can obscure the fact that what distinguishes Shakespeare's tragedies from everyone else's and prompts us to consider them together are not so much common denominators but rather the power of Shakespeare's language, his insight into character, and his dramaturgical inventiveness.[2]

Uneasiness with definitions of Shakespearean tragedy is of a kind with the uneasiness generated by definitions of tragedy itself; these often give a static impression of the genre and incline towards prescriptiveness, ignoring the fact that 'genres are in a constant state of transmutation'.[3] There is, however, a simple argument to be made in defence of genre criticism, namely that full understanding and appreciation of any piece of literature requires knowledge of its contexts, literary as well as intellectual and socio-political: in its relation to the author and his work, context informs, assists, stimulates, provokes. Thus knowledge of generic context helps us recognize not only what authors inherit but also what they invent and intend. So, too, familiarity with Shakespeare's tragedies as a whole enhances understanding of the meanings and the special nature of any one of them.

As practised in Renaissance England and in classical Greece and Rome, tragedy is an intense exploration of suffering and evil focused on the experience of an exceptional individual, distinguished by rank or character or both. Typically, it presents a steep fall from prosperity to misery and untimely death, a great change occasioned or accompanied by conflict between the tragic character and some superior power. It might be said, therefore, that conflict and change – the first intense if not violent, the second extreme – together constitute the essence of tragedy.

In his seminal account of the subject, Aristotle (fourth century BC) said that the success of a tragedy depends on its capacity to excite pity and fear, thereby effecting a catharsis of these emotions (*The Poetics*, chap. 6). Twentieth-century commentators have interpreted this as referring to the contrary responses of attraction and repulsion: pity draws us sympathetically to the protagonist, regretting his or her suffering as unjust or disproportionate; fear denotes an attitude to the protagonist of dissociation and judgement and acknowledges the rightness of what has happened. What Aristotle meant by catharsis has been the subject of much disagreement, but in contemporary usage the term usually implies a state of mind in which the powerful and conflicting emotions generated by the spectacle of great suffering are reconciled and transcended through artistic representation, so that a condition of exultant but grave understanding remains.

This rephrasing of Aristotle in conflictual terms may be ascribed to the fact that since the nineteenth century, when the nature of tragedy began to be studied as never before, the overriding emphasis has been on conflict, and the concomitant notions of contradiction, ambivalence, and paradox, as the genre's major characteristic. It is an emphasis which has been due entirely to the philosophers G. W. Hegel (1770–1831) and F. Nietzsche (1844–1900). According to Hegel, the characteristic conflict in tragedy is not between ethical right and wrong but between the personal embodiments of a universal ethical power, both of whom push their rightful claim to the point where it encroaches on the other's right and so becomes wrongful. The (usually violent) resolution of this conflict restores a condition of natural justice and confirms the existence of a just and divine world order.[4] Nietzsche rejected the idea of such an order, but he too saw 'contrariety at the center of the universe' and tragedy as a process involving the conflict and reconciliation of opposites: for him, these opposites are Apollo and Dionysus, the first symbolizing reason, control, and art, the second, passionate destructive energy, orgiastic abandon, and the self-renewing force of life itself.[5] Both thinkers were inspired by the pre-Socratic philosophers (sixth to fifth centuries BC) who held that the natural world is a system of 'concordant discord' animated by sympathetic and antipathetic forces personified as Love and Strife (War).[6] Despite substantial differences between their theories of tragedy, both Hegel and Nietzsche were prompted by their attraction to pre-Socratic cosmology to locate tragic events in a natural dialectic of destruction and renewal, and so to emphasize an ultimately positive dimension to tragedy. Perhaps, however, because they were so obsessed with Greek tragedy and Greek culture generally, both philosophers failed to discover that the essentially paradoxical view of nature fathered by the pre-Socratics was embedded in all Shakespeare's tragedies and was central to the intellectual inheritance of his contemporaries.

A. C. Bradley (1851–1935) rightly criticized Hegel for underestimating the action of moral evil and the final sense of waste evident in most tragedies;[7] but he concurred with him by making conflict a major theme in his own hugely influential account of Shakespearean tragedy. He contended, however, that the distinguishing feature of Shakespearean tragedy is not conflict between the tragic hero and someone else, or even between contending groups, but rather conflict within the hero, who is a man divided against himself. Bradley also adapted Hegel's dualist metaphysics, arguing that Shakespearean tragedy demonstrates the existence of an ultimate power which reacts violently against evil but in the process contradictorily and mysteriously destroys much that is good as well.[8]

In later versions of the conflict theory, tragedy (both Shakespearean and non-Shakespearean) has been identified as a genre which projects mutually incompatible world views or value systems;[9] and then again as one which exposes 'the eternal contradiction between man's weakness and his courage, his stupidity and his magnificence, his frailty and his strength'.[10] Shakespeare's tragedies have been seen as characterized by a disturbing conjunction of the lofty and the comic–grotesque, something which emphasizes the coexistence in the hero of nobility and pettiness and reinforces a largely pessimistic view of the way in which nature produces and destroys greatness.[11] The tragedies of both Shakespeare and his contemporaries have also been read in the light of Marx's materialist Hegelianism as embodying the contradictions and incipient collapse of feudalism and heralding the bourgeois revolution of the seventeenth century.[12]

II

The models of tragedy which influenced Shakespeare and his contemporaries were not Greek (the great tragedies of Aeschylus, Sophocles, and Euripides) but Roman and late-medieval: that is, the sensational and highly rhetorical plays of Seneca (apparently written for recitation), and the narrative verse tragedies popularized in England by John Lydgate's fifteenth-century *The Fall of Princes* and by the sixteenth-century, multi-authored collection known as *The Mirror for Magistrates* (1559). Written in the shadow of the emperor Nero, Seneca's tragedies are characterized by a preoccupation with horrific crimes and the tyrannical abuse of power. His protagonists are driven to murder by inordinate passions such as vengeful rage, lust, and sexual jealousy; most of them, too, unlike most of Shakespeare's heroes, are conscious wrong-doers. But they are driven by passions which seem humanly uncontrollable (ghosts, Furies, and meddlesome divinities spur them on) and are often cursed by the consequences of evils rooted in the past; thus despite their energies and their wilfulness they seem more the victims than the responsible agents of their fate. Another common characteristic is their compellingly assertive sense of selfhood; this may exemplify the Stoic notion of an indestructible personal identity (as in *Hercules Oetaeus*) but more often it is a perversion of that ideal (as in *Thyestes* and *Medea*). Seneca's tragic heroes and heroines see their crimes as defiant expressions of self and unfold this impassioned selfhood in long and rhetorically elaborate monologues and soliloquies. Like their victims, they regularly hyperbolize their feelings by projecting them on to the 'sympathetic universe' and by calling in rage, grief, or despair for nature to revolt against earth, for primal Chaos to come again.[13]

The Fall of Princes narratives shared Seneca's fascination with power and its abuse. Like him too, but far more insistently, they emphasized the insecurity of high places and the rule of fortune or mutability in worldly affairs: indeed, in these narratives the notion of tragedy is almost reducible to that of catastrophic change. Moreover, fortune and its capricious turns are now explained in Christian terms as a consequence of the Adamic Fall, which brought change and misery into the world. Thus the treacheries of fortune are afflictions which everyone is liable to, irrespective of his or her moral condition. The main concern of the *Mirror* authors, however, was political as well as ethical: to show that fortune is an instrument of divine justice exacting retribution for the crimes of tyrannical rulers and over-ambitious or rebellious subjects.

Tragic theory in the sixteenth century consisted mainly of a set of prescriptive rules derived from Senecan and Fall of Princes practice. Critics such as Puttenham and Sidney emphasized that tragedy is 'high and excellent' in subject and style, does not meddle with base (i.e., domestic and plebeian) matters or mingle kings and clowns. It uncovers hidden corruption and shows the characteristic conduct and the deserved punishments of tyrants. Dealing with 'the dolefull falls of infortunate & afflicted Princes', it 'teacheth the uncertainty of this world, and upon how weak foundations gilden roofs are builded'. It excites feelings of 'admiration and commiseration', wonder and pity.[14]

Shakespeare's affinities with Senecan and Fall of Princes tragedy, and with sixteenth-century tragic theory, will be apparent as we proceed. But we must begin by emphasizing difference. Like almost all contemporary playwrights who wrote tragedies for the public stage, Shakespeare departed strikingly from classical practice and Elizabethan theory by his inclusion of comic elements and plebeian characters. This characteristic was due to the influence of the native dramatic tradition (the mysteries and the moralities), which habitually conjoined the sublime and the homely and made its devils and villains either ludicrous fools or mocking comedians. It seems unlikely, however, that Shakespeare's inclusion of the comic in his tragedies signifies a reluctant pandering to popular taste; although he never overtly justifies this practice, the self-reflexive aspects of his art show that early in his career he reflected deeply on the nature of tragedy and evolved a sound rationale for his mixed practice. A Midsummer Night's Dream and Romeo and Juliet, written at approximately the same time, and strikingly similar in style and plot (young love rebelling against patriarchal control), insinuate that in real life the comic is always on the verge of the tragic, and vice versa, and that comedy and tragedy must acknowledge that fact by the controlled inclusion of their generic opposite. Theseus's reaction to Bottom's comical tragedy – 'How shall we find the concord of this discord?' (5.1.60) – draws attention to the extraordinarily mixed nature of A Midsummer Night's Dream itself and implies by its phrasing that justification for the mixed mode will be found in the correspondence of the play's art to nature – that unstable order of concordant discord (or discordant concord) constituted of opposites (the four elements, qualities, and humours) whose changing relationships are governed by Love and Strife. In Romeo and Juliet, what seems like a romantic comedy in the making suddenly hurtles towards tragedy with the violent death of the great jester, Mercutio; for this defiantly unclassical procedure Friar Lawrence's discourse on the contrarious and paradoxical dynamics of nature offers a lengthy if indirect justification (2.2.1–30).

As well as serving to extend the scope of tragedy beyond anything attempted in Greece or Rome, Shakespeare's comic element functions as a safety valve forestalling the kind of inappropriate laughter that scenes of great tension and high passion are likely to provoke.[15] Comedy is woven into the fabric of the drama, too, being psychologically consistent with the satiric, mocking, or deranged aspects of the tragic and villainous characters, and functioning always as thematic variation and ironic counterpoint in relation to the tragic narrative. It may even (as in *King Lear*) intensify the effect of heroic suffering.

A comic safety-valve was particularly desirable, for Shakespeare not only followed Senecan tradition by focusing on passion-driven protagonists but also departed from classical practice by presenting scenes of violent passion onstage instead of confining them to narrative report in the classical manner. Comic incident provided much needed relief from the kind of spectacular scenes in which his plays abound, scenes where rage and hatred, long festering or suddenly erupting, explode in physical conflict and bloodshed. From the beginning (in *Titus Andronicus*, *Romeo and Juliet*, and *Julius Caesar*), Shakespeare sought to present in the opening scene a state of conflict either between the protagonist and his community, or between two sections of the community (one associated with the protagonist, the other with his chief antagonist); and as Bradley intimated, these conflicts relate to a conflict of loyalties, values, or conscience within the protagonist himself.

Where Shakespearean tragedy seems most obviously related to the Fall of Princes tradition, and to Elizabethan theorizing on the genre, is in the intensity with which it focuses on the phenomenon of change. But change here is not just one of worldly fortunes; it is above all else interpersonal, moral, and psychological change. An essential part of the hero's experience is the horrified discovery that the world he knows and values, the people he loves and trusts, are changing or have changed utterly. He feels cheated and betrayed 'to the very heart of loss'.

Hamlet expresses his sense of overwhelming change in eloquently cosmic terms: '[T]his goodly frame, the earth, seems to me a sterile promontory. This most excellent canopy, the air, look you ... this majestical roof fretted with golden fire – why, it appears no other thing to me than a foul and pestilent congregation of vapours' (2.2.282–6). Based on the four elements, the imagistic pattern here shows that Hamlet construes change in terms of the premodern model of contrarious nature; in consequence, he tends to see change antithetically, from one extreme to the other. And this mode of thinking is entirely characteristic of the tragedies. The great storm passages in *Julius Caesar*, *Othello*, and *King Lear*, where 'the conflicting elements' (*Tim.* 4.3.231) are thrown into wild disorder, function as central symbols for a pervasive sense of violent change and confusion, a technique reinforced by sustained use of elemental imagery elsewhere in each play. Whereas Seneca's tragedies invoked a general correspondence between disorder in the human and the natural world, in Shakespeare's tragedies the instabilities, ambiguities, and contradictions (as well as the fruitful harmonies) of human nature and history are precisely coextensive with those of nature.[16]

The extent to which the principle of polarized transformation affects Shakespeare's tragedies can be gauged if we consider the link and parallels between his first and his last tragedy. In *Titus Andronicus* (4.4.62–8) a comparison is made with the historical hero of *Coriolanus*, and for obvious reasons. In each case Rome suddenly becomes so hateful to its great champion that he joins forces with its enemies. Identified during the Renaissance as the archetypal city of order and civility, and associated specifically with law and oratory, Rome becomes in *Titus* a 'wilderness of tigers' where justice is mocked and the pleading tongue ignored or brutally silenced; and this decline into barbarism is symbolized by the marriage of the Roman emperor to Tamora, queen of the Goths. As in *Coriolanus*, too, it is apparent that the disaster which befalls Rome stems from the fact that its respect for the humane qualities which underpin its civility is no greater than – is in fact dependent on – its famed regard for martial valour. Each play depicts the collapse of an order in which these ethical opposites have hitherto been kept in balance; in the elemental terms used throughout *Coriolanus*, fire, signifying martial rage, eclipses water, signifying pity: 'I tell you, he doth sit in gold, his eye / Red as 'twould burn Rome' (5.1.64–5).

Transformation of the community and its representative hero are intimately and causally connected. But the overriding emphasis is on that of the hero: it is the primary source of that 'woe and wonder' which Shakespeare acknowledges at the close of *Hamlet* to be the characteristic emotional effect of tragedy. In play after play, the extreme and unexpected nature of the change which overtakes the hero is underlined by the bewildered comments of those who know him best. And even the unreflective Coriolanus identifies this personal transformation as a universal propensity in nature. In a world of 'slippery turns', he muses, 'Friends now fast sworn, / Whose double bosoms seem to wear one heart... break out / To bitterest enmity', while 'fellest foes... by some chance, / Some trick not worth an egg, shall grow dear friends':

> So with me.
> My birthplace hate I, and my love's upon
> This enemy town.   (4.4.12–24)

Because the transformed hero is driven to act with the utmost brutality against one or more of those to whom he is bound by the closest ties, some are inclined nowadays to conclude that his alleged nobility is being exposed as superficial or in some sense inauthentic. Such a conclusion implies that the pity, wonder, and fear which the plays provoke in performance are symptoms of sentimental misapprehension on the part of the audience; it rules out the possibility of seeing the fall of the hero as genuinely tragic.

Behind Shakespeare's delineation of the hero's moral fall lies a conviction that 'In men as in a rough-grown grove remain / Cave-keeping evils that obscurely sleep' (*Luc.* 1249–50). One might regard this conviction as an essentialist evasion of such questions as historical contingency and the effects of cultural conditioning on character. Othello's murder of Desdemona, for example, might be explained solely in terms of his own particular make-up and unusual situation: a proud, middle-aged African warrior, married to a beautiful young Venetian lady, socially and sexually insecure, and terrified by the humiliating thought of cuckoldry. But there is quiet play in *Othello* on the relation between the words 'general' and 'particular', and it has the effect of hinting that 'the General' is not just a uniquely flawed stranger ('an erring barbarian') but a representative human being as well; such hints are reinforced by Iago's reminder that 'there's many a beast in a populous city, / And many a civil monster' (4.1.61–2). When the mad Ophelia says, 'We know what we are, but know not what we may be' (4.5.44), she is recalling not only the baker's daughter who became an owl but also the refined prince of noble mind who killed her father and contemptuously lugged his guts into the neighbour room; and who himself had reminded her father that 'it was a brute part' (*Ham.* 3.2.101) of the 'gentle Brutus' (*JC* 1.2.71) that killed his friend in the Capitol. The notion of cave-keeping evils in every human being was one which Shakespeare clearly took for granted.

And the cave-keeping evil can emerge with shocking abruptness. The sheer speed with which Othello's love and nobility are turned to hatred and baseness is sometimes taken as incontrovertible proof that both (if genuine at all) were exceptionally fragile. But with Shakespeare the speed of the hero's transformation is a theatrical device emphasizing both the extremity of the change and the vulnerable nature of all love and all nobility, indeed of all human worth. France observes in amazement that Lear's affection for his favourite daughter turns by way of 'the dragon...wrath' to black hatred in a 'trice of time' (*Lear* 1.1.116, 210); and concerning Coriolanus, suddenly 'grown from man to dragon', Sicinius asks: 'Is't possible that so short a time can alter the condition of a man?' (*Cor.* 5.4.7–8).

III

Shakespearean tragedy is centrally concerned with the destruction of human greatness embodied in individuals endowed with 'sovereignty of nature' (*Cor.* 4.7.35): men who are instinctively referred to as 'noble' (in the moral or characterological sense) by those who know them, even their enemies. However, what constitutes true nobility in action invariably proves problematic for the hero, especially when he becomes entangled in the ethical contradictions associated with the notion of 'honour'. Shakespeare habitually exposes to ironic critique a conception of nobility – and so of honour – which is based exclusively on individualist self-assertion and warlike valour; nobility so conceived is implicitly equated with potential barbarism, a denaturing of the self. The tragedies encode an ideal of true nobility that was entirely familiar to his audience. Its origins lie in the humanist notion of an educated aristocracy as delineated in Sir Thomas Elyot's *The Governor* (1531) and Baldassare Castiglione's *The Courtier* (1528); in the chivalric ideal of the knight – especially as interpreted by Chaucer in *The Knight's Tale* – as both valorous and compassionate; and in the classical ideal of the soldier–statesman, everywhere implicit as a standard of judgement in Plutarch's *Lives of the Noble Grecians and Romanes* (trans. North, 1579) and embodied in his characterization of Pericles. The common factor in this long and mutating tradition is the assumption that although the nobility as a class are soldiers by profession, the complete nobleman is one who excels in the arts of both war and peace: he is skilful with sword and tongue and unites in his character the qualities we designate as 'masculine' and 'feminine'. Shakespeare articulates this ideal in both *1 Henry VI* (describing the Duke of Bedford) – 'A braver soldier never couchèd lance; / A gentler heart did never sway in court' (3.6.20–1) – and *Richard II* (describing Richard's father) – 'In war was never lion raged more fierce, / In peace was never gentle lamb more mild / Than was that young and princely gentleman' (2.1.173–5). Like Chaucer in *The Knight's Tale*, Shakespeare sometimes associates the dual nature of the aristocratic hero with the myth of Mars and Venus; and he does so because of that myth's well-known interpretation as an allegory of nature's concordant discord. Like Chaucer, too, he likes to play on the social and behavioural meanings of the word 'gentle' as a reminder that a fiery spirit is only half of what is expected in a princely gentleman.

The villain–hero of *Richard III* is by his own admission a man only 'half made up', framed by nature for 'Grim-visaged war' and not for love (1.1.9–21); the other tragic protagonists have passionate natures capable not only of heroic wrath and striving ambition but also of great love, and consequently of intense suffering: symptomatically, the first of them (Titus) is a grieving father who 'hath more scars of sorrow in his heart / Than foeman's marks upon his battered shield' (*Tit.* 4.1.126–7).[17] The hero's fall involves a self-betrayal or loss of identity which constitutes a breakdown in the balance of a richly endowed nature, one in which feeling is so powerful that it is never far from the point of destructive excess. It is this nature which gives rise to the notion that what makes the tragic protagonists great is also what destroys them; 'strengths by strengths do fail', says Aufidius, struggling to understand Caius Martius Coriolanus (*Cor.* 4.7.55), the man who has the god of war and wrath inscribed in his name. Others may give these characters prudent advice on how to avoid impending disaster, but Romeo's answer to such advice is telling: 'Thou canst not speak of what thou dost not feel' (3.3.64).

Loosely speaking, then, anger and ambition (including pride, a sense of honour, and the desire for glory) and, on the other hand, love and grief, are the passions whose overflow brings disaster; and it should be stressed that the first pair are to be seen initially in as positive a light as the second. Following the Stoic philosophers of old, Elizabethan moralists defined anger as a brief madness; but the 'noble anger' which Lear invokes (2.4.269) is a traditional feature of the hero, being symptomatic of courage and a sense of both justice and personal worth. The concept of noble anger also points to the affinity between tragic and epic or heroic literature: 'the wrath of Achilles' is the subject of Homer's *Iliad,* it drives the action of Seneca's *Troas* in the person of Achilles's avenging son Pyrrhus, and Pyrrhus is a character with whom Hamlet consciously identifies; indeed Reuben Brower has claimed that 'all tragic heroes in European literature are measured against Achilles'.[18] As for ambition, the dangers to society which its unbridled forms constituted was a familiar subject in Shakespeare's England; but equally commonplace was the notion that 'ambition [is] the soldier's virtue' (*Ant.* 3.1.22–3; cf. *Oth.* 3.3.355).

In these attitudes to passion we are confronted with a mindset, characteristic of the period and well fitted to tragedy, which greatly admires and greatly fears excess: where a soldier can be praised because 'his captain's heart... burst[s] the buckles on his breast' (*Ant.* 1.1.6–8) and condemned because he 'cannot / Buckle his distempered cause within the belt of rule' (*Mac.* 5.2.15); where lovers who defy society are indicted of blind folly and honoured as 'pure gold' because they show that love of its very nature transcends limit (*Rom.* 2.1.175–7, 5.3.298). Othello's claim that he was vulnerable to Iago and his message of hatred because he 'loved not wisely but too well' has been viewed with disdain by many critics. If it merits disdain, however, so too does the claim of Timon, the great philanthropist whose boundless kindness undoes him and turns his love of his fellow-men into a raging hatred: 'unwisely, not ignobly, have I given'. But a cynical response to Timon's claim is precluded by the compassionate exclamation which his change inspires in his long-suffering steward: 'Poor honest lord, brought low by his own heart, / Undone by goodness!' (4.2.37–8).

Along with extreme feeling comes extreme action. The violent acts of Shakespeare's noble heroes can be linked generically to the monstrous crimes of ancient myth rendered familiar in the Renaissance through the tragedies of Seneca and the *Metamorphoses* of Ovid. They may therefore have seemed rather less astonishing to a contemporary than they do to a present-day audience. However, beginning with Titus, the noble Roman who kills his son and daughter, Shakespeare seems to invite the charge of implausibility by stressing the shocking nature of these violent deeds. Othello's suffocation of Desdemona in her bridal bed is hardly more terrible than the way Brutus – 'the noblest Roman of them all' – bathes his hands exultantly in the blood of the friend he has stabbed to death. And yet Shakespeare will always re-emphasize the fallen hero's nobility, his greatness of heart. Sometimes the contradiction located in such characters is expressed in boldly paradoxical terms: 'You have deserved nobly of your country, and you have not deserved nobly' (Cor. 2.3.78–9; cf. Ant. 5.1.30); but the more typical emphasis, implicit or explicit, and one which helps to make such behaviour credible, is on the inherent frailty of all humans, including the finest: 'a noble nature / May catch a wrench' (Tim. 2.2.204–5; cf. Ant. 5.1.31–3).

Shakespeare seeks to render the brutal actions of the noble hero plausible and potentially forgivable in other ways. First of all, there is the continuous reminder of an intrinsically unstable natural order in which things can rapidly 'decline' to their 'confounding contraries' (Tim. 4.1.19). More obviously, the fatal act is often unpremeditated and rash, the product of an unbearable access of passion, or of temporary madness or something close to madness. Or the hero may be the victim of some self-deception which enables him in his own mind to accommodate the fatal act to his moral sense, so that what he does seems to him both just and necessary, even a ritual sacrifice performed for the good of the community. Or he has the pure misfortune of being faced with the one challenge that his nature and experience do not equip him to deal with.

He may also be the victim of one or more artful manipulators who know him better than he knows himself: close associates or seeming 'friends / Who can bring noblest minds to basest ends' (Tim. 4.3.465–6). The figure of the manipulator in Shakespeare's tragedies is descended by way of the morality Vice from the devil of Christian mythos, the tempter who deploys the arts of the orator and the actor in making evil seem good to his deluded victim. The manipulator is granted heroic status in the devilish protagonist of Richard III ('the wonder at a capacity greater than one would expect is the feeling most often inspired by the heroic');[19] but his characteristic role is the secondary one of an agent provocateur who operates on the passions of the hero and also, it may be, on others whose susceptibility to his wiles confirms the hero's representative nature. The manipulator sets about changing the hero in full consciousness of what he or she is doing and may even observe the ongoing process with scientific detachment: 'Work on, / My medicine work!' (Oth. 4.1.42–3; cf. JC 1.2.308–10).

In Seneca's tragedies there is usually a companion figure who warns the protagonist against the dangers of succumbing to passion; the Chorus too sometimes moralizes on the Stoic ideal of emotional detachment and control. Some of the protagonists' victims, and in the case of Hercules, the protagonist himself, meet death with an equanimity which exemplifies the Stoic ideal of constancy in the face of the worst that fortune or tyranny can offer. Partly because of Seneca, but partly too because it was deeply embedded in Christian thought and Renaissance culture, Stoicism impinges on the passionate world of Shakespearean tragedy in a number of ways. There are counsellor figures such as Friar Lawrence, John of Gaunt, and Menenius, who plead for patience and restraint (Iago appropriates this role with demonic skill). And there is the figure of Horatio, more an antique Roman than a Dane in his attitude to suicide and in the impression he gives of being one who 'in suffering all, suffers nothing'.

The hero's attempts at self-control are often evidence of his pre-tragic self: Romeo as 'a virtuous and well-governed youth', Hamlet as 'the soldier's, scholar's eye, tongue, sword', Othello as the imperturbable leader in the thunder of battle. These attempts serve also to emphasize by contrast the explosive power of the emotions which have begun to rack him. He may oscillate between moments of Stoic calm and passionate rage and grief; or his rages may hover uncertainly between the kind of rational, heroic anger approved by the Stoics and blind, vengeful fury. Hamlet dwells repeatedly on the conflicting values of impassioned, 'honourable' action on the one hand and rational control and Stoic resignation on the other (critics disagree on whether this dialectic is resolved in the end or not). Blending Stoic and Christian virtue, Lear proclaims that he will 'be the pattern of all patience and say nothing' in response to the cruelty of his daughters; but he has to pass through madness before the great rage subsides in him, and even then the calm is shortlived. The *Lear* world is one whose 'strange mutations' repeatedly shatter the armour of patience.

Shakespeare unquestionably admired much of the Stoic inheritance, but he also exposed the inadequacy of its more extreme attitudes to emotion. Thus Brutus's Stoic *apatheia* makes it possible for him to suppress his natural tenderness and murder his friend. *Hamlet* hints at a profoundly subversive point made by the Duchess of Gloucester in *Richard II* when Gaunt tells her they must wait patiently for God to exact justice on Richard: 'Call it not patience, Gaunt, it is despair' (1.2.29). Anger and lust tear the nation and its two leading families apart in *King Lear*, yet the posture of Stoic detachment self-consciously adopted by the grievously wronged Edgar is quickly rendered irrelevant by a recognition that the human heart, with its capacity for both love and hate, pity and rage, is the source of all that is best as well as all that is worst in human nature; thus the detached Edgar in the end enters the lists (both literally and metaphorically) and demonstrates his fitness for rule by virtue of his just anger and his compassionate love. It is not Coriolanus' ability to subject his notorious wrath to the claims of reason that saves Rome and redeems (and destroys) him, but an access of that natural gentleness which his mother's extreme version of Roman culture precluded. The symbolic geography of *Antony and Cleopatra* emphasizes a cultural clash between control and passion, Stoic and Epicurean. At one level, Rome and what it stands for triumphs over Egypt; but at another level the clash is resolved in a synthesis which proclaims the partiality of each set of values: that synthesis being the suicidal marriage of the Roman general and the Egyptian queen.

IV

The combination of truthfulness and formal perfection with which the spectacle of suffering and evil is presented in great tragedy is one reason why we derive both pleasure and satisfaction from what should in theory depress us. Another reason is the fact that most great tragedies, and Shakespeare's in particular, concur with the maxim that 'there is some soul of goodness in things evil, / Would men observingly distil it out' (*H5* 4.1.4–5). The ending of *Antony and Cleopatra*, with its note of triumph and exultation, is an extreme example of this aspect of Shakespeare's tragic practice. Varying greatly in degree of importance from one play to another, the positive aspect of tragic events manifests itself in several ways. Most obviously, there is the restoration of social order, with an emphasis on reunification and reconciliation. In *Romeo and Juliet*, the feud that divides the city and destroys the lovers is visibly ended with the mutual embrace of their remorseful fathers. In *Hamlet*, the enemy of the state becomes its saviour; in *Lear*, Albany changes sides and helps instal the virtuous Edgar as king; in *Macbeth*, the alienated nobility are reunited with their ruler, who gives 'thanks to *all at once*, and to *each one*' (5.9.41). In *Timon of Athens*, Alcibiades makes peace with the Athenians whom both he and 'transformèd Timon' grew to hate, declaring, 'I will use the olive with my sword / Make war breed peace, make peace stint war, make each / Prescribe to other as each other's leech' (5.5.19, 87–9). In the major Roman tragedies, the enemy of the dead hero is magnanimous in victory and acknowledges his nobility; a kind of reconciliation.

More important altogether are the reunions and reconciliations achieved by the protagonists themselves. Like Antony and Cleopatra, Romeo and Juliet are bonded in death, triumphing over those forces within and without which threatened to divide them. Hamlet exchanges forgiveness with Laertes and dies at one with his mother; the repentant Lear and Gloucester are forgiven by their wronged children; Othello begs and receives forgiveness from his wronged friend, Cassio, and dies 'on a kiss' beside Desdemona; Coriolanus takes his mother's hand and so forgives and is forgiven by Rome. Timon, however, dies solitary and unforgiving, making

> his everlasting mansion
> Upon the beachèd verge of the salt flood,
> Who once a day with his embossèd froth
> The turbulent surge shall cover.
>
> (5.2.100–3)

Yet Alcibiades suggests that nature forgives Timon, and he signals for others to do likewise when he looks at the dead hero: 'rich conceit / Taught thee to make vast Neptune weep for aye / On thy low grave, on faults forgiven. Dead is / Noble Timon' (5.5.80–5). The reconciling process entails confirmation of the hero's nobility as well as forgiveness for his rash and ignoble acts.

The most important distillation from the experience of things evil is understanding, or what in Aristotelian terminology is called 'recognition'. The journey of Lear and Gloucester from blindness to vision foregrounds a spiritual process which affects most of Shakespeare's tragic characters in some degree; it includes even Macbeth, who realizes that the crown which he coveted cannot compare in value with love and friendship lasting into ripe old age. Perhaps we should feel uneasy about Hamlet's insistence that Rosencrantz and Guildenstern are not near his conscience, and his public assertion (contradicting what he said in private to his mother) that it was not he but his madness that killed Polonius. Is he in this respect somewhat like Brutus, who dies failing to perceive that the killing of his friend for the crime that he *might* commit was profoundly wrong? We may be on surer ground when we note Hamlet's recognition in Act 5 (based on a new-found belief in Divine Providence) that it is not for him to choose the time for justice; a recognition which ultimately allows him to die at peace with himself. Othello's recognition of error and guilt is so great that he refuses divine mercy and commits suicide in the conviction that he merits the torments of Hell. Some have accused him, however, of essential blindness at the end, noting his failure to see that even if Desdemona were guilty of adultery it would still have been wicked to kill her. However valid in itself, the point is of doubtful dramatic relevance; to argue thus is to introduce a kind of mundane calculus which seems out of place in a tragedy of titanic emotion. On the other hand, the failure of the tragic hero to achieve complete recognition need not constitute a limitation in the play itself; the understanding which matters is that which the playwright enables the audience to achieve. But such understanding characteristically involves an awareness that there is no univocal answer to some of the questions – moral or metaphysical – raised by the tragic action.

By far the most positive aspect of Shakespearean tragedy is the final restoration of the protagonist's nobility, shown by the manner in which he meets death. The quality usually involved here is that of constancy, which signifies truth to self and one's values: a spiritual triumph over the forces of change. Exemplified in the deaths of Senecan characters such as Hercules and Polyxena, and in that of the historical Cato (Brutus's father-in-law), constancy was the supreme virtue in Stoic and neo-Stoic thought. But religious persecution gave it a special significance in the sixteenth century, as both the Protestant and Catholic martyrologies of the time vividly indicate. A notion of great importance in the long tradition of the noble death is that of dying 'like oneself'; and 'like a man' as distinct from a beast, upright and unflinching, with the kind of self-conscious decorum imputed to the first Thane of Cawdor: 'Nothing in his life / Became him like the leaving it' (*JC* 5.4.25; *Mac.* 1.4.7–8).

In its most extreme form, constancy involves suicide, signifying a calm refusal to submit to a superior force and live in misery, dishonour, or disgrace. Brutus and Cassius are obvious examples, but the cases of Romeo and Juliet and Antony and Cleopatra are more truly Shakespearean, since they locate personal identity in the human bond and emphasize the dual nature of the self. Hearing of Juliet's death, Romeo stoically defies the stars and decides to join her; his conduct here contrasts vividly with the adolescent and indeed bestial frenzy of his first reaction to bad news, and marks his attainment of manhood. And Juliet, having already overcome her terrors of isolation in the tomb in order to be true to Romeo, is no less 'manly' and decisive than Romeo in taking her life beside him. Hinted at here is an idea which is fully developed in the suicides of Antony and Cleopatra, each of whom learns from and imitates the other in death; suicide thus symbolizes a union of opposites by means of which the full potential of the noble self is disclosed. Othello's hell is that he is eternally separated from Desdemona; yet his dying on a kiss carries the suggestion of an 'atonement' (see 4.1.230) coextensive with the reintegration of self achieved by acknowledging and punishing the erring barbarian that he had become.

The theatricality of all these suicides, especially Othello's, is part of the Stoic style and can be matched in Seneca by, for example, the spectacular deaths of Astyanax and Polyxena, the second of which actually takes place in an open theatre where 'every heart / Was struck with terror, wonderment, and pity'.[20] Claims that we should take the theatricality of Shakespeare's suicides as self-deceiving egotism ignore not only the Stoic tradition in pagan literature but, more importantly, the Christianized Stoicism exemplified in the political executions, martyrdoms, and martyrologies of the sixteenth century. As their accompanying woodcuts vividly indicate, the narratives of execution in John Foxe's *Book of Martyrs* are as theatrical in conception as anything in Seneca; so too was the carefully studied manner in which Mary Queen of Scots and many other persons of high rank met their end on the scaffold in Tudor England. It was an age which gave substance to the observation, 'More are men's ends marked than their lives before' (*R2* 2.1.11).

V

Far more important than the composed ending in Shakespearean tragedy, however, is the central experience of suffering and distress. 'Is there no pity sitting in the clouds / That sees into the bottom of my grief?' asks Juliet in despair (*Rom.* 3.5.196–7). As early as *Titus Andronicus*, Shakespeare gave much attention to scenes where the protagonist cries out in anguish to human or divine witnesses of his or her misery, emblematizing thus the relationship between the play itself and the audience whom the dramatist seeks to fill with woe and wonder. Shakespeare conceives of his tragic characters as individuals to be remembered less for their errors and misdeeds than for the sufferings and griefs they endure in consequence. Prompted in this by Seneca's rhetorical bravura, but vastly surpassing it in dramatic intensity, Shakespeare's eloquence expends itself with astonishing bounty and ever increasing poignancy on the lament of the lacerated heart. Even Macbeth, the relentlessly clear-eyed murderer, utters cries of unassuageable pain which ensure our compassion: 'Canst thou not minister to a mind diseased, / Pluck from the memory a rooted sorrow ... ?' (5.3.41–2).

The causes of suffering in Shakespeare's tragedies are diffuse and seem to involve large abstract forces as well as human error, weakness, and malice. His characters frequently invoke fortune in such a way as to grant her the status of a mysterious supernatural being with a cruelly unpredictable personality. In addition, his plots are sometimes informed by a principle of ironic circularity which seems to testify to the presence of the capricious goddess and her famous wheel. Unlike the authors of the Fall of Princes narratives, however, Shakespeare usually intimates that the changes which are imputed to treacherous fortune are of human origin, and more precisely that her inconstancy corresponds with that of mutable human nature. The case of Richard II is exemplary: his fall from power (symbolized by his voluntary descent to 'the base court') is preceded by a scene in which he swings up and down repeatedly between wild optimism and total despair.

Accident – Richard's delayed return to England, the mistimed encounters in *Romeo and Juliet*, Emilia's discovery of the handkerchief – may contribute to the advancement of the tragic plot, but it would not have the malign impact it does without the characters being what they are. In that sense, character is fate: one's own character interacting with that of others.

Fate, in the sense of a predetermined order of events, is less frequently invoked but sometimes powerfully suggested. In *Julius Caesar* and *Hamlet*, an impression of impending disaster is established by ominous occurrences which provoke fearful speculation in the dramatis personae. What is most notable about such speculation, however, is that it initiates a continuing process of inquiry and interpretation focused mainly on the uncertain significance of what certain individuals mean or intend. Even as Cassius intimates to Casca that disorders in the natural and the supernatural world prefigure what Caesar will do to Rome, thoughtful spectators will respond to his 'But if you would consider the true cause...Why all these things change from their ordinance...To monstrous quality' (1.3.62–8) by answering that he himself is in process of effecting such a change in Rome and Romans. In *Macbeth* 'the weird sisters' who contrive the hero's downfall merely point him in the way he was already inclined to go (like the 'fatal' dagger); moreover, their treacherous double-talk matches the doubleness in his own and in all nature: 'Double, double toil and trouble'.

And yet there is a very important sense in which circumstances conspire to produce a situation in which disaster seems inevitable. Hamlet is trapped in a situation where to do nothing is to encourage the spread of evil and to act is to become part of it: 'O cursèd spite / That ever I was born to set it right' (1.5.189–90). In *Othello*, chance contributes uncannily to the fulfilment of a doom adumbrated in a series of ominous or ironic observations at the start of the play; but the most cursed spite of all is that the trusting Othello should have as his confidant a man like Iago, without whom the tragedy is inconceivable. Hamlet offers what looks like Shakespeare's explanation for the fall of all the tragic heroes when he speaks of noble and gifted men who are born with some vicious mole of nature ('wherein they are not guilty'(1.4.25)) that brings ruin upon them; but more often it is arguably their good qualities which, in the given circumstances, prove fatal and become or engender defects. What Iago says of his plan to exploit 'the inclining Desdemona' is applicable also to his attack on the nobly trusting ('free and open') Othello: 'out of her own goodness [I will] make the net / That shall enmesh them all' (1.3.381, 2.3.328–9). Friar Lawrence comes nearer than Hamlet to the causal centre of Shakespearean tragedy when he observes – while philosophizing on the paradoxes of nature – that 'virtue itself turns vice, being misapplied' (2.2.21).

In the pagan universe of *King Lear* the gods are continually invoked as participants in the tragedy. Their existence, however, is implicitly called in question by the fact that the good and bad events imputed to them are shown by the immediate dramatic context to be of very human origin. Significantly, the deity who is invoked most solemnly and characterized most fully is Nature, a figure whose generosity and ferocity, kindness and cruelty, accounts for everything that happens in Lear's kingdom. The habit of finding causes for human misery outside the realm of nature is shown here to be part of the confusion in which most of the characters live. Lear points in the right direction when he speaks to the warring elements and asks: 'Is there any cause in nature that makes these hard-hearts?' (3.6.34–5).

In Christian theology, Divine Providence signifies God's ordering of a world rendered imperfect by the Fall, a mode of government which uses all acts and happenings, both good and bad, for an ultimately just and benevolent purpose. In Shakespeare's tragedies and tragical histories with a Christian setting, Divine Providence is invoked with varying degrees of emphasis and conviction. At the end of *Romeo and Juliet* the Friar says that '[a] greater power than we can contradict' has thwarted his plan to use the marriage of the lovers as a means of reconciling the two families; presumably he would agree with the Prince, who adds that Heaven has, instead, used the deaths of the lovers both to punish the feuding families and to end their discords. But the Friar has shown himself to be a natural philosopher rather than a theologian, and a more satisfactory explanation for the tragedy and its outcome can be found in his disquisition on nature's dialectical order, where medicines can prove poisonous and poisons medicinal.

Although saturated with doubt and uncertainty, *Hamlet* comes close to a firm providentialism; puzzlingly so. Horatio believes that 'Heaven will direct' his 'country's fate' (1.4.68) and Hamlet in the last act begins to see the controlling hand of Providence in his rash and bloody deeds. There can be little doubt that many in Shakespeare's audience would have internalized the Hamlet–Horatio understanding of the tragedy (they have been told by the hero and his friend 'what the show means'); but we can be sure that others would have found it strange that after all Hamlet's sufferings and scruples Divine Providence has arranged for Denmark to be ruled by a violent opportunist with no respect for international law or human life. Moreover, the ghost is the most palpable sign of the supernatural realm; and not only is it entirely ambiguous ('from heaven or from hell'), it is driven by distinctly human passions and recruits Hamlet to its cause by invoking two conceptions of nature, one associated with 'foul crimes', the other with filial love. Here, as in the incantations and 'natural magic' (3.2.243–8) of the player Lucianus, whose divinity is witchcraft's Hecate, the supernatural points us back to the unpredictable forces in nature; when light comes, Hamlet's 'erring spirit' returns to its habitation 'in sea or fire, in earth or air' (1.1.134). So whatever significance is attached in the tragedies to fortune, fate, the gods, and God, the crucial fact is that these always function in complete consistency with, and can easily be construed as projections of, the workings of nature in the actions of men and women.

Despite its inherent thrust towards violent confusion, nature is implicitly understood as an order; and that order is seen primarily in terms of Time. If it is possible to answer Bradley's question, What is the ultimate power in Shakespeare's tragic world?, the most reasonable answer would seem to be nature in its temporal dimension. In premodern cosmology, time is the measured movement of the elemental world and, like it, discloses a cyclic pattern of binary and quadruple opposites: day and night, spring and autumn, summer and winter. Accordingly, the confusion of night and day is a characteristic feature of Shakespeare's tragic world. Violent action being often nocturnal either in conception or execution, night is conceived as a time of rest and peace violated and as a symptom of chaos: the imagery of *Julius Caesar*, *Othello*, and *Macbeth* involves the mythical identification of Night and Hell (Erebus) as the children of Chaos. More importantly, the deeds which generate the tragic action are untimely or mistimed in the sense that they are dilatory or (much more often) either rash or cunningly swift.

Tragic catastrophes, too, reveal the corrective action of time. It is corrective first of all in the sense that it is retributive: untimely acts, whether tardy or rash, are punished in kind. Richard II 'wasted time' and then took from Hereford and 'from Time / His charters and his customary rights'; and 'now doth time waste' him (2.1.196-7, 5.5.49). Cassius kills Caesar 'in the shell' (before his presumptive crime is committed) and then has to kill himself on his own birthday: 'Time is come round, / And where I did begin, there shall I end...Caesar thou art revenged' (2.1.34, 5.3.23-5, 44-5). There is a comparable sense of symmetrical justice in Macbeth's recognition, 'Time, thou anticipatest my dread exploits' (4.1.143). Variously accented, the pattern of Time's justice can be detected in most of the tragedies. However, this is not to imply that there is a neat overall distribution of justice in most of the tragedies. The villains get their deserts, but it cannot be said that the tragic characters are always responsible for what befalls them, nor even that the issue of responsibility is a primary concern. It can be argued indeed that the disproportion in Shakespearean tragedy between culpable error (where there is any) and consequent suffering, and between the sufferings of the noble and the wicked, is so great as to preclude any idea of justice and rationality. But that is surely too simple, however much it might coincide with how we ourselves would interpret the same events. It would be more appropriate to say that Time – much like Bradley's undefined 'ultimate power' – acts retributively through a convulsive action which sweeps away all but the most fortunate and the most astute.

Time's action is corrective also in the sense that it is restorative, a force for renewal. The cyclic and dialectical order of nature entails that the positive undertone in Shakespeare's tragic endings is a necessary and logical counterpart to the negative undertone in his comic endings. Nevertheless, the overall impression in the tragedies is of a world where Time is put disastrously out of joint with terrifying ease, and can only be set right again at huge cost. George Chapman's aphorism, *The use of time is fate*, is very apt in relation to Shakespearean tragedy, especially if we stress the ominous note in the phrasing.

VI

Over the centuries, Ben Jonson's claim that Shakespeare is not of an age but for all time has been continuously endorsed in different ways. Jonson, however, was not denying that Shakespeare addressed the specific concerns of his audience in ways they understood. Historically minded critics rightly remind us that his plays were inevitably shaped to a very considerable extent by the particular experiences, institutions, and ideas of the age in which he lived. One of the many advantages in approaching the plays from the perspective of Tudor–Jacobean politics and ideology is that we begin to perceive just why tragedy flourished to such an extraordinary degree in the period; for at every level, it was an age characterized by conflict and change: intense, heroic, painful, bitter, and violent.

The splitting of Christianity into two hotly antagonistic sects during the sixteenth century had a profound effect on England. The nation was torn between Catholic and Protestant claims to religio-political supremacy, a division which fuelled three rebellions, three attempted invasions, and several assassination attempts on Elizabeth. Moreover, the religio-political division split families and friends, gave rise to cruel personal betrayals, resulted in numerous executions for treason (seven hundred 'at one fell swoop' in 1570), and left men like John Donne uneasy in conscience after their pragmatic shift from one faith to the other: 'O to vex me, contraries meet in one.'[21]

Interconnected with the Reformation was the decline of feudalism, the rise of authoritarian monarchy, and the waning power of the old aristocracy. It has been plausibly argued therefore that Shakespeare's tragedies reflect 'a tragic view of the decline of feudalism' and that his heroes 'are all living in a new world and are smashed by it'.[22] Insecure as well as authoritarian, and creating unity by coercion and persecution, the Tudor regime severely reduced the freedoms of all its subjects; it thus created an environment in which the inherited tragic themes of tyranny, injustice, revenge, and the outraged revolt of the alienated individual had special resonance.

If the Reformation brought about an intensification of religious faith for many, the spectacle of two kindred theologies diabolizing each other necessarily generated an overwhelming sense of religious doubt in the minds of others. Moreover, the 'wars of truth' extended into philosophy, political theory, and science, where Montaigne, Machiavelli, and Copernicus boldly attacked ancient convictions. Sir Thomas Browne was surely in tune with the time when in 1635 or thereabouts he recalled that the wisest thinkers 'prove at last, almost all Scepticks, and stand like Janus [the double-faced deity] in the field of knowledge'. Looking back on the period, he saw it as a time of violent and tragic disunity. And like Shakespeare, he appealed to the contrarious model of nature as one way of making some sense of it all: 'this world is raised upon a mass of antipathies' and man himself is 'another world of contrarieties'.[23]

It is certainly true that we will never approach a full understanding of Shakespeare's tragedies if we ignore their historically specific filiations. The fact remains, however, that the greatness of these plays has been acknowledged for centuries by audiences and readers in diverse cultures who have relatively little knowledge of that kind. And they do so for the simple reason – I conclude by recalling the obvious – that Shakespeare not only engaged with but went through and beyond the contemporary to capture in brilliantly realized characters and deeply moving scenes some of the most persistent aspects of human nature and experience: the strength and the vulnerability, the goodness and the wickedness, of men and women; the desolation and courage of the individual at odds with society; the cruel injustices and the terrifying uncertainty of life itself.

NOTES

1. Kenneth Muir, *Shakespeare's Tragic Sequence* (London: Methuen, 1972), pp. 12, 16.
2. Dieter Mehl, *Shakespeare's Tragedies: An Introduction* (Cambridge University Press, 1986), p. 7.
3. Alistair Fowler, *Kinds of Literature: An Introduction to the Theory of Genres and Modes* (Oxford: Clarendon Press, 1982), p. 24. Cf. Raymond Williams, *Modern Tragedy* (London: Chatto and Windus, 1966), pp. 15–46.
4. *Hegel on Tragedy*, ed. Anne and Henry Paolucci (New York: Harper and Row, 1975), pp. 62, 67–71, 89, 237.
5. Friedrich Nietzsche, *'The Birth of Tragedy' and 'The Genealogy of Morals'*, trans. Francis Golffing (New York: Doubleday, 1956), pp. 19, 33–6, 42, 50, 64.

TOM MCALINDON

6. See my *Shakespeare's Tragic Cosmos* (Cambridge University Press, 1991), pp. 11, 261–2.
7. *Oxford Lectures on Poetry* (1909; London: Macmillan, 1962), pp. 83–4.
8. *Shakespearean Tragedy* (London: Macmillan, 1905), lect. 1.
9. Una Ellis-Fermor, 'The Equilibrium of Tragedy', *The Frontiers of Drama* (London: Methuen, 1948), pp. 127–47. See also Bernard McElroy, *Shakespeare's Mature Tragedies* (Princeton University Press, 1973), pp. 1–28.
10. F. L. Lucas, *Tragedy in Relation to Aristotle's Poetics* (London: Hogarth Press, 1927), pp. 55–6.
11. A. P. Rossiter, *Angel with Horns: Fifteen Lectures on Shakespeare* (London: Hutchinson, 1961), pp. 265–72.
12. Catherine Belsey, 'Tragedy, Justice and the Subject', in *1642: Literature and Power in the Seventeenth Century*, ed. Francis Barker (Essex, 1981), pp. 166–86; Jonathan Dollimore, *Radical Tragedy: Religion, Ideology and Power in the Drama of Shakespeare and his Contemporaries* (Brighton: Harvester Press, 1984).
13. On Seneca and the 'sympathetic universe', see Thomas G. Rosenmeyer, *Senecan Drama and Stoic Cosmology* (Berkeley, Los Angeles, and London: University of California Press, 1989).
14. George Puttenham, *The Arte of English Poesie* (1589), ed. G. D. Willcock and A. Walker (Cambridge University Press, 1936), p. 26; Sir Philip Sidney, *An Apology for Poetry* (1595), ed. Geoffrey Shepherd (London: Nelson, 1965), p. 118.
15. Roland Mushat Frye, *Shakespeare: The Art of the Dramatist* (London: Allen and Unwin, 1982), p. 116.
16. See my *Shakespeare's Tragic Cosmos*, chap. 1.
17. On passion and suffering as marks of greatness in the hero, see especially Rossiter, *Angel with Horns*, p. 264, and Robert Kirsch, *The Passions of Shakespeare's Tragic Heroes* (Charlottesville and London: University of Virginia Press), 1990. See also my 'Tragedy, *King Lear*, and the Politics of the Heart', *Shakespeare Survey* 44 (1992), 85–90.
18. Reuben A. Brower, *Hero and Saint: Shakespeare and the Graeco-Roman Heroic Tradition* (Oxford: Clarendon Press, 1971), p. 31.
19. Eugene M. Waith, *Ideas of Greatness: Heroic Drama in England* (London: Hutchinson, 1971), p. 106.
20. *The Trojan Women*, lines 1179–80; in Seneca, *Four Tragedies and Octavia*, trans. E. F. Watling (London: Penguin, 1966), p. 203.
21. Donne, 'Holy Sonnets' no. XIX. But see especially no. XVIII.
22. Bertolt Brecht, *The Messingkauf Dialogues*, trans. John Willett (London: Methuen, 1965), p. 59.
23. *Sir Thomas Browne, The Major Works*, ed. C. A. Patrides (Harmondsworth: Penguin, 1977), pp. 144–5, 148.

2

RUSS McDONALD

The language of tragedy

In the middle of *The Second Part of King Henry the Fourth*, during the long nocturnal tavern scene, Shakespeare abruptly alters the elegiac mood by introducing a new character – Pistol. Significantly, his entrance is announced in advance: as soon as his name is mentioned Doll Tearsheet denounces him as 'a swaggering rascal' and 'the foul-mouthed'st rogue in England'. Her complaint instantly identifies his essential attribute, for like so many secondary characters in the second tetralogy, Pistol speaks a distinctive language.

> PISTOL What, shall we have incision? Shall we imbrue?
> [*Snatches up his sword.*]
> Then Death rock me asleep, abridge my doleful days!
> Why then, let grievous ghastly gaping wounds
> Untwind the sisters three; come, Atropos, I say!
>
> HOSTESS Here's goodly stuff toward!   (2.4. 157–61)

'Stuff' indeed. Attempting to pass himself off as a valiant warrior, the coward has filched the rhetoric of a hero, and we need look no further for the source of his grandiloquent speech than the Elizabethan playhouse. Pistol wants to sound like a Marlovian hero – in one of his first speeches he misquotes Marlowe's Tamburlaine – and thus assembles his speeches with the verbal materials of the tragedian. Since parody or caricature exaggerates and thus identifies the fundamental properties of a style, Pistol's extravagant, pretentious, colourful speech provides an appropriate introduction to the language of Shakespearean tragedy.

Before considering the authentic idiom that Pistol counterfeits, it will be helpful to glance briefly at the growth of tragedy as a theatrical phenomenon in the last decades of the sixteenth century. Thanks partly to the emergence of a few brilliant playwrights, particularly Thomas Kyd and Christopher Marlowe, the English theatre made enormous presentational, social, commercial, and poetic advances at the end of Elizabeth's reign. By 1603 the

tragic actor, whether he spoke Shakespeare's verse or Ben Jonson's or someone else's, sounded radically different from his counterpart of thirty years
earlier. To a considerable extent the spoken words sounded different because,
as the sixteenth century gave way to the seventeenth, the world being spoken
of was changing, becoming ever more alien, confusing, and disturbing. The
language of English tragedy at this crucial moment was shaped by a wide
range of cultural phenomena: the rise of literacy, the emerging artistic dignity of the English language, the emerging existential dignity of the human
being, corresponding scepticism about such an evaluation, the accelerating
reassessment of monarchical, ecclesiastical, and divine authority, and the
concomitant upheaval in the political, religious, social, and philosophical
spheres. Although I shall touch on such trends and movements, they are
treated more thoroughly elsewhere in this volume.[1] My aim is to elucidate
Shakespeare's response to such developments as it manifests itself in the
speech of his principal tragic characters.

Hamlet, Othello, and their theatrical kin are among the most charismatic
speakers in all of world drama, and this essay is an attempt to identify and
analyse the sources of their unexcelled authority. In one sense such a taxo-
nomic effort is inherently vain, in that Shakespeare's tragic language works
just as the rest of Shakespeare's language works: the dynamic effect of pat-
terned words upon the listener's mind is much the same whether the speaker
is Petruchio or Portia or King Lear. And yet the visionary propensities of
the tragic heroes, the extremes of tragic action, and the historical–cultural
sovereignty of the tragic mode help to generate a distinctive poetic intensity.
Lofty diction, repetition of words and syntactical patterns, classical allusions,
rhetorical questions, sophisticated metrical schemes and effects, poetic and
thematic recapitulation, overstatement – all these characteristics mocked in
Pistol's outbursts constitute the 'stuff' of Shakespearean tragic speech. After
the two initial efforts in the early and mid-1590s, *Titus Andronicus* and
Romeo and Juliet, the playwright committed himself in mid-career to the
darkly sceptical mode of tragedy. That turn coincides with his attainment
of poetic maturity, with his having mastered and developed the technical
practices and formal innovations inherited from his theatrical predecessors:
blank verse as a medium for poetic drama, for example, was less than fifty
years old when Shakespeare wrote *Hamlet*. This technical proficiency afforded him the means of articulating with unparalleled force the terms of
the tragic paradox – that the sources of human greatness and the sources of
human failure are identical. And the artistic manifestation of that paradox
is that the limits of language are set forth in language of almost illimitable
power.

Antecedents and commentary

Two distinct traditions shaped the way English writers thought about tragedy in the middle of the sixteenth century. The first is the native strain deriving from the medieval stories and poems typified in John Lydgate's *The Fall of Princes* (1431). The public thrilled to these tales, which their authors regularly describe as 'tragedies' but which resemble classical tragedy much less than they do the Christian tradition of *contemptus mundi*. In the English popular mind, devoted as it was to 'this proliferating body of mortuary verse,'[2] the term 'tragedy' meant simply a spectacular fall from high place. In the dramatic tradition, 'tragedy' usually meant Roman tragedy, specifically and almost exclusively the plays of Seneca. The Elizabethans automatically identified Senecan drama with blood, vengeance, violent death, and supernatural intervention. For present purposes, the more significant Senecan characteristic is the prominence of sublime expression. In the *Apology for Poetry* (pub. 1595), Sir Philip Sidney famously praises Sackville and Norton's *Gorboduc*, the first important English stage tragedy, because 'it is full of stately speeches and well-sounding phrases, climbing to the height of Seneca's style'.[3] It is worth pausing here to heed Sidney's figurative language, particularly 'stately' and 'climbing'. From the sixteenth century to the twenty-first, metaphors of altitude are inescapable in discussions of tragic language. 'Stately', meaning 'majestic' or 'regal', invokes height in relation to social class. The decorum of tragic language, of Seneca's style in particular, is aristocratic, refined, associated with and limited to the small world of the court. And Sidney's use of such descriptive terms is utterly conventional and consistent with the attitudes of the period.

Thomas Newton introduces his 1581 edition of *Seneca His Tenne Tragedies* by defending the Roman's works against charges of immorality. At just about that time opponents of the stage were busy attacking the London theatres as showcases of depravity, condemning plays and players for providing instruction in vice. Seeking to refute such criticism by asserting the morality of drama, Newton ascribes great moral efficacy to Seneca's style, and his commendation provides a typical example of early modern rhetoric about dramatic rhetoric:

> For it may not at any hand be thought and deemed the direct meaning of Seneca himself, whose whole writings (penned with a peerless sublimity and loftiness of style), are so far from countenancing vice, that I doubt whether there be any among all the catalogue of heathen writers, that with more gravity of Philosophical sentences, more weightiness of sappy [vigorous, juicy] words, or greater authority of sound matter beateth down sin, loose life, dissolute dealing,

and unbridled sensuality; or that more sensibly, pithily, and bitingly layeth down the guerdon [reward, consequences] of filthy lust, cloaked dissimulation, and odious treachery, which is the drift whereunto he leveleth the whole issue [i.e. the resolution] of each of his tragedies.[4]

The sentiments and the language of Sidney and Sidney's contemporaries – not to mention Polonius, who approvingly mentions Seneca's 'heavy' style – are clearly and forcefully expressed here. Newton establishes the morality of the dramatic enterprise in the series of adverbs that describes the excoriation of vice, 'sensibly, pithily, and bitingly', but even more relevant is his figurative analysis of the style: 'peerless sublimity', 'loftiness of style', 'weightiness', 'sappy words'.

The nobility of tragic language is intimately connected with the aristocratic pedigree of tragedy as an artistic form. Renaissance literary critics were no less hierarchical than political writers or religious apologists, and tragedy stood near the very top of the order of fictional or poetic forms, second only to the epic. Virtually everyone in the period who writes about tragedy invokes its exalted status: Sidney ('the high and excellent tragedy'), Roger Ascham ('the goodliest Argument of all'), William Webbe ('bringing in the persons of Gods and Goddesses, Kynges and Queenes, and great states'), George Puttenham ('besides those poets *Comick* there were others who served also the stage, but medled not with so base matters'), Kyd's Hieronimo ('Fie! comedies are fit for common wits;...Give me a stately written tragedy').[5] The tragic playwright addresses, and addresses self-consciously, fundamental problems of human experience – the inevitability of death, the desire for transcendence, the vanity of terrestrial aspiration, the consequences of pride, heroic self-assertion, the effects of evil in the world. Such heavy matters require heightened, uncommon language.

The burgeoning of Elizabethan tragedy owed much to the invention of a poetic language suitable for it – unrhymed iambic pentameter, or blank verse. Until poets and playwrights began to experiment with blank verse and made it the standard for Renaissance tragedy, those writers who sought to tell tragic stories were hampered by the available poetic forms, as we hear in John Studley's translation of a passage from Act 3 of Seneca's *Agamemnon* (1566). Miserable humans are happy to be summoned

> By death, a pleasaunt port, for aye in rest them selves to shroude,
> Where dreadfull tumultes never dwell nor stormes of fortune proude:
> Nor yet the burning firy flakes of Jove the same doth doubt,
> When wrongfully with thwacking thumpes he raps his thunder out:
> Heere Lady Peace th'inhabitours doth never put in flight,

Nor yet the victors threatning wrath approching nygh to sight,
No whyrling western wynde doth urge the ramping seas to praunce,
No dusty cloude that raysed is by savage Mimilaunce,
On horseback riding rancke by rancke, no fearce and cruell host,
No people slaughtred, with their townes cleane topsie turvey tost.[6]

The point of citing such a passage is not to gain a cheap laugh at Studley's expense or to belittle him for not being Marlowe or Shakespeare. Writers like Studley were admired in their day, and their translations are notable because they attest to the poetic taste of the age just prior to Shakespeare's and to the kind of verse considered appropriate for the highest form of drama.

In Studley's case the poetic crudeness (which sometimes approaches burlesque) is attributable in part to the modest talents of the translator, but such apparent ineptitude owes much to the comparatively undeveloped state of English poetry. Studley's translation is hampered by his chosen prosodic form: the fourteen-syllable or septenary line almost inevitably tends to split in two, producing a clumsy and puerile-sounding monotony, and this long line also gives the ham-handed alliterator more space and material – more syllables – with which to embarrass himself. Further, the unremitting jingle of the rhymes enhances the impression of naiveté. As poets and dramatists were happily beginning to discover, the unrhymed ten-syllable line, neither so long as to split nor so short as to sound juvenile, provides a more congenial medium than fourteeners for extended flights of English verse.

Thomas Sackville and Thomas Norton seem to have been the first to write blank verse for the theatre in *Gorboduc, or Ferrex and Porrex*, their tragedy about English politics, specifically the problem of royal succession, composed at the beginning of Elizabeth's reign and published in 1562. Although their poetry is significantly less complex and polished than that to be heard fifty years later, it is serviceable and relatively easy on the ear:

O my beloved son! O my sweet child!
My dear Ferrex, my joy, my life's delight!
Is my beloved son, is my sweet child,
My dear Ferrex, my joy, my life's delight,
Murdered with cruel death? O hateful wretch!
O heinous traitor both to heaven and earth!
Thou, Porrex, thou this damned deed hath wrought;
Thou, Porrex, thou shalt dearly bye [pay for] the same.
Traitor to kin and kind, to sire and me,
To thine own flesh, and traitor to thyself,
The gods on thee in hell shall wreak their wrath.

(4.1.23–33)[7]

27

Representing English blank verse in an early manifestation, this passage presents to the ear possibilities that later poets would enthusiastically develop.

The lack of rhyme in poetic drama would probably have puzzled the first audiences of *Gorboduc*. Tragedy demanded verse, not the quotidian prose of comedy, and verse usually supplied some form of end rhyme. Sackville and Norton create their poetic effects not with rhymed line-endings but with noticeable repetitions and other rhetorical turns, tropes that assert themselves without rudely clamouring for attention. The tendency of the pre-Shakespearean poets to stop at the end of a line is audible, but it is striking that these writers are unusually alert to the possibilities of rhythmic variation in the line. The frequent pauses within the pentameter line are remarkable because they are rare in such early blank verse. Here they serve to accent the repetitions achieved with appositives and doubled nouns: 'my joy, my life's delight' or 'to kin and kind, to sire and me'. In other words, the ordering effect of the decasyllabic rhythm is supplemented with and supported by other shaping patterns. It is just these variations that will, in the hands of the later poetic innovators, break the monotony of dramatic dialogue organized into endlessly repeated ten-syllable units. Until the arrival of Shakespeare, the most gifted and significant of those theatre poets was Christopher Marlowe.

Marlowe showed his theatrical contemporaries how to characterize the tragic hero by means of language, creating a dignified verse style appropriate to his subjects. *Tamburlaine*, his first great success, opens with a prologue consciously asserting theatrical originality and poetic superiority. The audience will be rescued 'From jigging veins of rhyming mother wits' and invited instead to 'hear the Scythian Tamburlaine / Threatening the world with high astounding terms' (Prologue, 1, 4–5).[8] Explicitly advertising novelty, the playwright rejects sing-song rhyme in favour of the more neutral and more modern medium of blank verse. In a series of tragedies written for the celebrated tragedian Edward Alleyn at Henslowe's Rose playhouse, Marlowe was the first English poet to introduce great flexibility into the rigid blank-verse line of the 1570s and '80s.[9] Building upon the example of Sackville and Norton and exploiting the latent variety in their lines, he experimented boldly with the rhythmic possibilities of iambic pentameter, inserting pauses at various points in the line and exaggerating the aural effect of such stops. Above all, he consciously played with the inherent tension between the poetic frame and the semantic energy of the sentence: the intellectual hunger of a Doctor Faustus and the gleeful vengeance of a Barabas, the Jew of Malta, for example, tend to push the sentences so hard as to threaten the regularity of the pentameter. Marlowe's other major contribution was to demonstrate the appeal of majestic diction. The *Tamburlaine* Prologue means what it says in promising 'high astounding terms'. Everywhere the audacious young playwright indulges his fondness for the exotic proper noun, either of place – *Persepolis, Trebizon, Bithynia, Campania, Elysium* – or of person – *Bajazeth, divine Zenocrate, Usumcasane, Ithamore*. Rather than dispense entirely with the rhetorical patterns and artificial verbal structures that stiffen the verse of his predecessors, he summons them for particular theatrical effects without allowing them to tyrannize over the structure of his verse.

These and other Marlovian innovations are significant in moving dramatic speech to a new level of sophistication and possibility. The poet complicates the use of dialogue, for example, enhancing verisimilitude by allowing characters to speak *to* each other rather than *past* each other. But perhaps most important is that Marlowe figures words explicitly as weapons. This equation has become axiomatic, and yet it is impossible to consider the subject without stating it plainly: in Marlowe, language is power. Tamburlaine, for example, talks his way into geopolitical supremacy, control of words symbolizing other forms of domination – political, sexual, emotional, financial – and usually his characters know it. The extraordinary self-consciousness about language that we observe in Marlowe's speakers is a clue to his vital role in changing the English theatre. Even before Marlowe's death in 1593 Shakespeare the novice was beginning to exploit some of these same ways of thinking about theatrical representation, and in just a few years Shakespeare had created some of his greatest successes with Marlowe's poetic and theatrical tools. It is idle to speculate on what Shakespeare's verse would have looked like had Marlowe never written a play, but it seems indisputable that the young Shakespeare was enthralled by the Marlovian poetry he heard declaimed from the stage of the Rose.

'The style that shows'

Familiarity with earlier Elizabethan plays (or sonnets, or prose fiction, or any other literary form, for that matter) makes it easier to overcome one of the greatest obstacles to appreciating Shakespeare's tragic language: its obvious and unapologetic artificiality. In this respect, as in many others, it is like everything else he wrote. Ordinary people in Elizabethan England did not sound like dramatic characters. Hamlet and Doctor Faustus and Volpone talk the way they do because their creators have selected and arranged the raw linguistic materials, have 'wrought' the words into art. And the extremes of tragic emotion and eloquence of the heroes' speech make the stylization especially conspicuous. One of Shakespeare's primary contributions to the development of English drama was his capacity for making dramatic speech sound 'natural'. He extends Marlowe's technique of having his persons engage with one another's speech, interacting directly and responding to or modifying the utterance of the conversational partner. His construction of their speeches also makes characters seem dynamic, as they change their minds in mid-speech or work through an idea rather than merely expound it.

And yet for all this verisimilitude, Shakespeare's tragic speakers still employ many of the same rhetorical patterns audible in the language of John Lyly and Thomas Kyd and their Tudor predecessors. Such obviously arranged verbal structures are most easily discerned in his early plays, particularly the histories. In *3 Henry VI*, for example, the doomed King Henry imagines a meeting which decides his future, the participants being his Queen Margaret and the Earl of Warwick:

> Ay, but she's come to beg, Warwick to give:
> She on his left side, craving aid for Henry,
> He on his right, asking a wife for Edward;
> She weeps and says her Henry is depos'd,
> He smiles and says his Edward is installed
>
> (3.1.42–6)

Here the oppositions and complements are well suited to the subject of the passage, the complementary nature of royal politics, specifically the fall of one king with the rise of another. Characteristic syntactical forms include the similarly shaped lines, particularly with antithetical contents, the reiterative diction ('and says her.../...and says his'), and the obviously 'poetic' or 'arranged' sound of the passage. In the early comedies, too, the give-and-take of flirtation and courtship is often represented in symmetrically arranged phrases and words. Although the 'flowers of rhetoric' become less pronounced as Shakespeare gains experience, he never abandons artifice altogether but depends upon subtler, less exposed forms of verbal patterning.

Renaissance playwrights wrote for audiences who relished 'the style that shows'.[10] Shakespeare in the tragedies depends upon conventional rhetorical forms and overt structures not because he can't escape them but because he likes them, and his taste reflects his culture's unashamed delight in craft. People in early modern England took pleasure in art that was obviously art: they expected to see evidence of labour, they relished the highly wrought object, they delighted in the ornamented sentence, the intricate phrase, the clever rhyme. Thus Ben Jonson's poem that prefaces the 1623 Folio praises Shakespeare's 'well turned, and true-filèd lines'. Such an attitude also accounts for the sixteenth-century humanists' general preference for Virgil over Homer, since the *Aeneid* was thought to be more polished and artful than its more primitive Greek antecedents.[11] To look at Elizabethan tragedy under this lens is to recognize one of its principal appeals, that its noble characters and extreme actions gave opportunity for highly wrought, extravagant declamation. Sidney's praise of 'stately speeches and well sounding phrases, climbing to the height of Seneca's style' in *Gorboduc* reveals the expectations that audiences brought with them to the public theatres. It was for such ears and tastes that Shakespeare created the eloquent heroes of the tragedies.

The heroic register

The sound of any Shakespearean tragedy is dominated, of course, by the extraordinary voice of the tragic hero.[12] Each of the title characters speaks distinctively, such is Shakespeare's gift for individualizing them linguistically, but they do share some common rhetorical traits, and it will be worthwhile to identify and illustrate some basic features of the heroic style. This sort of enterprise must be approached with caution, however. First, each of the protagonists is so vividly particularized that lumping all together can seem to misrepresent their modes of expression. Second, in addition to differences from play to play, there are variations within each play: the hero is by no means the only speaker of exalted or impressive verse. Since the tragic mode implies an elevated verbal decorum, most members of the cast speak a relatively formal, dignified style of poetry. And given the extremity of the passions represented, as well as the rank of the characters, many supporting players speak an appropriately noble language – Claudius, Bolingbroke, Macduff, Octavius, Volumnia. Finally, any such taxonomy is bound to be unsatisfying. Knowing and naming components cannot account for the mysterious power of Hamlet's speech, or that of any of his tragic counterparts: poetry is much more than the sum of its parts. Still, we can say that the keynote in tragedy is set by the tragic hero, and that keynote is hyperbole.

When Sidney asserts that tragedy should 'stir the affects [emotions] of admiration and commiseration', 'admiration' is synonymous with 'wonder', and the hero's poetic flights are one of the poet's most effective tools for stimulating such a response.[13] They confer upon the protagonist what we would call charisma, a verbal authority that supplements and reinforces the natural attractions of the lead actor, be he Burbage or Branagh. In Shakespearean tragedy the sound and fury signify something: the heroic idiom is calculated to suggest the visionary propensities of the tragic hero. Heightened speech attests to idealism, aspiration, the desire for transcendence. The dimensions of this heroic vision are suggested in Brutus's refusal to swear an oath to assassinate Caesar:

> What need we any spur but our own cause
> To prick us to redress? What other bond
> Than secret Romans that have spoke the word
> And will not palter? And what other oath
> Than honesty to honesty engaged
> That this shall be or we will fall for it?
> Swear priests and cowards and men cautelous,
> Old feeble carrions, and such suffering souls
> That welcome wrongs: unto bad causes swear
> Such creatures as men doubt. But do not stain
> The even virtue of our enterprise,
> Nor th'insuppressive mettle of our spirits,
> To think that or our cause or our performance
> Did need an oath.   (JC 2.1.123–36)

This is the hero's early, idealistic mode. It is marked by command, by self-assertion, by rejection of the common or conventional. Poetry and vision convert murder into sacrifice, conspiracy into a sacred cause. Hamlet, Macbeth, Coriolanus, all speak in similar accents.

During the course of each tragic narrative the heroic voice changes radically in response to conflict and suffering. This linguistic alteration signifies the metamorphosis by which the hero is transformed into his opposite. It is clearly audible in Mark Antony's language after the battle of Actium:

>   All is lost!
> This foul Egyptian hath betrayèd me.
> My fleet hath yielded to the foe, and yonder
> They cast their caps up and carouse together
> Like friends long lost. Triple-turned whore! 'Tis thou
> Hast sold me to this novice, and my heart
> Makes only wars on thee. Bid them all fly;
> For when I am revenged upon my charm,
> I have done all. Bid them all fly. Begone! [Exit Scarus]
> O sun, thy uprise shall I see no more.
> Fortune and Antony part here; even here
> Do we shake hands. All come to this? The hearts
> That spanieled me at heels, to whom I gave
> Their wishes, do discandy, melt their sweets
> On blossoming Caesar; and this pine is barked,
> That overtopped them all. Betrayed I am.
>   (Ant. 4.12. 9–24)

Experience and the tragic environment exert a pressure on the hero that magnifies, intensifies, and violently changes the tones of speech. In Antony's

register changes character

case the language is no longer magnanimous and self-assured, but vindictive, cruel, and to some extent desperate. He reaches for the poetic conventions that will furnish him with a language appropriate to adversity, e.g., apostrophe ('O sun'), personification ('Fortune and Antony'), images ('cast their caps up'), grand metaphors ('this pine is barked'), imperatives ('Bid them... Bid them'), rare diction ('spanieled', 'discandy'), extravagant alliteration ('Like friends long lost. Triple-turned...'), rhetorical questions ('All come to this?'), syntactic inversion ('Betrayed I am'), and other forms of patterning and intensification.

Othello offers an even clearer paradigm of this verbal mutation. The Moor owes his success before the Senate to the same rhetorical powers that won the heart of Desdemona and that he then proceeds to turn against himself. The sonorous verbal music of the opening becomes, by the middle of the third act, destructive, vengeful, and bombastic, and in the fourth act glorious poetry yields to prosaic gabbling and filthy images hurled at his innocent wife. Such audible variations not only support but help to create the arc of each hero's experience. Hamlet's assault on Ophelia in the Nunnery Scene (3.1), for example, or his vulgar treatment of his mother in the Closet Scene (3.4) are as brutal as some of his other speeches are sensitive and lyrical, one register depending upon the other for its impact.

Usually the tragic hero regains poetic authority and power just before the end, before death. Othello in his final speech, 'Soft you; a word or two before you go', has recovered some control of the rhythms and imagery that were so initially winning. Even King Lear, perhaps the most reduced and damaged of the tragic protagonists, attains a degree of eloquence and authority in the speech to Cordelia about their living 'like birds in the cage' (5.3.8–19). *Ex* Then in his final moments he unleashes another kind of affective power in the imprecations and wrenching pleas over her lifeless body. In each play the hero's eloquence results from the poet's manipulation of patterns: the establishment and subsequent modification of these expected forms signal or underscore the emotional, psychological, and spiritual permutations that so thoroughly move the audience.

'Big and boisterous words'

Of the particular elements from which Shakespeare fashions his heroes' extraordinary speech, one of the most potent is diction. As William Webbe wrote in 1586, 'To the tragical writers belong properly the big and boisterous words.'[14] Shakespeare's heroes are bigger than life, and putting the matter bluntly, they use bigger words than other characters, magnificent polysyllables that contribute substantially to their eloquence: Othello's

'Anthropophagi' and 'chrysolite'; Hamlet's 'the Everlasting', 'malefactions', and 'consummation / Devoutly to be wished'; Richard II's 'Discomfortable cousin' and 'glistering Phaeton'; Romeo's 'o'erperch' and 'unsubstantial Death is amorous'; Juliet's 'cockatrice'; Macbeth's 'multitudinous seas incarnadine', 'Tarquin's ravishing strides', and 'If th' assassination / Could trammel up the consequence'; Lear's 'cataracts and hurricanoes'; Coriolanus's 'acclamations hyperbolical'; Cleopatra's 'make / My country's high pyramides my gibbet'. Some of these, such as 'o'erperch', 'incarnadine', and 'assassination', seem to have been Shakespeare's invention, or in some cases his adaptation of an existing word. Many were as unusual and striking in his day as they are in ours. Just as his heroes are magnified by the presence of foils and opposites – Hamlet and both Horatio and Polonius, Macbeth and Banquo, Lear and Kent or the Fool – so the hero's speech stands out by virtue of its difference from the languages spoken around him. The poet has selected verbal elements that connote distinction and rarity: such splendid diction is to common speech as the hero is to common people.

The dazzling word, like a precious gem, benefits from an appropriate setting, and much depends upon placement. Webbe goes on to say in his brief comments on 'big . . . words' that 'Examples must be interplaced, according fitly to the time and place.'[15] As some of the phrases cited above will have indicated, Shakespeare often underwrites the equation of speech and stature by locating exceptional words against a relatively neutral background. Richard II's eloquent metaphor for his downfall is one such passage, in which the stunning phrase is embedded among monosyllables: 'Down, down I come, like glistering Phaeton' (3.3.178). So it is in Romeo's 'shake the yoke of inauspicious stars', the hard consonants of the first monosyllables preparing for the sibilant sweep of the last two words. Romeo's phrase also illustrates another typical form, an impressive adjective linked with a plain noun. Often the adjective is Latinate and the concluding noun Anglo-Saxon in origin, although sometimes the combination is reversed. In Romeo's final soliloquy alone we find 'inauspicious stars' accompanied by a multitude of such contrasting doublets: 'betossèd soul', 'triumphant grave', 'slaughtered youth', 'unsubstantial Death', 'everlasting rest', 'world-wearied flesh', 'righteous kiss', 'engrossing Death', 'true apothecary'. This characteristic verbal device creates a systole–diastole rhythm, another long–short pattern that mimics other forms of rhythmic contrast, most notably the iambic structures of which the lines are made.

But no one, not even an eloquent Shakespearean hero, speaks this way all the time. For all their command of a brilliant vocabulary, these characters may, especially at moments of extreme passion, express themselves with unwonted simplicity. A striking form of this tactic is the unlooked-for series of powerful monosyllables:

> OTHELLO Damn her, lewd minx! O, damn her! damn her!
> (3.3.476)

> LEAR Why should a dog, a horse, a rat, have life,
> And thou no breath at all? (5.3.279–80)

> MACBETH ... a poor player
> That struts and frets his hour upon the stage
> And then is heard no more. (5.5.23–5)

> RICHARD III Chop off his head! (3.1.193)

> HAMLET To be, or not to be (3.1.56)

These simple nouns and verbs are powerful, to be sure, but subtle poetic forces are at work to complicate their plainness. The apparently lone mono-syllables are supported by an array of rhythmic devices, particularly du-plication or reiteration. The verbs in Macbeth's image ('struts and frets') are acoustically matched; Othello's outburst depends upon a triply repeated verb and the unexpected spondee ('lewd minx'), a foot that breaks the iambic pattern with two syllables of identical weight; the repeated article in Lear's question separates and emphasizes the iambs; and the most famous of all Shakespearean phrases benefits from its opposed infinitives, duplicated with a difference.

Such phrases also register powerfully because their simplicity contrasts so markedly with the surrounding poetic grandeur. Othello's blunt curse, the first example, follows several rhythmically propulsive speeches, one of which develops the elaborate simile comparing his 'wide revenge' to the 'icy current and compulsive course' of the Pontic Sea. Macbeth's monosyllabic doublet 'struts and frets' occurs in the soliloquy that begins with the famously reiter-ated polysyllables, 'Tomorrow and tomorrow and tomorrow', and proceeds to 'the last syllable of recorded time'. An obverse but no less impressive in-stance occurs in the last act of *Othello*, in the opening lines of 'It is the cause, it is the cause, my soul': as one critic puts it, 'In Othello's priestlike speech before the sacrifice of Desdemona forty monosyllables fall like the water-drops of Chinese torture before the crowning grandeur of "monumental alabaster." '[16] This juxtaposition of the majestic and the simple exemplifies a larger principle, one that governs not only verbal registers but also such fea-tures as scenic arrangement, contrasting characters, and comparable plots. All these combinations fall under the category of rhythm.

The most pervasive form of rhythm found in tragedy is the pulsating beat of the blank verse. In its basic pattern the poetry spoken by the tragic heroes is no different from that given to Titania or Bolingbroke or any verse speaker from any other kind of play. But by the time Shakespeare commits himself to the tragic mode, i.e., by mid-career, he has already developed a sophisticated, tractable approach to the pentameter line, and this flexible command of verse structure permits him to adapt and shape dramatic speech according to the demands of character and narrative. Considering the state of English blank verse in 1590, it is astonishing to observe how far he had pushed the boundaries of the form by 1600, his first decade of composition. He was able to rely on the audience's familiarity with the underlying beat, both the give and take of the iambs and the general length of the pentameter line, so that when he came to write *Hamlet* his profound understanding of the relation between sound and sense allowed him to modify the line for specific effects. The major tragedies exhibit an unparalleled intuition of how acoustic variation and irregularity make meaning.

The sound of Hamlet's speeches, to take one of the most audible examples, profits from Shakespeare's experiments with enjambment, with variously and multiply segmented lines, with reversed feet, and with other rhythmic subtleties.

> I am dead, Horatio. Wretched queen adieu.
> You that look pale, and tremble at this chance,
> That are but mutes or audience to this act,
> Had I but time, as this fell sergeant death,
> Is strict in his arrest, I could tell you –
> But let it be.   (5.2.312–17)

The tactics by which Shakespeare slackened and varied the relative uniformity characteristic of early English dramatic verse are clearly exhibited here. The first line begins by eliding two words ('I am') into one syllable, then quickly performs another elision as the 'i-o' of Horatio is reduced to one syllable. Including the stop at the end of the line, the speaker must pause four times: the medial period divides the line in two, and a comma sub-divides each half. The second line begins with a trochaic inversion ('Yóu thăt'); the fourth adds a spondee ('thís féll sérgeănt') to promote a crucial metaphor; the fifth appends an additional syllable to the end; grammatical intrusions disrupt the rhythmic uniformity ('I could tell you'); and only one line allows the sweep of an unbroken pentameter.

Such hesitations and rhythmic instability focus the ear on Hamlet's dying words, of course, and many other passages reveal, in their distinctive rhythmic imprint, a similarly intimate relation to their narrative context. We might note Macbeth's verbal disarray when, after having killed Duncan, he justifies his killing the guards who have apparently killed the king:

> Who can be wise, amazed, temp'rate, and furious,
> Loyal and neutral, in a moment? No man.
>
> (2.3.101–2)

or Coriolanus's emotional division over having to ask for the consulship:

> [I] for your voices have
> Done many things, some less, some more. Your voices!
> Indeed, I would be consul.   (2.3.115–17)

or Cleopatra's

> Give me my robe. Put on my crown. I have
> Immortal longings in me.   (5.2.274–5)

Repeatedly local meanings are thus enhanced by the poet's manipulation of sound. The rhythmic baldness of Coriolanus's last five words establishes the opposition of talk and action, the contrast between the reiterated 'voices' of the previous lines and the 'Indeed' of the conclusion.

Particular significance, however, is much less important than the larger rhythms to which sound and sense contribute. The extraordinary metrical variety that Shakespeare achieves in the tragedies is only one component in a larger musical structure. This pervasive system is not much commented on, but it is vital in our experience not only of the tragic voice but also of its echoes produced throughout the play. Hamlet's short phrases and broken lines play off our memory of contrary rhythms we have been assimilating from the beginning of the play. 'But let it be. Horatio, I am dead, / Thou livest' (5.2.317–18) depends for its effect upon our having absorbed such expansive phrases as 'Whether 'tis nobler in the mind to suffer / The slings and arrows of outrageous fortune' (3.1.57–8). The tragedies offer what we might call dramatic polyphony, a simultaneous sounding of different voices, accents, patterns, and tempi. Lear's extravagant outbursts, from the early speech about 'the barbarous Scythian' (1.1.110) to 'Blow winds, and crack your cheeks! Rage, blow' (3.2.1), require the counterpoint of Cordelia's 'Nothing' (1.1.82, 84), the Fool's jingling reversals, and Edmund's verbal bravado. The alternation between verse and prose is another manifestation of this rhythmic pattern, as is the contrast in tempo between differently paced lines of blank verse within the same play, or between the same speaker's use of different styles and speeds.

Often a single speech exhibits a deliberate acceleration and accumulation of verbal power that seems uniquely Shakespearean. Mark Antony's famous soliloquy just after the assassination of Julius Caesar, beginning 'O, pardon me, thou bleeding piece of earth' (3.1.254), palpably increases in velocity as it moves towards its rhythmic climax. Other familiar examples would be Othello's 'Farewell the tranquil mind! Farewell content!' (3.3.348–57), Lady Macbeth's 'Come, you spirits / That tend on mortal thoughts' (1.5.40–54), or Coriolanus's 'You common cry of curs' (3.3.120–35). In these cases, and others like them, clauses and phrases of approximately the same length follow one another in succession, generating something like a perpetual motion machine that pushes the listener forward to the memorable conclusion. Also, a lightening of punctuation seems to intensify the reiterative pulsating of the iambs. This sudden intensification in a crucial speech promotes increased tension and power in the play as a whole.

Such manipulation of tempo signals another rhythmic effect, here perceptible in Othello's repetition of 'Farewell' and in the harsh alliteration of Coriolanus's line. The reproduction of various sounds certainly creates poetic coherence, binding together words and phrases, but a more important function is that it increases the formality and thus the gravity or momentousness of a speech. By this point in his career Shakespeare knows the difference between stiffness and formality, and thus the rhetorical schemes and self-conscious patterns of the early plays have yielded to the extravagant but more spontaneous repetitions of the tragic figure in conflict. To look at the pressure points in most of the tragedies is to notice how frequently such acoustic duplication appears at such moments.

CLEOPATRA   Where art thou, Death?
Come hither, come! Come, come, and take a queen
Worth many babes and beggars.

CHARMIAN   O, temperance, lady!
(*Ant.* 5.2.45–7)

'Temperance' is exactly what the tragic figure disdains: extravagance makes the character exceptional, and this magnificent intemperance is heard in such effusions as the four instances of 'come' in the second line, or the alliterative 'queen [with its embedded 'w'] . . . worth' and 'babes and beggars'. So significant and widespread is such pleonasm that many of the passages already cited depend upon it, from Richard II's 'Down, down I come, like glistering Phaeton' to Macbeth's 'Tomorrow, and tomorrow, and tomorrow'.

Figures and their function

To first-time readers or playgoers, the highly figurative texture of Shakespeare's plays is most immediately impressive and can make the verse appear unduly ornamented and disorienting. So it seemed to no less a critic than John Dryden:

> [His] whole style is so pestered with figurative expressions that it is as affected as it is obscure...'Tis not that I would exclude the use of metaphors from passions, ... but to use 'em at every word, to say nothing without a metaphor, a simile, an image, or description, is I doubt to smell a little too strongly of the buskin.[17]

Dryden and the Augustans who followed him especially deplored Shakespeare's practice of mixing images and piling metaphor upon metaphor, probably because such fluent or mercurial treatment violated their taste for discrete categories of action and thought. But these objections, which motivated eighteenth-century editors' attempts to 'clean up' and regularize the Shakespearean text, serve ironically to prove the centrality of figurative language in it. Prose speakers in comedy and tragedy also use imagery constantly, Iago being one of the most notorious of such speakers, and so do we all, even in ordinary conversation. But in poetry, particularly the heroic style, the images and image clusters colour and thereby intensify the passionate verse.

The first effect of figurative language proceeds from the materiality of the image, the way that an image *as an image* stimulates the reader's imagination and enriches the texture of speech. This ornamental or affective value is suggested by the Elizabethan poetic theorist and cataloguer George Puttenham when he asserts that 'figurative speeches [are] the instrument wherewith we burnish our language', that the excellent poet will produce verse that 'is gallantly arrayed in all his colours which figure can set upon it'.[18] This is not to imply that even in this limited sense images perform no thematic work: on the contrary, they establish atmosphere, modify our perception of character, comment on the action, and otherwise contribute in a multitude of ways. But many images do not primarily serve to elucidate another thing; instead, they make a powerful impact on their own.

Images can forcefully affect the senses of the imaginative mind. Shakespeare often seeks a visceral effect, attempting to move the audience by means of word pictures and their associations. Pictorial or other sensory images account for some of the most memorable and characteristic passages in the tragedies:

Hamlet's disposal of the body of Polonius:

> I'll lug the guts into the neighbor room.
> (3.4.213)

The Nurse's recollection of Juliet's weaning:

> For I had then laid wormwood to my dug,
> Sitting in the sun under the dove-house wall.
> (1.3.27–8)

Cleopatra's angling for 'tawny finned fishes':

> My bended hook shall pierce
> Their slimy jaws (2.5.12–13)

Aufidius's greeting to Coriolanus:

> Let me twine
> Mine arms about that body, whereagainst
> My grainèd ash an hundred times hath broke
> And scarred the moon with splinters.
> (4.5.103–4)

Enobarbus's lengthy and detailed recital of Cleopatra's river journey:

> The barge she sat in, like a burnished throne
> Burned on the water. The poop was beaten gold;
> Purple the sails, and so perfumèd that
> The winds were lovesick with them. The oars were silver,
> Which to the tune of flutes kept stroke (2.2.201–5)

And yet as luscious as the sounds and pictures may be, even those images employed for their material effect are likely, as the barge speech indicates, to be exploited for their symbolic possibilities.

All language, linguistic theorists contend, is in some sense metaphoric: a word is a verbal sign, an image, that calls to mind – through a process of symbolic representation – the object or concept it names.[19] Therefore poets, attracted to the materiality of language as well as to its symbolic capacities, are naturally drawn to metaphor because it multiplies what the ordinary word can do. Metaphor was known to humanist rhetoricians as 'the figure of transport', since in the process of apprehension the perceiver's mind is moved, impelled from one image to another. Abundant figurative language is vital to the great arias because in those crucial moments of passion speakers seem transported beyond themselves and seem to carry the audience with them. Shakespeare's metaphoric practice is once again especially conspicuous in the early work. *Romeo and Juliet*, for instance, is saturated with figures, particularly metaphors that beget other metaphors. Readers can recall their own favourite metaphoric clusters from this lavishly figurative play: perhaps the religious discourse with which the lovers flirt on first meeting; the heavenly bodies, flowers, lights, colours, and other beauties of the balcony scene; Juliet's 'Gallop apace, ye fiery footed steeds', with its multiple, vivid comparisons ('thou wilt lie upon the wings of night / Whiter than new snow upon a raven's back'); the oxymoronic combination of images – e.g. 'fiend angelical' – that express Juliet's irreconcilable feelings about her husband just after the death of Tybalt (3.1.1). Metaphoric intensity is so prominent in *Romeo and Juliet* probably because the playwright was still discovering his gift for figuration and the story he chose to dramatize stimulated him to use it liberally.

A flair for metaphor is one trait that distinguishes the speech of the great tragic heroes and enriches the poetic texture of the middle and later tragedies. Metaphor and simile account for some of the most famous phrases and passages in the canon: 'the slings and arrows of outrageous fortune' with which Hamlet struggles (3.1.57–8); Othello's 'subdued eyes' that 'Drops tears as fast as the Arabian trees / Their medicinable gum' (5.2.346–7); Macbeth's 'I am in blood / Stepped in so far that should I wade no more, / Returning were as tedious as go o'er' (3.4.136–8). Such figuration contributes much to the monumental, irresistible sound of the hero's voice. But in the mature tragedies it does much more than that: metaphor is one of the primary means by which Shakespeare creates unity of effect and thus intensifies the affective power of these great plays. Unity is such a fundamental artistic principle, one that artists and critics worry over, because the strategies that promote unity help to concentrate meaning. In *King Lear*, the savage conditions of the playworld are given vivid reality for the audience because the playwright describes the characters and their actions as tigers, vultures, kites [birds of prey], 'pelican daughters' [spilling the blood of the parent], vultures, monsters, 'monsters of the deep', rats, serpents, asses, dragons, bears, hogs, foxes, she-foxes, lions, boars, fitchews [polecats], horses, multiple species of dogs, centaurs, fiends, and cannibals. Whatever his theme Shakespeare always represents the significance of that topic in a network of meaningful figures. *Coriolanus*, his late Roman tragedy, is a hard play, both in the sense of its difficulty and in its tough, unyielding tone: its hero is proud, unpleasant, and hard to like, keeping his distance both from others and from the audience. Thus it is apt that the language of the play strikes us as somewhat rigid. G. Wilson Knight, one of the twentieth-century critics most sensitive to poetic imagery, gives a persuasive account of this correspondence between image and theme:

> We are in a world of hard weapons, battle's clanging contacts...the sicken-
> ing crashes of war...The imagery is often metallic – such as 'leaden pounds'
> (III.i.314), or 'manacles' (I.ix.57) or 'leaden spoons, irons of a doit' (I.v.5),
> or as when Coriolanus's harshness forces his mother to kneel 'with no softer
> cushion than the flint' (v.iii.53)...Hostile cities are here ringed as with the
> iron walls of war, inimical, deadly to each other, self-contained. Thus our city
> imagery blends with war imagery, which is also 'hard' and metallic. And that
> itself is fused with the theme of Coriolanus's iron-hearted pride.[20]

Such a symbolic network enriches the play's interest in the problem of Coriolanus's masculinity, his effort to remain untouched by other beings, particularly the weak ones, more particularly women. An even more impressive and
detailed symbolic structure informs *Macbeth*: blood. Blood not only gives
rise to a complex network of related figures but also reveals the playwright's
concern with such central issues as kinship and country. In every play the
figurative patterns generate a symbolic world, an imaginary realm in which
the means of comparison – in *Coriolanus*, the metallic images – take on an
existence of their own and thus fortify the meaning of the tragic action.

'The self-conscious sleepe'

The contribution of these technical features to the voice of the tragic
hero is less significant, finally, than one indispensable quality – verbal self-
consciousness reflecting the poet's sensitivity to the uses of language. The
modern world, given our technological advances and other cultural developments, seems dominated by visual images, and the supremacy of the eye
may have dulled our acoustic sensitivities, at least compared to those of
our early modern ancestors. With print in its adolescence, Shakespeare's
England was largely an oral culture; consequently, the ability to do things
with words was a coveted talent. The early modern feeling for words and
verbal patterns is related to the increasing dignity of the English language,
considered unsuitable for serious writing until well into the sixteenth century. As translators began to render the Bible into English, and as poets and
scholars began to explore the expressive possibilities of their native tongue,
educated English people began to take pride in their language. They fretted
over it, relished it, sought to polish it, called attention to its felicities and
opportunities for creativity and communication. This public consciousness
meant that Shakespeare could have expected his audience to notice and take
pleasure in linguistic virtuosity. And since tragedy occupied so exalted a position on the critical scale, the mode was especially hospitable to rhetorical
ostentation.

Such verbal brilliance becomes a matter of alarm to Shakespeare around mid-career, just as he turns wholeheartedly to the creation of tragedy. In *Julius Caesar* (1599), young Antony's language is flamboyant and self-aware, particularly in the funeral oration, with its ironic digs at Brutus and the conspirators as 'honourable men'. Thus his eulogy contrasts pointedly with his adversary's prose defence of the assassination, for Brutus subordinates virtuosity to virtue, style to substance. However, Brutus's disdain of rhetoric also implies a kind of reverse virtuosity, a pride in undecorated statement. This juxtaposition of opposing forms embodies Shakespeare's growing doubts about pyrotechnical speech, suspicions he had begun to explore in the history plays, tentatively in *Richard III* and then more profoundly in the second tetralogy (1595–9).

All these anxieties come to fruition in the tragedies that immediately follow *Julius Caesar* – *Hamlet* and *Othello*. One of Hamlet's principal appeals is his sensitivity to language and his self-conscious manipulation of it:

> GERTRUDE Hamlet, thou hast thy father much offended.
> HAMLET Mother, you have my father much offended.
>
> (3.4.9–10)

Hamlet cannot resist showing off. His punning first line, 'a little more than kin, and less than kind' (1.2.65); his reply to Polonius's question about what he is reading, 'Words, words, words' (2.2.189); and his insolence to Claudius about the dead Polonius being 'At supper. ... Not where a eats, but where a is eaten' (4.3.17–19) – these are sophomoric applications of formidable linguistic prowess, a talent that Shakespeare both admires and deplores. Indeed, the prince's self-awareness about his words is a synecdoche for his larger existential difficulty, the potentially paralytic effects of self-consciousness. While Othello is not as verbally adroit, he too is knowing about his particular form of verbal showmanship. His apology to the Senate, 'Rude am I in my speech' (1.3.81), is a rhetorical tactic, the manoeuvre of a sure-handed storyteller who knows how to manipulate his audience and whose defence of his marriage is anything but unpolished: on the contrary, the tale of Othello's wooing is a brilliant performance, romantic, poetically powerful, convincing to the audiences on stage and in the theatre. Above all, the speaker is aware of his talent. The 'self-dramatizing' tendencies that T. S. Eliot and others have noticed in Othello – they intend the phrase pejoratively – hint at the hero's irresistible inclination to use such virtuosity against himself. According to the paradox that underlies most of Shakespeare's work in this mode, the tragic fact is that the hero who uses his talent to conquer others also employs it to undo himself.

Most of the tragic protagonists who follow Othello are not represented as rhetorical show-offs; in these later tragedies the self-consciousness is patently that of the playwright. King Lear and Macbeth, for example, are powerful speakers, but they are less obviously attentive to language as language than their earlier counterparts. Shakespeare, however, is no less interested in language as a human problem. To start with, other verbal dandies begin to appear, Iago being the model of villainous eloquence. In *King Lear*, Goneril and Regan evince a kind of glee in their flattery of their father, while Edmund in his soliloquy on primogeniture (1.2.1–15) takes delight in the pliability of the word, particularly in the quibbles on 'bastard' and in his mockery of that 'fine word, "legitimate"'. Since Coriolanus is so absolute in his mistrust of language, the role of the self-conscious talker is taken by his mother, Volumnia, whose name indicates her passion for words. Having used her tongue incessantly, she concludes her loquacious plea that Rome be spared with an ironic look at her own prolixity: 'I am hushed until our city be afire, / And then I'll speak a little' (5.3.181–2). In *Antony and Cleopatra* Mark Antony reappears, older, more experienced, and manifestly less impetuous, but he is still conscious of his rhetorical gifts and his charismatic power. And Cleopatra, of course, is one of Shakespeare's most beguiling speakers. The arts of language are among Egypt's great attractions, along with music and other sensuous pleasures: much of her charm arises from her ear for language – 'he words me, girls' (5.2.190) – and her awareness of her verbal command.

The tragedy of language

Shakespeare's tragic conception of human experience must be seen, at least in part, as predicated on the failings of language itself. Throughout the Middle Ages and into the Renaissance, a bedrock of Christian doctrine was the linguistic catastrophe attendant on the Fall. Prelapsarian speech had been perfect and thus unmistakably clear, whereas in the fallen world language had become unreliable, potentially fraudulent, and dangerously ambiguous. The story of the Tower of Babel in Genesis 11 elaborated on the linguistic chaos to which fallen humanity was subject, and Reformation theologians regularly deplored their necessarily faulty medium of communication. At the same time, however, Shakespeare's culture had also inherited from the earlier Tudor humanists a faith in eloquence and in the power of language to educate, to civilize, and thus to help redeem the fallen race. In this respect Shakespeare's tragedies are faithful registers of a significant cultural division. They are among the most complex and subtle representations we have of this early modern ambivalence towards language. And that ambivalence extends beyond speech to the playwright's doubts about the theatre and his deeply divided estimation of the human species.

The tragedies everywhere imply an authorial obsession with the capacity of language to damage, deform, and mislead. Shakespeare's thinking about his medium seems to darken appreciably as his career proceeds from Hamlet, who loves words, to Coriolanus, who loathes them. When Hamlet laments, in his second major soliloquy, that he 'Must like a whore unpack [his] heart with words', he identifies his own particular vulnerability, the propensity to substitute language for action and to exercise his gift for words to the point of self-indulgence and self-delusion. *Coriolanus*, written at the end of the tragic sequence, examines the opposite problem: the Roman soldier despises language so thoroughly that he cannot move into the parliamentary realm of politics ('Parliament' is from French *parler*, to talk). He confesses that, while he sought out warfare, he 'fled from words', and he objects to the recitation of his deeds, resents hearing his 'nothings monstered'. This last phrase captures his mistrust of language, specifically its inherent failure to represent the world accurately. The man of action cannot tolerate the slippage or lack of correspondence between sign and signified.

Between the extremes of *Hamlet* and *Coriolanus* stand the other tragic heroes, all inhabiting a world in which language is to some degree the enemy. Each play depicts a slightly different form of linguistic treachery, although certain pernicious modes of speech and many of the same woeful consequences recur again and again. *Othello* exhibits the power of words used maliciously, or, putting it another way, the danger of fiction in the hands of the wicked. A manipulator such as Iago can make words distort the truth, pierce the heart, and destroy the innocent. Similarly, Edmund invents and employs such lies in *King Lear*, a play that begins with two lessons in the art of fiction, Goneril's and Regan's extravagant and empty declarations of love for their father. Cordelia suffers because she rejects such empty signs, refuses to use 'that glib and oily art / To speak and purpose not' (1.1.219–20). Since the evil of flatterers, or 'mouth-friends', is the focus of the first half of *Timon of Athens*, it is not surprising that Timon should figure his suicide as a rejection of speech: 'Lips, let sour words go by and language end' (5.1.210).[21] Further instances might be adduced – Cassius's dishonest exploitation of Brutus's idealism; Hamlet's lashing out at Ophelia; Othello's insulting Desdemona in the brothel scene (4.2); or, in *Coriolanus*, the tribunes' inciting the people to taunt the hero into self-defeat. Each case represents the dangerous malleability of words, their utility as instruments of evil.

Language is not merely the apparatus of the evil, however, but is itself treacherous and unreliable, even in the hands of the good or the well-meaning. Even when not maliciously intended, not employed as outright lies, words may be empty or misleading, as Shakespeare's complex portrait of Othello himself may prompt us to suspect. His romantic speech is colourful, even enthralling, but his self-dramatizing manner hints that his language may be hollow, an instrument of deception – especially self-deception – and that Iago may be partly right when he refers to the Moor's style as 'bombast'. As Puttenham puts it in *The Arte of English Poesie*, 'generally the high style is disgraced, and made foolish and ridiculous by all words affected, counterfeit, and puffed up, as it were a windball carrying more countenance than matter...'[22]

Flatterers and liars can succeed because words are inherently limited in their capacity to represent the world. A measure of Lear's tragic pain is his discovery of the distance between sound and sense:

> They flattered me like a dog, and told me I had the white hairs in my beard ere the black ones were there. To say 'ay' and 'no' to everything that I said 'ay,' and 'no' too was no good divinity. When the rain came to wet me once and the wind to make me chatter, when the thunder would not peace at my bidding, there I found 'em, there I smelt 'em out! Go to, they are not men o' their words: they told me I was everything; 'tis a lie, I am not ague-proof.
>
> (4.5.95–107)

The mad king's ordeal on the heath, when he commands the elements to destroy the wicked world, teaches him not only the consequences of flattery but also the futility of language divorced from power. The world survives 'the pelting of this pitiless storm'(3.4.29); Lear's words have no effect. Even more bitterly tragic is the insufficiency of words to do good. Cordelia knows that feelings cannot be adequately expressed, that she cannot describe the bond of love between child and parent: 'I cannot heave my heart into my mouth' (1.1.86–7).

In *Macbeth* language is more sinister still, the tool of demonic forces and the means of error and deceit. There Shakespeare looks sceptically at the properties of language that permit its misuse, reacting with disgust and sympathy at the fatal vulnerability of even the greatest among us. The Porter's joke about the damned 'equivocator' arriving at hell's gate – he 'could not equivocate to heaven' (2.3.7–10) – is a darkly ironic expression of the multiple dangers that pervade the play: double talk, slithery language, wicked persuasion, lies. To overcome Macbeth's high-mindedness, Lady Macbeth resolves to 'chastise with the valour of [her] tongue' (1.5.25) everything that prevents him from killing the king. She bullies and ridicules him, using contemptuous terms to belittle his manliness: 'beast', '*infirm* of purpose', as timid as 'the poor cat i'th'adage'. Macbeth is finally destroyed and his bloody career halted by a pair of prophecies: that 'none of woman born / Shall harm Macbeth' (4.1.79–80), and that 'Macbeth shall never vanquish'd be until / Great Birnam wood to high Dunsinane hill / Shall come against him' (92–4). Both promises are deceptive, seeming to offer invulnerability and yet fulfilling themselves in unexpected ways. Macbeth learns too late his error in trusting 'th' equivocation of the fiend / That lies like truth', of believing the 'juggling fiends... / That palter with us in a double sense' (5.8.19–20). The wordplay that delightfully animates the comic realms of *Much Ado About Nothing* and *Twelfth Night* has turned dangerous, and fatal ambiguity is everywhere: in the double meanings of words; in the riddling prophecies; in the duplicitous terms of Lady Macbeth's welcome to Duncan, that 'All our service / In every point twice done and then done double' (1.6.16–17) would be insufficient; in the witches' incantation, 'Double, double toil and trouble'.

Macbeth's 'Tomorrow, and tomorrow, and tomorrow' speech (5.4.18–27) urges a despairing assessment of all language: 'life' is nothing more than an empty verbal construct, 'a tale / Told by an idiot, full of sound and fury / Signifying nothing'. This dark passage, however, has proved to be among the most powerful and enduring of Shakespeare's words. The playwright was able to conceive of language in the darkest possible light, to identify the conditions of a tragic world with the verbal medium that constitutes it, and to imagine a character whose nihilism condemns even the means of expressing itself. But clearly he also appreciated the complementary position, recognizing that language had the capacity to fix such a dark point of view in a beautiful and lasting verbal artifact. Words are not entirely destructive but can be used creatively within the tragic narratives: in seeking to relieve his father and save the king Edgar modulates his speech, taking on the accents of disparate social classes; Emilia in *Othello* resolves to speak the truth despite the fatal consequences; Macbeth articulates the searing effect of evil on his soul; Volumnia persuades her stubborn son – at the cost of his life – to spare the city that has rejected him. Cleopatra constructs a 'monumental recreation of Antony' in the great speech to Dolabella (5.2.76–92), a word-picture that has been called 'the great generative act of the play'.[23] After the tragedies Shakespeare will devote himself to romance, and Cleopatra's creativity represents a step on the way to the affirmations of that mode.

Hamlet regrets unpacking his heart with words, but the forms in which he expresses his misery comprise some of the most meaningful verbal configurations ever created. This is one of the great paradoxes of Shakespearean tragedy, that language may convey its own failures and inadequacy in a form that is more than adequate, even triumphant. Thus Shakespeare's ambivalent conception of language, of his own artistic medium, corresponds exactly to the mixed view he takes towards his tragic protagonists: foolish and heroic, estimable and contemptible, undercut by the very quality that distinguishes them. This mixed assessment is congruent with the philosophical or religious contrarieties that had emerged from both medieval scholasticism and Tudor humanist thought and that characterized English literate culture at the beginning of the seventeenth century: the principle of the dignity of man, on the one hand; on the other, the belief in human depravity. All the tragedies invite the audience to entertain both positions, the infamy and the glory of the race, and the validity of each is encoded in Shakespeare's words.

Having begun with Pistol, I conclude by recalling another of Shakespeare's tragic pretenders. In the first rehearsal scene of *A Midsummer Night's Dream* Bottom covets the part of a tyrant – 'I could play Ercles rarely' – and proceeds to illustrate his gift for Herculean declamation. Bottom understands the prestige and the supreme power of the tragic idiom: even fools know that there is something special about the tragedies, something unavailable in the other modes. Shakespeare's command of language is one source of that distinction.

NOTES

1. See the essays by Hattaway, Diehl, Paster, and Belsey, elsewhere in this volume.
2. Alfred Harbage, 'Introduction' to *Twentieth-Century Views of Shakespeare's Tragedies* (Englewood Cliffs, NJ: Prentice-Hall, 1964), p. 3.
3. *English Renaissance Literary Criticism*, ed. Brian Vickers (Oxford: Clarendon Press, 1999), p. 381.
4. 'To the Right Worshipful Sir Thomas Henneage, Knight', in Thomas Newton's *Seneca His Tenne Tragedies* (New York: Alfred A. Knopf, 1927; rpt University of Indiana Press, 1932), p. 5.
5. The first quotations are cited from Vickers, *English Renaissance Literary Criticism*, and from *Elizabethan Critical Essays*, ed. G. Gregory Smith (Oxford: Clarendon Press, 1904), 2 vols.: Sidney (Vickers, p. 363); Ascham (Vickers, p. 19); Webbe (Smith, I. 249); Puttenham (Smith, II. 27). The lines from *The Spanish Tragedy* are cited from Thomas Kyd, '*The First Part of Hieronimo'and* '*The Spanish Tragedy*', ed. Andrew S. Cairncross (Lincoln: University of Nebraska Press, 1967).
6. Quoted from Newton's *Seneca*, p. 123.
7. *Gorboduc, or Ferrex and Porrex* in *Drama of the English Renaissance: The Tudor Period*, ed. Russell A. Fraser and Norman Rabkin (New York: Macmillan, 1976).
8. *The Complete Works of Christopher Marlowe: Tamburlaine the Great Parts I and II*, ed. David Fuller (Oxford: Clarendon Press, 1998). I have modernized the spelling.
9. George T. Wright, *Shakespeare's Metrical Art* (Berkeley and Los Angeles: University of California Press, 1988), p. 98.
10. Richard Lanham, *The Motives of Eloquence* (New Haven: Yale University Press, 1976), p. 1.
11. See Vickers, *English Renaissance Literary Criticism*, p. 623 n. 51.

12. 'Hero' is a problematic term. It seems to carry a positive valence – 'protagonist' is less evaluative – and it may appear to exclude those central figures who are women. But it is less cumbersome than the alternatives, and it is appropriate here because the hero's language is in the heroic register and sets the tone for the linguistic decorum of tragedy.

13. See J. V. Cunningham, *Tradition and Poetic Structure* (Denver: Alan Swallow, 1960), pp. 181ff.

14. *A Discourse of English Poetry*, in *Elizabethan Critical Essays*, ed. Smith, 1. 292.

15. *Ibid.*, p. 292.

16. George Rylands, 'The Poet and the Player', *Shakespeare Survey* 7 (1954), 31.

17. Quoted in Kenneth Muir, 'Shakespeare's Imagery – Then and Now', *Shakespeare Survey* 18 (1965), 46.

18. *The Arte of English Poesie*, in Vickers, *English Renaissance Literary Criticism*, p. 236.

19. See Terence Hawkes, *Metaphor* (London: Methuen, 1972), *passim*.

20. *The Imperial Theme* (London: Methuen, 1965), pp. 155–6.

21. I have adopted 'sour words', an emendation often accepted by editors; NCS prints the Folio's 'four words'.

22. Cited in Vickers, *English Renaissance Literary Criticism*, p. 231.

23. Janet Adelman, *Suffocating Mothers: Fantasies of Maternal Origin in Shakespeare's Plays, 'Hamlet' to 'The Tempest'* (New York and London: Routledge, 1992), p. 187.

3

DAVID BEVINGTON

Tragedy in Shakespeare's career

In one sense, Shakespeare wrote tragedies throughout his career. To be sure, among the plays classified as tragedies in the great Folio edition of 1623, only *Titus Andronicus* (c. 1589–92) and *Romeo and Juliet* (1594–6) were written before 1599. Yet Shakespeare certainly pursued tragic themes and consequences in his early historical plays. The title page of *The First Part of the Contention betwixt the Two Famous Houses of York and Lancaster*, published in 1594 as a somewhat shortened version of what was to appear in the 1623 Folio as *The Second Part of Henry the Sixth*, announces among its subjects 'the death of the good Duke Humphrey', the 'banishment and death of the Duke of Suffolk', and 'the tragical end of the proud Cardinal of Winchester'. *The True Tragedy of Richard Duke of York, and the Death of Good King Henry the Sixth*, published in 1595 as a version of what was to appear in the 1623 Folio as *The Third Part of Henry the Sixth*, describes itself as a tragedy in that quarto title. So does *The Tragedy of Richard III*, registered and published in 1597 after having been written in about 1592–4. *The Life and Death of King John* (written in about 1594–6 and first published in the 1623 Folio) and *The Tragedy of Richard the Second* (registered and published in 1597) are similarly characterized as tragedies on their title pages, at least (in the case of *King John*) by the implications of tragedy in the King's 'death'.

To say that the early history plays explore tragic themes and consequences is not, however, to establish in Shakespeare's writing at this juncture a clear sense of tragedy as a genre. In all of these plays, as David Kastan has argued,[1] history is an ongoing and open-ended project that eclipses tragic form. Classical literary criticism, from Aristotle on down to the early modern period, afforded no precedent for 'the history play' as a dramatic structure; hence Francis Meres's categorization of all the plays of Shakespeare that he lists in 1598 as either comedies or tragedies.[2] *Richard III* in his taxonomy is a tragedy, while *Henry IV* is a comedy. These rough-hewn approximations make sense, but do not allow for the conception of 'the history play' as a genre in its own right. 'The history play' remains a different sort of classification, based primarily on subject matter in a way that comedy and tragedy are not; the English history play is a play about English history.

As such, the history play's commitment to tragedy remains radically ambiguous. *Richard III* is about the rise and fall of Richard, Duke of Gloucester, who became king; it is also about the accession to power of Henry Tudor, Queen Elizabeth's grandfather. The idea of 'tragedy' here seems indebted to the overarching scheme of the medieval English cycle plays, in which human failure and death are ultimately to be understood as a part of a larger cosmic plan aimed at eventual restoration of order and harmony. This is not to argue a theological providential reading of Shakespeare's first tetralogy, or to see the account as allegorical. Yet these plays do interpret English history in such a way as to suggest that Richard's diabolical evil leads ultimately to his own downfall, having in the meantime inflicted on the English nation a scourging that it has richly earned through factionalism. The Earl of Richmond represents a deliverance and a new beginning under the Tudor monarchy. *The Tragedy of Richard II* similarly ends in the ascension of the Lancastrian king whose son will be Henry V. Tragedy is a prelude to historical change.

Shakespeare appears to owe his conception of tragedy in these early history plays not only to the English cycle plays (and to the larger cosmic idea of Christian history to which they are in turn indebted), but also to the tradition of the Fall of Princes. As enunciated in Chaucer's Prologue to 'The Monk's Tale',

> Tragedie is to seyn a certeyn storie,
> As olde bookes maken us memorie,
> Of hym that stood in greet prosperitee,
> And is yfallen out of heigh degree
> Into myserie, and endeth wrecchedly.[3]

Chaucer proceeds to illustrate this commonsense view of tragedy with illustrations of the fall of men and angels in divine and human history, from Lucifer and Adam to Samson, Hercules, Nebuchadnezzar, Nero, Antiochus, Alexander, Julius Caesar, Croesus, and still others. The idea of such a dolefully edifying catalogue is derived from Boccaccio's *De casibus virorum illustrium* and from the *Roman de la Rose* (5829–6901).[4] Boccaccio supplies the plan of the tale, with a similar catalogue of falls of great men; the *Roman* (indebted in turn to Boethius' *De consolatione philosophiae*)[5] supplies the motif of Fortune as the capricious goddess upon whose turning wheel no human can depend.

The list of fallen angels and men in Chaucer and Boccaccio contains some who are evil and villainous (Lucifer, Nero, Antiochus). As a result, the idea of tragedy bears little relation to Aristotle's definitions and classifications of tragedy in the *Poetics*, where the overthrow of a bad man is seen as distinctly less 'tragic' than the downfall of an essentially good man in whom can be identified a '*hamartia*' (variously translated as 'tragic flaw' and 'tragic error'). Instead, the prevailing view of tragedy in the Middle Ages becomes that of an edifying instance of the instability of fortune. Chaucer's essential definition is that the protagonist falls from high to low and ends wretchedly. The reader is invited to learn from such instances what it is to pin one's hopes on worldly advancement and one's own fatal pride.

This conception of tragedy continues strong into the late Middle Ages and early modern period, in John Lydgate's *The Fall of Princes* (1430–8), and in ever-expanding versions of *A Mirror for Magistrates*, begun (but prohibited from being published) in 1555 by William Baldwin and others, then published in 1559, 1563, 1574, 1578, and 1587, each time with additions. Tracing a direct line of descent back to Chaucer and Boccaccio, this compilation came to include exemplary 'Complaints' of Henry Duke of Buckingham (by Thomas Sackville) and Jane Shore, among others. New material contributed in the later editions by John Higgins and Thomas Blennerhasset took the story back to the legendary kings of early Britain, like Locrine, Lear, and King Arthur. The subject, increasingly, was English history and legendary history, in a form that was readily at hand to dramatists (Shakespeare most of all) eager to exploit a growing fascination with English national identity in the time of the Spanish Armada – 1588, just one year after the publication in 1587 of a major edition of *A Mirror*, as well as of the second edition of Holinshed's *Chronicles*.[6]

To be sure, *A Mirror for Magistrates* duplicated a good deal of the information Shakespeare could also have found in the chronicles of Holinshed and Hall, but it also firmly established a model of tragedy as applied to the history of England's royal families. This model offered a 'mirror' of the instability of fortune and the inevitable punishment of vice. Shakespeare's *Henry VI* plays and *Richard III*, insofar as they are tragedies, repeatedly illustrate this formula in the rise and fall of Henry VI, Richard Plantagenet, Duke Humphrey of Gloucester, the Dukes of Suffolk and Clarence, Edward IV, Hastings, Rivers, Grey, Buckingham, and many others. *Richard III* is, in these terms, the culmination and epitome of the model that Shakespeare inherited from a long tradition of the Fall of Princes. The model served him as a conceptual framework around which to dramatize civil conflict and provide a moral commentary which would have been familiar to his audiences.

As a basis for writing tragedy, on the other hand, its purposes were limited. It focused on political struggle to the virtual exclusion of the domestic and personal. The criteria of evaluation through which an audience might experience tragic emotion were largely those of judging success or failure in the performance of public duty. The audience is invited to deplore cynical manipulation of the political process as something to be punished by the workings of the plot, however engaging the manipulator (such as Richard III) might prove to be. Even a basically good-hearted man whose fall is due to what could be viewed as a tragic flaw, like Duke Humphrey of Gloucester in *Henry VI Part II*, appears more as a victim of conniving than as a tragic protagonist working out his own destiny; his story, however 'tragic' in the trite sense of *A Mirror for Magistrates*, is subsumed into a larger narrative of England's struggle for national identity. This narrative is ultimately comic in finding a positive and edifying outcome – 'comic' in the sense that Dante's *Divina Commedia* is comic.

Concurrently with his early history plays, Shakespeare seems to have been thinking about a strikingly different conception of the tragic offered by Seneca's tragedies and Seneca's English imitators. Thomas Kyd's *The Spanish Tragedy*, first published in 1592 after having been written and acted as early as 1586 or 1587, was a major theatrical event in London during Shakespeare's first years in the city. Here was a model that was distinctly tragic in form, and wildly popular.[7] Just as he tried his hand at Plautine comedy in *The Comedy of Errors* during these same years, Shakespeare apprenticed himself to neo-classical Senecan tragedy in *Titus Andronicus* (c. 1589–92).

The parallels between *The Spanish Tragedy* and *Titus Andronicus* are so extensive, indeed, that we cannot be sure when Shakespeare is modelling his writing on Seneca and when on Kyd. Certainly Kyd was the closer at hand for Elizabethan audiences. The success of the genre of the revenge tragedy, in the early 1590s and on down for another generation, points to a formula that worked theatrically. As a pattern for tragedy, on the other hand, it has its limitations. The increasingly remorseless conduct of the protagonist as revenger comes at the expense of sympathetic identification. The emotional effect in the catastrophe is more ironic than personally tragic; Titus is the cunning avenger more than the fallen hero struggling to understand his destiny and his place in an uncertain cosmos. This is a problem to which Shakespeare will return in *Hamlet*, with stunning success. *Titus Andronicus*, for all its brilliance of effect and powerful theatrical moments, seems content to succeed in the way that Kyd had succeeded earlier.

Romeo and Juliet, the other play prior to 1599 that was published as a tragedy in the 1623 Folio, explores a strikingly different approach to tragedy. It is no revenge tragedy, even if a vendetta between two families is the ugly problem that the two lovers must face; vengeful street-fighting repeatedly sets in motion the fateful trajectory that the play must follow. Nor is the play a mirror for magistrates, clearly. To a remarkable extent, it is *sui generis* as a dramatic genre. Pragmatically, its conception of tragedy comes from its sources, which are non-dramatic: Arthur Brooke's long narrative poem in English called *The Tragical History of Romeus and Juliet* (1562), and, behind it, Matteo Bandello's *Novelle* of 1554, Pierre Boaistuau's French translation (1559), and, still further back, Luigi da Porto's *Novella* (c. 1530), Masuccio of Salerno's *Il Novellino* (1476), and so on back to the *Ephesiaca* of the fifth century AD. The much-admired story of two lovers destined to suffer the consequences of their families' animosity had grown in successive stages, adding new characters like Mercutio and the Nurse. As Brooke's title indicates, the word 'tragical' seemed an appropriate designator.

Shakespeare, then, inherited the 'tragic' dimensions of the story he chose to dramatize about fated young lovers. The idea of tragedy came with the sources, and it is not one for which either the Fall of Princes or revenge tragedy provided a formula. Nor does the pattern owe anything to classical and neo-classical theories of tragedy. The play's protagonists are young persons, unremarkable other than for the poetic intensity of their passion. Their families are not patrician; indeed, the plan to marry Juliet to Count Paris underscores a hope for social advancement that is appropriate to the Capulets' status as one of two 'households' in Verona. The families are well-to-do, able to employ a number of servants and put on impressive parties, but they are not from the ruling elite. The dual protagonists spend little time exploring the existential dimensions of the universe and their place in it, even if Romeo does exclaim at one point 'Then I defy you, stars!' (5.1.24).

Perhaps we can call *Romeo and Juliet* a 'love tragedy'. The need for such an improvised characterization bespeaks a sense of the anomalous. Sometimes the play is paired with *Antony and Cleopatra* as a later, more mature play about tragic protagonists,[8] but even at that the pairing seems a little desperate. *Antony and Cleopatra*, for all its fine comic scenes involving the queen of Egypt, is an unmistakably tragic action dramatizing great figures of the classical past in a way that classical theorists of drama would recognize, even if they might tear their hair out at the play's lack of chronological and geographical unity. Romeo and Juliet, contrastingly, are ordinary people.

Moreover, a major portion of the play is funny and delightful in the vein of the romantic comedies that Shakespeare was writing at about the same time, such as *A Midsummer Night's Dream* and *Much Ado about Nothing*. We are warned that disaster is looming, of course, by the Prologue and by the violence with which *Romeo and Juliet* begins, and yet the play's first two acts wonderfully evoke the ecstasy of falling in love, the playful adolescent camaraderie of the young men, and the domestic imbroglios of a large extended family. The bawdry is as colourful as anywhere in Shakespeare, chiefly in scenes involving the Nurse and Mercutio. Plainly, Shakespeare has no interest in adhering to the strictures of neo-Aristotelian theorists insisting that tragedy not be adulterated with comedy.

The play announces itself as about 'a pair of star-crossed lovers', prompting us to ask what it means to be 'star-crossed', and whether that phrase can be seen as a kind of synonym for tragedy. The answer, in this resolutely non-classical play, is as varied as the story itself. The hostility between the families must serve as a major cause of tragedy here, and yet we see that good-hearted persons on both sides of the quarrel are determined to stop the carnage. Mere accident plays an important part: if the Friar's letter had got to Romeo in time, or if the Friar himself had arrived at Juliet's tomb before Romeo killed himself, tragedy could have been averted. Misunderstanding is no less crucial: if Juliet's family had known of her secret marriage to Romeo, presumably they would not have insisted on her marrying Paris. The father's anger at Juliet's waywardness in refusing to take up so promising an offer of marriage (3.5) shows him to be choleric and dictatorial as patriarch of the family, and yet we see his intemperance with the ironic understanding that he really is trying to do what he thinks best. All these are factors that seem quite external to the young protagonists, and thus do not bear heavily on tragic choice in a way that we see in Aeschylus' *Oresteia*, for example.

At one moment in *Romeo and Juliet*, to be sure, tragic choice does become crucial. It is when Romeo determines that he must kill Tybalt in revenge for the death of Mercutio. We see him giving in to peer pressure and the contagious atmosphere of macho loyalties to one's friends, at the expense of the softer and more charitable ideas of turning the other cheek that he has begun to learn from his love of Juliet. We see Romeo struggling with this choice, and regretting that choice in the immediate aftermath of Tybalt's death, even if Romeo tries to blame it on something outside himself: 'O, I am fortune's fool!' (3.1.127). This is a fine moment, and suggests that Shakespeare is searching for a tragic pattern that will deeply explore the connection linking choice and fate and character. At the same time, Shakespeare seems drawn to the story of *Romeo and Juliet* by other considerations, by a vision of young love as all the more exquisite for being misunderstood by an unfeeling world. In such a picture there is only limited room for an exploration of the inner self in relation to destiny. To talk about *hamartia* in *Romeo or Juliet* is, by and large, an exercise in futility. Such an approach imposes criteria on a play whose interests lie elsewhere, in the essentially beautiful pain of suffering for having fallen in love.

Shakespeare's disparate ventures into tragic expression in the years prior to 1599 suggest that he had not yet found the model or models he was looking for, or, more positively, that he was exploring tragic and near-tragic possibilities in the romantic comedies and English history plays for which he was rapidly becoming famous. In comedy, his inclination from the start was to threaten and complicate his comic world with tragic potential. *The Comedy of Errors* (c. 1589–94), despite its farcically Plautine plotting, is framed by the pending execution of old Egeon that is resolved only by the conclusion of the comic plot. This same formulation can be applied to *The Merchant of Venice* (c. 1596–7), in which Shylock's seemingly irresistible assault on the life of Antonio is foiled by the heroine of the love plot, and to *Much Ado About Nothing* (1598–9), where the terrible wrong done to Hero by Don John's slander and the assent of Claudio, Don Pedro, and even Hero's father to the undeserved accusation lead to her apparent death and to Benedick's resolution to challenge his best friend to a duel. Virtually all of the gentlemen are at the point of killing one another until the bumbling Dogberry and his Watch discover the truth, thus prompting the penance of those who have so erred in their faith. Even *A Midsummer Night's Dream* (c. 1595) darkens its comic vision with a perception that fairy magic can be malign. The banishment of the virtuous Duke Senior and his followers to the Forest of Arden in *As You Like It* (1598–1600) bespeaks a fallen world of ingratitude and treachery; Orlando's brother Oliver plans the death of his hated sibling by means of a rigged wrestling match. In his comedies generally, Shakespeare is continually fascinated by tragic possibility as a way of defining a human potential for failure that is redeemed solely by a comic and restorative move towards charity and forgiveness that is vested chiefly in Shakespeare's romantic heroines.[9]

The obsession of the so-called 'problem plays' in pursuing still further a problematic and even pessimistic view of human nature needs to be understood in the context of Shakespeare's full engagement with tragedy as a formal genre in the years beginning with 1599–1601. *Julius Caesar*, publicly acted at the new Globe Theatre in 1599, is set in the ancient classical world of Rome. Shakespeare had experimented with this setting in *Titus Andronicus*, albeit in a fictional guise derived from his various sources for that play. Now, in 1599, he chose to dramatize one of the climactic and enduringly memorable scenes of Roman history. Both plays display a fascination with the spirit of Rome as material for tragical discourse. Roman history was, for the Shakespeare and his contemporaries, the sole earlier civilization of which they had much knowledge. Through various legends about the founding of Great Britain by the grandson of Aeneas, Britain considered itself a scion of Rome and a direct inheritor of its culture. A story about the overthrow of a senatorial republican tradition by a strong single military leader was, moreover, a story that was bound to resonate in an England uncertain of its own political destiny at the end of Queen Elizabeth's reign, no matter how different the situation after Caesar's assassination might be from that of monarchist England.

What the story of Caesar's assassination offered Shakespeare was a chance to explore the tragic dimensions of that great account quite distanced from the moral and Christian imperatives of English history. *Julius Caesar* is a history play, but it is one that need not end in any providential sense of history as a confirmation of God's handiwork. Even in the English history plays, Shakespeare had done much to question such imperatives, but they were a given of his sources. In *Julius Caesar* he is free to delineate a radically different pattern of historical process. Indeed, as John Velz has shown,[10] that process in *Julius Caesar* is essentially one of undulation, in which one leader or one kind of governmental structure succeeds a predecessor and then yields to a successor without any clear sense of progress or even of plan. History is change; it is unstable; the outcome of a particular moment depends on the charisma or perhaps the luck of the individual leader.

The consequences of such an existential view of human history for tragedy are profound. Brutus, whom traditional neo-Aristotelian criticism inevitably singles out as the play's tragic protagonist,[11] is a man of noble and even worthy intentions whose seemingly best qualities help to undo him. Keenly aware of his descent from the first Brutus (Junius) who had liberated his city from Tarquinius Superbus, Brutus is selflessly devoted to public service but also proud. A devoted Stoic, he thinks himself invulnerable to flattery, but is for that very reason an easy target for the insinuations of those like Cassius who know how to appeal to Brutus's sense of his own integrity. A defender of republicanism, Brutus nonetheless assumes command of the revolutionary conspiracy he has been asked to join and proceeds to overrule his compatriots with a series of disastrous decisions: spare Mark Antony after the assassination, allow Antony to speak at Caesar's funeral, fight with Antony and young Octavius at Philippi in disregard of Cassius's judicious warnings of their military unpreparedness for the battle. Brutus's attempt to restore republicanism is undone by the very qualities that make him a great man: he sees the necessity of assassinating Caesar, but refuses to shed blood further than is necessary, and then grants Antony permission to speak at Caesar's funeral out of a sense of fair play and decency (along with his own proud sense that what he will have to say will silence any answer that Antony might give). Here is a tragedy at once personal and political. It illustrates the Fall of Princes, while at the same time it discovers tragic meaning in the protagonist himself. The ironies of history are best displayed in this leader of the cause of republicanism, who gives his life in a supreme effort, the result of which is to repress still further the liberties that Brutus held so dear.

Though Brutus is usually interpreted by neoclassical criticism as the play's tragic protagonist, other figures are also remarkable studies in tragic character. Julius Caesar is like Brutus in more ways than either of them recognize. Unshaken of purpose, holding steady when other men waver, Caesar is also deaf to counsel when he most needs it. Physically he is both the mightiest man of the world and a frail human being who cannot compete with Cassius in swimming the Tiber, and who must turn his head to one side when the senators address him because he is deaf in one ear. Like Brutus, he considers himself above flattery, and is for that reason prone to it; as Decius Brutus observes, 'when I tell him he hates flatterers, / He says he does, being then most flattered' (2.1.208–9). Caesar is superstitious, even though he professes to scorn the interpretation of omens and signs. Like Brutus, Caesar is counselled by a wise and compassionate wife, who futilely urges him not to go to the Capitol on what they both know to be a fateful day. His character is his destiny. Shakespeare's astute strategy of pairing Brutus and Caesar in adjoining scenes (2.1 and 2.2), as these great men ignore their wives' urgings and march to their destinies, underscores the ironic and repetitive patterns of history through which this tragedy unfolds.[12] The great men of this play are victims of their own hubris, and experience a kind of blindness at the crucial moment of their destinies that is remarkably like that which the ancient Greeks called *até* or blind infatuation.

In *Hamlet*, written shortly after *Julius Caesar*, Shakespeare revisits the revenge-play motif of *Titus* in a way that transforms it into tragic greatness. A seemingly inherent problem in the formula of the revenge play, as we have seen, is that the protagonist, in his obsessive drive for necessary revenge, becomes dehumanized and unsympathetic to such a degree that the cathartic effect of tragedy is diverted into the kind of savage and wanton destruction we see in the end of *The Spanish Tragedy*, where the spirit of Revenge is not satisfied until nearly every person of the play lies dead onstage. *Hamlet* does not shy away from this problem. Hamlet himself is unquestionably hardened and even coarsened by his killing of Polonius (however mistaken in its object), his sending of Rosencrantz and Guildenstern to their deaths, his responsibility however indirect for the madness of Ophelia, and still more. The stage at the end of *Hamlet* is littered with corpses. Hamlet is the avenger, and as such he stands in a line of inheritance that is bloody.

To grasp the extent of this hold over the play exerted by the revenge tradition, we can look not only to the earlier revenge play that Shakespeare had written but also to his sources for *Hamlet*. The *Historia Danica* (1180–1208) of Saxo Grammaticus is unapologetically violent. Undeterred by any moral scruples, facing a cunning enemy in his uncle Feng, young Amlethus senses that he is being spied upon during his interview with his mother in her chamber. Finding the hidden courtier, Amlethus stabs the man to death, drags the body forth from the straw in which it has been concealed, cuts the body into morsels, boils them, and flings the bits 'through the mouth of an open sewer for the swine to eat'. Sent to England, as in Shakespeare's play, he arranges for the death of his escorts by substituting in their papers a forged document ordering their execution in his stead. Returning to Jutland a year later, after having married the king's daughter, Amlethus encourages the court to indulge in a wild drinking party, imprisons the drunken courtiers in a large tapestry stitched for him by his mother, and then sets fire to the palace.[13]

The later versions of the story to which Shakespeare was more directly indebted, including Belleforest's *Histoires Tragiques* (1576) and a lost anonymous play of *Hamlet* of the early 1590s, did little to ameliorate the carnage. What Thomas Lodge recollects from that theatrical experience is 'the vizard of the ghost which cried so miserably at the theatre, like an oyster wife, "Hamlet, revenge!" ',[14] while Thomas Nashe speaks of the lost play as 'English Seneca read by candlelight'.[15] Later revenge plays as well, after Shakespeare's *Hamlet*, feature protagonists whose cunning overwhelms their (presumably) better natures; John Marston's *Antonio's Revenge* and *The Revenger's Tragedy* (perhaps by Thomas Middleton) are cases in point. Shakespeare's *Hamlet* is unique not only in being one of the finest tragedies ever written, but also in its attempts to exculpate and humanize the revenger. The play's greatness and the humanity that Shakespeare bestows on his protagonist are not unrelated.

Shakespeare's way of humanizing his revenger is to present a Hamlet who is thoughtful, introspective, witty, capable of enduring friendships, deeply moved by the need for human affection both in his family and in romantic attachments, and philosophically inquisitive. Ever since Coleridge, criticism of this play has been plagued by the notion that Hamlet's humanity renders him incapable of action,[16] despite the play's plentiful evidence to the contrary in his slaying of Polonius, his resolute behaviour at sea, and still other forthright actions. The observation seems more appropriate to Coleridge (and to Goethe and Hegel) than to Hamlet. In the context of our present argument about Shakespeare's developing sense of tragic form, a dramaturgical interpretation presents itself: the humanizing of Hamlet is the strategy needed to counter the dehumanizing thrust of the revenge tradition.

Viewed in this light, Hamlet is bound to question his own motives and the certainty of the information he has seemingly received about his father's apparent murder. His hesitancy and self-castigation are the appropriate responses in a student of philosophy who is also heir to the Danish throne. Shakespeare adroitly takes advantage of his play's location in Denmark (which is to say that he does not alter the location, as he certainly could have done) in order to present us with a world that stands between Scandinavia to the north (a land of pagan legends of revenge, prominently including that narrated by Saxo Grammaticus) and Europe to the south, bifurcated in our imagination between the Paris of pleasurable pursuit and the Wittenberg of scholarly learning and theology. Hamlet the man and *Hamlet* the play stand between these worlds. The pagan ethic of revenge, on the one hand, demands of Hamlet that he revenge the 'foul and most unnatural murder' of his father (1.5.26). The civilized world of Europe, on the other hand, brings with it Christian imperatives against suicide and murder. Hamlet is a Christian; he is also his father's son. Here, then, in Shakespeare's solution to the problem of sympathetic identification posed for him by the revenge-play tradition, Shakespeare found his most intensely satisfying pattern for the depiction of the tragic individual. Hamlet's internal conflict, in which civilized decency is posed with seemingly irreconcilable opposition against the need for brutally direct action, is the stuff of tragic greatness.

The danger in this pattern, on the other hand, is that the protagonist might turn out to be ineffectual, pitiable in his inability to act, unable to find a way out of his dilemma – the Hamlet of Coleridge's imagination. Shakespeare's dramaturgical solution to this is again integral to what makes this play so great as tragedy. Hamlet does find a solution, or, rather, one is found for him. Paradoxically, after he has flailed about in an attempt to carry out his father's commission and has managed in the process to kill the wrong man – a move that, as Hamlet sees, he will have to pay for – Hamlet submits himself to the will of Providence and is thereupon handed the solution he has devoutly sought for but has been unable to find on his own initiative. Without his connivance – a connivance that would inevitably smack of premeditation to commit murder – Hamlet finds himself in a fatal duel with Laertes that leads further to the death of his mother, the public exposure of Claudius's villainy, and thus the occasion for a violent act against Claudius that is essentially unpremeditated. The act seems fully justified to us as audience by the powerful emotions of the final scene. Hamlet comes to understand his fate and to see a pattern in the human suffering that has seemed to him earlier so pointlessly brutal. At the same time, the ending he did not devise for himself brings about his own death – a death he has longed for, yet without the suicidal self-infliction that his Christian teaching forbids. Even if Horatio offers a more sceptical reading of Hamlet's history, one in which 'carnal, bloody, and unnatural acts' have prevailed along with 'accidental judgment' and 'casual slaughters' (5.2.383–4), the play's ending notably strives towards philosophical comprehension of human suffering and evil. It is here that we find the catharsis so richly evident in *Oedipus Tyrannos*, and lacking in *Titus Andronicus*.

Once Shakespeare had succeeded so brilliantly with tragedy in *Hamlet*, the way may have seemed open for him to concentrate on what had eluded him earlier, or had seemed less pressing in terms of his own artistic agenda. Perhaps, as Richard Wheeler has argued, this turning point in his artistic career can best be understood as a grappling with new and deeply personal problems that Shakespeare had been unready to face in his younger years.[17] Having successfully manoeuvred the strategies of male maturation and courtship in his earlier plays, and having begun to explore darker themes in his Sonnets, particularly the agonies of betrayal and jealousy, Shakespeare was at a point where he could choose no longer to present female infidelity as primarily a phantasm of the diseased male imagination, but as something that could actually occur. The Dark Lady of the Sonnets is unfaithful in a way that Hero of *Much Ado* simply was not.

The 'problem plays', in this view, are of critical importance. Manifestly, in them Shakespeare is exploring the porousness of the generic boundaries between tragedy, history play, and comedy. A tragic outcome so threatens the major personages of *Measure for Measure* (1603–4) that the Duke, for all his secretive manipulations, is stymied in his attempt to save the life of Claudio until a prisoner providentially dies in the prison. The problematic nature of marriage in this play, and in *All's Well That Ends Well* (c. 1601–5), is inseparably linked to the human propensity (especially among males) for forced seduction, bribery, and attempted murder. Angelo's anguished discovery of his own diseased cravings produces soliloquies that are fully tragic in tone. The mutual recriminations of Claudio and his sister Isabella are as searing as anything Shakespeare wrote in his tragedies, and as fully revelatory of human failure. The Duke's meditation on the vanity of human wishes in his counselling of Claudio (3.1.5–41) to 'Be absolute for death' is no less tragic, even if its tragic import is qualified by the Duke's disguise and his announced intent to be a rescuer. *All's Well*, like *Much Ado*, invokes a mock death in its attempt to recuperate the undeserving hero through penance. *All's Well* shares with *Measure for Measure* the employment of an ethically dubious bed trick. *Troilus and Cressida* (c. 1601–2), the most problematic of these 'problem plays', defied the attempts of the Folio editors to find a tidy place for it in their generic categories: manifestly a history play about the Trojan war, it ends with the tragic death of Hector and with the failure of the love affair of its title figures, and yet spares the lives of most of its characters in a standoff that is more akin to satire than to tragedy; the hovering figures of Thersites and Pandarus strongly reinforce this satiric tone. Fittingly, *Troilus and Cressida* ended up in the Folio edition between the histories and the tragedies, unpaginated, ceaselessly enigmatic.

If, then, Shakespeare was ready to investigate human failure in a fully tragic dimension as never before, and with the very real successes of *Julius Caesar* and especially *Hamlet* as vital encouragement to proceed, we may well imagine a Shakespeare who now was ready to tackle the tragic dilemmas that his own advancing age must have compelled him to face: sexual jealousy in marriage (in *Othello*), the ingratitude felt by children towards their aging parents (*King Lear*), the insane promptings of ambition (*Macbeth*), midlife crisis (*Antony and Cleopatra*), bitter resentment towards persons who fail to show proper gratitude and reciprocity for a lifetime of generosity (*Timon of Athens*), and, again, resentment towards a city that has not been properly grateful to its leading general and fledgling political leader (*Coriolanus*).

This list of tragedies is remarkable in its own right as Shakespeare's greatest achievement. It is also remarkable for its variety of tragic experiences and tragic forms. *Othello* (c. 1603–4) is a play that might well illustrate Shakespeare's understanding of Aristotle's definitions of tragedy, if we had any reason to think that Shakespeare cared about Aristotle and the critical tradition that descended from him. Othello is a mighty figure in the heroic mould of classical tragedy, even if his being black marks him as a stranger. He is a good man in most ways: brave, capable of great leadership, strong in his affections, loyal, ordinarily calm under stress. His devotion to Desdemona is all-encompassing; indeed, it is the intensity of his love for her that prepares the extent of his fall into misery and self-hatred. If one looks for a *hamartia* or tragic flaw, Othello's characterization of himself as 'one that loved not wisely but too well' is readily at hand; he is one 'not easily jealous but, being wrought, / Perplexed in the extreme' (5.2.354–6).

The play's cathartic experience is deep, and depends on the protagonist's belated recognition of the wrong he has committed. The irrational fury that has seized Othello and has led to such a terrible crime is not unlike the *até* that afflicts Agamemnon in Aeschylus' *Oresteia*; it is an insanity from which the protagonist recovers too late, so that we are allowed to see the causal relationship between character and destiny. A larger scheme of justice ultimately prevails: Othello denounces his terrible act, clears Desdemona of any wrong, rediscovers his love for her even though she cannot be restored to him as his living wife, and (like Oedipus) punishes his own crime. The pattern of tragic recognition is not unlike that so admired by Aristotle and his followers; the tragic effect works on us in ways that Aristotle ably describes.

Macbeth (c. 1606–7) is another Shakespearean tragedy that is not unduly distorted by applying the framework of Aristotle's *Poetics*. Macbeth is an aristocratic figure of great personal bravery and public reputation. At the start of the play, he is the loyal soldier of his kind-hearted king. He is a man of poetic sensitivity and extraordinary insight into his own emotional drives. We are invited to sympathize with him, even in his torments of guilt, and to see things through his eyes. His *hamartia*, if we wish to call it that, is his intense ambition, combined with a dependence on the fatal urgings of his wife on the occasion of Duncan's visit to their castle. He knows his obsessive desire for the kingship is wrong, and yet his susceptibility to that desire makes him prone to the suggestions of his wife and the three Weird Sisters. The sisters know how to insinuate with him because they can read his heart and know that the longing to seize power by whatever means necessary has visited him long before they make known their enigmatic and seductive half-truths about his advancement from Glamis to Cawdor and thence to king.

Macbeth is thus an otherwise good man afflicted by a tragic flaw. Our understanding of the meaning of his tragedy lies in our perception of the necessary and just relationship between that craving and his ultimate fate. This pattern again sounds Aristotelian in its working out of discovery and recognition. As in *Othello*, order is restored through the punishment of the protagonist and the reaffirmation of political and social stability. At the same time, we must recognize that the terms of the tragic flaw in *Macbeth* are Christian and moral in a way that they are not in fifth-century Greek tragedy. Oedipus's *hamartia* has nothing to do with guilt or sin; his killing of his father and marrying his mother are polluted acts that he has committed however unintentionally, and he must pay for them, but he is not a sinner. Macbeth is a sinner, and he knows it: even before he kills Duncan, he confesses that Duncan's virtues will plead, 'like angels, trumpet-tongued, against / The deep damnation of his taking-off' (1.7.18–19). To see *Macbeth* as a kind of object lesson illustrating one of the Ten Commandments, 'Thou shalt not kill', would be to reduce the play to a platitude, perhaps, but this would not misrepresent the nature of Macbeth's *hamartia*. It is ambition, or Pride, the deadliest of the Seven Deadly Sins; it is the sin of Lucifer. The elucidation of meaning in Macbeth's tragedy thus depends on moral cause and effect in a way that Greek tragedy does not. The fact that Macbeth is a sympathetic character capable of a close marital relationship with his wife makes his fall into sin all the more terrifying, since it implies that, but for the grace of God, there go we as well. The cause and effect of sin and punishment in *Macbeth* thus reads as a kind of translation of Greek *hamartia* into terms that are more morally comprehensible to a Christian civilization.

The Aristotelian formula does not apply, on the other hand, to a play like *Romeo and Juliet*, where the protagonists are, by and large, innocent victims, even martyrs, to the unfeeling world that surrounds and engulfs them. Romeo is briefly caught up as agent of his own tragedy, but incidentally and as part of a larger pattern of guiltless suffering. Hamlet, too, despite the efforts of much criticism to shape him in the mould of *hamartia*, and despite his many failures of *caritas*, is better seen as one who must bear on his shoulders the 'slings and arrows of outrageous fortune' (3.1.59). He must die that the truth may be known and the debt of vengeance paid, not in relation to any crime of his own but that of his uncle. Denmark is 'an unweeded garden' (1.2.135) not through Hamlet's means, and yet he must die. Without in any way allegorizing this narrative, we can perceive that it bears a structural similarity to the story of Christ's suffering and death. That is to say, the meaning in tragedy resides not in a cause-and-effect discovery through which the protagonist comes to understand his own frightening inner self and to see a cosmic need for fall and punishment; rather, it is a tragedy of sacrifice. With it comes finally a cathartic sense of compensation and ultimate reward, if only the reward of knowing that one has tried to better a fallen world. As Capulet says at the end of *Romeo and Juliet*, the lovers are 'Poor sacrifices of our enmity' (5.3.305). The parents' rage has been such that, 'but their children's end, naught could remove' (Prologue, 11).

This distinctly non-Aristotelian tragic pattern, of a seemingly necessary sacrifice that atones for and partly ameliorates the wretched condition of humanity, can account for much that happens in *King Lear* (c. 1605–6). Lear himself, as protagonist, is one in whom one can easily find a *hamartia*; he is choleric, imperious, domineering, deaf to counsel, fatally wrong in his judgements of his daughters. His failures lead with exemplary directness to his fall from power. Yet we respond at once to his cry of pain that he is 'a man / More sinned against than sinning' (3.2.59–60). The inversions of madness and sanity, seeing and blindness, justice and tyranny that so overwhelm us in this play bring with them the perception that Lear does not deserve what happens to him. Accordingly, we must look for tragic meaning elsewhere than in a formula of crime and punishment. What is true of Lear is also true of Gloucester; however badly he misjudges his sons and persecutes Edgar, the blinding of this defenceless old man with the connivance of his illegitimate son Edmund, and the charitable sorrow with which Gloucester accepts blame for his own failures, create for him the role of sacrificial victim. The meeting of these two ruined old men at Dover (4.6) evokes our pity so compellingly that we nearly forget what they have done to bring this on themselves.

Even more so, those who win our unhesitating sympathy are sacrificial figures. However much Cordelia may have prompted Lear into banishing her, however much she may have wished to make clear to him that she had to have a life of her own, she does return from France to save him. She does the very thing she told him she wouldn't do: she puts her marriage and her very life at risk, because the things that her sisters are doing to her father are intolerable. There are times when one must stand up and be counted, at whatever cost to oneself, and Cordelia has the immense courage to do this.

So have Edgar, and Kent, and the Fool. They and Cordelia must make their choices to suffer for goodness in the face of an indifferent universe where the gods do not seem to care and indeed may not exist. Under these circumstances, what moral guidelines can be discovered to govern human action? Edmund embodies the principle that a naturalistic universe invites and even demands a naturalistic response; if there are no gods, if moral principles are mere contrivances of human culture, then why not proceed ruthlessly to obtain what one wants? Goneril and Regan, though less able than Edmund to verbalize philosophical and moral principles, act on the same basis of anarchic opportunism. Yet they are all struck down, by their own hands, and by the desiccating force of inward corruption that (in the apocalyptic vision of this play) necessarily attends on heartless self-sufficiency. Cordelia, Edgar, and Kent suffer, but they have made the choices by which they know they must live. Tragic meaning, in this devastating play, resides somewhere in this recognition that evil is its own worst reward and that the only way to be able to live with oneself as a human being is to embrace the role of sacrificial victim, suffering in order that an idea of goodness may not perish.

Antony and Cleopatra (1606–7) breaks away from the Aristotelian definition of tragedy in still another way. It is, first of all, a play that defies all classical and neo-classical strictures about the unities of time, place, and action, but that is of less importance than its conception of the main characters. By deploying dual protagonists, it wonderfully complicates the tragic formula. Traditional criticism has usually solved this problem by centring on Antony alone as the tragic protagonist; he is, after all, a male, and he is the subject of Plutarch's *Life of Antony*.[18] Not surprisingly, the traditional interpretation of him as tragic figure confirms Plutarch's view: Antony is a great general of personal courage, vitality, and charisma, but he is a man who throws away everything out of his infatuation for a trull. Cleopatra is an amazing woman, to be sure, but in Plutarch she represents fleshly temptation through which the great man is diverted from his appointed task. This is a perfect formula of *hamartia*; it sees moral and just cause and effect in Antony's downfall.

The trouble is, of course, that it fails to do justice to Shakespeare's amazing play. Shakespeare dramatizes the Plutarchan perspective, all right, but as an ideology against which to measure the daring of the lovers and of the poet who created them. All that can be said against the lovers is true: Antony deserts duty and hates himself for it, he is untrue to Octavia in despite of his oaths to her, and he is unmanned by Cleopatra, who, for her part, is presented as cunning, seductive, and deceiving.[19] Yet out of this story of human failure Shakespeare dares to imagine a spirit of greatness, a sharing of experiences between a man and a woman that transcends boundaries of gender, and a defiance of normal worldly expectations that entirely alters the nature of the tragic experience. This is no simple moral lesson in which we see *hamartia* leading to its necessary consequences. Instead, we are invited to admire a Cleopatra who is grandly capable of a noble resolution through which she will be able to call 'great Caesar ass / Unpolicied' (5.2.307–8). Antony and Cleopatra are not sacrifices like Romeo and Juliet, since they are far from innocent, but they do insist on being 'past the size of dreaming' (5.2.96). As such, they share with other tragic protagonists in Shakespeare a wish to challenge and surmount the dead weight of a world that imposes such a fearful cost on those who do not follow the world's ways.

Shakespeare's tragedies of disillusionment, *Timon of Athens* (c. 1605–8) and *Coriolanus* (c. 1608), suggest by their deep misanthropy a kind of sad and even bitter conclusion to Shakespeare's exploration of the genre of tragedy. What vision of tragedy is possible, we are invited to ask, after *King Lear*, *Macbeth*, and *Antony and Cleopatra*? Shakespeare writes as though the desolate conclusions found especially in *Lear* leave no further room for hope. Turning again in these plays to the ancient classical world where, as in *Julius Caesar*, he could step aside from Christian imperatives and ameliorating visions of human history, Shakespeare ponders human ingratitude with unsparing candour. Timon and Coriolanus are alike in their outspokenness, their disappointment in human behaviour, their mistrust of ordinary people. The protagonists are ultimately extreme and unattractive in their rejection of human consolation. Timon and Coriolanus are admirable in their relentless refusal to deceive themselves through illusion, but for them, and indeed for us, very little is left. Timon cuts off all human contact; Coriolanus not only leaves his family and his mother, but finds himself on the verge of attacking his own city of Rome, with his family among the intended victims. He is pulled back from matricide and wife-slaying not by an ennobling tragic vision but by the irony of a situation that paralyses him into helplessness: 'O Mother, Mother! / What have you done? Behold, the heavens do ope, / The gods look down, and this unnatural scene / They laugh at' (5.3.182–5). Shakespeare's final tragic vision is dispiriting indeed. He surveys the desolation found also in *Lear* but without the sacrificial and cathartic ending that offers some atonement. These tragedies of disillusionment offer scepticism as the only honest answer to humanity's tragic dilemma.

Without the romances to which Shakespeare turned in his last years as a writer, the vision would be bleak indeed. These plays are needed to repair and recuperate the tragic failures that this essay has been investigating. They do so by confronting tragic possibility, as the earlier romantic comedies had done. In fact they do so with a new intensity. *Pericles* (1606–8) deals with incest more relentlessly than the earlier plays, and allows the titular hero to suffer for the apparent abandonment of his wife at sea. *Cymbeline* (c. 1608–10) features the death and gross disfigurement of Cloten, along with the apparent death of Imogen, to the extent that the play was catalogued in the Folio as a tragedy. *The Tempest* (c. 1611) plays out its perfect comic structure on the island against a backdrop of political duplicity and attempted murder in mainland Italy, to which the unreconstructed Antonio and Sebastian will presumably return. Uniquely, *The Winter's Tale* (c. 1609–11) misleads its audience into an assurance that Queen Hermione is actually dead, since her spirit appears to Antigonus in requesting that he save the life of her daughter. The deception is needed to produce the splendid ambiguity surrounding Hermione's coming to life as a statue: is it an illusion staged for Leontes's spiritual edification, or a miracle of the dead restored to life? Certainly it is a *coup de théâtre*, one in which Shakespeare's supple exploration of the ambiguous boundaries between tragedy and comedy is perfectly encapsulated. To the end of his career, his interest is in mingled forms.

NOTES

1. David Scott Kastan, *Shakespeare and the Shapes of Time* (Hanover, NH: University Press of New England, 1982).
2. Francis Meres, *Palladis Tamia* (London, 1598).
3. *The Riverside Chaucer*, ed. Larry D. Benson (Boston: Houghton Mifflin, 1987), 'The Monk's Prologue', 1973–7, 3163–7.
4. Giovanni Boccaccio, *De casibus virorum illustrium (Concerning the Falls of Illustrious Men)*, mid-fourteenth century, and Guillaume de Lorris and Jean de Meung, *Le Roman de la Rose*, translated in part by Chaucer as *The Romaunt of the Rose*.
5. Anicius Manlius Severinus Boethius, *De consolatione philosophiae*, early sixth century.
6. See Claire McEachern, *The Poetics of English Nationhood, 1590–1612* (Cambridge University Press, 1996), and Richard Helgerson, *Forms of Nationhood: The Elizabethan Writing of England* (University of Chicago Press, 1992). The debate about nationhood also importantly involves Benedict Anderson, *Imagined Communities: Reflections on the Origin and Spread of Nationalism* (London: Verso, 1983).
7. Fredson Bowers, *Elizabethan Revenge Tragedy, 1587–1642* (Princeton University Press, 1940).
8. See Franklin M. Dickey, *Not Wisely But Too Well: Shakespeare's Love Tragedies* (San Marino, CA: Huntington Library, 1957).
9. Robert Grams Hunter, *Shakespeare and the Comedy of Forgiveness* (New York: Columbia University Press, 1965). On the transitional years 1500–1601, see Harley Granville-Barker, 'From *Henry V* to *Hamlet*', *Proceedings of the British Academy* 11 (1925), 283–309.

10. John Velz, 'Undular Structure in *Julius Caesar*', *Modern Language Review* 66 (1971), 21–30.

11. See, for example, Ruth M. Levitsky, ' "The Elements Were So Mix'd..." ', *PMLA* 88 (1973), 240–5, and Reuben A. Brower, *Hero and Saint: Shakespeare and the Graeco-Roman Heroic Tradition* (Oxford: Clarendon Press, 1971).

12. Norman Rabkin, 'The Polity', *Shakespeare and the Common Understanding* (New York: Free Press, 1967), pp. 105–21.

13. Saxo Grammaticus, *Historia Danica* (1180–1208), in Geoffrey Bullough, *Narrative and Dramatic Sources of Shakespeare*, 7 vols. (London: Routledge and Kegan Paul, 1966), vol. VII.

14. Thomas Lodge, *Wit's Misery, and the World's Madness* (London, 1596).

15. Thomas Nashe, *Epistle* prefixed to Robert Greene's *Menaphon* (London, 1589).

16. *Coleridge on Shakespeare: The Text of the Lectures of 1811–12*, ed. R. A. Foakes (Charlottesville: University Press of Virginia, 1971), and Ernest Jones, *Hamlet and Oedipus*, rev. edn (New York: 1949, 1954).

17. Richard P. Wheeler, *Shakespeare's Development and the Problem Comedies: Turn and Counter-Turn* (Berkeley: University of California Press, 1981).

18. See Linda T. Fitz, 'Egyptian Queens and Male Reviewers: Sexist Attitudes in *Antony and Cleopatra* Criticism', *Shakespeare Quarterly* 28 (1977), 217–316.

19. See Janet Adelman, *The Common Liar: An Essay on 'Antony and Cleopatra'* (New Haven: Yale University Press, 1973) and Linda Charnes, *Notorious Identity: Materializing the Subject in Shakespeare's Plays* (Cambridge, MA: Harvard University Press, 1993), pp. 103–47.

4

MICHAEL WARREN

Shakespearean tragedy printed and performed

Throughout the twentieth century critical and popular opinion regarded Shakespeare's tragedies as his highest achievement; there is no sign that their pre-eminence will be modified in the twenty-first. In a largely secular world they have been invested with the status of secular scripture, often treated with reverence as spiritual masterpieces of transcendent literary art rather than as great plays written about four hundred years ago. The texts have some-times appeared like sacred objects, especially in collected editions. Certainly the discussion of individual plays (sympathetic or hostile) has often been conducted as if the text of each were definitively established, canonically determined, and available for exegesis.

However, such is not the case. The notion of a single authentic text belongs to the tradition of reading plays rather than that of performing them in the playhouse, where performance admits variation. The texts of Shakespeare's tragedies, as of all of his plays, are unstable. The modern editions that we study are derived from documents of doubtful origin and imperfect execu-tion about which there is less external evidence than we desire. Those early documents are constantly re-edited in the light of new knowledge, new the-oretical concerns, and new hypotheses. The reading texts of the plays have changed and developed since their first publication; the texts of the plays have never been and cannot be truly fixed, although editions are frequently quite similar.

It will be advantageous to begin an introduction to the texts of Shakespeare's tragedies by reviewing briefly the facts about the plays' earliest publication.

Titus Andronicus is usually regarded as the earliest tragedy that he wrote. It was the first of the tragedies to be published and was, as far as we know, also the first of Shakespeare's plays to be published; even of that we cannot be truly certain, for all the details of Shakespeare's early career are not known. Only his poem *Venus and Adonis* had been published (1593) prior to the appearance of *Titus* in quarto in 1594; *Lucrece* appeared in 1594 also about the same time as *Titus*. Both poems were printed in London by Richard Field, a former resident of Stratford-upon-Avon, neither with the author's name on the title page, but each with a dedicatory letter to the Earl of Southampton signed by William Shakespeare. The title page of *Titus* bore the following words: 'The Most Lamentable Romaine Tragedie of Titus Andronicus: As it was Plaide by the Right Honourable the Earle of Darbie, Earle of Pembrooke, and Earle of Sussex their Seruants'. A notable inclusion is the names of the companies that played the play; a notable omission, by modern standards, is any reference to the playwright. The printer of that play was John Danter, who in 1597 also printed the next of Shakespeare's tragedies to appear, *Romeo and Juliet*. Its title page reads: 'An Excellent conceited Tragedie of Romeo and Iuliet. As it hath been often (with great applause) plaid publiquely, by the right Honourable the L. of Hunsdon his Seruants'. Again there is no identification of the playwright on the title page. In 1599 appeared a second printing of the play, still anonymously, this time by Thomas Creede, with a title page that reads: 'The Most Excellent and lamentable Tragedie, of Romeo and Iuliet. Newly corrected, augmented, and amended: As it hath bene sundry times publiquely acted, by the right Honourable the Lord Chamberlaine his Seruants'. The change of name of the acting company is not particularly significant: its sponsor had received a new appointment. However, the claim that the text is 'Newly corrected, augmented, and amended' and the assertion that it is 'As it hath bene sundry times publiquely acted' are important. The text that Creede printed was markedly different from that published in 1597; variation between the two texts is extensive, and Creede suggests that the earlier printing was deficient in length and in accuracy. Such distinction between texts presents challenges to the definition or even the description of a single entity called *Romeo and Juliet*.

A similar situation obtains with *Hamlet*, the next tragedy to be printed. In 1603 it appeared in quarto with a title page that reads: 'The Tragicall Historie of Hamlet Prince of Denmarke By William Shake-speare. As it hath beene diuerse times acted by his Highnesse seruants in the Cittie of London: as also in the two Vniuersities of Cambridge and Oxford, and else-where'. Shakespeare's name appears on the title page (it had appeared first in 1598 on that of *Love's Labour's Lost*); King James I had become the company's sponsor. The book was printed by Valentine Simmes, working for the publishers, Nicholas Ling and John Trundell. One of those publishers of the first quarto (Q1), Nicholas Ling, employed James Roberts to print a second quarto (Q2) late in 1604 (surviving copies are variously dated 1604 or 1605). Its title page reproduces the play's title and its author's name almost exactly, but instead of the identification of the play's performance history it states:

'Newly imprinted and enlarged to almost as much againe as it was, according to the true and perfect Coppie'. The differences between the two quartos are even greater than those between the two quartos of *Romeo and Juliet*. Not the least significant is the discrepancy in length: the first quarto is 2,221 lines of type, and the second quarto is 3,803 lines of type. In 1608 a quarto of *King Lear* was published with a bold and elaborately informative title page that begins with the playwright's name: 'M. William Shake-speare: His True Chronicle Historie of the life and death of King Lear and his three Daughters. With the vnfortunate life of Edgar, sonne and heire to the Earle of Gloster, and his sullen and assumed humor of Tom of Bedlam: As it was played before the Kings Maiestie at Whitehall vpon S. Stephans night in Christmas Hollidayes. By his Maiesties seruants playing vsually at the Gloabe on the Bancke-side'.

These are the only tragedies of Shakespeare published before his death in 1616. Prior to his death both *Titus* and *Romeo* were reprinted, the former in 1600 and 1611, the latter in 1609. A second quarto of *Lear* was published after his death: in 1619 Thomas Pavier reprinted the text of Q1 *Lear* with a title page that bears the false date 1608. In 1622, a year before the publication of the First Folio (F1), a fourth quarto of *Romeo* was published, but, more importantly, a quarto of *Othello* appeared: 'The Tragœdy of Othello, The Moore of Venice. As it hath beene diuerse times acted at the Globe, and at the Black-Friers, by his Maiesties Seruants. Written by William Shakespeare'.

The other five tragedies – *Julius Caesar, Macbeth, Antony and Cleopatra, Timon of Athens*, and *Coriolanus* – did not see print until the publication of the First Folio in 1623: 'Mr. William Shakespeares Comedies, Histories, & Tragedies. Published according to the True Originall Copies'. Among the tragedies the Folio places *Troilus and Cressida* and *Cymbeline*, which are rarely considered as such, and which I shall not consider. The Folio provides the sole authoritative text for these five plays. In relation to the plays already published in quarto, the First Folio presents complications. In each case except *Romeo*, where the Folio text is close to that of Q2, there are significant and important variations between the Folio text and the earlier quarto record. The text of *Titus* contains a scene that is not in Q1 and its later reprints. If Q1 and Q2 *Hamlet* present radically different texts, the Folio *Hamlet* presents a third. The Folio *King Lear* contains material not in Q1 and does not contain some material that is in Q1. The Folio text of *Othello* contains sequences and language that are not in Q1, but it also lacks material that is in Q1. All these five texts are thus manifestly unstable at source; each play exists in more than one state or condition. Moreover, the fact of the variant states of these texts places in question the nature of those texts that exist in one state or condition only. What state of the play does each represent? What states of each play do we lack?

One cannot but be struck by two aspects of this review: first, the apparently arbitrary nature of the publication of the plays; second, the frequency of significant variation in texts of plays published more than once.

The former should not be a matter of surprise. Shakespeare was a working dramatist; performance was the primary medium for making his creations public. Moreover, he wrote within a culture in which plays, even tragedies, were not accepted as high art on a par with epic poetry or the works of the classical authors. The playhouses were centres of noble achievement but in a popular culture environment, and actors and playwrights did not command the dignity frequently claimed for and often ascribed to poets; it is not surprising that Jonson's bold act of publishing his collected plays, poems, and masques in 1616, the year of Shakespeare's death, under the title *Workes* drew mocking comment in his time. However, not only was there no high status attached to plays, but there was not a sufficiently demanding reading public for play texts to drive a publishing economy. Peter W. M. Blayney has pointed out that in the first decade of the seventeenth century on average fewer than six new plays were published each year, and that for the publisher there was little prospect of early profit from a first printing.[1] The hope of the publisher was that a play would be attractive to a reading public and would occasion a second printing, which would yield a substantial profit. Scholarship has frequently suggested that by withholding their plays from publication companies protected their performance rights, but it seems more likely that publishers were not enthusiastic about paying companies or playwrights for the right to publish their works. An absence of obvious profit to the publisher meant that the company would gain no great sum from the sale of its play (compared to the income from performance). Blayney suggests that the chief reason that companies wished to see their plays in print may have been publicity (pp. 396–9).

The second matter, the variation between printed texts, is a crucial issue for Shakespeare studies. What did the sixteenth- or seventeenth-century book buyer receive when he or she made a purchase? What do we read when we examine such texts? In the case of each quarto that I have recorded above, the title of the play is listed with some authenticating detail – one or all of the author's name, the name of the acting company that played the play, or the occasion of the play's performance. In the Folio's preliminaries John Heminge and Henry Condell protest the perfection of the texts that the Folio presents: in their letter 'To the great Variety of Readers' they state that the plays that have been previously published 'are now offer'd to your view cur'd, and perfect of their limbes', while those that appear for the first time are 'absolute in their numbers, as he [Shakespeare] conceived the[m]'. However impressive these statements may be, examination of the texts suggests that Heminge and Condell were engaged in hyperbolic praise of the book's contents and that the plays are manifestly not perfect. Apparent imperfections in the texts and variants from earlier published states, for instance, provoke scholars to try to discover more about the sources of what was printed, and specifically what may be known about the origins of the copy from which the compositors set the text. If Q1 *Lear*, the 'True Chronicle Historie of . . . King Lear and his three Daughters', and F1 *Lear*, 'The Tragedie of King Lear', disagree in numerous ways, what is each? Where does each come from? In what sense is each or either *King Lear*? In what sense is there a single play called *King Lear*?

Textual scholars desire to understand what state or condition of a play its printing represents; by examining its features they attempt to establish the relation of the text to its authorial origins. In the absence of surviving examples of annotated printers' copy for a play, and with a limited number of extant playbooks or manuscript copies of plays to serve as guides, scholars work within a set of descriptive categories that are based on hypotheses about how plays were composed, what copies were made, and what materials were sent to printing houses. The conventional narrative distinguishes five basic forms of 'copy', the materials from which compositors set a play into type: (i) foul papers, authorial draft materials not in a finished state; (ii) fair copy, the finished state of the author's composition, which may have become or from which a scrivener may have produced (iii) the prompt-book, or 'the book of the play', the manuscript in the playhouse which bore the signature of approval of the Master of the Revels that authorized stage performance; (iv) transcripts prepared from any of these sources; (v) copies of an earlier printing of the play, possibly corrected by reference to 'the book of the play', or subjected to revision by the author or some other hand[s].

Each kind of copy is conventionally identified by particular features. For instance, the particular traits that identify a work as printed from foul papers include an observed level of confusion or absence of clarity in the language of a text that may be the consequence of the difficulty in the printing house of reading the working draft of the author as he writes, corrects, crosses out, rewrites, and introduces new material. A lack of specificity in stage directions (*Enter Gloster brought in by two or three*, in Q1 *Lear*) is interpreted as evidence of the vagueness of the composing author. Another indicator of foul papers is the presence of variant speech headings for a single role; in Q2 *Romeo* Lady Capulet is designated in the speech headings variously as *Wife*, *Old La*, *La*, *Mo*, and *M* (the last two indicating 'Mother'). Yet another is the presence of the actor's name in the text; in Act 4 Scene 5 of *Romeo* a Q2 stage direction reads *Enter Will Kemp*, presumably in the role of Peter coming to address the Musicians (Q 1 *Romeo* reads *Enter Seruingman*). Significance is attached to the presence of unusual spellings that resemble the idiosyncratic forms that appear in the Hand D section of *The Book of Sir Thomas More*, which has been identified by many as in Shakespeare's hand. This system of discrimination assumes that, by contrast, the practical demands of the playhouse would not tolerate such imperfection and inconsistency in the book of the play. The presence of stage directions indicating more specific actions is seen as evidence of playhouse origins of some kind; for instance, in F *Lear, Stocks brought out*, and *Alarum within. Enter with Drumme and Colours, Lear, Cordelia, and Souldiers, ouer the Stage, and Exeunt*, and *Exeunt with a dead March*. Scribal copying is detected from the presence of non-theatrical elements such as act-and-scene divisions, and also from the distinctive features of the work of a known scrivener. For instance, the habit of grouping the names of all characters in a scene at the beginning of the scene and also some punctuation habits, particularly the heavy use of parentheses, betray the hand of Ralph Crane in a number of texts of the First Folio.

A small but important group of texts does not conform readily to these categorizations, however. While the second quartos of *Romeo* and *Hamlet* correspond well to the model of foul papers origins, the first quarto of each play does not. In each case the first quarto prints a text that is significantly shorter than the second, is relatively of much poorer quality, and contains notable differences in major features of plot and action. They – along with five other texts in the Shakespeare canon – have become known as Bad Quartos, an unfortunately prejudicial term that was invented in 1909 by A. W. Pollard, who believed that they were unauthorized publications of 'pirated' texts.[2] Their textual origins have usually been identified in 'memorial reconstruction', the efforts of one or more actors to reproduce a text of the play as they had performed it without the aid of any authoritative document. However, although they have been dismissed as non-authoritative because of their reported (i.e., second-hand) nature, their stage directions have nevertheless been seen as preserving possible information about stage practice, since, it is presumed, the actors were recalling the details of their performance. For instance, where the Q 2 stage direction for Juliet's entrance to her wedding reads *Enter Iuliet*, the Q 1 stage direction reads *Enter Iuliet somewhat fast, and embraceth Romeo*. Similarly, when Ophelia enters mad for the first time, Q 2 *Hamlet* reads simply *Enter Ophelia*, but Q 1 reads *Enter Ofelia, playing on a Lute, and her haire downe singing*.

In recent years both the criteria for identifying the printers' copy of plays and the category of Bad Quartos have come under attack. Paul Werstine has

subjected the narratives of textual transmission to a sceptical criticism. He
has argued that in the absence of any surviving example of 'foul papers' the
ability of scholars to identify a text's origins in such material depends on
commitment to a system of hypotheses rather than on extrapolations from
observed data.[3] William B. Long has pointed out that thorough examination
of surviving playbooks indicates that they reveal no signs of the kinds of reg-
ularization and conformity in the service of clarity and efficiency that are the
criteria for discriminating text of playhouse origin.[4] Randall McLeod has
demonstrated that even prompt-books of twentieth-century productions do
not conform to conventional expectations of playbooks; he has noted that
they often confuse the name of the role with that of the actor of the role.[5]
With regard to Bad Quartos, Peter W. M. Blayney has refuted a foundational
aspect of Pollard's theory (1909) that stressed that they were unauthorized
or 'piratical' printings (pp. 383–4). The work of Laurie E. Maguire and Paul
Werstine has eroded the certainty of identifying their origins in memorial reconstruction; Werstine has shown that the evidence on which Q1 *Romeo* and
Q1 *Hamlet* have been identified as memorially reconstructed and the roles
of the reconstructing actors discerned does not hold up under examination.[6]
These texts remain troublesomely idiosyncratic. Nevertheless, in the absence
of any more persuasive or useful hypotheses, many textual critics and editors
continue to discriminate between texts by using the traditional categories.

The aim of the conventional hypotheses has been to identify the qualities of
the printed work and from the data to recreate the 'play', usually in the form
of the ideal authorial original. However, while the grounds for discriminating
the individual printed texts have been challenged, the concept of the authorial original has been subjected to scrutiny also, and in such a way that the
idea of the author as the site of interest for the textual scholar has been questioned. Two separate approaches produce this particular disruption. The first
involves attention to the prevalence in sixteenth- and seventeenth-century
playhouse culture of authorial collaboration. Gerald Eades Bentley asserts
that collaborative composition was common among professional dramatists;
he records his 'reasonable . . . guess that as many as half of the plays by professional dramatists in the period incorporated the writing of more than one
man' and that 'nearly two-thirds' of the plays mentioned in *Henslowe's Diary*
are the result of collaboration.[7] While no scholar explicitly advances the idea
of identifiable collaboration in the composition of the tragedies beyond the
presence of Middleton in *Macbeth* and probably *Timon*, Shakespeare's texts
are nevertheless perceived by many as far more permeable than those of the
conventionally conceived solitary author. With the loss of authorial sanctity
the play text becomes an entity separate from the author, whose original production is no longer the object of pursuit. The second influential approach

emphasizes that the very nature of a play as a theatrical form frustrates the idea of the defined single entity that can be realized by any kind of historical or archaeological investigation. In this way of thinking a play is an unfixed object always subject to change in performance and to modification over time in the playhouse. Accordingly, any scholarly approach that seeks to reproduce some text of original purity is not true to the historical and generic nature of the play: the play is always in flux and impure. What survive are just print manifestations of moments in the history of the play.

In such a context of destabilization not only are the principles of the establishment of the authorial text subject to rethinking, but new modes of presentation of whatever text is established are also entertained. Editing Shakespearean tragedy has always been a process of imposing order on the unruly or creating provisional truth in an environment of uncertainty. Editions have always varied in textual detail one from another, but recently the variation in presentation has become greater than in the past as editors grapple with questions of what they are to represent and how best to represent it. Most conventional editions still aim to reproduce as a reading text something that can be described as the 'ideal of the authorial fair copy'[8] with a critical apparatus that records the choices made. The Riverside edition, for instance, is of this kind, even conservatively preserving some unusual spellings within its general modernization and marking significant editorial interventions with brackets. By contrast, the Oxford *Complete Works* has as its objective the recreation of the text as it existed in the playhouse as the foundation of performance. Since its editors believe that the revision of *King Lear* produced two distinct performance versions of the play, the Oxford is notable as the first collected edition to publish two separate reading texts of *King Lear* printed sequentially as *The History of King Lear* and *The Tragedy of King Lear*. The Oxford texts are printed without textual apparatus, although a full discussion of the textual situation is to be found in the separately published *Textual Companion*. The New Cambridge Shakespeare presents another approach, publishing both conventional critical editions of the plays and a complementary series of critical editions of 'The Early Quartos', including Q1 *Hamlet*, Q1 *King Lear*, and Q1 *Othello*.[9] Some editions push beyond the conventional formats to draw attention to the textual history and the editor's practice. In the Arden 3 series of individual texts of plays some editors meet editorial challenges with arresting graphics. The edition of *Titus* prints the fly-scene (3.2) in a distinctive sanserif type that contrasts with the serif type used for the rest of the text, thus drawing attention to its F-only status. The edition of *Lear* presents only a single conflated text, but material that is exclusive to either Q1 or F is clearly identified by parenthetical superscripts of the appropriate letter.[10] It is not evident that any of these editions has abandoned the standard categories of the narrative of textual recension. However, in the New Folger Library Shakespeare series Barbara A. Mowat and Paul Werstine reject the standard narrative as insufficiently confirmed by evidence to be useful in identifying the source of the printer's copy for a text. Consequently they declare their ambition to present an edition of each play as a textual phenomenon, as manifested in one or more surviving printings and disengaged from the circumstances of its authorial origins.[11] They choose for their editions a format with markings designed to highlight their choices and introductions so that the constructedness of their work is always manifest. Such a reading text insists on its own provisionality; the editors seek to make the reader constantly aware of the unavoidable constitutive role of editorial activity that in most editions is only visible in the textual apparatus.

Other editions also seek to respond to the particularity of the material remains or to the perceived irreducibility of the phenomena to a single text. In their Shakespeare Originals series Graham Holderness, Bryan Loughrey, and Andrew Murphy present direct transcriptions of individual early printings, reducing editorial mediation to the minimum, and encouraging the reader's encounter with features of the 'unedited' text without engaging the costly process of photographic facsimile reproduction. In this context the problem presented by the two texts of *King Lear* has provoked instructive editorial design solutions. Michael Warren has produced parallel texts of Q and F in facsimile by cutting photographic images, thus retaining as far as possible the unedited features of the original print of both texts. René Weis has produced edited texts of both Q and F *Lear* and presented them in parallel format on facing pages. Stephen Orgel has edited each and presented them sequentially as in the manner of the Oxford *Complete Works* but with glossarial notes on the page. In *The Norton Shakespeare Based on the Oxford Edition* Stephen Greenblatt and his co-editors reprint the Q and F versions from the Oxford *Complete Works* on facing pages; a traditional Conflated Text succeeds them.[12]

Such variety is not a manifestation of prodigality or irresponsibility in scholarship. Rather it is an inventive response to current thinking about the nature of the historical remains, the purpose of editing, and the possibilities of the book format, albeit within the constraints of the economics of commercial publishing. An awareness of complexity and a scepticism about simple answers require that superficial representations of the phenomena be avoided, and the print medium be explored in imaginative ways.

Examples from four plays may illustrate the general issues that I have discussed above. Q 1 *Lear* (1608) contains about 283 lines that are not present in F *Lear* (1623); F *Lear* contains about 100 lines that are not present in Q 1 *Lear*; verbal variants between the two texts are numerous. There are two primary explanatory hypotheses for the variant states of the texts: first, that each is a degraded state of a lost complete original that contained all the mutually exclusive material; second, that each represents in some form a stage in the development or existence of the play. Texts that combine material from both printings, such as that in the Riverside edition, the Arden 3, or the Conflated Text in *The Norton Shakespeare*, represent the editorial consequences of the first mode of thinking. Dual text presentations, such as those of the Oxford *Complete Works* and that of Stephen Orgel, and parallel presentations, such as the editions by Warren and Weis and that in *The Norton Shakespeare*, reflect the second. The Folger edition represents an avoidance of choice in its resort to a concept of textuality. The New Cambridge Shakespeare series goes one step further by publishing separate editions entitled *The Tragedy of King Lear* (F) and *The First Quarto of King Lear* (Q).[13] To maintain the first position, which seeks to reconstruct the author's desired form of the play, one must assume that at any moment of disagreement between the texts one is correct and one incorrect, or alternatively that neither is correct. But that is not incontrovertibly the case with Q and F *King Lear*. If the two *Lear* texts are read with respect for their individual textual integrity it is possible to recognize that each has a characteristic dramaturgy and that each has the potential for the creation of a distinctive theatrical experience. Q 1 is distinguished from F by the presence of the mock trial and Edgar's soliloquy in 3.6, the conversation of the two servants after the exit of Regan and Cornwall in 3.7, much of the conversation of Albany and Goneril in 4.2, the complete scene between Kent and the Gentleman (normally numbered 4.3), and their further conversation at the end of 4.7. The presence or absence of these particular elements, which are only some of the most immediately conspicuous among many, affects aspects of stage action, characterization, and ultimately meaning in the literary or theatrical interpretation of each text. This will become evident from a discussion of two sequences in the last moments of each version of the play, occurring in both texts on the last printed page.

The death of Lear is portrayed in different ways in the two texts. All recent conflated editions of the play, assuming the inferior quality and greater corruption of the quarto text, reproduce in some form the Folio text of the event. Lear's last words are:

> And my poore Foole is hang'd: no, no, no life?
> Why should a Dog, a Horse, a Rat haue life,
> And thou no breath at all? Thou'lt come no more,

> Neuer, neuer, neuer, neuer, neuer.
> Pray you vndo this button. Thanke you Sir,
> Do you see this? Looke on her? Looke her lips,
> Looke there, looke there.
>
> *He dies.* (TLN 3277–83)[14]

In F and conflated editions the speech is succeeded by Edgar's 'He faints, my Lord, my Lord'. Kent then expresses his desire for release, 'Breake heart, I prythee breake'. But the quarto text presents a different sequence of events in relatively similar language. Lear's speech is shorter and in prose:

> And my poore foole is hangd, no, no life, why should a dog, a horse, a rat of life and thou no breath at all, O thou wilt come no more, neuer, neuer, neuer, pray you vndo this button, thanke you sir. O, o, o, o.   (L4r)

Here, after expressing his thanks, Lear does not draw the attention of others to Cordelia's lips, but instead utters a sigh or groan represented by 'O, o, o, o'. As in F, Edgar comments on the movement of Lear's fainting, but in Q Lear speaks again, uttering words that are ascribed in F to Kent: 'Breake hart, I prethe breake'. In this version Lear expresses his personal desire for his release and dies a willed death, not, as F may be interpreted as indicating, in some condition of happy illusion. These sequences present different scenarios for stage action; they permit different modes of interpretation of the characters' behaviour that are mutually exclusive; and they elicit possible different emotional and intellectual responses in readers and audiences to Lear's death.

The roles of Albany and Edgar are also affected by variation in a speech heading at the end of the play. In the familiar F reading that is customarily adopted by editors, Edgar speaks the last speech of the play:

> The waight of this sad time we must obey,
> Speake what we feele, not what we ought to say:
> The oldest hath borne most, we that are yong,
> Shall neuer see so much, nor liue so long.
>
> (TLN 3298–301)

The quarto prints the same speech with only one minor variation in punctuation, but it assigns the speech to *Duke*, that is Albany. The conclusions of the two texts are therefore different in a second respect; each presents a different interpretive opportunity. In both texts Albany has just invited Edgar and Kent to share Lear's kingdom: 'Friends of my soule, you twaine, / Rule in this realme [Q: kingdome], and the gor'd state sustaine' (TLN 3293–5); in both texts Kent declines the invitation. In F Edgar's response to Albany's invitation to rule is oblique but presumably positive. In Q, however, he is apparently unresponsive, and in the context of Albany's final speech his silence suggests that he is not accepting the throne. The quarto title page gives prominence to mentioning 'the vnfortunate life of Edgar'; the conclusion of the Q text can be interpreted as related to that statement. Although Edgar's life in the F text could be considered unfortunate – he has undergone a severe test, lost his father, and fought his brother to the death – it is not the epithet that seems appropriate to the man who assumes the throne at the end of the play. The two endings are irreconcilable; scholars may argue that one or the other is corrupt, but that is a judgement, not a necessary conclusion from the evidence. Each is justifiable theatrically and intellectually. There are grounds for identifying more than one text of a play called *King Lear*; *King Lear* is not a single stable entity.

Othello also exists in two states, the quarto of 1622 and the Folio of 1623, although the nature of the variance between the texts is different. The Folio text is longer and fuller than the quarto text and so has been chosen usually as the copy text for editions; there are numerous individual verbal variants between the texts. One set of verbal variants is of particular interest, notably oaths that are present in Q but not in F. For example, in Q the first line of the play reads 'Tvsh, neuer tell me, I take it much vnkindly', but in F the initial exclamation is missing; in the fourth line Iago says ''Sblood but you will not hear me', whereas in F he says simply 'But you'l not heare me'. The presence of such oaths in Q suggests that it derives from a manuscript that represents a state of the play that dates from before 1606 when the Act to Restraine Abuses of Players prohibited the uttering of oaths on the stage.[15] Their absence from F indicates its later origin. However, Q is also notable for the absence from it of several passages that are present in F, not least among them Desdemona's Willow Song in 4.3, Emilia's justification of women's sexual rights at the end of the same scene, and a number of other speeches of Desdemona and Emilia in the fourth and fifth acts that appear to have serial interpretive connections. Nevill Coghill and E. A. J. Honigmann have both proposed that the interrelation of these passages suggests a systematic development and revision in the F text rather than corruption or cutting in Q, although Honigmann has recently withdrawn his support of this position.[16] Whatever the case, two distinct texts of the play exist. It is scholarly hypothesis that determines the constitution of one or two versions of *Othello* from this material, just as in the act of conflating to produce a single *Othello* it will be scholarly judgement that will select one or the other reading where there are verbal variants.

The textual condition of *Hamlet* is still more complicated because there are three texts, Q1 (1603), Q2 (1604/5), and F (1623). I shall ignore in this case the complex relation of Q2 and F, in which the familiar pattern of presence and absence in both texts and of local verbal variants is apparent, and focus instead on the relation of Q1, the 'Bad Quarto', to the term *Hamlet*. Because of the fullness and comparative goodness of the Q2 text, the edited text of *Hamlet* is usually based on Q2 with additions from F.[17] However, there exists, challengingly, Q1, a much shorter, verbally less felicitous text that is nevertheless ascribed to Shakespeare on the title page. As I have indicated earlier, the origin and status of 'Bad Quartos' are uncertain; nevertheless, whatever its origins, Q1 testifies to a version of the play different in kind from either Q2 or F. F may lack Hamlet's fourth-act soliloquy, 'How all occasions doe informe against me' (printed in Q2), and Q2 may lack the second-act conversations concerning Hamlet's perception of Denmark as a prison and the adult players' discomfiture at the hands of boys' companies, but Q1 contains a whole scene between Horatio and the Queen that has no equivalent in either Q2 or F, that is not manifestly non-Shakespearean, and that alters the interpretation of the Queen's role in the rest of the play: in it Horatio informs her of the King's conspiracy to have Hamlet killed in England. The scene cannot be easily dismissed except insofar as it is part of the derided Q1 and as it is irreconcilable with the rest of the Q2/F text; it is worth considering that the book purchaser of *Hamlet* in 1603 believed that it was part of *Hamlet*. Standard conflated editions of the play are created by ignoring the challenge to their constructed unity that Q1 presents; although editors may borrow stage directions from it as a text with its origins in performance, they do so only after assigning it a status inferior to the Q2 and F texts. The scene of the Queen and Horatio is rarely printed and seldom acknowledged (see fig. 1).[18] It remains to assert that *Hamlet* is multiple, not a single fixed text.

By contrast with *Hamlet* there is only one text of *Macbeth*, so that no acts of comparison serve to complicate the identification of the work. However, the constitution of the work as Shakespearean is not simple. At two points in the Folio text the stage directions make reference to songs of which only a few words are supplied. In Act 3 Scene 5 F reads *Sing within. Come away, come away, &c.* In Act 4 Scene 1 a stage direction reads *Musicke and a Song. Blacke spirits &c.* Both appear to refer to songs by Thomas Middleton from his play *The Witch*. The date of composition of Middleton's play is unknown, though it is usually placed later than that of *Macbeth*. How these songs relate to the text of the play is not clear, since the references are very abbreviated.[19] However, it is noteworthy that the only source of information that establishes the foundation for a text of *Macbeth* manifestly contains non-Shakespearean elements. It is probable that there was a state of *Macbeth* that at some time did not contain the material derived from Middleton, but it is lost to us.

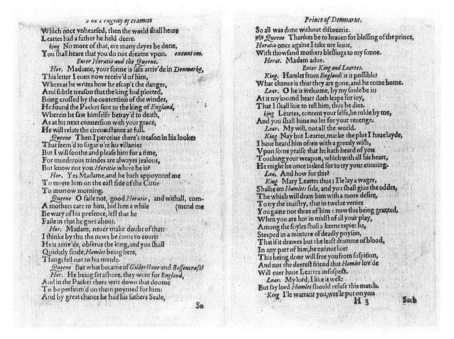

Figure 1 *Hamlet*, 1603 Quarto. Sigs. H2v–H3r.

Even though the text of *Macbeth* is single, the nature of what we know as *Macbeth* is not simple.

With the inclusion of the material from *The Witch*, the text of *Macbeth* appears to be associated with playhouse practice after initial composition; it may reflect what audiences saw at some time between 1606 and 1623. The record of performances of Shakespeare's tragedies before the closing of the theatres in 1642 is disappointingly slim. The title pages cited at the beginning of this essay provide information that may or may not be reliable about performances of *Titus*, *Romeo*, *Hamlet*, *Lear*, and *Othello*, or at least about the companies that performed them. There were three performances of *Titus* at the Rose playhouse and two at Newington Butts in 1594. A Swiss visitor to London, Thomas Platter, saw *Julius Caesar* at the Globe on 21 September 1599, and recorded that the actors performed a dance after the play; *Julius Caesar* was also played at court in the winter of 1612–13, at St James's Palace in 1637, and at the Cockpit in 1638. *Othello* was performed at court on 1 November 1604, at Oxford in September 1610 (Evans, *Riverside*, p. 1852), again at court in the winter of 1612–13, in 1629 at either the Globe or the Blackfriars, in 1635 at the Blackfriars, and in 1636 for the king and queen at Hampton Court. *Hamlet* was played twice on shipboard off Sierra Leone on 5 September 1607, and 31 March 1608, and at Hampton Court in 1637. A provincial company in Yorkshire performed *King Lear* in 1610 (Halio, *Tragedy*, p. 34). There are no surviving references to performances of *Antony and Cleopatra*, *Coriolanus*, or *Timon of Athens*. Few reports give insight into the nature of performances. A member of the audience for *Othello* in Oxford in 1610 described in a letter the moving quality of the actor playing Desdemona dead (Evans, *Riverside*, p. 1852), and the astrologer and alchemist Simon Forman recorded in his *Book of Plaies* his recollections of a performance of *Macbeth* at the Globe on 20 April 1611; he describes the Witches as 'women feiries or Nimphes'.[20] But what exactly was played on any occasion – the relation between the published text and the performance – is not known. If from the remark of the Chorus in the opening speech of *Romeo and Juliet* that he introduces 'the two houres trafficque of our Stage' (Q2) one is tempted to generalize the conventional length of presentation, then no audience can have seen all of Q2 or F *Hamlet*, both plays well in excess of 3,500 lines. Texts that editors have identified as of playhouse origins do not indicate how the play may have been played. Stephen Orgel suggests that the play performed was always shorter than the written text.[21] William B. Long (p. 116) has suggested that playbooks that do not provide adequate guides to playing by modern standards were nevertheless sufficient to the needs of the actors who knew how to use them, to play their contents. We have to conceive of a creative environment markedly different from our own.

The desire of textual and historical scholarship is for certainty, but in contemplating the text of Shakespearean tragedies scholars work with a perplexing body of relatively fragmentary information, and generalizing narratives are frequently perilous; in regard to performance the information is extremely limited. The forms in which we conventionally read the plays may enable acts of interpretation, but it is imperative that we acknowledge the provisional and constructed nature of those forms.

NOTES

1. Peter W. M. Blayney, 'The Publication of Playbooks', in *A New History of Early English Drama*, ed. John D. Cox and David Scott Kastan (New York: Columbia University Press, 1997), p. 385.
2. Alfred W. Pollard, *Shakespeare Folios and Quartos: A Study in the Bibliography of Shakespeare's Plays, 1594–1685* (London: Methuen, 1909).
3. Paul Werstine, 'Narratives about Printed Shakespeare Texts: "Foul Papers" and "Bad" Quartos', *Shakespeare Quarterly* 41 (1990), 67–86; and 'Plays in Manuscript', in *A New History of Early English Drama*, ed. Cox and Kastan, pp. 481–97.
4. William B. Long, '"A Bed / for Woodstock": a Warning for the Unwary', *Medieval and Renaissance Drama in England* 2 (1985), 91–118.

5. Randall McLeod, 'The Psychopathology of Everyday Art', in *The Elizabethan Theatre IX*, ed. G. R. Hibbard (Port Credit, Ontario: P. D. Meany, 1986), pp. 100–68.
6. Laurie E. Maguire, *Shakespearean Suspect Texts* (Cambridge University Press, 1996); Paul Werstine, 'A Century of "Bad" Shakespeare Quartos', *Shakespeare Quarterly* 50 (1999), 310–33.
7. Gerald Eades Bentley, *The Profession of Dramatist in Shakespeare's Time* (Princeton University Press, 1971), p. 199; see also Jeffrey Masten, 'Playwrighting: Authorship and Collaboration', in *A New History of Early English Drama*, ed. Cox and Kastan, pp. 357–82.
8. Fredson Bowers describes the process of editing as the application of critical principles 'to the textual raw material of the authoritative preserved documents in order to approach as nearly as may be to the ideal of the authorial fair copy by whatever necessary process of recovery, independent emendation, or conflation of authorities', *Textual and Literary Criticism* (Cambridge University Press, 1966), p. 120.
9. *The Riverside Shakespeare*, general and textual editor G. Blakemore Evans with the assistance of J. J. M. Tobin (Boston: Houghton Mifflin, 1997); *The Complete Works*, gen. eds. Stanley Wells and Gary Taylor (Oxford: Clarendon Press, 1986), pp. 1025–98; Stanley Wells and Gary Taylor with John Jowett and William Montgomery, *William Shakespeare: A Textual Companion* (Oxford: Clarendon Press, 1987; rpt with corrections, New York: W. W. Norton, 1997); *The First Quarto of Hamlet*, ed. Kathleen O. Irace (Cambridge University Press, 1998); *The First Quarto of King Lear*, ed. Jay L. Halio (Cambridge University Press, 1994); *The First Quarto of Othello*, ed. Scott McMillin (Cambridge University Press, 2001).
10. *Titus Andronicus*, ed. Jonathan Bate (London: Routledge, 1995); *King Lear*, ed. R. A. Foakes (London: Thomas Nelson, 1997).
11. Barbara A. Mowat and Paul Werstine, 'An Introduction to This Text', *Hamlet* (New York: Washington Square Press, 1992), p. xlix.
12. *The Parallel 'King Lear' 1608–1623*, prepared by Michael Warren (Berkeley: University of California Press, 1989); *'King Lear': A Parallel Text Edition*, ed. René Weis (London: Longman, 1993); *'King Lear': The 1608 Quarto and 1623 Folio Texts*, ed. Stephen Orgel (New York: Penguin Putnam, 2000); *The Norton Shakespeare Based on the Oxford Edition*, ed. Stephen Greenblatt, Walter Cohen, Jean E. Howard, and Katharine Eisaman Maus (New York: W. W. Norton, 1997), pp. 2307–553.
13. *King Lear*, ed. Barbara A. Mowat and Paul Werstine (New York: Washington Square Press, 1993); *The Tragedy of King Lear*, ed. Jay L. Halio (Cambridge University Press, 1992); *The First Quarto of King Lear*, ed. Jay L. Halio (Cambridge University Press, 1994).
14. TLN (Through Line Numbers) is the system developed by Charlton Hinman in *The Norton Facsimile: The First Folio of Shakespeare* (New York: W. W. Norton, 1968) to designate locations within individual Folio plays by line of type (spoken text or stage direction).
15. E. K. Chambers, *William Shakespeare: A Study of Facts and Problems*, 2 vols. (Oxford: Clarendon Press, 1930), I. 98–9.

16. Nevill Coghill, *Shakespeare's Professional Skills* (Cambridge University Press, 1964), pp. 164–202; E. A. J. Honigmann, 'Shakespeare's Revised Plays: *King Lear* and *Othello*', *The Library*, 6th ser., 4 (1982), 142–73; Honigmann expresses his doubts about the evidence for revision in *The Texts of 'Othello' and Shakespearian Revision* (London: Routledge, 1996), pp. 7–21.

17. The Oxford *Complete Works* prints a text based on F, printing the Q2-only material as 'Additional Passages'; in the Oxford Shakespeare *Hamlet*, ed. G. R. Hibbard (Oxford University Press, 1987), that material appears in Appendix A, 'Passages Peculiar to the Second Quarto'. Although based on the Oxford edition, *The Norton Shakespeare* reintroduces the passages into the body of the text but in italics.

18. The scene may also be located in *The Tragicall Historie of Hamlet Prince of Denmarke*, ed. Graham Holderness and Bryan Loughrey (Hemel Hempstead: Harvester Wheatsheaf, 1992); *The First Quarto of Hamlet*, ed. Kathleen O. Irace (Cambridge University Press, 1998); and in *The Three-Text Hamlet: Parallel Texts of the First and Second Quartos and First Folio*, ed. Paul Bertram and Bernice W. Kliman (New York: AMS Press, 1991).

19. For a full discussion see A. R. Braunmuller, 'Thomas Middleton's Contribution to the Folio', in his edition of *Macbeth* (Cambridge University Press, 1997),' pp. 255–9.

20. All information about performances derives (unless otherwise stated) from Chambers, *William Shakespeare*, II. 303–53.

21. Stephen Orgel, 'The Authentic Shakespeare', *Representations* 21 (1988), 97.

5

HUSTON DIEHL

Religion and Shakespearean tragedy

Shortly after Elizabeth Tudor became England's queen in November 1558, the Acts of Supremacy and Uniformity were passed, effectively outlawing the practice of Roman Catholicism in England and making Elizabeth I head of the Church of England. By establishing Protestantism as the official state religion, Elizabeth hoped to put an end to the religious conflicts that had divided the English people and disrupted the realm ever since her father, Henry VIII, defied the Pope by divorcing Catherine of Aragon in 1534. In what is known as the Elizabethan settlement, she reversed the policies of her Catholic half-sister Mary I, who reigned from 1553 to 1558. Mary's marriage to Philip of Spain had forged an alliance between England and the most powerful Roman Catholic country on the continent. As queen she had attempted to return England to the Roman Catholic faith after a period of intense reform activity that occurred during the six-year reign of Mary and Elizabeth's younger half-brother, Edward VI (1547–53). With the Elizabethan settlement England became a predominantly Protestant country after many turbulent years of religious strife.

Five and a half years after Elizabeth's ascension to the throne, William Shakespeare was born in Stratford. England's most illustrious playwright thus belonged to the first generation of English people who lived their entire lives in an officially Protestant country, required by law to practise the established state religion. We do not know anything directly about Shakespeare's religious beliefs, though some scholars have speculated that members of his family were recusants, Roman Catholic believers who refused to conform to the Protestant faith. But, whether he himself embraced, repudiated, or merely tolerated the teachings of the Anglican Church, the Protestant Reformation had a profound impact on his work.

In fact, as a London playwright active in the 1590s and early 1600s, Shakespeare would have been keenly aware of the way these religious reforms affected his profession, for the very conditions under which he worked were shaped by them. Because he wrote for the commercial theatre, his livelihood depended on his ability to appeal to the interests and tastes of London's citizens, many of whom harboured intense anti-papist sentiments, identified Protestantism with the English nation, and viewed the world through the lens of their Anglican faith. To avoid offending his monarchs (Elizabeth I, and, later, James I, both Protestants) and patrons (many of whom championed Protestant causes), Shakespeare also had to be attentive to the religious controversies of his day and alert to their political implications and social ramifications. Then, too, his theatre was subject to state-censorship laws that, among other things, outlawed plays that advanced Catholic doctrine and forbade theatrical representations of the divine in accordance with Protestant belief that such representations were idolatrous.[1] As a consequence of these laws, the biblical narratives of Christ's life and the sacred stories of the Virgin Mary and the Roman Catholic saints that had been the central subjects of English medieval drama were no longer considered appropriate theatrical material. Unlike his predecessors, Shakespeare could address religious subjects only indirectly.

But the impact of the Reformation on Shakespeare's theatre went far beyond the material conditions of the stage. If, as it appears, the Reformation was originally instigated by an elite group of intellectuals and political leaders and imposed from above, it nevertheless transformed the lives of ordinary English men and women, many of whom initially lamented the breakdown of the old order, the disruption of established ways, and the loss of cherished traditions (Duffy). Although the doctrinal controversies debated by theologians, the biblical scholarship produced by reform-minded humanists, and the political struggles waged between the English monarchs and the Pope were far removed from most people's daily lives, the Reformation profoundly altered the English people's devotional and ritual practices, putting an end to Roman Catholic traditions that had endured for more than a thousand years. It changed how they worshipped their God, how they confessed their sins, how they buried their dead, how they celebrated their holy days (holidays), how they practised charity, how they constructed their relationships to their families and communities, how they organized their days and ritual year, how they viewed the physical world, and how they understood their place in the cosmos.

Writing during a time of such radical changes, when so many long-held beliefs were being questioned, so many established traditions and institutions were being challenged, and so many familiar rituals were being outlawed or transformed, Shakespeare could hardly have ignored the impact that the Reformation had on England and its people. Indeed, as a native of Warwickshire (a rural county where people were more likely to cling to traditional religious rituals), a resident of London (a centre for reform activity), and a man of the theatre (an institution supported by Protestant patrons but also attacked by Protestant moralists, identified with the emerging Protestant English nation but also associated with a demonized Roman Catholic Church), he must have been acutely aware of the tensions produced by religious reform. Tragedy, especially, provided him a literary form in which he could reflect upon the disruption, uncertainty, violence, and loss caused by the Reformation and imaginatively engage the beliefs, rituals, habits, and moods of the new religion. Because it raises fundamental questions about the human condition, including questions about the nature of evil, the workings of fate, the mysteries of the supernatural, the consequences of human choices and actions, and the problem of knowledge, tragedy interrogates the core beliefs and assumptions of its culture. Shakespeare's culture is a predominantly religious one, and he therefore addresses these tragic concerns from the perspective of someone who is deeply cognizant of the religious beliefs and theological controversies of his day and fully engaged in examining their metaphysical, epistemological, and ethical dimensions. In addition, tragedy is closely aligned with the central, defining rituals of its culture. Because so many of those rituals in early modern English culture were religious ones that were in the process of being radically transformed, tragedy offers Shakespeare a medium through which he can explore that transformation.

The doctrinal differences between Protestants and Catholics may seem minor to readers living in today's secularized culture of the West, where one's religious beliefs are typically viewed as a private matter and where ecumenicalism, tolerance, and diversity are routinely championed. But these differences aroused strong passions in the sixteenth century, creating rifts in families, friendships, and political alliances and resulting in wars, conspiracies, riots, persecutions, and martyrdoms. Before turning to a discussion of how religion informs specific Shakespearean tragedies, I want to clarify those differences, giving particular attention to the central tenets of English Protestantism.

Although the Protestant Reformation had deep roots in various theological, political, and intellectual movements of the late Middle Ages, its inception is usually traced to the day in 1517 when Martin Luther posted his ninety-five theses against indulgences on the door of Wittenberg Cathedral. A German Augustinian monk and scholar well versed in medieval theology, Luther came to reject the Roman Catholic doctrine of good works that taught that the faithful could contribute in some degree to their own salvation by performing good works. Arguing that man lacks the free will to do good, Luther advanced the doctrine of justification by faith alone (*sola fides*). For him, Roman Catholicism misled the devout by engaging them in futile efforts to earn salvation, thereby diverting their attention from the central problem of faith, the challenge of believing in the words and promises of God.[2] One of the core beliefs of mainstream Protestantism, the doctrine of *sola fides* led Luther and other reformers to critique a range of Roman Catholic religious practices, including the buying and selling of indulgences and pardons, intercessory prayers, pilgrimages, and the veneration of images. Roman Catholicism taught that all these practices could aid salvation, but the reformers viewed them as mere externals that tempted people to trust in them, instead of putting their faith in God.

As Protestantism spread through many areas of Europe, it took distinctly different forms, depending on the relative influence of prominent theologians like Luther, Zwingli, and Calvin, as well as the particular political circumstances and social conditions of a given country or region. While the Reformation spawned a significant number of radical sects whose extreme beliefs were not accepted by more mainstream Protestants, most Protestants shared certain core assumptions. Virtually all insisted on the primacy of scripture and the centrality of the word of God. They therefore emphasized the importance of preaching the word, faulting Roman Catholics for privileging liturgy over preaching, and they advocated the use of vernacular languages in church services, instead of the traditional Latin of the Roman Catholic Mass, which most lay people could not understand. The reformers believed the Bible should be accessible to everyone, and, along with influential humanists whose philological scholarship called into question the accuracy of standard medieval Latin versions of the Bible, they undertook new vernacular translations of the Bible. In addition, their emphasis on the word led them to encourage literacy among classes of people who had not previously had access to even a rudimentary education.

Protestants also advocated a return to the practices of the 'primitive' or early church. They thus rejected those doctrines, rituals, and practices of the medieval church that they believed had no basis in scripture. Instead of the seven sacraments of the Roman Catholic Church, for instance, they argued that Christ instituted only two, baptism and communion. Although the various Protestant churches devised quite different ecclesiastical structures, all of them opposed the office of the Pope and renounced papal authority. In addition, Protestants strenuously objected to the monastic life and the practice of celibacy, arguing that the assumption that Catholic monks, friars, priests, and nuns could attain a purer or more holy state through adherence to monastic or clerical rules was a foolish delusion. Because they believed that the human will was inherently corrupt, they insisted that priests, too, were sinners and that not even the clergy could come close to attaining perfection in this world. Protestants therefore opposed many priestly functions that elevated the clergy above the laity, including the ritual of auricular confession, and they advocated a priesthood of all believers, arguing that there should be no intermediary between an individual and his or her God.

One of the most crucial points of contention between Protestants and Roman Catholics concerned the interpretation of the sacrament of communion. Protestants vehemently objected to the Roman Catholic Mass, and in particular the doctrine of transubstantiation, which taught that the sacramental bread and wine were mystically transformed into the true body and blood of Christ at the moment of the priest's consecration. They believed that priests misled the uneducated by nurturing the belief that the mere sight of the elevated host (the display of the consecrated bread) was powerful enough to assure one's salvation, and they objected to a number of Roman Catholic practices that they believed unnecessarily mystified this sacrament, obscuring its meaning. To undermine belief in the doctrine of transubstantiation, the reformers ridiculed the Catholic clergy in satires that accused priests of practising magic, mistaking a sign for the thing it signified, and even chewing and eating God. Protestants, however, did not agree among themselves about how to interpret this key sacrament, and influential reformers advanced competing theories, including consubstantiation (or real presence), virtualism, and memorialism.[3] In the Protestant English Church, the sacrament of communion, called 'The Lord's Supper', was generally interpreted in accordance with the theory of virtualism, defined as 'the belief that while the bread and wine continue to exist unchanged after the Consecration, yet the faithful communicant receives together with the elements the virtue or power of the body and blood of Christ' (Davies, p. 83). Debates about this sacrament, which focused on the rhetorical interpretation of Christ's words 'This is my body', were, to some degree, debates about the nature of representation.

One of the strongest continental influences on early English Protestantism was John Calvin, a French reformer who lived in exile in Geneva where many English reformers fled during the reign of Queen Mary. Calvin gave particular emphasis to the doctrine of election, which teaches that a few people, known as the elect, are predestined by God for salvation while the rest are reprobates, predestined to be damned. In advancing this doctrine, Calvin emphasized God's omnipotence and grace: while no one merited salvation or could attain it through good works, God nevertheless chose to grant it to an elect few. While Calvin saw this doctrine as providing comfort to the elect by assuring them of the certainty of their salvation through God's grace, it nevertheless aroused a distinct set of anxieties among the faithful, for how could one be certain that one was among the elect? And what kind of evidence might constitute assurance of salvation? These anxieties were primarily epistemological in nature: they raised questions about how people know and what can be known. The very notion of the reprobate, predestined to do evil, raised troubling ethical questions as well, for if someone is predestined by God to do evil, how then can he be said to exercise moral choice or to be responsible for his actions? And how can a belief in predestination be reconciled with Protestantism's insistence on the importance of repentance, moral reformation, and spiritual regeneration?

Many of the religious controversies of the earlier sixteenth century continued to vex theologians and believers after the Elizabethan settlement, and new, divisive religious controversies inevitably arose. Under the threat of persecution and imprisonment, Catholic recusants continued to practise the old faith in private, and some conspired with continental Catholics to overthrow the Protestant monarch and return England to Catholicism. Militant Protestants and nonconformists who were dissatisfied with the degree of reform in the Anglican state Church sought to institute further reforms of it and sometimes broke from it altogether, founding or joining various radical sects. Nevertheless, through such instruments as the Book of Common Prayer, a prescribed set of church homilies, official catechisms, the Geneva Bible and, in 1611, the King James Bible, the Church of England began to forge a common religious culture among the English people.

The degree to which Shakespearean drama is a product of that evolving religious culture is often underestimated in our more secular age. In the past twenty years scholars have tended to focus on the political and social dimensions of Shakespearean drama, examining issues of power, gender, sexuality, class, and race. Recently, however, there has been a growing recognition of what Claire McEachern has called 'the massive centrality of religion to this period's cultural imagination and production'.[4] This recognition has led to a re-examination of the relation between the religious culture of early modern England and the secular drama of the commercial, popular London stage. Scholars are beginning to consider, among other things, how various religious discourses inform the plays of Shakespeare and his contemporaries; how Protestant notions of inwardness and the self contribute to Shakespeare's portrayal of character; how providential theories of history find expression in dramatic narrative; how the rhetoric and performative aspects of Protestant preaching influence the stage; and how key religious conflicts of the Reformation are re-enacted or rehearsed on the stage. Some are asking as well how religious rituals and practices shape theatrical practices, including whether changes in the sacrament of communion might lead to changes in the nature of dramatic representation and whether Protestant iconoclasm might affect the status of theatrical spectacle. In the remaining part of this essay, I will situate three of Shakespeare's major tragedies – *Hamlet, Othello, and King Lear* – in the religious culture of early modern

England in order to show how each is in part a product of the Protestant Reformation.

When the reformers defied the edicts of the Pope, questioned the rules of clerical discipline, put obedience to God's word above obedience to a secular king, taught children to reject the religion of their parents, celebrated the rebellious acts of Protestant martyrs, and advocated a priesthood of all believers, they called into question established authority (from the Pope to the village priest, the Roman Catholic monarch to the father who remains loyal to the old religion). At the same time, they sought to inculcate obedience to the reformed church and the Protestant monarch, to institute new forms of religious discipline, and to teach reliance on the authority of the Bible. Writing about the structure of the Protestant family, the historian Steven Ozment speculates about how the Reformation might have complicated a young person's relation to authority. 'What must have been the long-term effect on children', he asks, 'when criticism and ridicule of traditional authority were constantly drummed in their heads, while at the same time they were assured of the infallibility and certitude of the new faith?'[5] Because it denies the legitimacy of traditional authority figures and yet insists on the authority of the word of God and celebrates the assurance of faith, early Protestantism, Ozment implies, nurtures both defiance and obedience, scepticism and certainty, doubt and faith.

Shakespeare explores this Protestant paradox in *Hamlet*, a play that is filled with cryptic allusions to the Protestant Reformation and infused with the questioning spirit of early Protestantism. His profoundly sceptical protagonist wrestles with the contradictory demands of competing authorities, including his dead father, his king (who is both his stepfather and paternal uncle), and his own conscience (which must answer to God the Father). Summoned home to the Danish court from his studies in Wittenberg, a university affiliation that surely signals his engagement with the revolutionary ideas of Protestantism, Hamlet is torn between his propensity to question all authority and his strong sense of filial obligation, an obligation that seems to require him to obey his father's ghost and take revenge on Claudius, but also one at odds with his intellectual nature. His task is complicated by the competing claims of rival authorities and his deep suspicion that every authority figure may be a hypocrite or fraud.

When Hamlet first sees the Ghost, he desperately seeks to understand his harrowing encounter with the supernatural, asking:

> what may this mean,
> That thou, dead corpse, again in complete steel,
> Revisitst thus the glimpses of the moon,

Making night hideous, and we fools of nature
So horridly to shake our disposition
With thoughts beyond the reaches of our souls?
Say, why is this? Wherefore? What should we do?

(1.4.51-7)

Although he seems here to appeal to the authority of the Ghost and initially promises to act swiftly to right the wrong the Ghost claims he has suffered, Hamlet subsequently feels compelled to find persuasive proof of the Ghost's allegations before he acts, and much of the play depicts his efforts to determine the validity of the Ghost's tale. Indeed, he recognizes that the Ghost itself may be unreliable, perhaps a demonic tempter or a hallucination rather than the actual ghost of his father (2.2.575-80). In the end, Hamlet decides to put himself at risk in the duel with Laertes not because of his reliance on any human authority, paternal ghost, or his own reason but because of his faith in a divine authority. 'There's a divinity that shapes our ends', he tells Horatio after escaping from the boat taking him to England with the warrant for his death, 'Rough-hew them how we will' (5.2.10-11). Laying aside his suspicions and checking his inclination to speculate, test, observe, and interpret, Hamlet articulates a belief in God's particular plan for him, asserting, in an allusion to Matthew 10:29, that 'There's a special providence in the fall of a sparrow' and concluding, 'The readiness is all' (5.2.157-8, 160). At this moment Shakespeare's most intellectual, sceptical, and self-reflective hero chooses to act solely on the basis of his faith in what cannot be known, proven, or rationally explained.

In its portrayal of this conflicted and paradoxical character – a youthful rebel striving to obey, a sceptic seeking certitude, an intellectual who acts on faith – the play of *Hamlet*, I am suggesting, explores the psychological pressures early Protestantism exerted on the individual. Although it is neither polemical nor doctrinal, it addresses the challenge of living in a post-Reformation world complicated by the competing demands of rival authorities, unsettled by the disruptive questions of people taught to be sceptical of received wisdom and traditional ways, and energized by a new emphasis on faith.

Protestantism's emphasis on faith raised compelling epistemological issues for people living in countries that embraced reform, issues that Shakespeare repeatedly engages, most notably, perhaps, in his tragedy of *Othello*. When the reformers challenged the validity of all external aids to faith, declared belief in the efficacy of sacred relics a superstition, accused priests of practising magic, insisted on the primacy of the word, and embraced the doctrine of justification by faith alone, they undermined the traditional means by which the English people had sustained faith in their God. Whereas, in the fifteenth century, the pious were encouraged to perceive 'the visible and tangible reality' of an 'incarnate Saviour' in devotional images, relics, and sacraments and to view the physical world as one 'saturated with sacramental possibility and meaning', the Protestant reformers dismissed this way of thinking as superstitious and idolatrous.[6] Citing St Paul, who defined faith as 'the evidence of things not seen' (Hebrews 11:1), they required people to maintain faith in an invisible God without relying on any visible evidence or intermediary aids.

Othello, a play about the passionate love between an 'exotic' Moor and a beautiful Venetian noblewoman, would seem to be an unlikely vehicle for an examination of these religious issues. But, in its depiction of a man who trusts a handkerchief he claims has magical powers instead of the word of the woman he loves, Shakespeare's tragedy explores the very epistemological issues that animate Reformation debates about the role of images in the practice of faith. Do objects have magical or efficacious powers, and if so, on what grounds can those powers be verified? Do visible things have any place in the exercise of faith? What role, if any, does sight play in establishing the truth? How can one distinguish between true and fraudulent evidence? Can anything be known for certain? Although *Othello* is a secular drama about erotic desire, sexual jealousy, and marital discord, its tragic story thus resonates in a particularly powerful way with early Protestantism's teachings about faith, evidence, magic, and images. Indeed, Shakespeare signals his interest in these theological issues by appropriating the language of religious discourse. In its references to magic and bewitchment, cunning beauty and stony hearts, strangers and whores, 'trifles light as air' and 'proofs of holy writ', and 'enfettered' and 'ensnared' souls, this play draws on key words and metaphors in Protestant tracts attacking religious images.[7]

Many scholars have argued that the handkerchief is far too trivial an object to serve as credible evidence of Desdemona's infidelity, and they thus declare the plot of *Othello* flawed. But if we consider Desdemona's handkerchief in the context of the Reformation controversy over images, a controversy that profoundly altered the way the English people understood the relation between the visible world and God, we can begin to see why Shakespeare might have chosen a handkerchief to serve as the 'ocular proof' that Othello trusts, imperilling his soul. In Shakespeare's day, sacred images and relics, including a number of handkerchiefs, were being systematically attacked by reformers who viewed them as impediments to faith. Far from being considered insignificant objects, many lay people fervently believed they had efficacious powers (for example, the power to save, to heal, to protect, or to make fertile). According to the reformers, these images were dangerous because they tempted people to put their trust in visible objects instead of an invisible God and to believe in magic rather than having faith in God's word. They embarked on a campaign to discredit thousands of relics and devotional images, exposing them as fraudulent and impotent. In fact, they set out not only to demystify these images, but to destroy them, and much of the sacred art of the medieval English Church fell victim to outbreaks of iconoclastic violence. The reformers did not, however, question the validity of all sacred images. Indeed, they argued that some images – including the rainbow that appeared to Noah and the handkerchiefs that Paul used to cure the sick – function as powerful signs or 'remembrances' of God's love and grace, signs that have the capacity to renew faith.

By giving the handkerchief such a central role in Othello's tragedy, Shakespeare is thus able to examine issues of critical importance in post-Reformation England. Employing a relentless dramatic irony, he shows how Iago manipulates what Othello sees, exploiting the Moor's belief in the magical powers of the handkerchief, arousing doubt in the very love for which the handkerchief was a 'remembrance', tricking him into accepting a visible object as the 'ocular proof' of his wife's betrayal. Othello's failure to have faith in the woman he so passionately loves and his readiness instead to believe what he sees with his eyes are tragic. His vulnerability to Iago's diabolic temptation to doubt Desdemona raises disturbing questions about whether faith can be sustained in the absence of any visible evidence, questions that speak to the epistemological anxieties aroused by Protestant efforts to abolish relics and remove devotional images from the Church.

In *Othello* Shakespeare invokes magic and acknowledges its allure even as he relentlessly demystifies it. *King Lear*, in contrast, presents a world already stripped of magic, a disenchanted world where, in the absence of any evidence of a caring God and in the face of unfathomable evil, characters raise profoundly disturbing questions about the moral regulation of the universe. What role, if any, does a God or gods play in the affairs of humans? Are there supernatural forces that control the human world, or is misfortune solely the consequence of individual actions? Are there 'natural' bonds between children and parents – loving bonds that it is 'unnatural' to violate – or are human beings, by nature, appetitive and motivated primarily by self interest? Is any belief in a moral order, a benevolent God, or a natural goodness a delusion?

These questions assumed a particular urgency in the years immediately following the Protestant Reformation. When the reformers reinvigorated the notion of original sin, adamantly insisting that everyone is depraved by nature and sharply critiquing the Catholic ideals of celibacy, monasticism, and good works that imply otherwise, they inevitably cast suspicions on all actions of the human will. Furthermore, when they denied the existence of present-day miracles, discredited such Catholic rituals as exorcism and auricular confession, and called into question the efficacy of the images that had comforted earlier generations, they disrupted practices that had enabled people to feel connected to God and empowered by that connection. As a result, Protestantism sometimes had the unintended effect of producing what Debora Shuger describes as 'a sense of the absence of God that verges on despair'.[8] She demonstrates how English theologians like Richard Hooker and Lancelot Andrewes 'struggle with the apparent lack of justice in history, with the failures of faith, with the fear that God is indifferent or hostile . . . with a sense of desolation' (*Habits*, p. 70). No longer accessible through mediating images, saints, or priests, God sometimes seemed distant and remote to early Protestants who fervently wished for a connection with him, and that remoteness, Shuger explains, aroused 'the terror of being unloved, alone in a hostile world governed by an indifferent God' (*Habits*, p. 73).

Although set in pre-Christian England, *King Lear* addresses the same anxieties and fears that Shuger finds expressed in the writings of influential English Protestant theologians like Hooker and Andrewes, who are Shakespeare's contemporaries. Lear's England is a country where the gods are repeatedly invoked but never manifest themselves, a country where the human capacity for evil is very much in evidence. To some degree, then, this tragedy may be said to explore the emotional impact of Protestant teachings on the men and women of post-Reformation England. Exposing the fragility of human bonds, the ferocity of human ambition, and the inadequacy of human justice, it dramatizes the suffering of two old men who, encountering their children's betrayal or apparent betrayal, struggle to comprehend 'filial ingratitude' (3.4.14). Although they cry out to the gods, they get no answers and receive no divine comfort; indeed, both could be said to confront 'the terror of being unloved, alone in a hostile world governed by an indifferent God'. The main narrative focuses on Lear's profound suffering as he grapples with fundamental questions about nature, justice, authority, love. Gloucester, a good but lesser man whose story mirrors Lear's, despairs, and his suicidal resignation serves as a foil to Lear's thunderous rage and tumultuous madness.

In telling the story of Gloucester, Shakespeare seems especially interested in the problem of despair, which was understood in the Renaissance in theological terms as the loss of all hope in God. After he is blinded and turned out on the heath, Gloucester feels, understandably, that the world he inhabits is governed by indifferent and uncaring gods. 'As flies to wanton boys are we to the gods', he laments, 'They kill us for their sport' (4.1.36–7). Unable to bear the desolation and abandonment he feels, he decides to kill himself by jumping off the cliffs of Dover. He employs Poor Tom to take him there, not knowing that the man he thinks is a crazed and destitute outcast is, in fact, his legitimate son Edgar in disguise. In a startling scene after the two have reached Dover, Edgar, still pretending he is Poor Tom, orchestrates a pseudo-fall, getting his father to believe he has jumped off the high cliffs and been miraculously saved by divine intervention when, in fact, he never leaves flat ground.

After Gloucester 'jumps' and realizes he has survived, Edgar, dropping the voice of Poor Tom, pretends that he is a stranger who has watched Gloucester's leap from below. Describing Poor Tom (that is, his own, earlier fictional persona) as a horned 'fiend', he proclaims Gloucester's survival 'a miracle', and assures his father 'that the clearest gods, who make them honours / Of men's impossibilities, have preserved thee' (4.5.73–4). Persuaded that the gods have in fact miraculously freed him from a devil and saved his life, Gloucester vows to 'bear / Affliction' (4.5.75–6) and recovers from his suicidal despair. Edgar tricks his father, he tells us, in order to 'cure' his despair (4.5.34), and his act thus raises significant questions about truth and illusion. Can deception ever be justified? Can a lie have a salutary effect? Might telling the plain truth sometimes be harmful?

This scene is remarkable in that it demonstrates how a theological belief (in this case, a Roman Catholic belief in present-day miracles) can be the product of human manipulation, theatrical illusion, and imaginative engagement with a fiction. Edgar plays upon his father's misconception that he stands at the edge of a dangerously high cliff; he exploits his father's desperate desire for some evidence that God cares about him; and he appeals to his father's traditional notions about demonic possession and miracles. Shakespeare reveals in this scene how deep is the human longing for a divine miracle, how unbearable life can be in a world where good seems absent, remote, hostile, or indifferent. He shows how easily people can be tricked into a false belief in miracles and asks whether, for some people at least, such a belief, however fallacious or delusional, is necessary.

In depicting the way Gloucester's need to believe in miracles is manipulated by Edgar, Shakespeare evidences a keen interest in the way a superstitious or erroneous belief is formed, an interest that was widely shared by post-Reformation thinkers. Shuger describes 'Hooker's sensitivity to how the mind projects what it wishes to believe into the text and then "discovers" there its own preconceits'. Noting how both Calvin and Bacon advance similar theories, she suggests that such concern may be the product of the Reformation, with its intensive critiques of Roman Catholic ideology and its proliferation of competing ideologies. 'One senses behind all three formulations', she writes, 'an emerging anxiety, perhaps generated by the need to account for the religious pluralism of post-Reformation Europe, about self-deception and ideological manipulation' (*Habits*, p. 259). *King Lear* registers that anxiety. By showing how easily Edgar can manipulate his father's preconceptions about miracles and devils, while revealing how Gloucester's desperate desire for concrete evidence of God's love makes him vulnerable to such manipulation, it raises unsettling questions about the nature and validity of religious belief.

The scene at Dover also explores the relation between religion and theatre, for the strategies Edgar employs to save his father from theological despair are inherently theatrical. Shakespeare addresses here a significant anti-theatrical bias in early Protestantism. When the reformers condemn the images, vestments, rituals, ceremonies, and spectacles of the Roman Catholic Church, they associate all these things with theatre, insisting that they are mere trifles and meaningless trumpery. When they attack the Roman Catholic clergy, they accuse priests of deceiving the faithful by practising a kind of fraudulent theatre, tricking people into false beliefs. And when they refute the Roman Catholic doctrine of transubstantiation, they ridicule it as an elaborate theatrical illusion. English anti-Catholic polemics repeatedly attempt to discredit Roman Catholicism by identifying it with a theatricality understood to be seductive, duplicitous, and inauthentic.

In a fascinating essay Stephen Greenblatt examines the way the scene at Dover calls attention to both religious and theatrical illusions. He points out how Edgar's 'counterfeit miracle' resembles a Roman Catholic exorcism, and he shows how Shakespeare draws on an anti-Catholic book about Jesuit exorcisms, Samuel Harsnett's *A Declaration of Egregious Popish Impostures*.[9] Harsnett, a Protestant polemicist who taps into the anti-theatrical bias in early Protestant culture, denounces the spectacular exorcisms performed by Jesuit priests as fraudulent theatre. In contrast to Harsnett, however, Shakespeare does not, in Greenblatt's view, simply demystify the ritual of exorcism. Rather, he appropriates it – with its original meaning 'emptied out' – for the stage, in effect preserving the theatricality of Roman Catholicism in a new, secular form that contains its seductive power by acknowledging its illusory nature (p. 126).

Greenblatt's analysis of this scene is a compelling one, but I would argue that it overstates the extent to which Edgar's elaborately staged 'miracle' illuminates Shakespeare's own theatrical enterprise. There is no doubt that this scene makes its audiences aware of the way Shakespeare's own theatre engages them. Edgar accomplishes his deception of his father in much the same way that a playwright would convince his audience that a bare, flat stage is a towering cliff, setting the scene with language that encourages the blind Gloucester to imagine he stands on a high precipice:

> How fearful
> And dizzy 'tis, to cast one's eyes so low
> The crows and choughs that wing the midway air
> Show scarce so gross as beetles.
> . . .
> The murmuring surge,
> That on the unnumbered idle pebble chafes,
> Cannot be heard so high. I'll look no more,
> Lest my brain turn, and the deficient sight
> Topple down headlong. (4.5.11–24)

In this scene, then, Shakespeare demonstrates the dramatist's persuasive powers even as he acknowledges the theatre's illusory nature. Although he does not ask his audience to accept his fictions as truth, he seems here to suggest a kinship between his own and Edgar's theatre and between both and the theatricality of a Roman Catholic exorcism.

But Edgar's theatre is only one of many kinds of theatricality represented in *King Lear*, and this play gestures towards the anti-theatrical sentiments of early Protestantism as well as the theatrical rituals of Roman Catholicism. While the well-intentioned Edgar employs a theatrical ruse in an effort to comfort his father, his villainous brother Edmund employs an equally cunning theatrical trick to con his father and frame his brother, staging a fake murder plot that is so convincing Gloucester disowns his legitimate and loyal son. And Lear's evil daughters Goneril and Regan give a perfectly calibrated, but entirely hypocritical, performance at the abdication ceremony, while Cordelia, the child who truly loves her father, is unable, or unwilling, to perform the role of the obsequious daughter even though she knows that playing such a part will guarantee her inheritance. In addition, circumstances force both Edgar and Kent to play fictional roles. But while each takes on the disguise of a social inferior, Edgar uses the highly theatrical persona of a crazed, demonically possessed beggar as a means of self-protection, whereas Kent adopts the persona of a plain-spoken and effective servant in order to continue to serve the king who had banished him. And, of course, the Fool is by profession an entertainer, one who, though he has no social power, possesses the freedom to tell Lear the truth about his folly. *King Lear* thus repeatedly calls attention to its own theatricality, and it holds up for examination markedly different aspects of the theatre and widely divergent motives for acting.

Perhaps most intriguing is the way it juxtaposes Edgar's theatrics to Cordelia's resistance to the theatrical, a juxtaposition that raises provocative questions about the legitimacy of theatre and the effectiveness of plain speaking, the power of ritual performance and the value of inwardness.

Edgar's theatrical scheme, undertaken out of pity for his father, works, but it is effective because it protects a deluded Gloucester from the truth. In contrast, Cordelia's uncompromising insistence on speaking the truth infuriates the father she loves, setting in motion the tragic action of the play. The two virtuous children thus employ opposing strategies, and the play probes the relative merits of each, asking whether Cordelia's plain speaking is heroic or foolish, whether Edgar's theatrical deception is admirable or unacceptable, and whether it is necessary for Cordelia to violate her father's ceremony or for Edgar to trick his father.

These questions are at the heart of Reformation debates about spirituality and religious practices. Edgar's staged exorcism and elaborately conceived, ritual challenge of Edmund in the final act serve to associate Gloucester's elder son with the rituals and theatricality of Roman Catholicism, perhaps even evoking a deep nostalgia for lost rituals and old ways. Cordelia's plain speaking, in contrast, aligns Lear's youngest daughter with early Protestantism, for plain speaking is a Protestant ideal. The English reformers advance an ethos of plainness based on the person of Jesus and identified with the qualities of inwardness, guilelessness, and truthfulness. They also embrace a rhetoric of plainness that privileges feeling over artful rhetoric, speaking the truth over cunning, authenticity over theatricality. In sixteenth-century narratives commemorating Protestant martyrs, plainness (as both an ethos and a rhetoric) is one of the central attributes of the men and women who resisted Roman Catholic authorities.[10]

If, at the beginning of this play, her plain speaking and truth-telling enrage Lear, in the end, these same attributes help Cordelia restore her father's sanity. When she reconciles with him, she does not resort to manipulative fictions or staged miracles, as Edgar does, but rather comforts him directly, guilelessly, and with great feeling. Her moving response to Lear's assertion that Cordelia, unlike her sisters, has some cause to reject him is utterly simple and heartfelt: 'No cause, no cause' (4.6.74). Repeating two, common, monosyllabic words as she weeps, she is able to express what she feels in an honest, forthright, and totally convincing way. Or, more accurately, the actor playing Cordelia is able to persuade the audience that what Cordelia speaks comes from her heart and is therefore authentic. Shakespeare thus uses a Protestant aesthetic of plainness to create the impression that his own theatre – in marked contrast to Edgar's elaborately staged fiction – is not theatre at all, but natural and true. In this reconciliation scene Shakespeare thus creates a different kind of theatre from the kind Edgar employs, one that draws on Protestant notions of plainness, inwardness, and authenticity. By claiming for the stage the very qualities that many reformed theologians assume are antithetical to it, he undermines the efforts of Protestant polemicists like Harsnett to associate theatricality with fraud, deception, and inauthenticity and to align it with the Roman Catholic Church.

In *Othello* and *Hamlet*, as well as in *King Lear*, Shakespeare challenges the anti-theatrical sentiments of early Protestantism, but he also demystifies a theatricality associated in his culture with Roman Catholicism. His plays could even be said to contain an anti-theatrical strain in the way they expose and condemn the fraudulent theatricality of villains like Goneril and Regan, Edmund, Iago, and Claudius. But Shakespeare actively seeks to dissociate his own theatre from empty ceremonies, superficial spectacles, magical illusions, and deceptive theatrical tricks, and he claims for the theatre an ethical purpose and an emotional power that seem to align it with early Protestantism. In *Hamlet*, for instance, he explores the possibility that a dramatic representation might have the power to arouse the conscience of a guilty man. When Hamlet stages 'The Murder of Gonzago', the play re-enacting his uncle's murder of his father, Claudius bolts from the room and, when he thinks he is alone, falls on his knees in prayer, admits his guilt, and attempts to repent. Rather than deluding its audiences, playing here arouses guilt, elicits self-examination, and reveals wrongdoing.

Rejecting any simple dichotomy between theatre and truth, Shakespeare's tragedies raise provocative questions about inwardness and theatricality, plainness and cunning, truth and illusion. How can inward truths manifest themselves except through visible signs and externals? Does plain speaking itself constitute a theatrical performance? How can someone know the difference between the authenticity of a virtuous person and the fraudulent posture of a villain like Iago, who maliciously poses as a plain-speaking and honest man? Can a fiction convey the truth? Can a theatrical illusion serve a moral purpose? Shakespeare provides no simple answers to these questions, but his interest in them, like his interest in authority, scepticism, faith, magic, false belief, and despair, indicates how fully his tragedies engage the religious controversies spawned by the Protestant Reformation.

NOTES

1. Eamon Duffy, *The Stripping of the Altars: Traditional Religion in England, c. 1400–1580* (New Haven: Yale University Press, 1992), p. 580.
2. Steven Ozment, *The Age of Reform 1250–1550* (New Haven: Yale University Press, 1980), pp. 233, 243.
3. For a detailed discussion of the eucharistic controversy, see Horton Davies, *Worship and Theology in England from Cranmer to Hooker 1534–1603*, 5 vols. (Princeton University Press, 1970), I. 76–123.
4. 'Introduction', *Religion and Culture in Renaissance England*, ed. Claire McEachern and Debora Shuger (Cambridge University Press, 1997), p. 10.

5. Steven Ozment, *When Fathers Ruled: Family Life in Reformation Europe* (Cambridge, MA: Harvard University Press, 1983), p. 172.
6. Gail McMurray Gibson, *The Theater of Devotion: East Anglian Drama and Society in the Late Middle Ages* (University of Chicago Press, 1989), pp. 15, 66.
7. Huston Diehl, *Staging Reform, Reforming the Stage: Protestantism and Popular Theater in Early Modern Drama* (Ithaca: Cornell University Press, 1997), pp. 125–55.
8. Debora Shuger, *Habits of Thought in the English Renaissance: Religion, Politics, and the Dominant Culture* (Berkeley: University of California Press, 1990), p. 70.
9. Stephen Greenblatt, *Shakespearean Negotiations: The Circulation of Social Energy in Renaissance England* (Berkeley: University of California Press, 1988), pp. 94–128.
10. For a detailed discussion of the rhetoric of plainness, including its relevance to *King Lear*, see Kenneth J. E. Graham, *The Performance of Conviction: Plainness and Rhetoric in the Early English Renaissance* (Ithaca: Cornell University Press, 1994).

6

MICHAEL HATTAWAY

Tragedy and political authority

Shakespeare's tragedies are usually remembered for the central characters
for whom they are named. However, the fact that all of their heroes are
what in the period were termed 'princes', occupying the power centres of
their realms, means that these narratives of usurpation and death are also
anatomies of political crises. In setting out contexts for his tales of woe
or wonder Shakespeare reveals himself to have been as curious about the
make-up of courts and kingdoms as he was about the psychology of individuals. The sufferings of great men and women in Shakespearean tragedy
derive from conflicts, the analysis of which inevitably entails a consideration
of 'the properties of government'[1] – its characteristics and its proprieties.
In 1589, at about the time Shakespeare was beginning to write, George
Puttenham observed that 'poets... were the first lawmakers to the people,
and the first politicians, devising all expedient means for th'establishment
of commonwealth'.[2] Although in his tragedies Shakespeare may concentrate
far more on rulers than on the ruled, 'commonwealth' interests are inevitably
invoked by the fact that any act on the part of a king is *de facto* what, in
Hamlet, Claudius terms 'sovereign process' (4.3.65).

This theatrical scrutiny of sovereignty and rule, also practised by contemporaries like Kyd, Marlowe, Chapman, and Jonson, discomforted court,
Church, and City. In the context of the century of political division engendered by religious difference that followed the Reformation of Henry
VIII, 'matters... unfit and undecent... handled in plays', including 'both
Divinity and State', were, according to the Privy Council, likely to be in-
citements to rebellion and therefore of concern to both magistrates and min-
isters. In the City of London the Common Council was vexed by playhouse
'examples or doings of... unchastity, sedition, [and] suchlike unfit and un-
comely matter'.[3] Almost all of Shakespeare's tragedies have central characters who take arms against legitimate or established rulers. So although the
actions of the plays were historically remote, the appointment of officers to
'allow' texts before they were performed as well as conventions of theatrical

representation – performances were in modern dress – reveal that performances and publication of tragedies were regularly construed as potentially seditious interventions in the political life of the nation.[4]

The very fact of placing a tragic action at court was, because of the particular decorum of English tragedy, likely to demystify the authority of prince and courtiers. Tragedies of the English Renaissance, unlike most from continental Europe, mingle kings and clowns, and comic scenes in the tragedies provide not just comic relief but occasions for popular voices to baffle or scoff at their 'betters'. The Clown's jokes about deflated bagpipes in *Othello* (3.1) hint at the hero's impotence. When the Gravedigger hands him the skull of a nameless courtier, Hamlet reflects that it is 'now my Lady Worm's, chopless, and knocked about the mazard [head] with a sexton's spade. Here's fine revolution', he continues, 'and we had the trick to see't' (5.1.75–6). (This is one of the first uses of the word 'revolution' to designate the overthrow of a political regime.) Moreover, David Scott Kastan's argument about the oppositional nature of playing the king in a history play holds true for a tragedy: 'Whatever their overt ideological content, history plays inevitably, if unconsciously, weakened the structure of authority: on stage the king became a subject – the subject of the author's imaginings and the subject of the attention and judgement of an audience of subjects.' Robert Weimann has argued that theatrical representation is a symptom of a long-running post-Reformation 'crisis of authority'.[5] Even if, at the end of the play, some kind of public calm or *moral* order is restored, the representation of 'carnal, bloody, and unnatural acts' (*Ham.* 5.2.360) is likely to have destabilized the audience's confidence in the *social* order on which it is based.

In his own lifetime Shakespeare's tragedies were not set apart from other genres that opened more obviously on to political life: the categorization of texts by the editors of the Folio as comedies, histories, and tragedies raises critical and historical problems. The Roman plays, which portray historical figures and which are so obviously concerned with issues of power, authority, and empire, are placed among the tragedies. Conversely, the 'history' plays are often designated as 'tragedies' in their titles (or in their quarto versions), and share as sources the chronicles of Hall and Holinshed with plays like *Macbeth* and *King Lear*. *King Lear* is designated as a history on the title page of its quarto version and as a tragedy in the Folio, and the full title of Shakespeare's most famous play in both its curtailed (Q 1) and most extended form (Q 2) is *The Tragical History of Hamlet*. Chains of causation that create tragedy in Shakespeare derive as much from situation – the feud in *Romeo and Juliet*, the unexpected love test that goes wrong at the beginning of *King*

Lear – as from what actors or readers deem to be the personality of the hero. (A situation is often what is designated in the texts by 'fortune'.)

Shakespearean tragedy, moreover, is the tragedy of a group as much as an individual. Conflicts of class or gender, contests between generations or within the family, unresolvable moral dilemmas, accidents (sometimes designated as 'fate') are as important to the unfolding of the tragic action as the consequence of the 'hero's' choice. This is what A. C. Bradley in 1904 described as 'action issuing from character' – a notion that encapsulated Romantic readings of the plays and set a restricting critical agenda centred around accounts of the 'characters' of Shakespeare's tragic heroes that endured for about eighty years.[6] Confronted with momentous events often magnified by supernatural portents, caught up in political change, or immersed, as most of them are, in rites of passage that mark a change in the nature of the self, it is as likely that characters in tragedy will act 'uncharacteristically' as 'characteristically'. The fact that tragedies may derive from uncharacteristic actions on the part of their protagonists is what sets them apart from moral fables where 'good' but 'flawed' individuals come to just but unhappy ends.

In his studies of the degradation of powerful men and women Shakespeare inevitably engaged not only with morality but with the nature of power and of political authority. Nearly all early modern discussions of these topics refer to the famous assertion of St Paul that secular power derived from divine authority: 'Let every soul [person] be subject unto the higher powers; for there is no power but of God, and the powers that be are ordained of God' (Romans 13: 1). That text stands not just as an 'idea' that individuals could choose to believe or disbelieve but as an ideological instrument: it is glossed in the Geneva Bible (1560) as *'The obedience to the rulers'* and in the Authorised Version (1611) as *'Subjection, and many other duties we owe to the magistrates* [those in authority]'. The passage was useful to princes who could claim that any attack on their person was a violation of a divinely sanctioned order. The homily or official sermon 'Against Disobedience and Wilful Rebellion' which, after the Northern Rebellion of 1569 and a Papal Bull of 1570 that excommunicated Elizabeth and absolved her subjects from allegiance,[7] was added to the collection of homilies issued in the reign of Edward VI, argued that rebellion was 'an abominable sin against God and man'. Moreover, given that the person of the monarch was held to be a manifestation of the timeless spiritual body of the kingdom (see below), any attack on the monarch could be construed, as the homily indicates, as an attack on the nation: 'the wrath of God is kindled and inflamed against all rebels, and ... horrible plagues, punishments, and deaths, and finally eternal damnation ... hang over their heads'.[8] We hear of prodigious disasters from the Old Man in *Macbeth* (2.4). Regicide was akin to deicide: both crimes were of a different order to homicide. In *Hamlet* Claudius argues that divine authority even offers protection to the monarch:

> What is the cause, Laertes,
> That thy rebellion looks so giant-like? –
> Let him go, Gertrude. Do not fear our person.
> There's such divinity doth hedge a king
> That treason can but peep to what it would,
> Acts little of his will.   (4.5.120–5)

However, towards the beginning of the sixteenth century political historians, most famously Niccolò Machiavelli, had begun to anatomize the constitution of the states of Europe and Asia, past and present, and showed that authority derived not from God but from the constitution of the state as well as from the means whereby a monarch had obtained the crown. The power of a consul holding office for only one year in the Roman republic was different in nature from that of a king who reigned for life, and the authority of a ruler who had seized power by force was different from that of a prince who had inherited authority upon the death of a parent. Pragmatic comparisons between different political systems revealed that authority might be secular rather than divine in origin. A prince, as Machiavelli pointed out, had to create an image for himself, take care about the ways in which he was perceived by his subjects. Even if he could not have the wisdom of a fox and the boldness of a lion he should imitate those who did:

> It is not ... necessary for a prince to have ... the above named qualities, but it is very necessary to seem to have them. I would even be bold to say that to possess them and always to observe them is dangerous, but to appear to possess them is useful. Thus it is well to seem merciful, faithful, humane, sincere, religious, and also to be so; but you must have the mind so disposed that when it is needful to be otherwise you may be able to change to the opposite qualities.[9]

We can see why Hamlet inveighs against 'seeming' and why the Player King is not just a strolling actor but a figure for all those with authority in Denmark. Moreover the roles politicians had to assume in order to protect their standing could take over their 'selves'. Richard III recognized this when, at the end of the play, he found his self-fashioned fictive self had taken over his essential or 'natural' self:

> What? Do I fear my self? There's none else by.
> Richard loves Richard, that is I am I.
>
> (*R3* 5.3.185–6)

Hamlet's 'antic disposition' (1.5.172) not only provided in feigned madness a fool's cover for the truth-telling of a malcontent but created out of a sweet prince something of a monster, careless of the lives of those about him. ('Antic' in the period had connotations of grotesquerie and monstrosity as well as of clownage, and could designate figures who were half-man and half-beast.)

Moreover, if a prince did not reign by the consent of his or her subjects, it was apparent that might was a more necessary adjunct for rule than right. Alternatively it could be expedient to derive authority from *ragione di stato* or political necessity rather than from moral legitimacy. This kind of political analysis seemed dangerous, and the word 'politician', newly imported from France according to Puttenham, rapidly acquired a pejorative meaning.[10] In the gravedigger scene Hamlet reflects over another skull: 'This might be the pate of a politician...one that would circumvent God, might it not?' (5.1.66–7). So it may not be surprising that in *Julius Caesar* Cassius, although convinced that the cause of the state and specifically the freedom of the Roman citizenry is threatened by the quasi-divinity of Julius Caesar, feels it necessary to legitimate his insurrection by drawing the noble Brutus into his conspiracy.

Materialist and 'Machiavellian' analyses of power gradually came to stand alongside those that pronounced it divine in origin. In a work that used to be ascribed to Sir Walter Ralegh, a certain T.B., in *Observations Political and Civil*, described 'authority' as 'a certain reverend impression in the mind of subjects and others touching the prince's virtue and government. It resteth chiefly in admiration and fear...[Authority] is reinforced and enlarged by power, without which no prince can either defend his own or take from others...Power and strength is attained unto by these five ways, viz., money, arms, counsel, friends, and fortune.'[11] This makes no reference to a divine origin for power and matches the radical claim made at the beginning of *1 Henry VI* when a messenger points out that English misfortunes in battles against the French derive not from the moral sin of treachery, which would conventionally provoke condign punishment from God, but from 'want of men and money'.[12]

Now the endings of *Hamlet*, *Macbeth*, *King Lear*, and, eventually, *Romeo and Juliet* turn in part on the outcome not only of battles but of duels or judicial combats. A duel was a species of trial, a demonstration that a claim to honour was authentic or divinely ordained. It could also destabilize the authority of the king, since duels operated by a code of honour which he might not be observing himself and sought a judgement that was not under his control. Yet in most performances of these struggles there seems little evidence of a divinely ordained outcome, the working of what Hamlet, following

Calvin, termed 'special providence' (5.2.192). In a playhouse these are, and can only be, like wrestling matches, feats of physical violence, and any claim by interested parties that in these broils hazard plays no part, that they are theodicies or justifications of the ways of God to men, seems highly dubious.

It had, however, pleased Sir Thomas More and the chroniclers Edward Hall and Raphael Holinshed who followed him to read the battle of Bosworth (where Elizabeth's grandfather, Henry Tudor, the future Henry VII, defeated the last Plantagenet, Richard III) as a theodicy. But, given the obvious pre-cariousness of those who had seized power, it is not surprising that while Shakespeare was writing his tragedies, Tudor and Stuart monarchs claimed to hold authority primarily by virtue of inheritance. During the reign of Eliza-beth, subjects were reminded of this constantly, particularly in the iconology of royal pageants and at the tilts held every year on the anniversary of her succession. Yet the claim of the later Tudors to authority by inheritance was weak: Elizabeth herself had been declared a bastard by parliament in 1536 and came to the throne only because of the early death of her half-brother Edward VI and the childlessness of her half-sister Mary I. The mother of King James, Mary Queen of Scots, had been executed by Elizabeth. So although the story had long been exposed as a myth, it pleased English monarchs to be celebrated as descendants of Brutus, grandson of Aeneas, a prince of Troy.[13] In some respects, Shakespeare's chronicles of the usurpation of the throne of Richard II by Henry Bullingbrook and, at the beginning of his career, of the Wars of the Roses (when the lineal descent of King Henry VI, scion of the House of Lancaster, proved a weak weapon against the forces of the House of York), must have appeared exceedingly provocative. When, in what its first edition calls *The Tragedy of King Richard II* (1595), Bullingbrook as-cends his throne as Henry IV there is no sign of divine displeasure. The play seems to have appeared so threatening to the regime – Elizabeth on several occasions identified herself with Richard – that it was not until its fourth edition (1608) that the deposition scene was printed, although in the mean-time it may have been performed.[14] Macbeth assassinated his way to the throne of Scotland: his comrade in arms Banquo, whose rectitude contrasts with that of the hero, was ancestor to King James (before whom the play may have been performed in 1606) and bore testimony to his descendant's moral legitimacy.[15] (James had escaped assassination in the Gunpowder Plot of 1605.)

The tragedies of Shakespeare and his contemporaries, moreover, reminded their audiences that kings could become tyrants. Kyd's *Spanish Tragedy* dis-played the plight of Hieronimo, who was crazed by his inability to find justice at court, supposedly the fount of justice, but in this case irredeemably polluted. (Hieronimo's predicament resembles that of Hamlet.) The emergence of princes as obviously evil as Saturninus in *Titus Andronicus*, Richard III, Macbeth (or Jonson's Sejanus) turned rebellion from sin to sanctioned political action. In fact, St Thomas Aquinas had argued that subjects had a right to depose a king who became a tyrant,[16] and texts that emerged during the French Wars of Religion (which lasted roughly forty years from 1562), notably the *Vindiciae contra tyrannos* (1579) probably written by the French 'politique' historian Philippe Duplessis-Mornay, contested the assumption of the Tudor *Homilies* that all rebellions are sins against God. The surge of interest in the 1590s in the writings of Tacitus, who exposed the corruption of imperial Rome, and the chronicling of violence and excess in the tragedies of Seneca also demonstrated that rebellion by subjects could be the correct course of action. In 1600 William Barclay generated the word 'monarchomachist' to designate any writer who justified the right to resist, although it does not imply a denial of the validity of monarchy.

A subject had to be certain that it was his conscience and not ambition that incited him to take arms against an erring prince. Even then the end might not justify the means. Saturninus and Tamora had brought about the rape and mutilation of Lavinia, daughter to Titus Andronicus. The banquet at the end of *Titus Andronicus* in which Titus serves Tamora the flesh of her sons in a pie in imitation of the way Atreus revenged himself upon Thyestes for seducing his wife – the subject of Seneca's *Thyestes* – reveals that, although the morality of Titus's revenge may be understandable, the quaintness of its manner is repulsive. Cases of conscience were made more intricate if rebellion was fomented by revenge upon the private person of the king. Hamlet, finding his own situation mirrored in that of Fortinbras of Norway, had to consider whether to move against Claudius:

> Rightly to be great
> Is not to stir without great argument,
> But greatly to find quarrel in a straw
> When honour's at the stake. (4.4.52–5)

His quizzical juxtaposition of a 'great argument' and a 'straw' exposes the sometime contradiction between acting morally or legally and acting honourably. Hamlet's decision to stand firm for family honour, to avenge the cuckolding of his father by his uncle, generates the pile of corpses at the end of the play which to many may reveal that vengeance indeed was the prerogative of God (see Romans 12: 19).

Authority figures in Shakespeare's time may have been particularly open to criticism because they were perceived as the fountainheads of power and justice: their actions were not yet subject to checks and balances by parliament or an independent judiciary, nor was the royal household or the court designed to function as a civil service. Indeed, an English 'state', defined according to Quentin Skinner as 'a form of public power separate from both the ruler and the ruled, and constituting the supreme political authority within a certain defined territory',[17] had not come into being. This was made explicit by Sir Thomas Smith in 1583: 'To be short, the prince is the life, the head and the authority of all things that be done in the realm of England.'[18] In his tragedies Shakespeare indicates that the actions have their origins not in divine providence but in a decision of the king.

However, although, as we have seen, monarchical power theoretically derived from God, and although 'early modern Englishmen were more used to thinking in terms of duties than of rights',[19] few Elizabethans would have believed that a monarch had an absolute right to do whatever he or she liked. While popular maxims such as 'The king can do no wrong' and 'What the king wills, that the law wills' are recorded from the 1530s, throughout the period 'ancient rights' of subjects and parliament (often unspecified) were frequently invoked: authority needed to be legitimated.[20] Certainly what emerges from an attentive reading of Shakespeare's tragedies is that they place as much emphasis on the duties as on the rights of kings. At the time Shakespeare was writing his tragedies Richard Hooker was arguing that the king had to be subject to the law:

> where the law doth give dominion, who doubteth but that the king who receiveth it must hold of it and under the law according to that old axiom *Attribuat rex legi quod lex attribuit ei potestatem et dominium* [May the king attribute to the law that power and dominion that the law attributes to him] and again *rex non debet esse sub homine, sed sub Deo et lege* [the king ought not to be subject to a man but to God and the law].[21]

These historical realities notwithstanding, many critics of Shakespeare have invoked concepts of 'divine right'. It is worth noting that the phrase occurs in no Shakespearean text, and it is crucially important to distinguish between a divine right to rule (i.e., to reign as an anointed king) and a divine right to act – perhaps against the interests of Church and people. The notion of divine right had really been brought into being by Henry VIII's claim to be entitled to appoint bishops in place of the Pope. It is generated by the presence within one political system of both secular and religious powers. Hooker insists that an English king does not have a divine right to meddle in ecclesiastical affairs[22] – although this is not really a topic in Shakespearean tragedy. In a speech to parliament on 21 March 1610 King James set out an 'axiom of divinity':

That as to dispute what God may do is blasphemy . . . so is it sedition in subjects to dispute what a king may do in the height of his power. But just kings will ever be willing to declare what they will do if they will not incur the curse of God. I will not be content that my power be disputed upon, but I shall ever be willing to make the reason appear of all my doings and rule my actions according to my laws.[23]

In fact James's analogy between himself and God subverts his power because he concedes that his authority is not absolute but subject to his ruling justly under the law. In Shakespeare there is always an implicit appeal from the political to the moral or the spiritual – his kings are not possessed of an unquestionable 'divine right'.

Some of Shakespeare's tragedies went further and implicitly questioned whether inherited monarchy was the best or 'natural' form of government. Neither the word 'republic' nor its derivatives appears in any Shakespearean text: the *OED*'s earliest citation of the word dates only from 1603 (although the word was common in Renaissance Latin texts). Yet *Julius Caesar* (1599) invokes the virtues of republicanism, hinting that the conversion of Rome into an empire under Caesar might bring back the excesses of monarchical tyranny. These had been displayed in Shakespeare's *Rape of Lucrece*, the 'Argument' of which notes how the rapist, the son of the last of the Roman kings, Tarquinius Superbus, had been rooted out of Rome by Junius Brutus, ancestor of the Brutus in *Julius Caesar*. It was obvious that Machiavelli favoured the liberty and self-government of the Roman republic over any other form of state, and his contemporary, Sir Thomas More, chancellor to Henry VIII, owed far greater allegiance to a *Res Publica Christiana* than to any monarch.[24] In Shakespeare the word 'commonwealth' signals analogous secular values, although among the tragedies the word appears only in the Roman plays.

It is especially notable that in four of his tragedies, *Titus Andronicus*, *Julius Caesar*, *Hamlet*, and *Coriolanus*, Shakespeare shows political authority emerging from forms of election rather than inheritance or *coups d'état*. The fact that Hamlet's Denmark had a hybrid constitution, an elective monarchy, is central to the political and moral concerns of the play. Claudius, who, it turns out, was a regicide and probably an adulterer was, arguably, a good king. He was above all a peacemaker, exercising diplomatic powers to deflect invasion from Norway while maintaining a strategic deterrent. The electors of Denmark, it is hinted, while ignorant of his crimes, may have done well to choose him in preference to his nephew, whose threats to his companions – 'By heaven, I'll make a ghost of him that lets me' (1.4.85) – reveal a nature as choleric as it is melancholic. Even after he has encountered the warlike Fortinbras, who was prepared to sacrifice 'twenty thousand men'

(4.4.60) in order to avenge his family's honour, Hamlet lends his dying voice to the election of the Norwegian to the throne of Denmark. In many productions of the play Fortinbras is portrayed as a belligerent monster whose accession will harm the commonweal. George Chapman was to write poems and plays about whether great men could or ought to be good men: Hamlet was 'good' by virtue of agonizing over the moral choices open to him but, arguably, showed few of the 'great' qualities necessary for strong and peaceful rule. The relation between goodness and greatness had been investigated by Machiavelli and his contemporaries; their writings indicate a challenge to the pieties of Christian humanism which held that only a good man could be a great man.

The action of *King Lear* is defined by polarities of goodness and greatness, power and authority. Lear's intention is to abdicate, surrender his monarchical power to his daughters and their husbands. It may well be that the division of the kingdom was regarded by the play's first audiences as an act of folly likely to destabilize England's political order. An academic play, Thomas Norton and Thomas Sackville's *Gorboduc*, performed at the Inner Temple in 1562, had chronicled the miseries of civil war caused by King Gorboduc's decision to divide his realm between his sons. Eubulus, whose role resembles that of Kent in Shakespeare's text, speaks out:

> Pardon I crave, and that my words be deemed
> To flow from hearty zeal unto your grace
> And to the safety of your commonweal:
> To part your realm unto my lords your sons
> I think not good for you, ne yet for them,
> But worst of all for this our native land.
> Within one land one single rule is best:
> Divided reigns do make divided hearts.
> (1.2.253–60)[25]

Even if Lear's abdication in favour of three putative heirs was not self-evident folly, the play conducts a subtle examination of the relationship between power and authority. Having handed over his power to Albany and Cornwall the king, now politically impotent, seeks to retain authority. His authority is recognized by his faithful retainer Kent but denied by Oswald, who, along with Goneril and Regan, finds Lear's conspicuous display of authority, in particular his retinue of knights, superfluous to his new station. Any director of the play is going to have to decide how riotously these knights should behave: if their conduct matches the nuisance that Goneril describes (1.3.6) an audience is likely, for the moment at least, to sympathize with the daughters against the patriarch. The implications are conspicuous:

a king may owe his power to his office rather than to any virtue or moral strength. The *reductio ad absurdum* is that any evil person may be invested with a form of legitimated power by virtue of the ceremonies of office – in Elizabethan English the word 'ceremony' could designate not just ritual practices but regalia. A famous story of Queen Elizabeth's chief minister, Lord Burghley, makes the point: 'At night when he put off his gown, he used to say, lie there, Lord Treasurer',[26] an anecdote in which the separation of man from mantle may signify the separation of authority from power. When Lear cries 'Off, off, you lendings' (3.4.102) he is seeking to rid himself of the trappings of a power which at that moment he sees as able to lead only to corruption.

In this play one of the functions of Edmond is to expose the impotence of those who claimed that the stability of the state rested upon ancient custom and a system of civic law that was validated, as Richard Hooker argued in 1593, by being derived from 'natural law', which itself derived from divine law.[27] Edmond worships an opposing kind of nature (*Lear* 1.2.1–22), a goddess of force and self-interest or 'commodity'. By contrast Lear, in his conversation with Gloucester when the latter thinks he has been miraculously saved from suicide, reveals that, having put off the 'lendings', he may have internalized a kind of moral authority:

LEAR ... Thou hast seen a farmer's dog bark at a beggar?
GLOUCESTER Ay, sir.
LEAR An the creature run from the cur, there thou mightst behold the great
    image of authority. A dog's obeyed in office.
        Thou rascal beadle, hold thy bloody hand.
        Why dost thou lash that whore? Strip thy own back.
        Thou hotly lusts to use her in that kind
        For which thou whip'st her. The usurer hangs the
            cozener.
        Through tattered clothes great vices do appear;
        Robes and furred gowns hide all. Plate sin with gold,
        And the strong lance of justice hurtless breaks;
        Arm it in rags, a pygmy's straw does pierce it.
        None does offend, none, I say none.   (4.5.147–60)

At moments like this we might consider that Lear has achieved what Aristotle considered to be central to the tragic experience, *anagnorisis* or recognition, in this case a recognition that emerged from his suffering.

In *Measure for Measure* an articulate woman, Isabella, demolishes the authority of Angelo by the use of a conceit that matches the anecdote about Burghley:

> But man, proud man,
> *Dressed in a little brief authority*,
> Most ignorant of what he's most assured,
> His glassy essence, like an angry ape
> Plays such fantastic tricks before high heaven
> As makes the angels weep, who, with our spleens,
> Would all themselves laugh mortal.
>
> (2.2.121–7, emphasis added)

Her indictment swirls out to include not only all magistrates but all males. In the tragedies the claims to moral authority by men are exposed time and again. The treatment of Ophelia by Hamlet and by her father turns her mad. If the nineteenth century saw Ophelia as a chaste and sweet victim of circumstance, more recent productions have given us Ophelias whose madness is fuelled by a misandry engendered by righteous anger that is the obverse of Hamlet's misogyny shaped by inchoate desire. In the mad scene she sings of a maid whose honour was lost to a man:

> By Gis [Jesus], and by Saint Charity,
> Alack, and fie for shame,
> Young men will do't if they come to't –
> By Cock, they are to blame.
> Quoth she, 'Before you tumbled me,
> You promised me to wed.'
> He answers –
> 'So would I ha' done, by yonder sun,
> And thou hadst not come to my bed.'
>
> (4.5.58–66)

The song may refer to herself and Hamlet, or, possibly, to a stage in the relationship between Gertrude and Claudius before the murder of Hamlet's father. But what is significant is its exposure of the double standard: a man gains honour among his own sex by virtue of sexual conquests, while by the same activity a woman loses hers. (Earlier Hamlet had claimed that the need to revenge himself had made him 'like a whore, unpack [his] heart with words' [2.2.538] – just like Ophelia?)

Utterances of this kind, spoken in madness, led to George Orwell's famous observation that Shakespeare was 'noticeably cautious, not to say cowardly, in his manner of uttering unpopular opinions...Throughout his plays the acute social critics, the people who are not taken in by accepted fallacies, are buffoons, villains, lunatics or persons who are shamming insanity or are in a state of violent hysteria...And yet', Orwell continues, 'the fact that Shakespeare had to use these subterfuges shows how widely his thoughts ranged. He could not restrain himself from commenting on almost everything, although he put on a series of masks in order to do so.'[28]

Because it was clear that Tudor kings had to rule within the law, and perhaps as a consequence of the spread of rationalist political history that exposed the material bases of monarchical power, part of a movement described by Max Weber as 'the disenchantment of the world',[29] emphasis continued to be laid on the mystical status of monarchy. In *Henry V* the king reflects that kings are 'twin-born with greatness' (4.1.222), a reference to the fiction that a king had 'two bodies', the 'body politic', a sacramental and immortal body that partook of divinity, and the 'body natural', his body as a man. Shakespeare played with the notion in *Richard II* and made of the emblem of doubleness a figure for self-division within his heroes.[30] It generates Hamlet's quibble to Rosencrantz and Guildenstern who are seeking the body of Polonius:

> HAMLET The body is with the king, but the king is not with the body. The
> king is a thing –
> GUILDENSTERN A thing, my lord?
> HAMLET Of nothing. (4.2.24–6)

Hamlet implies that iniquity has cost Claudius the mystic body of kingship, and implies that it ought now to be his – but he, of course, has been neither elected nor crowned.

The coronation had a sacramental dimension which is perhaps why Shakespeare and his contemporaries mostly refrained from including coronations in their plays: to have done so would have invited censorship.

> Our kings therefore, when they take possession of the room they are called into,
> have it pointed out before their eyes, even by the very solemnities and rites of
> their inauguration, to what affairs by the said law their supreme authority and
> power reacheth. Crowned we see they are, and inthronized, and anointed: the
> crown a sign of military, the throne of sedentary or judicial, the oil of religious
> or sacred power.[31]

Macbeth's attack on the body of King Duncan appears to Macduff as 'sacrilegious murder [which] hath broke ope / The Lord's anointed temple and stole thence / The life o'th'building' (2.3.59–61). Later Malcolm describes the goodness of King Edward of England, an obvious contrast with the degradation of Macbeth, manifest in Edward's ability to cure scrofula by touch – the disease was known as 'the King's Evil':

> 'Tis called the Evil.
> A most miraculous work in this good king,
> Which often since my here-remain in England

I have seen him do. How he solicits heaven
Himself best knows, but strangely visited people,
All swoll'n and ulcerous, pitiful to the eye,
The mere despair of surgery, he cures,
Hanging a golden stamp about their necks
Put on with holy prayers; and 'tis spoken,
To the succeeding royalty he leaves
The healing benediction. With this strange virtue
He hath a heavenly gift of prophecy,
And sundry blessings hang about his throne
That speak him full of grace.   (4.3.148–61)

King James touched sufferers brought to him by the royal physician, although it was reported by the Duke of Saxe-Weimar that 'the ceremony of healing is understood to be very distasteful to the King, and it is said that he would willingly abolish it'.[32] By the time of the Commonwealth the habit was seen as a pseudo-miracle and representative of monarchical fraud.[33]

The Greek word *charisma* meaning a 'gift of grace'[34] only entered English in the 1640s when it designated a 'miraculous gift of healing'.[35] Julius Caesar enjoins his barren wife Calpurnia to touch Mark Antony when running through the streets of Rome as part of the feast of Lupercal (1.2.6–9), a ritual to ensure fertility that is reported by Plutarch.[36] But it is obvious that Caesar himself evinced what commentators after Max Weber now also call 'charisma', a capacity for inspiring devotion or enthusiasm through power of leadership. In the history plays kings acquire charisma through military valour, as do Othello and Coriolanus. However, the charisma of Othello is not sufficient for this noblest of Moors to be accepted into an exclusive Venetian family. Cominius thus describes the progress of Gaius Marcus, later graced with the cognomen Coriolanus:

                    He bestrid
An o'erpressed Roman, and, i'th'consul's view,
Slew three opposers. Tarquin's self he met,
And struck him on his knee. In that day's feats,
When he might act the woman in the scene,
He proved best man i'th'field, and for his meed
Was brow-bound with the oak. His pupil age
Man-entered thus, he waxèd like a sea,
And in the brunt of seventeen battles since
He lurched all swords of the garland. For this last
Before and in Corioles, let me say
I cannot speak him home. He stopped the fliers,
And by his rare example made the coward

Turn terror into sport. As weeds before
A vessel under sail, so men obeyed
And fell below his stem. His sword, death's stamp,
Where it did mark, it took. From face to foot
He was a thing of blood, whose every motion
Was timed with dying cries. Alone he entered
The mortal gate of th'city, which he, painted
With shunless destiny, aidless came off,
And with a sudden reinforcement struck
Corioles like a planet.   (*Cor.* 2.2.87–109)

The growth of man into an icon of magnificence is enhanced by the reference to the wounding of 'Tarquin', who, as we have seen, was a byword for tyranny. The celebration of this 'thing of blood' remembers not only Macbeth but another set-piece description of a type of valour. This is the description of Pyrrhus, avenging son of Achilles, that floods into Hamlet's mind when he is contemplating revenge upon his own father's murderer:

The rugged Pyrrhus, he whose sable arms,
Black as his purpose, did the night resemble
When he lay couchèd in the ominous horse,
Hath now this dread and black complexion smeared
With heraldry more dismal. Head to foot
Now is he total gules, horridly tricked
With blood of fathers, mothers, daughters, sons,
Baked and impasted with the parching streets,
That lend a tyrannous and damnèd light
To their lord's murder. Roasted in wrath and fire,
And thus o'er-sizèd with coagulate gore,
With eyes like carbuncles the hellish Pyrrhus
Old grandsire Priam seeks.   (*Ham.* 2.2.410–22)

To Hamlet's mind Pyrrhus has become a monster, a figure of a man without conscience or remorse. In the *psychomachia* (or struggle between good and evil) for the soul of the hero he stands as the antagonist of the Ghost who encourages his son to sweep to his revenge.

But if charismatic authority could be gained by valour, it was, when translated to the life of civil society, vulnerable. Shakespeare's tragedies often focus on the ability of warrior princes to rule successfully as kings of peace: Titus, Julius Caesar, Othello, Macbeth, Antony, and Coriolanus. In *Coriolanus* there is an important reflection on the loss of political authority by the tragic hero that is worth dwelling upon. Aufidius is reflecting on both the ability of Coriolanus to capture Rome and his previous inability to maintain authority there.

> I think he'll be to Rome
> As is the osprey to the fish, who takes it
> By sovereignty of nature. First he was
> A noble servant to them, but he could not
> Carry his honours even. Whether 'twas pride,
> Which out of daily fortune ever taints
> The happy man; whether defect of judgement,
> To fail in the disposing of those chances
> Which he was lord of; or whether nature,
> Not to be other than one thing, not moving
> From th'casque to th'cushion, but commanding peace
> Even with the same austerity and garb
> As he controlled the war: but one of these –
> As he hath spices of them all – not all,
> For I dare so far free him – made him feared,
> So hated, and so banished. But he has a merit
> To choke it in the utt'rance. So our virtues
> Lie in th'interpretation of the time,
> And power, unto itself most commendable,
> Hath not a tomb so evident as a chair
> T'extol what it hath done.
> One fire drives out one fire, one nail one nail;
> Rights by rights falter, strengths by strengths do fail.
>
> (4.6.33–55)

The speech stands as an important corrective to simplistic ascriptions of 'tragic flaws' to tragic heroes and readings of their stories that insist upon their consequent loss of authority, thus turning tragedies into moral fables. Aufidius does conjecture that Coriolanus might have been tainted with pride, but it is important to remember that 'tainted' in the period means 'infected' (*OED*, taint, vb. 4a): he does not say that Coriolanus was, in the words of Dickens's Mr Hubble, 'naterally wicious'.[37] The word from Aristotle that generated the notion of 'tragic flaw' is *hamartia*. Etymologically the word means 'missing the mark with a bow and arrow', an error but not necessarily a culpable one. It designates an action – an error or mistake – rather than a flaw in character. However, by the time of the translation of the New Testament from Greek, five hundred years after Aristotle, the word had changed its meaning to 'sin'.[38] Yet Aufidius, in his second stab at fixing Coriolanus's personality, does not insist upon wicked intent, simply on 'defect of judgement' and a failure to control events ('chances'). He then turns to what he calls 'nature': it is apparent from the context that the word here means 'role' or 'fictive self'. Coriolanus was unable to move 'from th'casque to th'cushion', translate his authority from the battlefield to the senate house. (Earlier in the play the hero made a boast: 'I play / The man I am' (3.2.14–15).) The indictment is even-handed: Coriolanus is worthy of merit, and Aufidius insists that men's virtues (here meaning 'strengths' [OED, virtue 1a]) are inevitably translated ('interpreted') in different ways at different periods and in different situations. A man whose rule is based on valour will not be highly regarded in time of war, his authority (the meaning here of 'power') will be as fragile as a wooden chair (with a hint of a throne of office). He ends by refusing to moralize: tragedy derives not from a contest between good and evil, as the moralists would have it, but from a conflict between right and right, a notion that adumbrates Hegel's model of tragedy as conflict between two self-validating ethical substances. In Sophocles' *Antigone* it was right for the heroine to wish to bury her brothers who had rebelled against Thebes – she owed a duty to her family. It was equally right for Creon to insist that their bodies be left unburied – he owed a duty to the city. It is right for Hamlet to seek to avenge his father, equally right for Claudius to seek to continue to occupy the throne of Denmark and save the country from the ravages of revenge.

By now we realize how complex are the meanings of the word that concludes the following passage:

LEAR What art thou?
KENT A very honest-hearted fellow, and as poor as the king.
LEAR If thou be'st as poor for a subject as he's for a king, thou'rt poor enough. What wouldst thou?
KENT Service.
LEAR Who wouldst thou serve?
KENT You.
LEAR Dost thou know me, fellow?
KENT No, sir; but you have that in your countenance, which I would fain call master.
LEAR What's that?
KENT Authority. (1.4.16–27)

Although poets, politicians, and moralists might dispute about the authority of monarchy and the nature of kingly power, the power of particular princes depended upon the way they could stage themselves to men's eyes, upon their ability to generate authority through performance. It is comparatively easy to establish ironical perspectives upon the monarchs and magistrates who people Shakespeare's plays, and yet experiences of charismatic performances by players of great 'countenance' (bearing or demeanour) may suggest something of the way in which princes of the early modern period could instil love and loyalty by their own roles in those rituals and ceremonies that constituted the theatre of the nation. Theatricality was an immensely important mechanism for sovereignty in a period that, as we have seen, was yet to see the development of state institutions.

Richard Burbage, the greatest of the player kings and the man for whom Shakespeare's tragic roles were contrived, inspired an anonymous funeral elegy when he died on 13 March 1619:

> He's gone, and with him what a world are dead,
> Which he revived, to be revivèd so
> No more: young Hamlet, old Hieronimo,
> Kind Lear, the grievèd Moor, and more beside
> That lived in him, have now forever died.
> Oft have I seen him leap into the grave,
> Suiting the person, which he seemed to have,
> Of a sad lover, with so true an eye
> That there I would have sworn he meant to die.
> Oft have I seen him play this part in jest
> So lively that spectators, and the rest
> Of his sad crew, whilst he but seemed to bleed,
> Amazèd, thought even then he died in deed.[39]

In terms of the opening conceit of the passage, the authority of Burbage created a 'world' just as the authority of a 'real' monarch created an order, of law and of justice, that would shape the realm. If authority could, to sceptical spectators, seem to reside in robes of office, a great player upon the stage of the world could 'suit himself' to his 'person' (here meaning 'role'), grow into the part to such a degree that he became himself what he conveyed, an icon of authority. Even if spectators realized that this role was false, played 'in jest', a 'lively' (here meaning 'energetic' as well as 'life-like') kind of 'monarchising'[40] could create its necessary effect upon the onlookers. We spoke of actors making kings their subjects: princes who played their parts in as lively a manner as Burbage could, contrariwise, turn spectators into subjects.

NOTES

1. *Measure for Measure*, 1.1.3.
2. George Puttenham, *The Arte of English Poesie* (London, 1589), pp. 4–5.
3. *English Professional Theatre, 1530–1660*, ed. Glynne Wickham, Herbert Berry, William Ingram, Theatre in Europe: A Documentary History (Cambridge University Press, 2000), pp. 74 and 94–5.
4. Richard Dutton, *Mastering the Revels: The Regulation and Censorship of English Renaissance Drama* (University of Iowa Press, 1991).
5. David Scott Kastan, ' "Proud Majesty Made a Subject": Shakespeare and the Spectacle of Rule', *Shakespeare Quarterly* 37 (1986), 459–75; Robert Weimann,

'Representation and Performance: the Uses of Authority in Shakespeare's Theatre', in *Materialist Shakespeare: A History*, ed. Ivo Kamps (London: Verso, 1995), 198–217.

6. A. C. Bradley, *Shakespearean Tragedy* (London: Macmillan, 1957 edn), p. 7.
7. For evidence that Shakespeare was brought up a Catholic and was therefore possibly unconvinced of the later Tudors' right to rule, see E. A. J. Honigmann, *Shakespeare: The 'Lost Years'* (Manchester University Press, 1985).
8. Cited in Robin Headlam Wells, *Shakespeare, Politics and the State* (Basingstoke: Macmillan, 1986), pp. 93–4; the author conveniently assembles extracts from many texts pertinent to this essay together with a useful commentary.
9. Niccolò Machiavelli, *'The Prince' and the 'Discourses'*, ed. Max Lerner (New York: Modern Library, 1950), chap. 18, p. 65.
10. Puttenham, *The Arte of English Poesie*, p. 122.
11. BL Add. Ms. 27320, ff.23–4; modernized from Tuck's citation of the passage in Richard Tuck, '*Power* and *Authority* in Seventeenth-Century England', *The Historical Journal* 17 (1974), 43–61.
12. See *1 Henry VI*, 1.1.69. I am using 'power' and 'authority' in their modern senses: in Renaissance texts the use of the words is not clear-cut. Either could be used, for example, to translate the Latin *potestas*: see Tuck, '*Power* and *Authority*'.
13. Patrick Collinson, 'History', in *A Companion to English Renaissance Literature and Culture*, ed. Michael Hattaway (Oxford University Press, 2000), pp. 58–70 at p. 66.
14. William Shakespeare, *King Richard II*, ed. Andrew Gurr (Cambridge University Press, 1984), pp. 6, 9–10.
15. See 1.3.65, 4.1.111–23 and William Shakespeare, *Macbeth*, ed. A. R. Braunmuller (Cambridge University Press, 1997), pp. 8–9.
16. See the passage from *On Kingship*, cited in Wells, *Shakespeare, Politics and the State*, pp. 91–2.
17. Quentin Skinner, *The Foundations of Modern Political Thought: The Age of Reformation*, vol. II of 2 vols. (Cambridge University Press, 1978), II, 353.
18. Sir Thomas Smith, *De Republica Anglorum [1583]*, ed. L. Alston (Cambridge University Press, 1906), pp. 62–3.
19. Kevin Sharpe, *Remapping Early Modern England* (Cambridge University Press, 2000), p. 54.
20. M. P. Tilley, *A Dictionary of the Proverbs in England in the Sixteenth and Seventeenth Centuries* (Ann Arbor: University of Michigan Press, 1950), K61 and 72.
21. Richard Hooker, *Of the Laws of Ecclesiastical Polity*, ed. Arthur Stephen McGrade (Cambridge University Press, 1989), Book VII, p. 40.
22. *Ibid.*, pp. 141–2.
23. King James, *Political Writings*, ed. Johann P. Sommerville (Cambridge University Press, 1994), p. 184; with this compare the discussion of John Donne's conception of royal prerogative in Sharpe, *Remapping Early Modern England*, p. 53.
24. J. H. Hexter, *More's 'Utopia': The Biography of an Idea* (New York: Harper and Row, 1952), pp. 93, 122.
25. *Minor Elizabethan Tragedies*, ed. T. W. Craik (London: J. M. Dent, 1974), p. 12.
26. Cited in William Shakespeare, *The Tempest*, ed. Stephen Orgel (Oxford University Press, 1987), 1.2.24–5n.

27. See Hooker, *Of the Laws of Ecclesiastical Polity*, Book 1.

28. George Orwell, 'Lear, Tolstoy, and the Fool' [1947], *Collected Essays* (London: Secker and Warburg, 1961), pp. 415–34, at p. 430.

29. Max Weber, 'The Evolution of the Capitalistic Spirit', *General Economic History*, trans. F. H. Knight (London: Weber, Allen and Unwin, 1928), pp. 352–69.

30. See Ernst H. Kantorowicz, *The King's Two Bodies: A Study in Mediaeval Political Theology* (Princeton University Press, 1957).

31. Hooker, *Of the Laws of Ecclesiastical Polity*, Book VIII, p. 147.

32. W. B. Rye, *England as Seen by Foreigners in the Days of Elizabeth and James the First* (London: John Russell Smith, 1865), p. 151.

33. See the passage from Arthur Wilson's *History of Great Britain* (1653), p. 289, cited in *Macbeth*, ed. Braunmuller, p. 244.

34. See *OED* 'charisma', a citation from 1644.

35. William Barclay, *De Regno et Regale Potestate adversus Buchananum, Brutum, Boucherium, & reliquos Monarchomachos* (Paris, 1600).

36. Cited in William Shakespeare, *Julius Caesar*, ed. Marvin Spevack (Cambridge University Press, 1988), pp. 156–7.

37. Charles Dickens, *Great Expectations*, chap. 4.

38. W. K. Wimsatt and Cleanth Brooks, *Literary Criticism: A Short History* (New York: Alfred A. Knopf, 1957), p. 39.

39. Wickham *et al.*, *English Professional Theatre*, p. 182.

40. See *Richard II*, 3.2.165.

7

CATHERINE BELSEY

Gender and family

A family dinner

The sound of trumpets ushers in the dinner guests. Dressed as a cook, an old soldier brings in the food. He greets the Emperor Saturninus and his wife with courtesy and encourages them to begin. The former Roman general's costume elicits a question, but since the guests already suspect that Titus Andronicus is not in his right mind, they do not press the point.

Over dinner, Titus turns the conversation to an episode in Roman history, when Virginius killed his daughter because she had been raped. Was this right, he wonders? Decidedly, the emperor assures him: she should not outlive the deed that shamed her. The old man takes this for authority, rounds on his own daughter and kills her then and there.

Self-evidently, this is *not* how families are expected to behave, and Saturninus says as much. However patriarchal Shakespeare's culture, or ancient Rome, come to that, this is 'unnatural and unkind' (5.3.4). But Lavinia too was raped, Titus explains, and begs his guests not to interrupt their meal, as if the summary execution of his daughter were no more than incidental. Her rapists, he discloses with apparent reluctance, were the empress's sons, Chiron and Demetrius. Surprised, Saturninus calls for the offenders to be brought before him at once. That will not be necessary, however, Titus laconically informs him:

> Why, there they are, both baked in this pie,
> Whereof their mother daintily hath fed,
> Eating the flesh that she herself hath bred.
> (5.3.59–61)

Drawing on the radical incongruity between cookery and carnage, the proprieties of hospitality and cannibalism, this scene represents a double horror: a father killing his own child; the spectacle of a mother devouring the sons that in nature she herself would once have once fed.

These days, perhaps only film in a line of descent from Martin Scorsese or Quentin Tarantino is equally stylized and sardonic in its treatment of the unthinkable. Julie Taymor's brilliant *Titus*, released in 2000, draws on the work of both to create a movie independent of either. But possibly our epoch has also become more receptive to the painful realization that the family often shelters remarkable cruelty, if not usually on quite this scale, between parents and children and, indeed, between parents themselves. The Victorians were not impressed by *Titus Andronicus*, but then the Victorians, officially at least, believed unequivocally in family values. We may want to, and most politicians tell us we should, but the emerging statistics for domestic violence and child abuse are making it harder to preserve our innocence.

Titus Andronicus is a play about two families, each unhappy in its own way. Oddly enough, the same observation applies in different terms to several of Shakespeare's tragedies. It fits, for instance, *Romeo and Juliet*, where the violence between Montagues and Capulets destroys the children of both; *Macbeth*, where the character of the hero's tyranny is thrown into relief by a direct contrast with the innocence of the Macduff family it destroys; or *Hamlet*, where the process of the hero's struggle to identify his own filial duty has direct implications for the family of Polonius, with tragic consequences for the prince himself.

Families, as we now know, construct positions for their members to occupy, including gender positions, but the family can be made to obscure the construction process itself by rooting it in 'nature'. Marriage, the cornerstone of the family, 'natural-izes' certain modes of behaviour: parental responsibility, sexual fidelity, heterosexuality itself.

We are the direct heirs of four hundred years of family values. But Shakespeare was not. Romantic courtship, marrying for love, and the loving socialization of children by two caring parents were new enough in his day not to pass for nature. Indeed, we might see Shakespeare's plays as contributing directly to the early modern process of naturalizing the affectionate nuclear family. But because this was a moment of change, they also make apparent to us now the anxieties provoked by the values themselves and the gender-models they construct.

It could be argued that this change in the understanding of the family can be traced within Shakespeare's work. His earliest tragedy raises some of the questions about the family and gender that the later tragedies will also address, but will answer differently in certain respects. As its climactic dinner party indicates, *Titus Andronicus* is a play about the appropriation of women, patriarchal power and family feuds; it is also, however, if more marginally, about domestic concord and familial love.

Courtship

The courtship practices the play depicts are remarkably perfunctory. As Titus Andronicus returns in triumph from the war against the Goths, he finds a contest between Saturninus and his younger brother Bassianus for the imperial throne. Saturninus wins with the help of Titus, and announces that as a reward, he will marry Titus's daughter:

> Titus, to advance
> Thy name and honourable family,
> Lavinia will I make my empress,
> Rome's royal mistress, mistress of my heart.
>   (1.1.242–5)

This is a strategic move for Saturninus: an alliance with the Andronici will secure the general's future loyalty. And, strategically too, Titus agrees to the match: in a world where names mean titles, and titles in turn are entitlements to property and influence, the family will surely benefit from the patronage of the emperor. No one consults Lavinia. She does not protest.

But Bassianus does. In a warrior society women are possessions. Rome, as many in Shakespeare's audience would know well, was founded on the appropriation of women, when Roman soldiers in quest of wives simply took them by force from their Sabine neighbours. Bassianus declares a prior claim to Lavinia:

> BASSIANUS Lord Titus, by your leave, this maid is mine.
> TITUS How, sir? Are you in earnest, then, my lord?
> BASSIANUS Ay, noble Titus, and resolved withal
> To do myself this reason and this right.
> MARCUS *Suum cuique* is our Roman justice:
> This prince in justice seizeth but his own.   (1.1.280–5)

Titus's brother Marcus usually represents the voice of sanity in this play: we take him seriously. Lavinia is already betrothed to Bassianus and Marcus confirms that she therefore belongs to him. The younger generation support this. Still no one consults Lavinia, though this time we may assume that she has given her consent to the betrothal. But the words used to claim her are proprietary, not romantic.

Cheated of one option, meanwhile, Saturninus promptly embraces another. He has already noticed the charms of the chief prisoner-of-war, Tamora, queen of the Goths. Briefly complimenting her with a comparison to Diana, goddess of chastity, he proposes to Tamora, acknowledging that this is a 'sudden choice', but no less determined for that (1.1.323). As a prisoner, Tamora has a great deal to gain by marriage to the emperor. The wedding is held without delay, though events will show that the new empress is no Diana.

Conversely, the short married life of Bassianus and Lavinia is apparently a happy one, though evidently not given over to sexual extravagance. When the next morning Saturninus makes a joke about young wives wanting to sleep late, Lavinia stoutly insists that she has been wide awake for two hours already.

Romance

How different, then, the story Shakespeare dramatizes in *Romeo and Juliet*, where the heroine is ready to call a lark a nightingale in order to keep her husband in her bed a little longer. Here the courtship process is intense, lyrical, passionate – and (almost) equal. At their first meeting, the lovers' exchanges compose a sonnet, in which Romeo speaks the first quatrain, Juliet the second. The remaining lines are evenly divided between them, and if Romeo initiates the dialogue here, while Juliet displays a degree of conventional coyness, she reveals her love to him without knowing it in the orchard, and then teasingly offers to stand on form and play hard to get, but only if it will intensify his courtship: 'I'll frown and be perverse and say thee nay, / So thou wilt woo; but else, not for the world' (2.2.96–7).

Moreover, in this play, where the lovers defy their parents and convention by their secret marriage, it is Juliet whose surprisingly eager and explicit expectations enable the audience to imagine their wedding night, as she appeals to the darkness that will cover them to

> learn me how to lose a winning match
> Play'd for a pair of stainless maidenhoods.
> Hood my unmanned blood, bating in my cheeks,
> With thy black mantle, till strange love grow bold
> (3.2.12–15)

Here, Juliet's father does his best to arrange a strategic alliance, but in vain. In this play it is the world of family feuds and the masculine obligation to avenge a wrong, precisely the values that seem to inform *Titus Andronicus*, which destroy a marriage based on love and reciprocity, made precious in the eyes of the audience by the romantic intensity of the poetry the lovers produce together.

Perhaps the most romantic of all Shakespeare's marriages is the elopement of Othello and Desdemona. Challenged to give a public account of her behaviour to the Senate, Desdemona does so fluently and without apology, explaining that, while she recognizes what she owes her father, she must now, like her mother before her, 'prefer' her husband (1.3.187). And when the Duke suggests that Othello should leave her at home on his journey to Cyprus, she takes part in the discussion to affirm her commitment, including her sexual commitment, to her new husband:

> That I did love the Moor to live with him
> My downright violence and scorn of fortunes
> May trumpet to the world. My heart's subdued
> Even to the very quality of my lord:
> I saw Othello's visage in his mind,
> And to his honours and his valiant parts
> Did I my soul and fortunes consecrate,
> So that, dear lords, if I be left behind,
> A moth of peace, and he go to the war,
> The rites for which I love him are bereft me,
> And I a heavy interim shall support
> By his dear absence. Let me go with him.
>
> (1.3.249–60)

The plain style of the speech ('I did love the Moor to live with him', 'Let me go with him') lays implicit claim to an equality with the Senate she addresses. Calm, authoritative, measured, Desdemona's rhetoric draws attention to the nature of the choice she has made between love and convention, passion and wealth. By marrying him, she has already dedicated to Othello her 'soul' and her fate; but left behind, she would lose the erotic 'rites' (or conjugal 'rights': the difference is not audible on the stage) which are her motive for loving him.

This is a strong statement, and some commentators have had difficulty with it, not least, no doubt, because Othello is black. The quarto text of the play, the first to be published, but after Shakespeare's death, intensifies the sexual component of Desdemona's speech. There lines 251–2 read, 'My heart's subdued / Even to the utmost pleasure of my lord.' Since the Folio version a year later has 'Even to the very quality', most editors have opted for this softened version. M. R. Ridley, however, the editor of Arden 2 (1962), not otherwise notable for his racial progressiveness, defied convention and gave the quarto reading.[1] But the most recent Arden reverts to the Folio version, on the grounds that 'utmost pleasure' 'might suggest sexual pleasure' (line 252n.). Yes, indeed it might. Since it also scans better, and has an equal claim to authority, we might well prefer it.

Whichever reading we choose, both Juliet and Desdemona display a sexual frankness which is evidently not inconsistent with early modern propriety.

Shakespeare was not a Victorian, and the polarized alternatives of demure virgin or voracious whore are not helpful in making sense of the plays. Evidently, early modern women were not expected to be sexless, though they were required to be faithful. Domestic conduct books of the period recommend that married sex should be pleasurable for both husband and wife.

Past and present

How should we explain the radical differences between *Titus Andronicus* and these two later plays? *Othello* is usually dated 1604, or a year or two earlier; *Titus* was probably first performed at least a decade before. Do the differences 'reflect' a cultural change in the understanding of love, marriage, and the place of women in both? A case could be made for this view. But cultural change on such a scale, especially in a world without television to bring the new values into every household, usually takes a little longer. (Every night on television fiction equates true happiness with reciprocal love between a heterosexual couple.) Meanwhile, *Romeo and Juliet* was probably staged only a few years after *Titus*.

There is a difference of genre, of course: *Titus* is usually thought of as a revenge play, in a line of descent from Kyd's *Spanish Tragedy*. It concerns the power relations in a warrior society, while the later plays are love stories centred on the home. But *Titus* locates its revenge plot in the relationship between two families, and the family is a prominent issue within it. Could there be an additional way of accounting for its apparent indifference to romantic love?

Everyone knows that Shakespeare's plays are hopelessly anachronistic. The clock that strikes in *Julius Caesar* is a classic instance. But have we, perhaps, allowed this knowledge too much sway? *Titus Andronicus* places strong emphasis on its Roman setting. In Act 1 alone there are no fewer than sixty-eight references to 'Rome', 'Roman', or 'Romans'. Locating the action in this way is helpful to the audience, of course, the equivalent of an establishing shot in the cinema, but it might be supposed that even the most inattentive would have taken in a mere setting rather more easily. All the literary references in this highly allusive play are to classical literature. The text is full of Latin tags, like the one Marcus invokes ('*Suum cuique* is our Roman justice'). And in a disarming touch, the play makes clear that Chiron the Goth learned Latin as a foreign language, just like any Elizabethan schoolboy, so that he is able to recognize (though not to interpret) the Latin quotation sent by Titus (4.2.20–8). The religion invoked is also Roman – the dead 'hover on the dreadful shore of Styx' until they are buried

(1.1.91) – though in one unexpected lapse Roman suddenly means Roman Catholic (5.1.76–7).

The last instance apart, or, indeed, included, since popery had been outlawed (if with some inconsistency) for more than half a century by the 1590s, is it possible that *Titus* deliberately sets its horrifying events in an alien culture, and that the society it depicts is defined precisely as archaic in respect of its domestic relationships, as well as in its invocation of the human sacrifice that seems to be required by Roman custom, the Stoical endurance of suffering with dignity and reticence, the tyranny of imperial rule, and the final regression to cannibalism? If this is a fictitious Rome, a conflation of Republican austerity, imperial decadence and a tribal culture that probably never existed at all, it is nonetheless coherently imagined, and a long way in most regards from Elizabethan London. If so, we may see its marriage customs as archaic too, though not, perhaps, so archaic that they were unintelligible to many in Shakespeare's audience, whose values did not necessarily match their actual habits. Arranged marriage was probably still the norm in practice, even though marrying for love becomes the ideal on the stage.

For that reason, *Titus Andronicus* offers a useful point of reference, an indication of what Shakespeare's culture felt it was in the process of leaving behind. Our difficulty now is to see just how much of what has become 'obvious' to us was less obvious then, and conversely, to distinguish between different moments of the West's cultural past, so that we are able to see what sense (or senses) these plays might have made in their own time.

Cultural subjects

However we read *Titus*, two separate sets of values were evidently available to its original audience. Each of these distinct worlds offers different modes of behaviour for men and women to enact. In one, men are expected to be proprietary and easily roused to violence; by contrast, women, or good women, at least, are silent and submissive. In the other, both men and women are rendered eloquent by love; their relationships are intimate, private, no one's concern but their own, if only others would leave them in peace. Different social arrangements involve different values as the condition of their existence, and virtuous conduct varies from one cultural moment to another.

The implication seems to be that human behaviour is not given in advance by identities prior to culture, but that, on the contrary, identity itself is to a high degree shaped by cultural values. Each relies on the other. There is no patriarchy without patriarchs, and no romance without romantics. New values do not come into existence unless people subscribe to them, reproduce them in their own understanding of themselves and their relationships.

It follows, then, that the spread of new values entails, perhaps over generations, new forms of subjectivity. At the same time, new values do not circulate themselves without inscription in cultural practices, including fiction. Arguably, if people had not seen romantic courtship at the theatre, they would never have thought of it on their own. Plays do not necessarily reflect behaviour; instead, perhaps they help to inculcate it.

If cultures both depend on and generate the subjects who reproduce them, so too, of course, do fictional genres. Love stories require protagonists who talk and act like lovers, not warriors. In Shakespeare's comedies love civilizes – or perhaps 'feminizes' – young men, turns them into poets and dreamers, and distracts them from the world of violence. Romeo fights Tybalt only with the greatest reluctance. The polar opposition between passive femininity and male violence depicted so sharply in *Titus* gives way to a degree of symmetry or even similarity between Romeo and Juliet so noticeable that in the nineteenth century the hero's part was commonly played by women.

Ironically, on Shakespeare's own stage the parallel is achieved by other means, since Juliet would, of course, have been played by a boy. The effect of this convention on the development of female roles in the period, and on audiences who took the convention for granted, is matter for speculation. The conclusions we reach will depend on our assumptions about the experience of watching a fictional performance. The identity of the actor, like the Epilogue or the Chorus, is both inside and outside the fiction. Perhaps it assumes a priority at certain moments, and seems a matter of indifference at others?

By focusing on the young, and not their fathers, *Romeo and Juliet* and *Othello* both depict and help to bring about a moment of cultural change, when the older generation takes for granted the obligation of parents to arrange the marriages of their children, and the younger generation perceives this practice as oppressive. But the change of values in society at large was not purely the result of fiction, nor was it simply the result of what we perceive as progress towards greater human happiness. On the contrary. The social project, diligently promoted by the Church, Reformers and moralists, was to stabilize the institution of marriage itself as the cornerstone of a more stable society. If couples married for love, so the story went, they would live together in harmony, and bring up their children in the fear of God and obedience to social convention. The loving family, Milton would later affirm, was 'the fountain and seminary of good subjects'.[2] And in this he echoed Shakespeare's contemporary, the Reformer William Perkins, who saw the family as 'the fountain and seminary of all sorts and kinds of life', since 'this first society is as it were the school wherein are taught and learned the principles of authority and subjection'.[3] Like the theatre, the state also had an investment in romantic courtship; it had yet to learn that, in the event, family values might prove themselves utopian.

Adultery

Strategic alliances designed to serve the interests of the dynastic family, indeed, were beginning to be perceived as distinctly unstable. The love stories that circulated most widely in the Middle Ages did not tell of courtship leading to marriage, but instead romanticized extra-marital passion. The loves of Tristan and Isolde, or Lancelot and Guinevere, threatened the very fabric of monarchy and the order it was required to secure. As many in Shakespeare's audience would know, both from Virgil's epic poem and Christopher Marlowe's recent tragedy of *Dido, Queen of Carthage*, Dido very nearly succeeded in deflecting Aeneas from his duty to found Rome. Desire was perceived as dangerous, and the practice of arranged and often loveless marriage must have seemed positively to enhance the appeal of adultery.

Tamora's marriage to Saturninus does not interrupt her sexual relationship with Aaron the Moor. The very next morning, she seeks him out alone in a secluded place, and invites him to emulate with her the secret pleasures of Dido and Aeneas in the cave. But for all the lyrical echoes of her speech (2.2.10–29), this is no romance. Aaron is presented as a devil (5.1.40, 45; 5.3.5, 11) who gladly claims responsibility for the rape and mutilation of Lavinia and for tricking Titus into chopping off his own hand. And he adds proudly,

> when I told the empress of this sport,
> She sounded [swooned] almost at my pleasing tale
> And for my tidings gave me twenty kisses.
> (*Tit.* 5.1.118–20)

The liaison between Aaron and Tamora constitutes a minor episode in a play crammed with appalling incident. But adultery is a central issue in *Antony and Cleopatra*, where the sympathies of the audience are harder to assess. Here too Dido and Aeneas offer a precedent. Preparing to kill himself, Antony foresees his reunion with Cleopatra in the Elysian underworld:

> Where souls do couch on flowers we'll hand in hand
> And with our sprightly port make the ghosts gaze.
> Dido and her Aeneas shall want troops,
> And all the haunt be ours.   (4.14.52–5)

This strange and delicate conjunction of the sensual (flowers and hands) with the insubstantial ('souls', 'ghosts', 'haunt') idealizes the passion it promises to seal at last in a spectral future. It also evokes the theatrical image of Cleopatra in the barge, which forms the prelude to their first meeting. Then too, she drew all eyes to her,

> and Antony,
> Enthroned i'th'market-place, did sit alone,
> Whistling to th'air, which, but for vacancy,
> Had gone to gaze on Cleopatra, too,
> And made a gap in nature.   (2.2.224–8)

This time Antony is alone. In Elysium, however, the lovers are together.

It would surely be difficult not to succumb to this, or to resist the power of this story of forbidden love, relating *Antony and Cleopatra* back to the medieval romances of doomed and tragic passion. And yet, when we look more closely, there are certain ironies here. Aeneas forsook Dido, who killed herself in despair. When they met in the underworld, she turned away. Misled, or self-deceived, Antony radically rewrites the well-known narrative.[4] Indeed, at this moment, he is literally misinformed, convinced by Mardian's false report of Cleopatra's death, her last and fatal seductive stratagem. The woman Antony imagines he will overtake in death (4.14.45) is at this moment hiding from his anger in her monument.

Compared with Cleopatra, 'Kingdoms are clay!', Antony declares (1.1.36). But in the very next scene news of trouble in kingdoms of the empire changes his mind: 'These strong Egyptian fetters I must break', he now insists (1.2.112). Fetters are iron shackles for the feet, designed to prevent prisoners from moving. Throughout the play, Antony oscillates between desire and politics, while Cleopatra, who has her own political interests, lies, cheats, and throws tantrums.

And yet the poetry consistently invests them with mythic status. Cleopatra in her barge outdoes paintings of the goddess of love herself, 'O'erpicturing that Venus where we see / The fancy outwork nature' (2.2.210–11). Even here, however, there is an implication that the picture improves on the thing itself, or that the spectacle Cleopatra herself creates is an effect of fantasy, not truth. In one sense, of course, it is: this woman who personifies the feminine is played by a boy, as the text itself obliquely reminds us (5.2.218–20). Antony is repeatedly compared with Mars, god of war (2.2.6; 2.5.117), but in the first instance the parallel is set in his heroic past, while his present condition is defined as 'dotage' (1.1.1–4).

Ovid tells the story of Venus and Mars in *The Metamorphoses*, one of the books used to teach little boys Latin. The goddess's husband, Vulcan the smith, skilful in metalwork, made a net of bronze as fine as a spider's web and spread it over their couch. When Mars and Venus next made love, they were caught by the net and held in position. Then Vulcan opened the doors to let in the other gods, who laughed, and entertained each other with the story for a long time to come (4.171–89).[5]

Does *Antony and Cleopatra*, which scales the heights of tragic poetry, also ask its audience to laugh at the lovers it depicts, caught in their own self-deceiving passion? Perhaps the continued fascination of the play for us now depends on the undecidable character of its attitude to adultery. Is this the greatest love story ever told, or a record of reciprocal misrecognition – or both? (Doesn't love always involve a degree of overvaluation?) Is Cleopatra, as she finally claims, a wife in all but name (5.2.286–7) or a remarkably accomplished courtesan – or both? And how different, once desire is understood to be a component of marriage, is one from the other?

Masculinity

Meanwhile, what are the alternatives for Antony? Cleopatra's rival is not primarily another woman, but the power-struggles of imperial Rome. Antony's strategic marriage to Octavia is intended to cement his relationship with Caesar, his partner and rival in the government of Rome. It fails to do so, of course, because the world of masculine competition is no substitute for the pleasures of Egypt, and the redoubled insult to Caesar's family when Antony betrays Octavia only intensifies the hostility between them.

Left to their own devices, it would appear, men quarrel. Bassianus and Saturninus contend for the throne; Chiron and Demetrius are ready to do battle over Lavinia. Montagues and Capulets fight as a matter of habit. Edmund is prepare to go to any lengths to get Edgar's inheritance; Claudius kills Old Hamlet for his.

Relations between men are commonly grounded in emulation. The word carries two apparently antithetical meanings, both appropriate, both intimately connected. It indicates, on the one hand, admiration and imitation, and on the other, rivalry. The person you want to excel is the one you respect most. It is because Caesar acknowledges Antony's heroism that he competes with him; a similar relationship develops temporarily between Cassius and Brutus in *Julius Caesar*. Iago hates Cassio because 'He hath a daily beauty in his life / That makes me ugly' (*Oth.* 5.1.19–20). Macbeth has Banquo murdered for fear of his virtue – 'and under him / My Genius is rebuked; as, it is said, / Mark Antony's was by Caesar' (3.1.54–6). Coriolanus has to beat Aufidius because he is the best.

In a world that sees war as heroic, true masculinity also means the ability to bear pain. If Titus is stoical in the face of almost unbearable emotional suffering, Antony's physical defeat of famine was once the admiration of the world. Despite his delicate upbringing, Antony, it seems, exceeded the animals in their ability to survive in hostile nature:

> Thou didst drink
> The stale of horses and the gilded puddle
> Which beasts would cough at.
> . . .
> On the Alps,
> It is reported, thou didst eat strange flesh
> Which some did die to look on. (*Ant.* 1.4.62–9)

And this without ever showing any distaste, or even losing weight (69–72)!

If women are to become consenting partners for men, perhaps one condition is that they too must endure pain without protest. Ironically, it is to prove herself a fit wife for Brutus, his friend and companion, able to share fully in his political secrets, that Portia has deliberately wounded her own thigh in *Julius Caesar*. Portia's act is usually read as a concession to Roman Stoicism, but isn't it as a perverse version of the same project that Cleopatra insists on fighting alongside Antony at Actium? Surely a corruption of this companionate ideal also drives Lady Macbeth when she urges evil spirits to 'unsex' her, to make her capable of taking an equal part in Duncan's murder, blocking all natural scruples, turning her life-giving milk bitter, 'That my keen knife see not the wound it makes, / Nor Heaven peep through the blanket of the dark, / To cry, "Hold, hold!" ' (1.5.40–54).

Lady Macbeth also perverts the meaning of manhood as a way of taunting her husband with cowardice. 'I dare do all that may become a man', he insists. 'Who dares do more, is none' (1.7.45). 'When you durst do it, then you were a man', she retorts (1.7.49). The challenge works, and Macbeth agrees to murder the king. 'Bring forth men children only!', he exclaims, in response to the ingenuity of her plan for the crime (1.7.73).

Lady Macbeth is wrong: masculinity is not by nature criminal, and it is not without feeling. When Macduff laments the slaughter of his family, Malcolm urges, 'Dispute it like a man' (4.3.220). Macduff replies, 'I shall do so; / But I must also feel it as a man' (4.3.224–5). The feeling, we are invited to believe, is what motivates his action.

And yet, strangely enough, the version of manhood urged by Lady Macbeth is not so far from the kind the play appears to endorse. The first words of the saintly Duncan are, 'What bloody man is that?' (1.2.1). The man is, it turns out, a soldier fresh from the battle, who recounts the exploit that so gratifies the king, Macbeth's combat with the traitor Macdonwald:

> brave Macbeth (well he deserves that name),
> Disdaining Fortune, with his brandished steel,
> Which smoked with bloody execution,
> Like Valour's minion, carv'd out his passage,
> Till he fac'd the slave:
> Which ne'er shook hands, nor bade farewell to him,
> Till he unseamed him from the nave to th'chops,
> And fixed his head upon our battlements.
> (1.2.16–23)

The sword 'smokes' with warm blood in the cold air; Macbeth 'carves' his way through the ranks, like a butcher; and he slits his enemy open, as if he were severing a row of stitches, upwards from the navel to the jaw. The difference between this and the murder of Duncan, apart from the fact that this is more bloodthirsty, is that the battle is legitimate. 'O valiant cousin! worthy gentleman'(1.2.24), comments the king, and promptly promotes him.

How are we to read this play, where the feminine is exiled or killed, witches should be women but have beards (1.3.44), Macbeth's wife demands to be unsexed in order to be a better partner in crime (1.5.39), and masculinity exceeds its own bounds – but only just – and becomes tyranny? What, in other words, are the proper limits of manhood?

'It will have blood, they say: blood will have blood', mutters Macbeth (3.4.122). Does he refer only to the murder of Banquo, or to the violence that prevails from the beginning? Would this proverb, in other words, serve as an epigraph to the whole play? Is Macbeth speaking simply of his plan to kill Duncan, when he reflects, 'we but teach / Bloody instructions, which, being taught, return / To plague th'inventor' (1.7.8–10)? Should we, perhaps, see killing, lawful and apparently heroic on the one hand, and criminal on the other, as in a way continuous? If so, though it differentiates between a good cause and a bad, perhaps the play also foregrounds the tragic potential of the militaristic values that require a real man to devote his energies to making 'Strange images of death' (1.3.95).

Values in conflict

This issue is directly engaged in the revenge tradition, where law and the readiness to act in what looks, in some ways, like a good cause, come into direct conflict with each other. Titus Andronicus, who has no hesitation in killing his own son when he violates his father's code of conduct, defers vengeance against the legitimate ruler until he is at least half crazed with grief. His 'piety' (1.1.118) impels him to obey the law. As Marcus explains, despite his sorrow, Titus is 'so just that he will not revenge'. And he appeals to the gods, 'Revenge the heavens for old Andronicus!' (4.1.128–9). If the heavens act at all, however, it is only to send him Tamora and her sons in disguise, and this looks more like an intervention from hell.

Here, the patient endurance of suffering replaces unlawful violence, at least in the first instance. In this light, it seems unlikely that Hamlet is contemplating suicide when he wonders which of his options is *nobler*:

> Whether 'tis nobler in the mind to suffer
> The slings and arrows of outrageous fortune,
> Or to take arms against a sea of troubles
> And by opposing end them. To die –
>
> (*Ham.* 3.1.57–60)

What the Ghost demands is the murder of Hamlet's uncle and his king. Which is right, unlawful masculine violence, or equally masculine endurance? But suffering what fortune sends is hard to distinguish in practice from cowardice, as Hamlet knows well:

> it cannot be
> But I am pigeon-livered and lack gall
> To make oppression bitter, or ere this
> I should ha' fatted all the region kites
> With this slave's offal.   (2.2.529–33)

On the other hand, if this image of violence is repulsive, the consequences are still more so so: 'To die – '. Revengers always die. But death, Hamlet reflects, is not the problem: to die is to sleep, no more than that. Who would not be willing to die, to escape the miseries of life, were it not that the murder of an uncle and a king, if not justified, also incurs punishment in the next life? In consequence, 'the dread of something after death . . . puzzles the will' (3.1.78–80). 'Thus', Hamlet inconclusively concludes, 'conscience does make cowards of us all' (83).

Feminization

Nineteenth-century writers and artists regarded Hamlet with profound ambivalence. Surely, they reasoned, a young man ought to obey his father? And surely, too, a proper man would polish off a bad king in no time? Laertes, after all, would cheerfully have broken sanctuary and 'cut his throat i'th'church' (4.7.125). But they also admired Hamlet's intellectual engagement with the issues and his philosophical range. We, with less conviction that fathers are always right, and more reservations about violence as the solution to all problems, might be inclined to admire more than we condemn.

In the nineteenth century Hamlet's hesitation was widely regarded as 'feminine', and like Romeo, he was commonly played by women. More recently, we might prefer to see a contradiction in the ideal of masculinity. An early modern man should both endure, like Titus, and act, like Macbeth. Both are noble. But even Macbeth needs considerable encouragement to kill a king. 'I do fear thy nature', his wife observes. 'It is too full of the milk of human kindness' (1.5.16–17). Only thirty lines later, she will repudiate the milk of her own 'woman's breasts' (1.5.47–8).

In a brilliant article which suddenly made obvious what we ought to have seen all along, Stephen Orgel explained that men in Shakespeare's time were in perpetual fear of feminization.[6] When Galenic physiology, and especially midwifery, thought of women as less perfect versions of men, possessing the same sexual organs, but with less heat to push them outwards,[7] there was, it seemed, always a danger that men would slide back towards imperfect femininity.

It's true, of course. This is what happens to Antony: the effect of his 'dotage', and his devotion to love's 'soft hours' (*Ant.* 1.1.45), is that he loses the masculine will to war and, in consequence, at Actium he follows Cleopatra from the battle, yielding the day to Caesar. Romeo in love is unwilling to fight his new cousin Tybalt, and Mercutio incurs his own death doing it for him:

> O sweet Juliet,
> Thy beauty hath made me effeminate
> And in my temper soften'd valour's steel.
> (3.1.104–6)

But my own doubt is whether this feminization is offered, even in its own period, as cause for alarm, or instead as a relief from the remorseless demands of male aggression. The feud in *Romeo and Juliet* is made to seem particularly pointless, and as Romeo points out, street brawling is against the law (3.1.87–8). Hamlet reproaches himself because all he does is talk and curse, like a whore or a kitchen-maid (2.2.538–40), but would we really expect the audience to find him less sympathetic than Laertes because he deliberates?

The test case must surely be Coriolanus, brought up by his mother, a woman who, ironically, out-Romes Roman military values, to personify all that is most violent in masculinity, at the expense of the civil virtues that courtship and marriage are seen to inculcate elsewhere. When his upbringing leads Coriolanus to join the Volscians and threaten war against Rome itself, only his family can dissuade him: two women and a child. He tries to hold out against his own natural impulse to give way to the 'woman's tenderness' they elicit in him (5.3.129):

> But out, affection!
> All bond and privilege of nature break!
> Let it be virtuous to be obstinate. (*Cor.* 5.3.23–5)

It would not be virtuous, however, but perverse, and his words make clear that Coriolanus knows that. It is hard to imagine spectators who would not sigh with relief when he relents, even though the text also makes clear that the Volscians will not let him outlive this betrayal of their cause (5.3.187–9).

In the event, what happens is worse: his rival, Aufidius, calls Coriolanus a 'boy of tears' (5.6.100). For the hero, this is unbearable, but for the audience? The spectacle of Aufidius emblematically standing in triumph on his dead body surely elicits, perhaps for the first time, our sympathy for a figure who has loved one aspect of masculine values not wisely, but too well.

Homoeroticism

A warrior society, which thinks heterosexual love softens heroism, depends on close ties of loyalty between men, and the values of such a society were evidently still part of the fabric of early modern culture. The relationship between Antony and Enobarbus is presented as jocular, but close. Hamlet trusts Horatio, much as knights must have trusted their friends to drag them off the field of war when things went badly, and promises to 'wear' him 'In my heart's core, ay, in my heart of heart' (3.2.72–3).

Were these friendships understood as including a homoerotic element? This question is extremely difficult to answer accurately at this distance of time, not least because it depends on access to what was implicit rather than explicit in what is said. What we know, or think we know, is that while homosexual acts undoubtedly took place, early modern culture did not identify individuals as gay or lesbian. Those identifications, which classify a person rather than a practice, and imply a fixity of preference unknown to earlier epochs, belong to the eighteenth-century 'science' of sexuality. We also know that, while 'sodomy' was defined in the statutes as an appalling crime, prosecutions for sodomy were extremely rare.

The main areas of interest for homoerotic criticism of Shakespeare are probably the Sonnets and the comedies. There are indications in *The Merchant of Venice*, for instance, of a possible conflict between friendship and marriage, especially now that wives were themselves becoming their husbands' best friends. The homosocial world of the warrior Coriolanus, however, knows no such contests. The hero, who addresses his wife, in public, at least, as 'My gracious silence' (2.1.148), is much more effusive in the excitement of military triumph towards his friend, Cominius:

> Oh, let me clip ye
> In arms as sound as when I woo'd; in heart
> As merry as when our nuptial day was done,
> And tapers burned to bedward. (1.6.29–32)

But how should we interpret this? From one perspective, the comparison affirms the heterosexual intensity of his marriage night. From another, it transfers the eroticism of that moment to an embrace with another man.

There is an exact parallel here with Aufidius's welcome to Coriolanus himself: 'More dances my rapt heart / Than when I first my wedded mistress saw / Bestride my threshold' (4.5.113–15). Their relationship follows the pattern of tragic love: hostility gives way to intensity and, in betrayal, a bitter disappointment that issues in lawless violence.

'Race'

Aufidius is a Volscian. Is he therefore less 'civilized' than the Romans? Cleopatra is Egyptian, a 'gipsy' (1.1.10), 'tawny' (1.1.6), or (possibly) 'black' (1.5.29); Tamora is white, but a Goth and therefore barbaric; Aaron is black. Does their foreignness, their otherness, compound their threat, and in particular, their danger to family values?

There can be no doubt that early modern England, with its developing sense of national identity, and an emerging white racism as the legitimation of a growing slave trade, regarded with mounting suspicion other 'races', who palpably subscribed to other values than their own. Cultural difference is easily frightening – to the degree that it demonstrates that there are other ways of ordering people's lives. And what is frightening is readily demonized. Aaron in particular, while a Moor, is also clearly a descendant of the Vice of the moral plays, the dashing, witty, calculating figure who seduces the representative human hero to his own damnation. The Vice, like the devil, his 'father', had long been represented as black, the traditional colour of inhabitants of the darkness of hell.

How, then, should we understand the irruption of racial otherness into the heart of the family in *Othello*? There can be no doubt that Othello's blackness is a significant component of the play. The first act alone is pervaded by hate-speech. Othello is identified as 'the thick lips' (1.1.65); 'an old black ram... tupping' the white ewe, Desdemona (1.1.87–8); a 'Barbary horse' who will give Brabantio's family 'nephews to neigh to you' (1.1.110–11). Desdemona is imagined in 'the gross clasps of a lascivious Moor' (1.1.124). Her father tells Othello he cannot believe that his daughter would voluntarily leave her home for 'the sooty bosom / Of such a thing as thou' (1.2.70–1).

This is not, of course, the whole story. The speakers are Iago, who hates him, Roderigo, who himself wanted to marry Desdemona, and Brabantio, the absurd father who would more properly belong in comedy (compare Egeus in *A Midsummer Night's Dream*) if the consequences were not so tragic. At his first appearance, Othello utterly fails to live down to his reputation. And the Senate will hear none of Brabantio's racist slurs. Convinced by Desdemona, who 'saw Othello's visage in his mind' (1.3.253), the Duke affirms, 'If virtue no delighted beauty lack / Your son-in-law is far more fair than black' (1.3.290–91).

But this proto-liberal colour-blindness is no match for the super-subtle Venetian racism of Iago. Gradually, all the main characters in the play become his dupes, until Othello himself comes to fear that his blackness makes him unlovable (3.3.267). The 'ocular proof' of Desdemona's infidelity that Othello demands (3.3.363) is, of course, as much an illusion as Iago's widely recognized honesty. Othello's own blind innocence (1.3.398–400) is matched by Desdemona's and Cassio's. Ironically, it is Iago's wife, who knows him best, who finally perceives the truth.

In my view, this play uniquely values the partnership it depicts with such idealism. But a marriage founded on passionate, idealizing love is correspondingly vulnerable to imagined betrayal. What destroys this one is not so much, I think, an instability intrinsic to an inter-racial marriage, as the shaping fantasies of white racism itself.

Parents and children

Othello and Desdemona do not live long enough to have children. Titus Andronicus, by contrast, has had twenty-six. He has lost twenty-one sons in five military campaigns; he himself kills another, when Mutius defends his sister's marriage to Bassianus. Of those that remain, two more are executed and the last banished in the course of Tamora's revenge; Lavinia is raped and mutilated by the Goths, Chiron and Demetrius. This is the insupportable sequence of wrongs Titus finally avenges when he induces the empress to dine on her own children.

But the story of Tamora's revenge begins when Titus ignores her plea to spare her eldest son, whose life the 'cruel, irreligious piety' of Rome demands as a blood sacrifice (1.1.133). 'And if thy sons were ever dear to thee, / O, think my son to be as dear to me' (1.1.110–11). But were his children dear to Titus? And in what sense? Titus's austere ethical code, the play repeatedly makes clear, comes first. He loves his children, but on condition that they reproduce his own values. (Is there a parody of this idea in Aaron's passionate love of his baby? It is, he claims, 'Myself, / The vigour and the picture of my youth' (4.2.109–10).)

The Andronicus family is dynastic: Titus backs lineage. Although Bassianus would make a better emperor, Titus supports the claim of the elder brother. His own children expect to kneel to him (1.1.164, 374 s.d.). If there is a glimmer of hope at the end of the play, it lies with the accession of Lucius, the surviving Andronicus, and the innocence of young Lucius, his son. (The survival of Aaron's baby, conversely, implies the continuation of evil in the world.)

At the same time, a new set of values is evident in the play. The younger generation are right to defend Bassianus, and Titus belongs to a vanishing order. Paradoxically, as a grandfather, he himself anticipates the new one, dancing young Lucius on his knee, singing to him and telling him stories (5.3.159–65). The new family will make children more precious, and idealize the love between parents and children as unconditional.

In that sense, *Titus Andronicus* anticipates *King Lear* more than a decade later. In both plays fathers expect the obedience of their children, and do not find it. The young inhabit a different world. But in *Lear* the tragedy is the outcome of an emotional intensity the dynastic family cannot sustain. What Lear wants is not just obedience, but unconditional love. Sadly, the family is not able to accommodate the exorbitant demands now placed on it. That way, the tragedy will demonstrate, madness lies.

NOTES

1. William Shakespeare, *Othello*, ed. M. R. Ridley (London: Methuen, 1962). For a discussion of the story to this point, see Anthony Barthelemy, 'Introduction', *Critical Essays on Shakespeare's 'Othello'* (New York: G. K. Hall, 1994), pp. 3–4.
2. John Milton, *The Complete Prose Works*, 8 vols., vol. 11, ed. Ernest Sirluck (New Haven, CT: Yale University Press, 1959), p. 447.
3. William Perkins, *Christian Oeconomie, Works*, vol. 111 (Cambridge, 1618), p. 671, Epistle Dedicatory (n.p.).
4. Coppélia Kahn, *Roman Shakespeare: Warriors, Wounds and Women* (London: Routledge, 1997), p. 131.
5. Ovid, *Metamorphoses*, with an English translation by Frank Justus Miller (Cambridge, MA: Harvard University Press, 1984).
6. Stephen Orgel, ' "Nobody's Perfect", or, Why Did the English Stage Take Boys for Women?', *South Atlantic Quarterly* 88 (1989), 7–29.
7. See Thomas Laqueur, *Making Sex: Body and Gender from the Greeks to Freud* (Cambridge, MA: Harvard University Press, 1990).

8

GAIL KERN PASTER

The tragic subject and its passions

The poet John Dryden, writing near the end of the seventeenth century, criticized Shakespeare for failing to respect the unity of character in his tragedies: 'The last property of manners is, that they be constant, and equall, that is, maintain'd the same through the whole design: thus when Virgil had once given the name of *Pious* to *Aeneas*, he was bound to show him such, in all his words and actions through the whole Poem.'[1] According to Dryden, the playwright is bound by the canons of realism – rules that characters as represented in literary works ought to manifest a high degree of psychological and behavioural consistency. Thus for Aeneas *to be himself* – to have the identity of Aeneas – he should be pious in mind as in deed. For Dryden, this artistic requirement is grounded in a conviction that real human beings *are* psychologically consistent and, as such, the autonomous source of their meanings. Self-sameness in a person's behaviours flows from an invisible self-identity. This inner identity is the product of a disembodied consciousness that sees the world as the objectified instrument of its own willed designs. The 'I' with which an individual represents him- or herself to the world is fully present to itself and thus can be held accountable for its words and deeds.[2]

This essay will argue that Dryden's demand for unity (or self-sameness) of character in Shakespeare is anachronistic, based on a conceptual distinction between emotions and the body, between psychology and physiology, that is foreign to early seventeenth-century conceptions of an inward self.[3] Dryden does not use the term 'psychology', a term that entered the English language only at the end of the seventeenth century and referred at that point to the philosophical study of the soul (psyche). But there can be little doubt that he would understand the psychological properties of 'human nature' in more or less modern, post-Enlightenment terms as instruments of a sovereign self, a disembodied consciousness.[4] They are immaterial and incorporeal – hence cumulative and consistent in outward expression over time.

But Shakespeare is unlikely to have imagined the workings of self or its near-synonym, subjectivity, in such disembodied terms or to have imagined that the emotions of his tragic protagonists occurred anywhere but in and through their bodies or that they occurred otherwise than materially. This does not mean Shakespeare and his contemporaries lacked a conception of inwardness. On the contrary, as Katharine Maus has argued, the idea of a 'socially visible exterior and an invisible personal interiority' – the idea of an own self – has 'a long history in the Western philosophical tradition'.[5] The problem is how to understand that inwardness in terms other than the disembodied ones of post-Enlightenment modernity. The difference arises because 'in vernacular sixteenth- and early seventeenth-century speech and writing, the whole interior of the body – heart, liver, womb, bowels, kidneys, gall, blood, lymph – quite often involves itself in the production of the mental interior, of the individual's private experience'.[6] Selfhood then, in early modern terms and as used in this essay, refers to a form of self-experience intensely physical in kind and expression. Indeed it is hard to overstate the implications of the period's persistent materialism of thought where conceptions of selfhood are involved. Even Hamlet's famous statement – 'But I have that within which passes show' (1.2.85) – refers not to an incorporeal site where a disembodied self might be located but, as David Hillman suggests, 'to a realm of specifically *corporeal* interiority contrasted with mere outward signs'.[7] Thus the language of self-experience in Shakespeare's plays expresses an understanding of the sources of self in which the modern separation of the psychological from the physiological had not yet happened. In the Galenic physiology, 'self' in behavioural terms was the product of invisible, mysterious interactions between an immaterial soul and its material instruments. These instruments included the faculties of reason, imagination, and will, the five senses, and the body itself. Experience of self arose through a baby's early identification with its body, but the culture's idea of bodiliness included much that we now designate as non-bodily. In this paradigm, emotions were transformative bodily events emanating from the heart as seat of the affections. The body and its emotions were understood to be functionally inseparable, with change in one realm producing change in the other.

An assumption that emotional change produces bodily alteration underlies Desdemona's reaction to the transformation in Othello: 'My lord is not my lord', she tells Cassio and Iago, 'nor should I know him,/Were he in favour as in humour altered' (*Oth.* 3.4.118–19). Her distinction between Othello's countenance and his mood is between two aspects of physical being – his unchanged face (which she can see) and his changed bodily disposition or 'humour' (which she cannot). 'Something sure of state', she goes on, '...Hath puddled his clear spirit' (3.4.134–7). Her imagery of the puddled spirit represents powerful feeling as a fluid changing in colour from clear to dark and in motion from flowing to stopped. It defines the onset of Othello's jealousy as the onset, literally, of physical disease. The physical model underlying ancient and early modern psychology is 'a simple hydraulic one, based on a clear localisation of psychological function by organ or system of organs'.[8] In other words, the bodily fluids that flowed from and to different bodily organs were thought to affect mood, disposition, desires, and emotions – sources of the self.

Desdemona's belief in the functional coexpressiveness of body and emotions suggests that Shakespeare would not have felt himself obligated, like Dryden, to equate character with the disembodied properties of constancy and equality. Desire for constancy is often the wish of Shakespeare's heroes, a hallmark of neo-Stoic behaviour that they aspire to but often fail to achieve. But constancy is desired because these heroes see themselves as vulnerable to passions having the power to transform or even dissolve them. Emotions were understood in the early modern period, as they are now, to be essential for survival – God-given equipment for producing the right responses of hate and love, fear and desire, fight or flight. But they were also thought, again as they often are now, to cloud the judgement, corrupt the will, and seduce the reason. The power accorded to the passions helps to explain why Stoicism, which advocated the suppression or transcendence of the passions altogether, was an important ethical counterforce in the period. As the English moral philosopher Thomas Wright explains, the passions are able to effect an almost metamorphic change in cognition, judgement, and behaviour:

> By this alteration which Passions work in the Wit and the Will we may understand the admirable Metamorphosis and change of a man from himself when his affects are pacified and when they are troubled; Plutarch said they changed them like Circe's potions, from men into beasts. Or we may compare the Soul without Passions to a calm Sea; with sweet, pleasant, and crispling streams; but the Passionate, to the raging Gulf swelling with waves, surging by tempests, menacing the stony rocks, and endeavouring to overthrow Mountains; even so Passions make the Soul to swell with pride and pleasure; they threaten wounds, death and destruction by audacious boldness and ire; they undermine the mountains of Virtue with hope and fear, and, in sum, never let the Soul be in quietness, but ever either flowing with Pleasure or ebbing with Pain.[9]

In Wright's account, passions are powerful forces whose role in the body is analogous to the role of weather in the natural order.[10] For the early moderns, believing strongly in a universe structured through analogy, such a correspondence was deeply meaningful. As the French philosopher Nicholas Coeffeteau explained, 'there were some which have believed that as there were four chief winds which excite divers storms, be it at land or sea; so there are four principal *Passions* which trouble our *Souls*, and which stir up divers tempests by their irregular motions'.[11] In a model of the human body expressing the cosmos, emotions cross the bodily interior as winds cross the earth. They are part of the material substance of a self continually moved and threatened with change by forces within and without the body.

Wright's vivid vocabulary here is easily applicable to Shakespeare's tragic protagonists. Wright describes a man as being 'himself' when his 'affects are pacified' and presumably under the control of his reason. Proper selfhood, then, involves reason, and reason helps to guarantee that self will be the same from one moment to the next. But the hyperbolic terms that Wright uses to describe the workings of the great passions – pride, pleasure, boldness, and ire – belong to the weather-tossed realm of tragic action. That tragic protagonists are souls moved by great passions is true almost by definition thanks to their position at the centre of worlds in crisis; their passions are oceanic as a matter of social scale no less than of immediate circumstances. Such figures do not avoid being changed by their great passions, but such change necessarily brings about change to others. This is true especially, as M. L. Lyon and J. M. Barbalet have shown, because 'emotion is best regarded not as an "inner thing" but as a "relational process" ' because 'emotion is not only embodied but [is] also essentially social in character'.[12] The social character of emotion is particularly true for the figures of Shakespearean tragedy. The passions of love and hatred, hope and fear, boldness and shame act like winds and tides within and upon the tragic hero because those passions are strong enough to cause changes of mood and disposition in his inward self and hence in his outward behaviour. But such emotions are relational because they cannot be understood by the tragic hero (or by us) apart from the particularized dramatic worlds in which they occur.

It is because of the emotions' transforming power that Shakespearean tragic heroes have to struggle so mightily to achieve self-control and the Stoic constancy that self-control helps to produce. Hamlet reserves a special praise for his neo-Stoic friend Horatio as one 'whose blood and judgement are so well commeddled, / That they are not a pipe for Fortune's finger / To sound what stop she please' (*Ham.* 3.2.59–61).[13] (Blood is metonymic here for emotion, the substance embodying the significance.)[14] In a corrupt kingdom such as Claudius's Denmark, the 'time' is politically 'out of joint' for Horatio just as for Hamlet because they are both subjects of the Danish state. Shakespeare signals this by having Horatio among the watch awaiting the Ghost and speculating about the political problems that have provoked its visitation. 'A mote it is to trouble the mind's eye', says Horatio calmly of the state's disorders (1.1.112). Because of his rationality and trustworthiness, it is Horatio whom Hamlet asks for help in interpreting Claudius's response to 'The Murder of Gonzago'. But Horatio is an onlooker of the tragic action. His constancy and rationality are easily attained – even in such troubled times. For Hamlet, such constancy signifies mostly as a behavioural ideal that he can only admire from a distance. Thus, if Horatio is an exemplar of Renaissance Stoicism, Hamlet himself stands as critique of Stoicism's political relevance and viability in a state founded on usurpation through murder. The passionlessness so admired by the Stoics does not serve as the springboard to action for a son obligated to feel and revenge his father's murder. For in this time out of joint, Hamlet knows himself 'born to set it right' (1.5.190); the son who bears the name of the father is the real target of the Ghost's midnight stalking and stern invocation to remember filial duty. After he has raged against her as representative woman in the nunnery scene, Ophelia bemoans his transformation from a self-possessed prince to a madman: 'O what a noble mind is here o'erthrown!' (3.1.144). But we as audience have not seen much evidence of the self-possession that she remembers as characteristic. Or we have seen it only in brief flashes – in the moments before Hamlet has learned to distrust his old friends Rosencrantz and Guildenstern, for example, or when he greets the visiting players. On the contrary, the disarray in Hamlet's clothing and appearance that Ophelia particularizes in her report to Polonius suggests the linkage thought to exist between inner turmoil and its socially visible manifestations. He was 'pale as his shirt, his knees knocking each other, / And with a look so piteous in purport / As if he had been loosèd out of hell / To speak of horrors' (2.1.79–82).

Because of the challenges entailed by his position, then, no less than of what an early modern audience might, like Ophelia, presume to be his innate nobleness, Hamlet sees himself with shame as Horatio's temperamental opposite – emotionally volatile, swinging wildly between melancholic lethargy and ineffectual rage. In Hamlet himself, this oscillation produces a self-portrait fuelled by contempt because control of one's emotions was a trait ostensibly belonging to the male elite and justifying their right to the mastery of others.[15] Loss of self-control threatens loss of social identity. Thus, in the bitter second soliloquy beginning 'O what a rogue and peasant slave am I!' Hamlet calls himself 'a dull and muddy-mettled rascal' (2.2.502, 519). The scornful phrasing represents the kind of abuse that would be directed from a high- to a low-born man. The descriptors link the rascal's sluggish and ineffectual disposition, his 'muddy' mettle, to his base birth. In such a one (in contrast to Horatio), blood and judgement are not equally co-meddled (or co-'mettled'). Thus Hamlet, perplexed by his continuing lethargy, berates himself for being one whose cognitive faculties are literally darkened (mud-died) and slowed by the workings of the melancholy humours bred of grief, lethargy, disappointment, misogyny, and thwarted ambition. His lack of pur-pose and inner strength – his lack of worthy 'mettle/metal' – is degrading for a king's son; hence it is a form of psychological servitude, transforming him from prince to 'rogue and peasant slave'.

In Hamlet, self-reproach expresses itself as the perception of mental and bodily defect – a cold and bloodless liver, a lack of bitter choleric humour: 'it cannot be / But that I am pigeon-livered, and lack gall / To make oppres-sion bitter' (2.2.529–30). Reasoning inductively from behaviour to the body, Hamlet rationalizes his lack of purposive activity, his seeming inability to rouse himself to a murderous revenge. In the depressed interaction between a grief-laden, 'muddy' mind and a body physiologically unproductive of the heat and blood required for action against the usurper–king, Hamlet finds a diagnosis, though not an excuse, for his inconstancy. Given what Hamlet sees as his reasons for failing to exact revenge, it is not surprising that his efforts to change himself and his situation take the indirect form of putting on a play. The depressed prince requires the mimetic actions of others – professional players uninvolved in the political crisis and merely eager for patronage – to stimulate himself and Claudius into direct confrontation. (And, even then, direct confrontation does not happen until the final moments of the play when Hamlet is already dying from the poison received at the tip of Laertes's poisoned foil.)

When, after startling Claudius into a display of guilt and alarm during 'The Murder of Gonzago', Hamlet begins to feel instilled with purpose, he perceives his momentary sense of triumph as a transformation in bodily self-experience, in temperature, and in emotional appetite: 'Now could I drink hot blood, / And do such bitter business as the day / Would quake to look on' (3.2.390–1). Perhaps some of this new energy prompts the stab through the arras that kills Polonius in the closet scene. But Hamlet's sense of purpose and motive carried within the body remains unsteady and tentative, as when he implores the Ghost not to look reproachfully at him,

> Lest with this piteous action you convert
> My stern effects. Then what I have to do
> Will want true colour: tears perchance for blood.
>
> (3.4.127–29)

It is as if the energy – the blood – required to stab Polonius has been ex-pended with the deed, leaving Hamlet still open to the Ghost's rebukes about his 'almost blunted purpose' (3.4.110). Yet, even in this volatile scene, it is always self-assessment of his bodily state that Hamlet relies on to express his emotions. Here, having impulsively committed murder, raged against his mother's choice of husbands, and spoken imploringly to a paternal ghost invisible to Gertrude, Hamlet nevertheless seeks to reassure his alarmed mother of his overall sanity. He compares the regular, even harmonious movement of his body's blood-flow to hers: 'My pulse as yours doth temperately keep time, / And makes as healthful music. It is not madness / That I have uttered' (3.4.141–3). And Hamlet is not alone, of course, in seeking bodily expression for the emotions. His wild, inconstant behaviour produces the symptoms – metaphoric and literal both – of hot bodily diseases in others: 'Do it England', Claudius exclaims in apostrophe after sending Hamlet off to execution abroad, 'For like the hectic in my blood he rages, / And thou must cure me' (4.3.61–3). Here, too, emotions are represented as both embodied and relational – even contagious – in nature.

Though Hamlet may be among the most volatile of Shakespeare's tragic heroes, others too demonstrate the materiality of early modern selfhood in verbal representations of their inward experience. Othello, convinced of Desdemona's infidelity, feels suddenly incapable of participating in any of the martial actions that formerly defined his place in the world:

> Farewell the neighing steed and the shrill trump,
> The spirit-stirring drum, th'ear-piercing fife,
> The royal banner, and all quality,
> Pride, pomp, and circumstance of glorious war!
> ... Farewell! Othello's occupation's gone
>
> (3.3.352–8)

His transformation from soldierly calm to jealous anxiety renders him unfit in his own eyes for military command of warfare. Later, resolved upon murder, he imagines all the afflictions he could have borne with constancy – sores and shames, total poverty, imprisonment, even scorn – all the afflictions, that is, other than the idea, graphically brought to him by Iago's images of Desdemona 'topp'd', of his wife's infidelity. He comes to feel that the decay of his love for Desdemona and his sense of her moral corruption are stored in the great receptacle of affections that is his heart.[16] Such an agonized self-perception renders him psychologically alienated from his own bodily substance, the substance in which his love for Desdemona was stored. His relation to himself is no longer a properly self-possessed interior 'here' but an alienated elsewhere, a 'there':

> But there where I have garnered up my heart,
> Where either I must live or bear no life,
> The fountain from the which my current runs

Or else dries up – to be discarded thence
Or keep it as a cistern for foul toads
To knot and gender in!   (4.2.56–61).

His sense of bodily foulness in this passage is a strong version of Hamlet's self-contempt as 'muddy-mettled rascal'. It follows logically from a grief and jealousy so strong that their workings have rendered the once-eloquent Othello wildly inarticulate, shouting to the bewildered Venetian visitor, 'You are welcome, sir, to Cyprus. Goats and monkeys!' (4.1.254). In the moments before her murder, Desdemona is alarmed to see the self-possessed man she had married gnawing his 'nether lip' and shaking with 'bloody passion' (5.2.43–4). In this circular logic, Othello's passion is 'bloody' because it is a violent one; and it is a violent one because jealous rage has literally heated his heart's blood, darkened and polluted his spirits, and readied him to prompt such a violent deed as murdering his new wife.

Indeed it is precisely the early modern belief in the continual interaction between emotions and the body that validates Iago's description of his plot against Othello as a poisoning. From this point of view, Othello's acceptance of Iago's insinuations against Desdemona is ingestion, a bodily incorporation of powerfully aversive words and images. They move from the ear to the mind to the rest of his body and work to change him, emotionally and physically. Spoken words, while not material entities themselves, were thought to produce material changes in the mind – and hence in the self that receives them. But the changes in Othello's emotions, cognition, and behaviour were transported by blood. 'The Moor already changes with my poison', Iago remarks:

Dangerous conceits are in their natures poisons,
Which at the first are scarce found to distaste
But, with a little act upon the blood,
Burn like the mines of sulphur.   (3.3.327–30)

Given the effect of such a poisoning on Othello's embodied self – the sulphurous burning of his blood, the agitation of his spirits – it is not surprising that loss of consciousness would mark one of the first stages of Othello's psychological journey from contented new husband to wife-murderer. 'Work on, / My medicine, work!' Iago gloats (4.1.42–3), having added to the poisonous effect of verbal images on Othello the psychological impress of the lost handkerchief, an image of the object whose loss and misunderstood recovery is also material to Othello's transformation by passion.

It would be reductive to read Shakespeare's tragic protagonists merely in terms of a struggle between reason and passion, as some early critics have done.[17] But this struggle did in fact preoccupy the moral philosophers of early modern Europe and helped to set the terms for their understanding of human choice and agency.[18] Wright, one of the most influential of such philosophers in England (at least to judge by the success and later editions of his 1604 *Passions of the Mind in General*), describes passions, in league with the senses, engaged in a continual struggle against rational self-government. Most men, says Wright, 'feeling this war so mighty, so continual, so near, so domestical that either they must consent to do their enemy's will, or still be in conflict resolve never to displease their sense or passions, but to grant them whatsoever they demand'.[19] But, as we have seen with Hamlet, tragic heroes are set apart from the ordinary run of men – by dint of hereditary rank, accomplishment, life experience, strength, bravery, ruthlessness, or some combination of these. The tragic hero's exceptionality is a dramatic given so that it may be tested, that it may fail, that it may triumph, that it may inspire in us such self-dissolving and self-forgetting emotions as admiration, pity, or even (as with heroes such as Macbeth, Antony, Coriolanus, or Timon of Athens) complex mixtures of contradictory emotions. Such figures are set apart further by the suffering reserved for them. The reasoning here sounds and is circular, if tragic actions, by definition, represent the extraordinary life circumstances of exceptional figures whose obligation to be self-controlled and whose capacity to act and suffer is accepted as greater than that of ordinary people. And the reasoning is notoriously masculinist as well, in that it tends to exclude women as historically significant agents in tragic actions, with rare exceptions (Shakespeare's Cleopatra being one, John Webster's Duchess of Malfi being another). Classic tragedy asks the ordinary men and women in a theatre audience to ratify this social selectivity and gender exclusion even as it requires them to identify with the tragic hero and feel the tragic emotions of pity and fear at his downfall.

In these tragic male protagonists, the struggle between reason and passion takes on a representative or exemplary character. In *Antony and Cleopatra* Caesar remembers the young Antony as a model of Stoic constancy and physical endurance:

> Thou didst drink
> The stale of horses and the gilded puddle
> Which beasts would cough at. Thy palate then did deign
> The roughest berry on the rudest hedge . . .
> . . . all this
> – It wounds thine honour that I speak it now –
> Was borne so like a soldier that thy cheek
> So much as lanked not.   (1.4.62–72)

The young Antony conquered physical appetite, according to this memorial narrative, by an act of will that put bodily need in service to the long-range goals of the Roman state with which he identified. His was a triumph of self-control, here over an aversion so profound that it was shared, Caesar asserts, by animals and men alike. Such Stoicism differs from the more ordinary brand of passionlessness that Hamlet praises in Horatio as almost a gift of nature because Antony's is achieved, is precisely *not* natural.[20] In such an attained self-control Caesar recognizes the mark of personal greatness and exceptional masculinity – here given military modelling ('borne so like a soldier'). Self-control earned the younger Antony his reputation ('honour') and justified his control over others.

What matters desperately now for Caesar, given what the Romans diagnose as Antony's anti-Stoic pursuit of pleasure with Cleopatra, is that their long-standing psychic and cultural investment in him as the exemplar of human dignity has come into question. For Caesar, Antony's affair with Cleopatra signifies an immersion in the present moment and irrational surrender to the demands of the body. John Gillies argues that 'at the simplest level, Egypt attacks Antony through his senses' while 'at another level, Antony's judgment is bewitched' by Cleopatra herself.[21] To accept Renaissance psychology in its own terms, however, means that we can understand these two 'levels' functioning as one – the sensory transformation in Antony's physical and emotional environment overwhelming his once-rational control and effecting profound changes in his behaviour and his response to the world. His immersion in temporality, too, represents a form of inconstancy, a trait synonymous with woman and justifying women's exclusion from historical process. It is only logical, then, that Caesar finds Antony hopelessly – perhaps irrevocably – feminized: he 'fishes, drinks, and wastes / The lamps of night in revel'. By doing so, he 'is not more manlike / Than Cleopatra, nor the queen of Ptolemy / More womanly than he'. He is 'the abstract of all faults / That all men follow' (1.4.5–7, 9–10), a man regressing into the ungendered state of boys who, 'being mature in knowledge, / Pawn their experience to their present pleasure / And so rebel to judgement' (1.4.31–3). His affair with Cleopatra thus threatens to destabilize the great organizing binaries (here represented by the difference of male and female, man and boy) by which Rome knows its dominant place in the world.

Much in the imagery and action of *Antony and Cleopatra* resists the disparaging reading of the lovers' story that Rome finds it necessary to promulgate. The play's triumphant representation of the Egyptian queen's 'infinite variety' which 'age cannot wither', 'nor custom stale' (2.2.245–6) serves to question Rome's reductive binarisms of West–East, male–female, reason–passion, discipline–pleasure, constancy–inconstancy. Convinced of her lover's personal greatness and her own, wilfully defiant of Roman behavioural codes, Cleopatra exempts him from any obligation to Stoic impassivity. For her, immersion in pleasure and present time is a privilege granted to those who rule, a sign not of ignoble subjection but of the scope of their command of others, even of the natural world. She differs powerfully from Caesar in regarding emotional display in Antony as in effect validated by his greatness, not destructive of it: 'Be'st thou sad or merry', she says to him in affectionate apostrophe, 'The violence of either thee becomes,/So does it no man else' (1.5.62–4). It is nevertheless true that Antony's oscillation between service to Rome and allegiance to Cleopatra works like an oscillation between incompatible identities that are produced behaviourally in response to the demands and values of others.[22] As Linda Charnes has argued, 'the real battle in this play, then – that between Caesar and Cleopatra – is staked out across the terrain of Antony's "identity": the set of representations, images, and narratives he needs to recognize himself as "Antony"'. She adds, 'Both Octavius and Cleopatra understand how susceptible Antony is to attacks on his "manhood".'[23] This is why Cleopatra can try to shame him by interpreting his emotions as reactions to Rome: 'As I am Egypt's queen,/Thou blushest, Antony, and that blood of thine/Is Caesar's homager' (1.1.31–3). After his and Cleopatra's final defeat by Caesar's legions and having been told erroneously that Cleopatra has killed herself rather than surrender to Caesar, Antony feels suddenly lost and insubstantial, as if his body were dissolving into air. He asks his boy Eros a question which sounds not at all rhetorical: 'Eros, thou yet behold'st me?' (4.14.1). He goes on to express the sensation of self-dissolution and loss of personal boundaries in a comparison of his bodily self to the clouds. Asking Eros to think about the motions of clouds changing from 'bear or lion,/A towered citadel, a pendent rock' (4.1.3–4), Antony comments:

> That which is now a horse, even with a thought
> The rack dislimns and makes it indistinct
> As water is in water.
> . . .
> My good knave Eros, now thy captain is
> Even such a body. Here I am Antony,
> Yet cannot hold this visible shape
>
> (4.14.9–14)

This speech is usually valued for its pathos and eloquence as Antony faces the shame of loss and the challenge of suicide. Yet this speech is also – perhaps paradoxically – a good example of the early modern self's sense of its physicality and embeddedness in the natural world. Antony's dis-identification with his body comes through a contrasting identification with the clouds. The shaming comparison of himself to clouds tells us that he has lost the capacity for the sustained, self-same, willed action synonymous with heroic masculinity, becoming as inconstant in his motions as they are. The clouds are Antony's body dissolving, his self-sameness melting away: 'black vesper's pageants', they betoken death imagined as vanishing into insubstantiality (4.14.8).

Yet the speech is equally extraordinary for what it represents as the agency *within* natural forces even as those forces – represented by clouds – symbolize Antony's loss of agency and of sustainable identification with a fixed bodily self. This paradox becomes clear in the degree of almost purposive power that Antony's verbs – 'dislimns', 'makes' – give to the clouds themselves. In them, continual self-obliteration is also continual refashioning; the clouds *make* their indistinction as an expression of their essential nature. The clouds mirror the continual remaking – 'even with a thought' – of embodied consciousness but in a way that mocks – even as it expresses – the self's longing for fixity. For Antony comes to realize that identity requires what the clouds do not – the 'firmness of identity provided by unwavering allegiance to a particular place'.[24]

We too may feel such evocative reciprocity between clouds and embodied consciousness to be problematic here as Antony seeks to reassure the boy Eros (and himself) that he retains faculties of personal agency. But his more powerful sense of self-loss and insubstantiality makes his capacity for self-murder questionable. Only when Eros summons his own will and kills himself rather than hold the sword for Antony is Antony able to take such 'brave instruction' (4.14.98). Even then, he bungles the job and ends up a living dead-weight, becoming so firmly identified with his body that he needs to be hoisted clumsily by Cleopatra and her women up into the monument in order to die there. As Cynthia Marshall suggests, 'wounded, bleeding, and lacking agency, Antony takes on a typically feminine position [and] ... troubles an audience's notions of what it means to be a (masculine) hero'.[25]

Rather than being sovereign (hence incorporeal) selves, then, we need to see Shakespeare's tragic heroes as beings in whom psychology and physiology have yet to be pried apart conceptually. Their behaviours express a physical, emotional, and psychological embeddedness in fictive worlds structured and made meaningful by correspondence between inner and outer, body and cosmos, emotions and weather. We need to define those worlds broadly enough so that we can place the natural as well as the cultural and social dimensions of those worlds in a historical frame. Once we have done so, then the intentions of the materialized self may be mirrored by such objects in the landscape as Othello's befouled cisterns or Antony's clouds in motion. In these more precise terms, the 'inwardness' of a Shakespearean tragic hero is neither an internal psychological space hollowed out by language nor merely a function of rhetoric, but a collection of the embodied faculties, capacities, intentions, and passions that together constitute individual agency. What we should expect, then, from such a reconstituted notion of tragic selfhood is not disembodied constancy and equality of manners, in Dryden's terms, nor even the unified selfhood so dear to humanistic thought, but a self in which continuousness of psychological identity is put under severe stress by psychological and physiological openness to a complex and painful environment.

By using the terms of Renaissance behavioural thought to reconceptualize the tragic self as a permeable and hence changeable one, we are able to see Shakespeare's tragic heroes moved, and even transformed, by passions understood as 'psycho-physiological' events embedded in an environment both natural and cultural. Self is not a condition of disembodied inwardness independent of the material world that it inhabits. Self is rather inhabited reciprocally by that world, shaped by its elements.[26] In the extreme cultural environments of Shakespeare's tragedies, such permeation can lead to radical displacements of agency and interiority, rendering the self nearly unrecognizable as the site of ordinary emotions, desires, and motivations.

In *Titus Andronicus*, for example, it is Titus's role at the beginning of the play to represent a mythically exaggerated version of Roman imperial will. Phallically potent, Stoic, sacrificially public-spirited, Titus is first presented to us less as an interiorized self than as the stern embodiment of Roman militarism, an allegory of iron will. His merit, he announces to the public assembled for his return, consists of forty years of military service and the fathering of twenty-five sons, all but four of whom have died in battle. When Titus greets the opened family tomb as 'sacred receptàcle of my joys, / Sweet cell of virtue and nobility' (1.1.92–3), Titus's hailing of the tomb functions to ratify Rome's successful ideological 'hailing' of him: he is the faithful scion and arm of the state, his past and future identity equated with the city's. The link between rule of others and rule of self, so key to the action in *Hamlet*, *Othello*, and *Antony and Cleopatra*, is here established in mythic terms, rather than psychological or even social ones, because it is linked to a sequence of events which lead to Titus's fatally illogical renunciation of the crown. Rome turns to Titus to 'help to set a head on headless Rome' (1.1.186). When Titus refuses to take up the imperial crown on the manifestly weak grounds that 'a better head her glorious body fits / Than his that shakes for age and feebleness' (1.1.187–8), he is setting aside the logic of his own identity and imperilling that of the civil body from which his own earliest experience of self and masculine agency arose.

It has not been usual among critics to see Titus's abdication here as an abdication of reason, a surrender to passion. Yet it may be productive to do so, because Titus's renunciation of patriarchal duty is like a renunciation of the will. His refusal of the crown not only signifies a slackening of his lifelong vigilance as guarantor of Rome's physical and moral wholeness but also leads directly to the dismemberments visited first upon Lavinia and Titus and then, in the boomerang logic of revenge tragedy, on the bodies of the surviving Gothic brothers. Katherine Rowe has suggested that 'Titus's actions in the opening scene make him as dangerous and unfit as Saturninus.'[27] Certainly, it is as an embodiment of overweening will that Titus himself initiates the play's cycle of dismemberment and revenge that will lead to his family's downfall and suffering. The play's action suggests that Titus has been too severe in his execution of military authority, much too rigid a guardian of Rome's boundaries. He mercilessly insists upon the ritual sacrifice of a Gothic prince, whose 'limbs are lopped, / And entrails feed the sacrificing fire' (1.1.143–4) as payment for his sons' lives. This insistence, so early in the play, has the effect of reconfiguring Titus's Stoic self-control as a species of primitive vengefulness, a displacement of the pain he has endured on to those held responsible for it. In the predatory calculus of this tragedy, it is as if Titus had decided that integrity of self (construed to include Rome's corporate body no less than his own and that of his family) could only be guaranteed by a dismemberment of others rationalized as Roman piety. This may be why he refuses to accept any principle of equivalence between the public service of Roman and of Gothic warriors even though the Gothic queen Tamora argues powerfully for one:

> But must my sons be slaughtered in the streets
> For valiant doings in their country's cause?
> O if to fight for king and commonweal
> Were piety in thine, it is in these
>
> (1.1.112–15)

For John Gillies, Titus commits a gross disregard of what Elizabethans might have regarded as 'natural piety'.[28] Titus's failure to recognize the possibility of heroic agency in the Other and decision to locate it solely in himself and by biological extension in his family leads directly to the vengeful acts of the Gothic princes – their rape and mutilation of Lavinia, the murder of her husband Bassianus, and the execution of two of Titus's sons. In Titus's self-interested figuration, the suffering Andronici remain human while their enemies render themselves bestial. He describes the city for which the Andronici have fought so stoically as a beast-infested wilderness lacking the traces of human ordering: 'Rome is but a wilderness of tigers? / Tigers must prey, and Rome affords no prey / But me and mine' (3.1.54–6). But for Titus to see himself and his family, the tiger's prey, as victims in these naturalized terms is effectively to de-politicize the meaning of his suffering – hence that part of his own complex responsibility for it. If Rome is a wilderness, he has helped to make it so – by denying the reality of Tamora's maternal suffering, by sacrificing her children for his own, by murdering his defiant son Mutius ('What, villain boy, / Barr'st me my way in Rome?' (1.1.290–1)), by choosing Saturninus over Bassianus as new emperor of Rome, and by allowing the stranger queen Tamora through marriage to be 'incorporate in Rome' (1.1.462). Though, as Douglas Green has argued, the play tries to deflect its criticism of Titus through exaggeration of the evil represented by Tamora and her male entourage, Titus's extreme wilfulness as patriarch, soldier, and elector is hard to overlook given the magnitude of the horrors that it inspires.[29]

The extremes of his subsequent suffering (passion in its literal sense from the Latin verb 'patior', to suffer, to endure) take Titus into an altered cognitive state, into a form of madness. Here too, as we have seen before in Othello, the body's sufferings work changes in the mind. Reality appears nightmarish – a 'fearful slumber' (3.1.251) – and Titus's own responses to it become wildly inappropriate. 'Why dost thou laugh?' his brother Marcus asks in bewilderment as Titus reacts with 'Ha, ha, ha!' to the soldiers' presentation of the executed heads of his sons (3.1.265, 264). He gives way to the passion of revenge in spectacular fashion – feeding the Gothic queen Tamora a dish baked from the heads of her sons. But to do so, we soon realize, is to become a mirror version of his enemies and to collapse the binaries of Roman–Goth, human–bestial, pious–vengeful that constitute the play's symbolic vocabulary. It also suggests that extreme suffering collapses the overwhelmed self back into its mutely expressive environment. This is what Titus seems to recognize in describing the handless, tongueless Lavinia as a 'map of woe' (3.2.12) who 'drinks no other drink but tears, / Brewed with her sorrow, mashed upon her cheek' (3.2.37–8).

As Elaine Scarry has suggested of the practice of torture, the reduction of the suffering body only to its experience and recognition of extreme pain entails an unmaking of the world. In political torture, the interactivity that constitutes normative social intercourse is radically dislocated. Agency devolves wholly to the torturer, suffering wholly to his victim. For the tortured, the basic faculties of self-articulation are lost to pain and dread; social identity as constituted by loyalties to others becomes an axis of extreme vulnerability; and identification with one's own body as anything other than the location of pain is no longer possible.[30] Given his partisan account of suffering as the exclusive property of the Andronici, Titus could not recognize himself as torturer, only as the tortured. Yet what he and all his enemies share is a grotesque affirmation of hypertrophied will as the locus of agency, and of suffering as the locus of bodily self-experience. Lavinia begs Tamora to be killed rather than raped by her sons. The bodily punishments they do inflict on her – rape and the mutilation of her tongue and hands – constitute a display of agency on their part as merely killing her could not. Their power is not merely over her body or even her will to resist, but over the male relatives entrusted with a personal and social obligation to protect her. As Green comments, Lavinia's 'mutilated body "articulates" Titus's own suffering and victimization'; she becomes the mirror in which he sees and thus remakes self.[31] For Titus and Lavinia, pain and mutilation institute an unmaking of the world which they counter with a mirror unmaking – tricking their enemies into their own undoing. For Lavinia does not, in the end, display merely the agential power of her father's enemies nor serve as eloquently mute symbol of her family's passion in suffering. By finally communicating the story of her rape and its perpetrators, by carrying her father's severed hand offstage in her mouth, even perhaps by being wilfully murdered by Titus himself at the end of the play, Lavinia signals a resumption of agency both for herself and her father – though on terms a modern audience finds difficult to countenance or understand except as a tragic action parodying its own tendency towards excess. What Lavinia and her father concoct – literally – is a cannibal feast which they describe to their victims just before killing them: 'Hark, villains', Titus tells Chiron and Demetrius with unmistakable glee, 'I will grind your bones to dust, / And with your blood and it I'll make a paste' (5.2.186–7). He insists not only on Tamora consuming her own flesh and blood, but being made to know it before she too is killed. If Shakespeare makes it almost impossible for us to sympathize with Tamora, he also lets us see her undergo, in horror, the climactic unmaking of *her* world.

The mutilations visited upon the bodies of the Andronici and the cannibal savagery that Titus's family visits upon the family of Tamora enact a grotesque version of the dissolution of the body which figures Antony's self-loss in the mirroring clouds in *Antony and Cleopatra*. In both tragedies, however, and indeed in all the tragedies discussed in this chapter, the experience of self entails identification with a suffering body at a moment in intellectual history when bodies were open and porous, when bodily substances were thought to be psychologically both formative and expressive, when fluids could express the full weight of a character's destiny. What I have sought to emphasize here is the materiality of embodied consciousness in Shakespeare's tragic heroes – a condition not peculiar to them of course but peculiarly significant in them as the central representatives of subjectivity in their plays. In this sense, my neglect of the representation of female subjectivity in these plays is almost more inevitable than accidental, for the masculinist bias in all these tragedies – not excepting *Antony and Cleopatra* – presupposes the centrality as well as the representativeness of the embodied consciousnesses of the male protagonists. (To recognize this is not, of course, to agree with it.) Finally, to recognize the embodiment of consciousness matters in Shakespeare's tragedies because a prior generation of critics and the many students who still read such criticism today have tended to see the 'tragic self' in transhistorical and essentialist terms. What this chapter has sought to demonstrate instead is the importance of understanding the dramatic construction of self historically, in a period before psychology and physiology had divided conceptually. The representation of subjectivity in Shakespeare's tragedies represents a way of thinking about inwardness in many ways fundamentally different from our own.

NOTES

1. John Dryden, 'The Grounds of Criticism in Tragedy', in *Troilus and Cressida, or Truth Found Too Late, A Tragedy*, in Dryden, *The Dramatic Works*, ed. Montague Summers, 6 vols. (London: Nonesuch Press, 1932), V. 19.
2. For a cogent presentation of this position, see Catherine Belsey, *The Subject of Tragedy: Identity and Difference in Renaissance Drama* (London and New York: Routledge, 1985), pp. 33–42.
3. *Discourse on Method* in *Philosophical Writings of Descartes*, 4 vols., trans. John Cottingham, Robert Stoothoff and Dugald Murdoch (Cambridge University Press, 1985), I. 127.
4. Dryden does not use 'psychology' because it had not yet come into general usage. The *OED* records the first use in 1653 in William Harvey's *Anatomical Exercises*, in which Harvey describes psychology 'as a doctrine which searches out mans Soul, and the effects of it' (sig. H8v).
5. Katharine Eisaman Maus, *Inwardness and Theater in the English Renaissance* (Chicago and London: University of Chicago Press, 1995), p. 12.
6. Maus, *Inwardness and Theater*, p. 195.
7. David Hillman, 'Visceral Knowledge: Shakespeare, Skepticism, and the Interior of the Early Modern Body', in *The Body in Parts: Fantasies of Corporeality in Early Modern England*, ed. David Hillman and Carla Mazzio (New York and London: Routledge, 1997), p. 91.
8. Katharine Park, 'The Organic Soul', in *The Cambridge History of Renaissance Philosophy*, gen. ed. Charles B. Schmitt (Cambridge University Press, 1988), p. 469.
9. Thomas Wright, *The Passions of the Mind in General*, ed. William Webster Newbold (New York: Garland, 1986), pp. 133–4.
10. See Andrew Wear, 'Medicine in Early Modern Europe', in *The Western Medical Tradition 800 BC to 1800 AD*, ed. Lawrence I. Conrad *et al.* (Cambridge University Press, 1995), pp. 255–64.

11. See Nicholas Coeffeteau, *A Table of Humane Passions*, trans. Edward Grimeston (London: 1621), p. 31.
12. M. L. Lyon and J. M. Barbalet, 'Society's Body: Emotion and the "Somatization" of Social Theory', in *Experience and Embodiment: The Existential Ground of Culture and Self*, ed. Thomas J. Csordas (Cambridge University Press, 1994), p. 57.
13. Michael C. Schoenfeldt, *Bodies and Selves in Early Modern England: Physiology and Inwardness in Spenser, Shakespeare, Herbert, and Milton* (Cambridge University Press, 1999), pp. 15–17.
14. This phrase borrows from Charles Taylor, *Sources of the Self: The Making of the Modern Identity* (Cambridge, MA: Harvard University Press, 1989), p. 189.
15. Schoenfeldt, *Bodies and Selves*, pp. 90–1.
16. On the heart as receptacle of feelings, see Robert A. Erickson, *The Language of the Heart, 1600–1750* (Philadelphia: University of Pennsylvania Press, 1997), pp. 11–15.
17. Lily Bess Campbell, *Shakespeare's Tragic Heroes: Slaves of Passion* (Cambridge University Press, 1930).
18. See Susan James, *Passion and Action: The Emotions in Seventeenth-Century Philosophy* (New York: Oxford University Press, 1997).
19. Wright, *Passions of the Mind in General*, p. 96.
20. John Gillies suggests that Shakespeare has several models besides Plutarch for Antony's Stoic control here, 'any number of literary journeys in which Stoic virtue is measured against exotic perils'. See *Shakespeare and the Geography of Difference* (Cambridge University Press, 1994), p. 118.
21. Ibid., p. 119.
22. As Cynthia Marshall has written, 'Antony is always someone else's version of Antony, never himself.' See 'Man of Steel Done Got the Blues: Melancholic Subversion of Presence in *Antony and Cleopatra*', *Shakespeare Quarterly* 44 (1993), 387.
23. Linda Charnes, *Notorious Identity: Materializing the Subject in Shakespeare* (Cambridge, MA: Harvard University Press, 1993), p. 112.
24. Charnes, *Notorious Identity*, p. 113.
25. Marshall, 'Man of Steel Done Got the Blues', 403.
26. See my 'The Body and Its Passions', in 'Forum: Body Work', ed. Bruce R. Smith, forthcoming in *Shakespeare Studies*.
27. Katherine A. Rowe, *Dead Hands: Fictions of Agency, Renaissance to Modern* (Stanford University Press, 1999), p. 77.
28. Gillies, *Shakespeare and the Geography of Difference*, p. 104.
29. Douglas E. Green, 'Interpreting "Her Martyr'd Signs": Gender and Tragedy in *Titus Andronicus*', *Shakespeare Quarterly* 40 (1989), 321–2.
30. Elaine Scarry, *The Body in Pain: The Making and Unmaking of the World* (New York: Oxford University Press, 1987).
31. Green, 'Interpreting "Her Martyr'd Signs" ', 322.

9

ROBERT N. WATSON

Tragedies of revenge and ambition

Revenge and ambition, past and present

Revenge and ambition had meanings in Shakespeare's world significantly different from what they mean now. Yet we can still easily recognize them in Shakespeare's plays, allowing us both an emotional connection to the human past, and an intellectual perspective on it.

Shakespeare's brilliant contemporary, Francis Bacon, called revenge 'a kind of wild justice',[1] and it must have been an important supplement to official justice in an era of very limited police powers and severely enforced social hierarchy. The Tudor monarchies made some progress in controlling lawlessness, but there must have been some basis for the persistent jokes about incompetent constables and watches in Elizabethan comedy. With so many crimes unsolved, so many criminals immune to punishment, and so many outrages (against women, the poor, and ethnic and religious minorities) not even considered crimes, it is hardly surprising that the public developed an appetite for revenge stories. A prime example is Thomas Kyd's *The Spanish Tragedy* (1587?), which showed Hieronimo cleverly feigning madness in order to uncover and punish the secret murder of his son by his social superiors. The huge commercial success of that story led to Shakespeare's *Hamlet* and dozens of other revenge plays in the period.

Ambition, too, was a particularly alluring and dangerous sin in Shakespeare's society, where radical economic, technological, and theological changes had unsettled people from hereditary roles that dated back to medieval feudalism. For the many who migrated to urban centres, there was neither a safety-net to prevent starvation nor a glass ceiling to prevent social climbing – only a scramble for money, status, and favours from the powerful. While the subtle refashioning of inward identity provoked soliloquies, the rapid refashioning of outward identity provoked civil authorities – desperate to preserve traditional order – to punish upstarts and innovators (even high-ranking ones such as Essex and Norfolk). The conservative tendency of

160

human culture must have been similarly punitive, in less official but more pervasive ways: in unsettled times, people reflexively conspire to ridicule new styles and penalize opportunists, and Elizabethan and Jacobean comedies (especially those of Ben Jonson) showed people doing so. Furthermore, in a society where status was so unstable, ambition often led to violent revenge, as duels over honour became an epidemic among the aristocratic elite.

In a broader sense, this period seems to have invented a new and inexhaustible kind of ambition – and defined it as fundamental to human nature. Against a classical and medieval notion of desire as finite, seeking its own end in satisfaction, Renaissance culture came to advocate a Romantic and modern notion of desire as an infinite regress, willing to invent further goals in order perpetually to forestall its own demise in stasis.[2] Christopher Marlowe's great overreachers, such as Tamburlaine and Faustus, explored the tragic implications of this discrepancy between what the aspiring mind could imagine and what the mortal body could accomplish. A similarly relentless desire propels Shakespeare's Macbeth into crime after crime, tomorrow and tomorrow, and unfulfilled into death.

Yet, important as understanding the immediate social and philosophical context may be, Shakespeare's tragedies of revenge and ambition have applications and resonances far beyond the historical circumstances of his culture. Impulses like the ones fuelling these tragedies are visible from the earliest recorded human histories to the most recent. Indeed, these impulses are easily visible in many non-human animals, as they punish those who have hurt or insulted them, and compete for dominance over the others of their species and gender. If it waddles and quacks like a vengeful or ambitious duck, perhaps it *is* a vengeful or ambitious duck. While much can be learned about Shakespeare's tragedies by learning the history of Shakespeare's society, and vice versa, these plays seem almost supernaturally capable of speaking to issues that transcend local circumstances and reach to fundamental questions of life, and of death. Neither the partisans of essentialism (the idea that there are universal truths and categories immune to cultural difference) nor those of constructivism (the idea that all human reality is produced by local ideological conditions) allow Shakespeare's tragedies their full stature and intricacy.

Unlike even the best of the other tragedians of revenge and ambition in this period – from the strong Elizabethan roots in Marlowe to the decaying Jacobean blossoms in John Webster – Shakespeare looks inside not only the psychological workings of his characters, but also the transactional complexities of revenge and ambition as moral problems. He offers, not merely the grand cautionary spectacle of falling greatness, not merely the gruesome cautionary spectacle of escalating vengeance, but insight into the ways different human individuals shape, and are shaped by, some fundamental impulses. By staging human stories, Shakespeare can provide an indispensable acknowledgement of moral complexity, and thereby a means of understanding and forgiving, that law itself cannot provide, and that not even such subtle and powerful philosophers as Kant (with his detailed argument for making punishments fit crimes) and Hegel (with his abstract argument for punishment as negating a negation of the moral order) have been able to generate.

Shakespeare's philosophy of revenge and ambition

Characteristically, Shakespeare's observation of human behaviour enables him to trace patterns for which science would provide a rationale and a vocabulary centuries later. Shakespeare watches politics so closely that he can also see the evolutionary biology which drives it. He can therefore answer a question that troubles readers of history, not just of history plays: what is so desirable about becoming king that it explains a man's willingness to destroy the peace of both his land and his mind in order to achieve it? This is a theological question as well as a political and psychological one: 'What is a man profited, if he shall gain the whole world, and lose his own soul?' (Matthew 16:26). In the case of Macbeth, the implicit answer lies in an innate craving for dominion and progeny that the ambitious man himself cannot fully understand, that drives him even against his own better reason – perhaps because his genes (as modern science would explain it) are designed to replicate themselves, indifferent to the self-interest of the transient creatures they build to serve their own appetite for survival and reproduction.[3] The irony is that Macbeth, in pursuing that goal so desperately, in a selfishly mechanical rather than co-operatively humane way, destroys his own chances for a place in the human future. Seemingly driven by instincts from an evolutionary phase when only the dominant male had reproductive privileges, reading both Scottish history and the survival of the fittest too crudely, in too narrow a sense, Macbeth overlooks the complex, collective aspect of species survival.

No less characteristically, Shakespeare takes very ordinary human situations and human impulses, magnifies them to the highest dramatic scale, looks for their deepest implications, and offers no simple moral. The plays reflect a persistent myth of ambition, a myth that entails a tragic paradox. The desire to transcend oneself, to become something greater than one was born to be, is a natural and seemingly noble human tendency; yet it becomes a means of self-destruction, a betrayal of nature and origins that invites primal punishment. Even where – as for Leontes in *The Winter's Tale* – the aspirations (towards purity and timelessness) are noble, and some of the resulting losses miraculously repaid, the tragic potential of ambition and the vengeful potential of nature remain painfully obvious.

One version of Shakespeare's philosophical myth looks pragmatic and political: his history plays insist that anyone who takes the throne without inheriting it will always be vulnerable to new usurpers, and will have trouble passing it on to his own offspring, but can never safely relinquish that throne, either. Another, parallel version of this myth seems Freudian (which is not really an anachronism, since Sigmund Freud derived it from reading classical and Shakespearean tragedy): as the psychoanalytic theories about oedipal complexes and castration anxiety would suggest, the son attempts to outdo the father, perhaps attempts (like Coriolanus) to reconceive and recreate himself through a symbolic courtship of a maternal figure. Ambition takes the form of a desire to be reborn in some chosen ideal form, autonomous and powerful, unlimited by inherited identity or social taboo. The father (or some trace of him) punishes the son, specifically by destroying (a kind of castration) the son's procreative powers. Shakespeare's ambitious men rarely succeed in generating heirs, perhaps as a poetically just punishment for disdaining the condition of their own births; and they exist in a perpetual state of anxiety and self-alienation, able neither to make their achieved identity perfect and permanent, nor to retreat safely back to their humbler natural condition. The effort to expand the self often ends up dividing it.

Beyond these frustrating reactions of the political and psychological systems, there remains the fact that changes made by force of individual human will and action do not stand up very well in geological time, which allows nature to erode all efforts back to ground level, by something like the laws of entropy. In a culture already strained by the long view back to the rediscovered classical past – Hamlet traces 'the noble dust of Alexander, till a find it stopping a bunghole' (5.1.172–3) – Shakespeare offers glimpses of an even longer view: Macbeth gazes towards infinite tomorrows that will reabsorb the strongest castle into the eternal forest (5.5.19–51). Tragedies of ambition, then, often become stories in which the natural or social order, aided by the divided human psyche, becomes the avenger.

The awkward dual mandate of this chapter thus has some compensating explanatory value. These two types of tragedy are reciprocal: one depicting the will to superior power, the other depicting an unwillingness to be overpowered. Tragedies of ambition depend on the protagonist's illusion that an exception can endure, that no mindless or jealous reflex in nature or heaven will produce a reaction equal and opposite to the heroic action, recapturing exertion as merely lost heat. Tragedies of revenge depend instead on the protagonist's illusion that things can and must be made even (an eye for an eye, a humiliation for a humiliation). The plays suggest that Shakespeare often thought of ambition as a doomed effort to rise above a position of equality, and of revenge as a doomed effort to restore equality. Aristotle thought of tragedy itself in a similar way: as a cathartic treatment designed to restore equilibrium. This does not mean, however, that Shakespeare's tragedies of ambition and revenge are inherently reactionary. Their superficial endorsement of a final return to normality co-exists – in a typical Shakespearean paradox – with a deep acknowledgement of the loss of human greatness, and the betrayal of an implied human essence, in the protagonist's inevitable fall from ambitious heights.

One dynamic definition of tragedy, derived from Hegel, describes it as a dramatic story in which the protagonist receives imperative but contradictory instructions from two superior forces, and is therefore doomed to destruction by whichever one he or she disobeys. These forces need not be deities, as they often are in classical literature; they can reflect the inconsistencies of a mixed culture. Both the local Anglo-Saxon warrior tradition and the recovered traditions of classical antiquity (except in Platonic and Stoic philosophy) endorsed instinctive desires to repay injuries, and to seek power and status over our fellow creatures. Yet the Christian ethos at the core of Renaissance culture praised pity, love, humility, and turning the other cheek, exalting as the greatest hero a sacrificial lamb who chose to abdicate his heavenly palace to suffer among the lowliest.

Tragic contradictions were everywhere in Shakespeare's London, provoking exalted ambitions and then taking revenge on those who pursued such ambitions. Protestant theology – the most obviously pressing cultural innovation – at once told Christians to aspire to direct communication with God, and told them to despair of ever knowing anything about Him; told them to focus obsessively on their prospects for eternal salvation, and to recognize that those prospects were beyond their power to control or even comprehend; to seek desperately, and yet to mistrust utterly, an inner conviction of divine favour. The terrifying instability of the new urban capitalist economic system – whose essence was to encourage but also punish ambition – was matched by the terrifying instability of this new belief system, which left many true believers vacillating wildly between a faith that God's love would exalt them beyond all comprehension, and a fear that God's just anger at such presumptuous sinners would damn them beyond any redemption. Nor were Catholics spared from the painful dialectic of ambition and revenge. Protestant spokesmen portrayed Catholicism (to which many of the English continued to subscribe) as allegiance to ambitious foreign political powers, justifying violent official retribution; and as an overweening attempt to control God and earn heaven, deserving punishment here in anticipation of punishment hereafter. Especially in the emerging urban settings of which Shakespeare's London was a prime example, old tribal systems of shame control ceased to function, and no fair and efficient system of official policing had yet arisen to take its place, only a tacit and hugely complicated system of power radiating downwards from a court that must, to most, have seemed no less mysterious, inaccessible, and arbitrary than the Reformation God.

Under all these circumstances, both ambition and revenge were extraordinarily tempting and difficult – perfect material for tragedy. Plays on those topics would have been deeply ambivalent experiences for Shakespeare's audience, whose loyalty would have remained divided between old and new models of heroism: warrior vs. sufferer, knowing one's place vs. overreaching it, believing vs. inquiring, the norm vs. the exception. Even the nascent conquest of nature by empirical science (including astrology and alchemy, as well as more modern-looking navigational and medical technologies) could look at one moment like glorious achievement, at the next like foolish or evil presumption, and at the next like mere fraud (the magic of Marlowe's Faustus sometimes seems to be all three at once). And the persistent bad seasons of flood and plague and famine in Shakespeare's England were not only harsh implicit rebukes to the promise that science would allow humanity to comprehend and rule the created world, but widely and explicitly preached as divine punishment of that ambition.

The remainder of this chapter will explore the relationships between classical and Renaissance tragedy, and the range of Shakespearean tragedies of revenge and ambition, before turning to two famous examples – *Macbeth* and *Hamlet* – to show how a culture's ambivalence about these topics can grow into tragic agony, and how Shakespeare combines the historical and trans-historical aspects of the vengeful and ambitious impulses.

The functions of tragedy and Shakespeare's development

Cultures exist largely to channel the infinite possibilities of the creative and self-conscious human mind into safely limited and shared channels, so that individuals can sustain sanity and communities can sustain co-operation. This is work better suited to myth-makers than law-makers; and when cultures cannot manage to resolve, or even afford to acknowledge, their internal inconsistencies, they delegate those tasks to tragedians. Art – a seemingly self-contained ritual form in which nothing material such as money or power is obviously at stake – provides a relatively safe territory for negotiating the contradictions. Indeed, this may explain why the only period of great tragic drama comparable to Elizabethan and Jacobean England was classical Greece, which was comparably beset by 'a growing discontinuity between forms of social mobility ... and the precarious consequences of that mobility which can result in destruction'.[4] Greece was also, like England, a naval power, and therefore regularly exposed to the disease of pluralism.

Classical stories of ambition were generally tragedies of revenge, in which the gods (or their reflections in nature) took vengeance on *hubris*, on the excessive pride of protagonists from Arachne to Oedipus to Pentheus. Under Christianity, this transaction reappears as the Fall, in which God punishes the presumption of humanity, both as individuals and as a species. In the Renaissance, tragedies of revenge often partake of ambition, since the avenger – from Kyd's Hieronimo to Middleton's Vindice to Webster's Bosola – is often seeking to overcome his powerlessness against a higher-ranking miscreant.

The chief classical literary source for Shakespeare's revenge tragedies lies in Seneca's ten tragedies, written during the first century AD, and translated into English around the time of Shakespeare's boyhood. These were passionate, violent stories, full of high rhetoric, in which the furious indignation of the revenger – often provoked (as in *Hamlet*) by a ghost or vision of a beloved victim – took aim not only at the perpetrator but at his entire extended family. This vengeance (again as in *Hamlet*) often required elaborate deception by the revenger, and finally provided some kind of poetic as well as practical justice.

Because Seneca wrote his plays to be read rather than staged, he could describe sensationally gruesome acts of violence without worrying about how they could be performed by actors or endured by spectators. His Elizabethan imitators went blithely ahead putting the same kind of violence into visible action. The resulting horrors are nowhere more obvious than in Shakespeare's earliest surviving tragedy, *Titus Andronicus*. The play is neglected enough, and the story remarkable enough, to merit a brief retelling here. Titus is a great Roman military hero of old-fashioned patriotic values who, to appease the spirits of his many sons killed battling the Goths, ritually executes a Gothic prince. The prince's younger brothers then ambush Titus's virtuous daughter Lavinia, slay her husband, toss his body into a pit, then rape her, cutting off her tongue and both her hands so that she can neither speak or write to accuse her attackers. When her brothers go looking for her, they fall into the pit with the corpse and, discovered there, are accused of being its murderer. A villainous Moor named Aaron tells Titus that he can save these sons only by cutting off one of his hands and sending it to the emperor, as a gesture of good faith, but the hand is promptly returned to him along with the heads of his sons. So he sadly carries one head offstage in his remaining hand, while his mutilated daughter carries off the severed hand in her teeth.

This all provides satisfactory revenge for Tamora, the queen of the Goths, but it provokes a massive counter-revenge in which Titus finally traps the rapist princes and slices their throats while his daughter holds a bowl with her stump arms to catch the blood, which he then mixes with a paste of their bones and (in a zany disguise as a chef) serves (in an echo of the classical Philomel myth) as a stew to their mother and imperial stepfather at a glorious banquet where Titus fatally stabs his daughter and Tamora, and is fatally stabbed in turn by the emperor, who is in turn fatally stabbed by Titus's surviving son, Lucius, who blurts the talionic formula:[5]

> Can the son's eye behold his father bleed?
> There's meed for meed, death for a deadly deed!
> (5.3.64–5)

The sheer amplification of violence in *Titus Andronicus* tends to preclude subtle modulations of voice, or of moral thought. Letting the good guys do what the bad guys did is an easy source of emotional gratification, but a peculiar way to celebrate ethical distinctions. Much of Shakespeare's subsequent career was shaped by his efforts to solve that problem – a problem especially tricky for a dramatist whose renowned ability to see all sides of a situation with equal clarity precluded the partisan distortions that conveniently disguise the amoral mirroring function of so many feuds. By turning the competing accusations into mere echoes of each other, Shakespeare (like a modern sound engineer) arranged for these justifications to cancel each other out, to make audible the cries of pain behind them.

In his first group of history plays, Shakespeare seems already to feel the limitations of revenge as a symmetrical, political practice. One does not even need to know the context to recognize the transaction:

QUEEN MARGARET: Thou hadst a Richard, till a Richard killed him.

DUCHESS: I had a Richard too and thou didst kill him;
I had a Rutland too, thou holp'st to kill him.

. . .

QUEEN MARGARET: Bear with me. I am hungry for revenge,
And now I cloy me with beholding it.
Thy Edward he is dead that killed my Edward;
The other Edward dead to quit my Edward;   (*R3* 4.4.42–64)

This is obviously a bad social system, and not so good as drama or poetry either (there is much more of this kind of forced parallelism in this scene).

Even in *Romeo and Juliet* a few years later, the older-fashioned speakers and situations produce this kind of revenge-rhyme:

LADY CAPULET: I beg for justice, which thou, Prince, must give:
Romeo slew Tybalt, Romeo must not live.

PRINCE: Romeo slew him, he slew Mercutio;
Who now the price of his dear blood doth owe?

LORD CAPULET: Not Romeo, Prince, he was Mercutio's friend;
His fault concludes but what the law should end... (3.1.180–5)

In this same play, however, we can feel Shakespeare searching for more complex motives and a more complex rhetoric to express them.[6] He rehearses that rhetoric in the voice of Juliet, as she tries to find a way out of a potentially unstoppable cycle of talionic violence, seeking somehow to replace it – as the play itself flirts with an escape from tragedy into comedy – with a rhetoric of love and forgiveness.

The diplomatic delicacy of this change is exquisitely delineated just after Romeo departs into exile. Juliet shows her wit by choosing words that simultaneously satisfy her mother's expectation that she would want to murder Romeo, for killing her cousin Tybalt, and her own need to express a different sort of desire for him. She tells Lady Capulet,

JULIET: God pardon him, I do, with all my heart:
And yet no man like he doth grieve my heart.

LADY CAPULET: That is because the traitor murderer lives.

JULIET: Ay, madam, from the reach of these my hands.
Would none but I might venge my cousin's death!

When her mother promises to satisfy what she assumes is Juliet's desire for 'vengeance' by having Romeo poisoned, Juliet answers,

Indeed I never shall be satisfied
With Romeo, till I behold him – dead –
Is my poor heart, so for a kinsman vex'd.
Madam, if you could find out but a man
To bear a poison, I would temper it,
That Romeo should upon receipt thereof
Soon sleep in quiet. O, how my heart abhors
To hear him named, and cannot come to him
To wreak the love I bore my cousin
Upon his body that hath slaughtered him!
(3.5.82–102)

This breathtaking piece of verbal tightrope-walking is possible only because the line between death-wishing and love-desire – between unrequited wrongs and unrequited love – is so blurred by this play's passions. Love does not simply negate revenge here; it steers the energies of revenge into the thinly veiled violence of sexual desire. Juliet will convert the poisonous humours that elicit death into the fluids that love-making elicits, leading to sleep, and to another kind of bearing and feeding.[7]

Shakespeare himself perfects this ambivalence, and provides closure to this topic, near the end of his career, by writing *The Tempest*, which appears to be a revenge tragedy that renounces its own genre. The hero Prospero decides not to enforce punishment on the traitors he has finally captured: 'At this hour / Lies at my mercy all mine enemies', he announces at the end of Act 4 (4.1.264–5). Yet, at the start of Act 5, in conversation with the spirit Ariel, Prospero declares, 'The rarer action is in virtue, than in vengeance. They being penitent, / The sole drift of my purpose doth extend / Not a frown further' (5.1.27–9). He moves the story from tragedy to comedy, from a story of death to a story of marriage, focusing on matching his daughter Miranda joyfully with Ferdinand, a project hardly compatible with taking brutal revenge on Ferdinand's father. In a sense, Prospero achieves what Romeo and Juliet died attempting: the conversion of vendetta – the merciless Italian morality of revenge – into wedding, into a morality of forgiveness and community. He is able to 'requite' Ferdinand's father for the restoration of his dukedom with new life, instead of for the usurpation of that kingdom with enforced death (5.1.169). (Revenge is notably forsworn in other late plays also: in *The Winter's Tale*, King Leontes's falsely accused wife and friend, Hermione and Polixenes, have good cause for vengeance and good positions from which to impose it, but finally allow the king's penitence to take the place of punishment.)

From the first plays to the last, then, revenge as a motive is everywhere in Shakespeare. Even in his comedies, characters such as Shylock in *The Merchant of Venice*, Oliver de Boys in *As You Like It*, and Malvolio in *Twelfth Night*, are ambitious and vengeful figures against whom some combination of virtue and nature takes a poetically just counter-revenge, imposing humiliation. This counter-revenge is often engineered by a female character, such as Portia in *The Merchant of Venice*, Maria in *Twelfth Night*, even Mistress Ford in *The Merry Wives of Windsor* – which may suggest the way women in Shakespearean comedy are associated with the restoration of commonsensical norms. In Shakespearean tragedy, revenge often seems merely a rationalization by an already malign spirit, such as Aaron in *Titus*, Iago in *Othello*, or Cornwall in *King Lear*. These villains – who are generally at least superficially ambitious – set out to punish what we are asked to see as goodness; sometimes they do so precisely because they too see it as goodness, as an innocence they cannot match, and can therefore only destroy.

An important sub-category of revenge tragedy is the malcontent plot –
made famous by Shakespeare's contemporaries such as Marston and
Webster, but clearly shaping Shakespeare's high-tragic villains Iago and
Edmund – in which someone unappreciated by the royal court, someone
with frustrated ambitions, decides to show the world his abilities in a destructive mode instead. Hamlet arguably flirts with this role; Macbeth plays
it; Don John in *Much Ado About Nothing* is a minimalist caricature of it.
The ambitions of Shakespeare's Richard III reflect some of this same resentment, a resentment which turns his political career into an act of vengeance
against a world that cannot love him, and – in a psychological turn typical
of Shakespearean drama – against a deformed self he himself cannot love.

Indeed, heroes can be vengeful as well, though rarely at their best moments.
Henry IV and Henry V both skilfully disguise their political desires as causes
of honourable vengeance. In *Julius Caesar*, Antony is certainly an avenger,
with Caesar's ghost as his guiding and aiding spirit. Romeo becomes one,
briefly but disastrously, in killing Tybalt. King Lear seeks revenge against his
bad daughters, Timon against his fair-weather friends, Coriolanus against
his Roman banishers, Othello mistakenly and effectually against his wife and
then legitimately but futilely against Iago for causing that mistake. In *Hamlet*,
Shakespeare provides us with his most explicit and extended exploration of
heroic revenge; indeed, the most self-conscious and morally intricate revenge
tragedy in the long, lively history of the genre.

The history of *Hamlet* and the functions of revenge

Hamlet has long stood as the most famous revenge tragedy in Western civilization. The entire history of that fame is a lesson in the tension between
locality and universality in the reading of Shakespeare. The play's opening
words – 'Who's there?' (1.1.1–2) – make a claim on every audience that orders this ghostly play to 'Stand, and unfold yourself.' Hamlet the character
says that the purpose of drama is to hold 'the mirror up to nature'. *Hamlet*
the drama holds a mirror up to us, in which even the most sophisticated critics have trouble seeing beyond their own reflections. So *Hamlet* is universal,
in that each individual or historical period tends to see it as the story of
all humanity; but local, in that each individual or historical period thereby
defines that story in its own terms.

The reception of *Hamlet* thus provides a kind of core sample of cultural
history. Shakespeare biographers read *Hamlet* as Shakespeare's metaphorical
autobiography: after all, Shakespeare liked to stage revealing plays, report-
edly played the ghost of Hamlet's father, had recently lost his own father,
and had a son named Hamnet who died young. Zealous Christians detect

a Christian parable. Theatre historians think the play must be understood as an artifact of the historical theatre, and modernizing directors insist it is incomprehensible unless converted into an entirely modern work. German authors see the play as quintessentially German, while French authors deem it French. When the legendary Sarah Bernhardt played Hamlet, she told an interviewer that Hamlet must have been a woman. The play functions as a projection, and an optical illusion, whether or not the 'illusion' called a ghost does (1.1.127).

The Romantics who commented on Shakespeare in the early nineteenth century were often morbidly sensitive intellectuals (such as Coleridge and Hazlitt in England, Goethe and Schlegel in Germany) trapped in the world of brutal action: poet–philosophers with too much brain-power and emotional delicacy for their own good. They perceived Hamlet as much the same, with Claudius's usurpation standing in for the French Revolution in particular and the Industrial Revolution in general. The problem with revenge, from this perspective, is that it does not withstand careful consideration. Hamlet repeatedly condemns himself for getting caught up in analysing revenge instead of performing it:

> Now, whether it be
> Bestial oblivion, or some craven scruple
> Of thinking too precisely on th' event –
> A thought which quartered hath but one part wisdom,
> And ever three parts coward – I do not know
> Why yet I live to say, 'This thing's to do,'
> Sith I have cause, and will, and strength, and means
> To do it.   (4.4.39–46; cf. 2.2.550–86)

Yet Hamlet may well have been right to hesitate. How can anyone rouse the moral certainty to commit murder, however compelling the cause may appear, if he suspects that 'nothing is good or bad, but thinking makes it so' (2.2.239–40) – let alone if he suspects that a number of innocent people, including his own school-friends, sweetheart, and mother, will be likely to be killed also in the process?

Furthermore, Shakespeare provides us with perspective – almost a scientific control group – by including two other sons also seeking to avenge their fathers' slayings. Fortinbras (whose father was killed by Hamlet's father in single combat) seems too cold, sending 'twenty thousand men' to death in fighting an otherwise pointless cause (4.4.60–5). Laertes (whose father was killed by Hamlet himself) seems too hot to notice that his honour is being destroyed by the effort to preserve it. Warfare itself – killing provoked by a sense of duty to ghosts of our fathers in armour – is brought into moral question, along with all the smaller-scale forms of revenge. *Macbeth* raises similar questions by showing that the same kind of brutal violence which makes Macbeth the greatest of heroes in the play's opening scene makes him the worst of villains a few scenes later. Is revenge any better an excuse for killing than ambition is, or vice versa? What excuse is good enough?

When another German cultural wave washed over England and America a century after Romanticism – Freudian psychoanalysis – it again stared into the Hamlet mirror and saw itself. In his unsophisticated but influential book *Hamlet and Oedipus*, Ernest Jones – a student of Freud's – argued that Shakespeare and Sophocles were drawing on the same sources and patterns of psychic energy. Hamlet cannot kill Claudius because he identifies with him too much. All Claudius has done is fulfil precisely Hamlet's own oedipal fantasies: his guilt-ridden, subconscious desire to murder his father and then marry his mother. The problem with revenge is thus that it is inextricable from suicide, as the 'To be or not to be' soliloquy suggests; the avenger now sees himself in the mirror. It is worth noting, however, that this most famous question in literature may not mean (as most people assume it does), 'Should I commit suicide?', but rather the question Hamlet goes on to consider: 'Should I survive by stoically accepting wrongs, or die performing revenge?'

Now, another century later, Hamlet again seems to mirror the latest cultural revolution, and becomes a study of information systems at their limits, of the problems of communicating data and perfecting equations amid realities that may never be more than virtual. The biggest theoretical questions currently haunting literary critics and historians and psychotherapists and Web-surfers cluster around the multiplicity and instability of truth. In an age obsessed with moral relativism and recovered-memory syndromes and deconstruction and multiculturalism, how can we know each other, or ourselves, or reality – especially through language, which programmes us in ways we can never get outside of? Now the problem with revenge is that – as the play keeps reminding us – we cannot understand ourselves, recognize our enemies, calibrate our actions, define morality, or intuit divine purposes surely and precisely enough to trust that our revenge will actually constitute justice.

Hamlet's task of revenge appears fairly neat: his target is high but not out of reach, he has multiple kinds of evidence convicting Claudius, and his own plausible claim to the throne gives his efforts legitimacy as well as a supplementary motive of ambition. But, as so often in Renaissance drama, revenge tends to overflow, inflicting collateral damage on by-standers, ruining the logic of redressed grievance and the aesthetic of restored symmetry. Long before he finally strikes down 'that murderous, that adulterate beast' (1.5.42), Hamlet has turned bitterly vengeful against several other people:

not just his mother (briefly) for her supposed complicity, but against several members of his own generation who he feels have become disloyal to him, allowing themselves to be manipulated by the powerful elders. He therefore turns his fatal anger against the lovelorn Ophelia, against the ambitious Rosencrantz and Guildenstern, and against the proud Laertes. That anger also nearly becomes deadly against himself; before he can even undertake violence against Claudius, his speech and actions are markedly suicidal.

Drawing on a strong scholarly tradition that associated revenge with impiety, excess, and madness in Renaissance culture,[8] one critic argues vigorously that Shakespeare would not have approved of Hamlet's extreme vengefulness, even against Claudius, and would not have assumed approval from the audience. Against the long tradition of Hamlet criticism that wonders why he is so hesitant to take revenge, this argument suggests he should (by all recorded Elizabethan norms) have been even more hesitant, leaving vengeance to God and never seeking to damn another human soul.[9]

In fact, the divine injunctions against human retaliation ('Vengeance is mine, saith the Lord' in the Old Testament, 'turn the other cheek' in the New) were widely quoted – and even more widely ignored. Hamlet expresses concern that God has forbidden suicide, but not that God has forbidden revenge. In any case, Hamlet's situation is ambiguous, since he pursues not only a personal vendetta on behalf of his family, which Elizabethan commentators condemned, but also official justice as a prince of the state, which they tended to approve. Shakespeare employs such ambiguities to prevent the audience from seizing on a simplistic moral view of the protagonist's dilemma, which must be irresolvable if it is to be fully tragic. Something similar occurs with the laws of succession in *Macbeth*, where Macbeth's ambition may or may not be legitimate, since Shakespeare carefully avoids specifying whether Duncan's son has any presumptive claim on the throne, or whether (as a kinsman and leading general of the king) Macbeth deserved a chance at the 'election'.

The platitudinous father Polonius advises Laertes, 'to thine own self be true' (1.3.78). That advice only highlights what a strange new world Shakespeare – and Hamlet, and Macbeth – actually inhabited. The legacy of paternal identity was often rendered irrelevant by socio-economic changes that drove people into cities where they had to make a living or make a name for themselves, rather than simply inheriting both. The revenge of Hamlet, by which he seeks to claim his father's legacy, thus becomes an especially interesting case. Since the emphatic public discourses of Church and state alike condemned it, the practice of revenge seems to mark a moment of individual and/or instinctual resistance to official influence[10] – perhaps an exception to theories (currently popular among scholars) that claim the self is entirely constructed by social authority, and that individuality and instinct are delusive myths when applied to human beings who are in the encompassing grip of their historical moment with its ideologies and epistemes.[11] If we combine that observation with the tendency (also strong in recent scholarship) to credit this play with the invention of modern inwardness, of unique personal subjectivity, we find *Hamlet* breaking both Renaissance orthodoxy and modern academic orthodoxy about that Renaissance orthodoxy. We find ourselves again focused on the character's unprecedented autonomy – his freedom of agency, his ability to explore inwardly. And yet, when called upon to act, he feels himself very far from free. Revenge is tragic because (like ambition) it divides the protagonist against himself, casting him in incompatible roles, and because it is philosophically as well as practically difficult; the drama of moral choice complicates and deepens the drama of active suspense.

While the task of blood-revenge was discouraged by Elizabethan authorities, it may have been stimulated by Elizabethan theology, less directly but no less forcefully, because vengeance was suddenly about the only thing mourners could do on behalf of the dead. The Catholic tradition of praying and paying to redeem loved ones from purgatory was outlawed and ridiculed by the Reformation (which got its start at Wittenberg, where Shakespeare tells us Hamlet has been educated); and promptly the Elizabethan stage began depicting characters using worldly revenge (as in *The Spanish Tragedy* as well as *Hamlet*) to redeem tormented ghosts. Laertes's vengeful fury is amplified by his resentment that neither Polonius nor Ophelia can be buried with the full traditional rites. If prayers for the dead were discouraged in churches, then revenge on behalf of a ghost would be performed in theatres; diplomacy with God would give way to war on human villains, who became the satisfyingly localized and assailable scapegoats for the crime of mortality. Beneath the surface horror of Renaissance revenge tragedy (and modern detective fiction) lies the reassuring implication that death is a contingent event – the strange result of crime rather than the normal result of time – and the consoling idea that death can in some sense be refuted by destroying its immediate cause. This version of homeopathic medicine, by which death cures death, partly explains the renewed appeal of the classical drama of blood-revenge.

It may also explain why blood-revenge often becomes almost comically extreme in Jacobean tragedy, as avengers seek a dosage adequate to achieve the desired cure; and why audiences tend to side with such avengers despite all the official admonitions to the contrary. It doesn't take a murdered beloved, only a dead one, to make us share the sense of betrayal and futility that generates dramatic avengers. As in Shakespeare's great cluster of tragedies of

1605–8 – *King Lear, Macbeth, Coriolanus,* and *Antony and Cleopatra* – what looks like a tragedy about a particular political crime at a particular historical moment proves to be also a tragedy about the painful contradictions of ordinary human life, full of high aspirations, but subservient to nature, and limited by mortality.

Coriolanus provides a revealing instance: a character whose huge ambitions manifest themselves in vengefulness against both his own common bodily needs and the commoners of his body politic, which conspire to resist his claim to be the perfect embodiment of Rome's martial ideal. Shakespeare here stages a historical incident, closely based on Plutarch, with clear links to the history of Shakespeare's own time: the rebellion of the ambitious Essex, the Midlands grain uprisings of 1606–7, the emerging anxieties about representative government. But the play takes on a mythical rather than a historical aura. The factual background and political analysis coexist synergistically here with an archetypal study of the costs and limits of ambition itself. Clearly the revenge taken against Coriolanus is at once that of a social underclass against aristocratic arrogance, and that of fundamental elements of his birth against the superhuman soldier he aspired to become. The mob finally destroys him on behalf of slain kinsmen ('He kill'd my son! – My daughter! – He kill'd cousin Marcus – he kill'd my father!' (5.6.121–2)), but also on behalf of the common nature he insisted on transcending: Coriolanus is executed for crimes against his own humankindness. Taking his mother and his son each by a hand, hearing the honorary name he achieved reduced back to his patronymic, Coriolanus is fatally obliged to acknowledge his identity as merely one link in a chain of mortal generations. In this, Coriolanus's tragedy most clearly resembles Macbeth's: a story of nature and its norms taking revenge on ambition.[12]

Macbeth and nature's revenge on human ambition

Fundamentally, *Macbeth* tells the story of a man whose ambitions (abetted and personified by his wife) lead him into 'unnatural' deeds, deeds for which nature, society, and the psyche all take a vivid and systematic revenge. At the beginning of the story, Macbeth understands that ambitious violations invite retribution:

> ... we but teach
> Bloody instructions, which being taught, return
> To plague th' inventor. This even-handed justice
> Commends th' ingredience of our poisoned chalice
> To our own lips.   (1.7.8–12)

When the murderous couple get a taste of their own bitter medicine, they discover that its side-effects are more pervasive than the dangerous precedent a king-killer sets for his own kingship. Ambition – rebelling against the nation's divinely given hierarchy – entails a series of violations of natural order, all of which return to haunt Macbeth as relentlessly as Banquo's ghost does. Macbeth embodies normal human competitiveness, but he does so in a situation which converts that impulse into a terrible and irredeemable reality, and in a universe that takes massive, ineluctable revenge on those who overstep the natural and traditional boundaries.

Shakespeare goes to considerable trouble, not only to make the crimes vividly brutal, but also to show that Macbeth gets just what he deserves – what, in fact, he asks for. Macbeth's crime *is* his punishment. He forfeits precisely the regenerative functions that he violated in murdering Duncan. To seize the throne, Macbeth must violate the healthy, orderly cycles of nature, and in each case he discovers that he cannot survive without the aspects of nature his ambitions obliged him to shatter. Having murdered sleep, he and his Lady endure an endless night of insomnia. Having tried to rob the next human generation of life and inheritance, they die prematurely and childless. Having blighted the agricultural health of their nation by murdering its life-giving figurehead, Macbeth finds his castle walls swarmed by an instantly resurgent forest – the same forest human ambitions had presumably cleared from that place to build the castle so long ago. The real avenger here appears to be nature itself, with the biological heir Malcolm as merely its stalking-horse.

The immediate result of yielding to ambition, of forcibly disturbing the hereditary order, of making himself into something he was not born to be, is that Macbeth becomes disastrously divided against himself. His manhood erases his humanity; his senses contradict each other; his hand and eye, face and heart, become deceptively discrepant. Ambition provokes an inward as well as an outward civil war. The boundary between self and other blurs nightmarishly; his 'single state of man' loses its 'better part of man' (1.3.140, 5.8.18); and 'all that is within him does condemn / Itself for being there' (5.2.24–5).[13] A similar syndrome of disorder and division pulls down his ambitious wife.

Macbeth's decision to indulge the ambitious appetite reads like an allegory of Freud's division of the self into three parts. Macbeth is the ego, held in check by the super-ego – the rules ingrained in our conscience to make social existence possible. Macbeth's soliloquy (in 1.7) catalogues those rules: protect your sleeping guests, your benefactors, and your kindred; never make the question of hierarchy into a bloody free-for-all; listen to the angels, who will reward your virtues and expose and punish your crimes.

At the end of the soliloquy, he recognizes that he has no valid reason to proceed, 'Only vaulting ambition, which o'erleaps itself / And falls on th' other'; Macbeth mocks himself as a man leaping proudly up on to horseback, only to discover that his momentum carries him inevitably towards a painful and humiliating fall off the other side. Ambition is as impractical as it is immoral, provoking a revenge as certain as gravity. Lady Macbeth refutes this conscientious argument in the voice of the conscienceless id, the individual appetite, coaxing the super-ego into dropping its defences. She makes fun of him for 'Letting "I dare not" wait upon "I would" ' (1.7.44); she then proves that a little wine and sexual provocation can wash away conscientious resistance.

In this sense, the portrayal of Macbeth's fate as poetic justice falls far short of tragic complexity. He is not caught between conflicting imperatives: all he has to do is ignore some obviously sinister advice and he will be able to settle into the sociable contented old age he envisions (5.3.24–6). The preceding summary of the primary moral argument of the play does virtually nothing to explain why people find *Macbeth* any more haunting than, say, the manipulative 'Goofus and Gallant' cartoons that have run for decades in *Highlights for Children* magazine, where the binary choice between good and bad is utterly simple, and pervades every aspect of conduct and appearance. This play has remained compelling because (as so often in Shakespeare's work) it also harbours a contrary morality, a revisionist fairy tale which turns into a horror movie, because the face of dear old Mother Nature melts into a blur and reshapes itself as an ugly witch who promised us glory, but in fact always had us trapped in a deterministic labyrinth. Virtue triumphs at the expense of *homo sapiens* and *homo faber*: our ability to imagine something better and plan towards it, our practical need for tools and clothing and housing.

That may be one reason why this play puts so much symbolic weight on weapons and garments and castles.[14] The individualistic philosophy infiltrating England from Renaissance Italy, as prominently articulated by Petrarch and Pico della Mirandola, argued that human beings were authorized to alter their given world, and to aspire above their given place in that world, by the fact that they were created without claws or fur or exoskeletons, and so needed artificial equivalents in order to survive. Anthropologists, sociologists, philosophers, and art historians – who agree on little else – agree that the human species defines itself by the way it distances itself from nature. 'Human nature' is an oxymoron, a contradiction full of tragic potential. Hamlet says, 'What is a man, / If the chief good and market of his time / Be but to sleep and feed? A beast, no more' (4.4.34). King Lear registers a similar complaint: 'Allow not nature more than nature needs / Man's life is cheap as beast's' (2.4.267). The advancing Birnam Wood evokes, in a dramatically accelerated form, the mindless relentless organic processes that eventually will swallow up everything human pride – or the human genome – has provoked us to build. Akira Kurosawa's superb Japanese film adaptation of *Macbeth*, *Throne of Blood*, emphasizes exactly this demoralizing moral.

There are certainly other ways to slant the moral of this story. If it had been told by an ordinary Elizabethan author, susceptible to conventional thought and eager to please the government, it would have been a simple celebration of benevolent power triumphing over diabolical ambition. Told by a more openly rebellious and Promethean spirit such as Christopher Marlowe or George Chapman, this might have been the story of a great soul's repression by a narrow and mechanical physical world. Shakespeare, as usual, tells it both ways at once, leaving us to decide whether we want to excavate a human tragedy out of a moralistic and didactic tale about the rise and fall of two evil-doers. Underneath the story of nature's vivid revenge against ambition lies a story of entropy's ponderous nullification of human enterprise.

Macbeth is thus broadly philosophical and psychological in its treatment of ambition and revenge. It suggests that, in a conservative universe – one where God or a reactionary society or the stubbornness of intentionless physics limits human freedom – ambitious desires invite a tragic confrontation with what Freud calls the reality-principle, which demands 'the abandonment of a number of possibilities of gaining satisfaction and the temporary toleration of unpleasure as a step on the long indirect road to pleasure'.[15] *Macbeth* is a tragedy of ambitions which override that principle, choosing short-term, selfish satisfactions over the compromises which sustain collective human life. That collectivity then exacts revenge.

Macbeth is also insistently historical. Even if we take the 'weird sisters' more as allegory than as a commentary on Renaissance witchcraft, we can still see them either as agents of *wyrd* – fate – or more locally as an embodiment of contradictions in the organization of a Renaissance English society that repeatedly aroused high aspirations and then took vengeance on those who pursued them. The changes in Shakespeare's world, like the witches in Macbeth's, generated a foggy, confusing moral landscape, and then destroyed people for not finding the same old path through them. They tempted people to ambitious activity with glorious prophecies – rule the world, know the universe – and then brutally punished them for not passively accepting their given conditions. The glorious aspirations of humanism, even the ordinary aspirations of humans, are hard to reconcile with Christian (and monarchical) principles that demanded not only humility, but even unquestioning acceptance of the will and the world of God and Kings.

With the official voices offering such mixed messages, people often turn to nature as an arbiter; but the definition of what is natural is itself inflected by local ideology. The world did not need Shakespeare to suggest that ambition was a wrongful and dangerous violation of some benevolent and divinely ordained order which conveniently included the established hierarchies. Elizabethan moralists were only too willing to send that message, and Elizabethan authorities (who had the most to lose in any breakdown of established hierarchies) made sure that was the message which appeared in print and echoed through churches.

Macbeth appears to participate in that process of ideological control, but may also offer a critique of it. As in much government propaganda about the value of accepting subjugation (by race, class, and gender) and of following conventional practices (in sexuality, work, and belief), the traditional is here equated with the natural, and hence with justice and divine intention.[16] We see a wise and powerful force, comprising God and nature and political legitimacy, taking poetically just revenge on Macbeth for his crimes against the pious and natural and political orders. Shakespeare also reminds us, though, that those orders rarely stay so perfectly aligned except in propaganda. Coded into that moralistic story is a story of moral ambiguity, less obvious but no less powerful, one sympathetic to the paradoxes entangling human beings generally and Shakespeare's contemporaries in particular. Here again, Shakespeare voices a human problem that stretches across the range of civilizations in time and space, but is amplified and inflected by circumstances local to Shakespeare and his audience.

Renaissance artists, scientists, and explorers heard a temptress's voice, a witch's voice, a Lady Macbeth voice, telling them that conquest and glory were within their reach, if they were only bold and manly enough to grasp them. Those same aspirations were then smothered by Protestant doctrines that insisted on humanity's helpless depravity, and by the stubborn limitations of ignorance, traditionalism, and finally mortality. Versions of Macbeth's temptresses – equivocal forces that provoked and then betrayed ambition, that 'palter with us in a double sense' (5.8.20) – were constantly being conjured by the rapidly shifting economic, scientific, and theological conditions of the people for whom Shakespeare was writing his plays. Like Marlowe's *Doctor Faustus*, Shakespeare's *Macbeth* often looks like an old-fashioned story about the olden days, a story of sinful ambition and holy revenge. But, even more craftily than *Faustus*, Shakespeare's great tragedy of extraordinary ambition comports a warning, even a mourning, about the ethical contradictions produced by ordinary living in the emerging modern world.

NOTES

1. This is the opening sentence of Bacon's 'Of Revenge', in his *Essayes* (London, 1625).
2. William Kerrigan, '*Macbeth* and the History of Ambition', in *Freud and the Passions*, ed. John O'Neill (University Park, PA: Penn State University Press, 1996), pp. 13–24, outlines this argument vividly.
3. Richard Dawkins, *The Selfish Gene* (New York: Oxford University Press, 1976), has made this theory accessible to a general audience.
4. George Thompson, *Aeschylus and Athens* (1941; rpt London, 1980), p. 2; paraphrased by John Drakakis, *Shakespearean Tragedy* (London: Longman, 1992), p. 7. Thompson is remarkably foresighted about the necessary balance between historicism and essentialism.
5. The law of the talion is the principle of symmetrical repayment: an eye for an eye. And another eye for that one: René Girard, *Violence and the Sacred* (Baltimore, MD: Johns Hopkins University Press, 1977), argues that breaking such cycles of mimetic violence is an essential function of tragedy.
6. Even here, Shakespeare arguably introduces some complexity by allowing Lord Capulet to speak on behalf of the young Montague, Romeo. Most editors, however, including the New Cambridge, accept the traditional (but by no means necessary) emendation of Q4 that puts this defence in the mouth of Lord Montague instead, trapping Shakespeare back in the world of predictable vindictiveness that he may have been trying to escape.
7. Lady Macbeth will attempt the opposite transformation, turning her milk to gall, and the milk of her husband's humankindness into bloody murder (1.5.48, 17).
8. Many classic works on English Renaissance drama have acknowledged a powerful Elizabethan orthodoxy against private vengeance; see Lily Bess Campbell, *Shakespeare's Tragic Heroes: Slaves of Passion* (Cambridge University Press, 1930), pp. 3–24; Willard Farnham, *The Medieval Heritage of Elizabethan Tragedy* (Berkeley: University of California Press, 1936), pp. 343–51; and Fredson Bowers, *Elizabethan Revenge Tragedy, 1587–1642* (Princeton University Press, 1940), pp. 3–61. For a brief summary of this tradition that also acknowledges an unabashed counter-tradition – 'Drake named the sea vessel he led against the Armada not *Forgiveness* or *The Turned Cheek* but *The Revenge*' – see Harry Keyishian, *The Shapes of Revenge* (New Jersey: Humanities Press, 1995), pp. 1–14.
9. Eleanor Prosser, *Hamlet and Revenge* (Stanford University Press, 2nd edn, 1971). Prosser draws on the scholarly tradition outlined in n.8 above to attack the standard assumption that Hamlet has a moral imperative to act. For a helpful and more recent look at this issue, see Roland Mushat Frye, *The Renaissance Hamlet* (Princeton University Press, 1984), pp. 22–37.
10. Catherine Belsey, *The Subject of Tragedy* (New York: Routledge, 1985), pp. 115–16.
11. The latter term, meaning the vocabularies of possible knowledge at different historical moments, is developed by Michel Foucault in *Les Mots et les choses* (Paris: Gallimard, 1966).

12. Robert N. Watson, *Shakespeare and the Hazards of Ambition* (Cambridge, MA: Harvard University Press, 1984), pp. 83–221, makes this argument about Coriolanus and Macbeth at greater length.
13. Cf. Sigmund Freud, *Civilization and its Discontents* (New York: Norton, 1961), p. 13, which explores 'states in which the boundary lines between the ego and the external world become uncertain or in which they are actually drawn incorrectly. There are cases in which parts of a person's body, even portions of his own mental life . . . appear alien to him . . .'.
14. See, for example, the classic studies by Cleanth Brooks, 'The Naked Babe and the Cloak of Manliness', from his *The Well-Wrought Urn* (New York: Harcourt Brace, 1947), and Caroline Spurgeon, *Shakespeare's Imagery and What it Tells Us* (1935; rpt Boston: Beacon Hill Press, 1958).
15. Freud, *Beyond the Pleasure Principle*, trans. James Strachey (New York: Liveright, 1961), p. 4.
16. See, for two prominent examples, 'Exhortation Concerning Good Order, and Obedience to Rulers and Magistrates' and 'A Sermon on Disobedience and Willful Rebellion', in *Sermons or Homilies Appointed to be Read in Churches in the Time of Queen Elizabeth of Famous Memory* (London: C. and J. Rivington, 1825), pp. 114–15; also Richard Hooker, *Of the Laws of Ecclesiastical Polity* (1594), Everyman's Library (London: J. M. Dent, 1907), p. 157.

10

CATHERINE BATES

Shakespeare's tragedies of love

'Tragedy of love' is to some extent a contradiction in terms. For love is the great force that unites and binds. It is what prompts a man to leave his father and mother and cleave to his wife. Celebrated traditionally in romantic comedy, love is the divine bond which leads to marriage and the creation of a new family. In forming the basic building block of the social group, love is not only a beneficial but a fundamentally creative force and as such it is opposed to all the forces of destruction. Love not only creates society, moreover, but seeks to preserve what it has made. It is therefore the great civilizing force, the energy that counters anarchy and chaos with order and degree (in primitive societies, marriage is always the first law). Love makes for civil conversation, courtesy, and good manners. It oils the wheels of social functioning and mitigates aggression and selfishness. When, in literature, love does encounter the forces of destruction it is generally in order to meet them head on and reverse them in a glorious moment of redemption. When Hero appears to die in *Much Ado About Nothing*, for example, or Hermione in *The Winter's Tale*, their later appearance alive, well, and still loving is made all the more poignant for our fear that they have been lost. Tragedy is averted as love's redemptive force wins out. Strictly speaking, the sleeping potion that Juliet takes in order to feign death should fall into this category too. It is a classic comic device, designed to flirt with tragedy only to defeat it the more triumphantly. When, instead, she wakes up not in Romeo's arms but in the family vault with her lover dead at her side it is a sign that things have gone doubly wrong. The forces of death have not only wrought destruction: they have, in destroying love, killed creativity itself. In tragedy things by definition go wrong but in love tragedy what goes wrong are the very best things – goodness, mercy, and love. The forces of redemption are shown to be inferior to the forces of death, as if God had lost out in his struggle against darkness and evil. The result is a degree of nihilism and despair that often surpasses that of the grimmest tragedy. Tragedies of love can leave us with a sense of generic outrage, as if something deep in the order of things has gone wrong and the comedic will towards forgiveness and redemption has been diabolically reversed. The death of Cordelia is a case in point. In the many versions of the Lear story available to Shakespeare, love and goodness finally triumph and the life of Cordelia is spared. It is his version alone which wrenches the story out of this comedic pattern, and the resulting sense of emotional and literary vandalism continues to make this one of the most painful scenes in the Shakespeare canon.

'Civilization', wrote Freud in a famous essay,

> is a process in the service of Eros, whose purpose is to combine single human individuals, and after that families, then races, peoples and nations, into one great unity, the unity of mankind. Why this has to happen, we do not know; the work of Eros is precisely this. These collections of men are to be libidinally bound to one another. Necessity alone, the advantages of work in common, will not hold them together. But man's natural aggressive instinct, the hostility of each against all and of all against each, opposes this programme of civilization. The aggressive instinct is the derivative and the main representative of the death instinct which we have found alongside of Eros and which shares world-dominion with it. And now, I think, the meaning of the evolution of civilization is no longer obscure to us. It must present the struggle between Eros and Death, between the instinct of life and the instinct of destruction, as it works itself out in the human species.[1]

For Freud, human civilization is nothing less than an ongoing struggle between the forces of life and the forces of death, and it is only because his words capture so well the subject matter of Shakespeare's love tragedies that I quote them here at such length. Love sponsors all the forces of life, creating human families and social groups in the teeth of man's instinct for destruction – both self-destruction and the destruction of the Other. It is the perpetual struggle between these two forces which creates that tense, uneasy and fragile achievement which is human civilization, and Shakespeare's tragedies of love are both a product of that civilization and a profound, not always comfortable, investigation into it.

Romeo and Juliet

Usually dated around 1595, *Romeo and Juliet* is Shakespeare's first proper tragedy of love, and from the opening lines of this early play it is clear that man's incivility to man is to be the drama's key issue:

> Two households, both alike in dignity,
> In fair Verona, where we lay our scene,
> From ancient grudge break to new mutiny,
> Where civil blood makes civil hands unclean.
>
> (Prologue, 1–4)

Shakespeare plays on the intrinsic instability of the word 'civil'. It is when the citizens' hands are turned against themselves that civility turns to civil war, the worst kind of strife, and we soon learn of three 'civil brawls' which have disturbed the city's streets (1.1.89). Shakespeare puns on the word throughout the play as if to emphasize that the precariousness of human civilization is embedded in language itself.[2] There is no word for 'civil' that does not contain the seeds of its own destruction.

Indeed, the world into which the play opens is one where the chaos caused by the internecine squabbling of the Capulets and the Montagues is matched by a linguistic disorder in which the pun is king. The play's first four lines of dialogue toss puns around like loose change – 'coals...colliers...choler... collar' – for here language is evidently a currency so light that even servants can be free with it (1.1.1–4). This is not the world of the humanistic 'golden sentence' in which word is tied securely to thing but a mercantile free-for-all in which the true masters are the linguistic prodigals.[3] Where words have lost their value, characters can afford to be profligate with them – like the garrulous Nurse whose flood and tumble of unedited utterance is only one step above mere noise. At the beginning of the play Romeo puns incessantly and not very well – 'You have dancing shoes / With nimble souls, I have a soul of lead' (1.4.14–15) – but it is Mercutio who really tops the bill as a 'gentleman...that loves to hear himself talk, and will speak more in a minute than he will stand to in a month' (2.4.147–9). An inveterate punster, Mercutio is playing with words right up to the end – 'you shall find me a grave man' (3.1.98). His Queen Mab speech is an exercise in spinning something out of nothing:

> ROMEO   Peace, peace, Mercutio, peace!
> Thou talk'st of nothing.
>
> MERCUTIO   True, I talk of dreams,
> Which are the children of an idle brain,
> Begot of nothing but vain fantasy,
> Which is as thin of substance as the air
>   (1.4.95–9)

Dazzling and mercurial, Mercutio's speech bursts with an inventiveness and delight in words that makes him the true heir to Spenser's Phantastes, the character who represents both the poet's greatest asset and his major liability – the imaginative faculty of the brain. Housed in a chamber that is painted in rainbow colours and which reverberates to the ceaseless buzz of flies, Phantastes is monarch of all 'idle thoughts and fantasies, / Deuices, dreames, opinions vnsound, / Shewes, visions, sooth-sayes, and prophesies; / And all that fained is, as leasings, tales, and lies'.[4]

In a world where words are, as here, loose, detached, potentially meaningless and by implication debased, it is hardly surprising that, as the Prince complains, the civil brawls that disturb his city are born of a single 'airy word' (1.1.89). Indeed, the fatal fight between Tybalt and Mercutio which sets what should, properly speaking, have been a romantic comedy lurching irretrievably in the direction of tragedy is generated by little more:

> TYBALT Gentlemen, good den, a word with one of you.
>
> MERCUTIO And but one word with one of us? Couple it with something, make it a word and a blow. (3.1.38–40)

In Shakespeare's time, a lack of respect for language was equivalent to a lack of respect for authority. 'Wheresoever manners, and fashions are corrupted', wrote Ben Jonson, 'Language is. It imitates the publicke riot. The excess of Feasts, and apparell, are the notes of a sick State; and the wantonnesse of language, of a sick mind.'[5] According to the tenets of Renaissance humanism, linguistic disorder and social disorder were effectively one and the same. If language were allowed to decline, the long-term effects were sure to be dire. History provided the lesson. 'When apt and good words began to be neglected and properties of those two tongues [Greek and Latin] to be confounded', noted Roger Ascham, Queen Elizabeth's own schoolmaster,

> then also began ill deeds to spring, strange manners to oppress good orders, new and fond opinions to strive with old and true doctrine, first in philosophy and after in religion, right judgment of all things to be perverted, and so virtue with learning is contemned, and study left off. Of ill thoughts cometh perverse judgment; of ill deeds springeth lewd talk.[6]

As the prop of civilization, language had the power to civilize the savage by teaching him how to speak (or to curse, in the case of Caliban). Since language was the vehicle for reason, it was able – in theory, at least – to subdue the barbarian and bring him to good order. 'Suche force hath the tongue', wrote Sir Thomas Wilson in his *Arte of Rhetorique* (1553), 'and such is the power of eloquence and reason, that most men are forced even to yelde in that, whiche most standeth againste their will.'[7] Renaissance literature and humanist education in logic and rhetoric aimed at nothing less.

It is appropriate, therefore, that the love of Romeo and Juliet – which has the potential, at least, to reconcile the warring families and so to civilize a broken state – should express itself above all by the effect that it has on words:

ROMEO If I profane with my unworthiest hand
This holy shrine, the gentle sin is this,
My lips, two blushing pilgrims, ready stand
To smooth that rough touch with a tender kiss.

JULIET Good pilgrim, you do wrong your hand too much,
Which mannerly devotion shows in this,
For saints have hands that pilgrims' hands do touch,
And palm to palm is holy palmers' kiss.

ROMEO Have not saints lips, and holy palmers too?

JULIET Ay, pilgrim, lips that they must use in prayer.

ROMEO O then, dear saint, let lips do what hands do:
They pray, grant thou, lest faith turn to despair.

JULIET Saints do not move, though grant for prayers' sake.

ROMEO Then move not while my prayer's effect I take.

(1.5.92–105)

This is the lovers' first exchange. At the Capulet feast, with Romeo still in perilous disguise and the pair not yet aware of each other's identity, the wondrous immediacy of their love expresses itself in a sonnet – one of the most condensed, rich and complex literary forms of the period. 'Is it not most delightfull', wrote Samuel Daniel, praising the sonnet form in *A Defence of Ryme* (1603), 'to see much excellently ordred in a small roome or little, gallantly disposed and made to fill vp a space of like capacitie?'[8] Romeo and Juliet intensify the language of their love in the manner of the Metaphysical poets, cramming every syllable with meaning and feeling. Shakespeare alters the standard ABABCDCDEFEFGG rhyme scheme of his own sonnets to repeat the B rhyme here, partly in order to condense the rhyme still further and partly to spell out quietly the action in which the sonnet culminates: 'this kiss, this kiss'. Surrounded by the bustle of the feast, the action of the scene is momentarily put on hold, crystallizing into a perfect sonnet, before it erupts into drama again with that fateful meeting of lips. And, although Juliet accuses Romeo of kissing 'by th'book' (110), this is manifestly not a staid, copy-book Petrarchism but rather a living moment, the intensity of which suddenly exposes as empty rhetoric Romeo's now scarce-remembered passion for Rosaline. By comparison with the holy words he exchanges with Juliet, Romeo's earlier protestations of 'devout religion' (1.2.88) for his 'saint' (1.1.214) now seem nothing but idolatry. The experience of real love massively expands the signifying power of words. The old Romeo was akin to Spenser's scorned courtier who 'himselfe doth [n]ought esteeme, / Unlesse he swim in love up to the eares'.[9] In such a world it is not only language but poetry that is debased. For Mercutio it is enough 'to pronounce but "love" and "dove"' to be a poet (2.1.10) or to copy 'the numbers that Petrarch flow'd in' (2.4.38–9). But now Romeo is coming to the experience of love from the inside and the effect is dramatic. The language of the play – heightened, lofty, and poetic – has long been commented on.

At the lovers' next rendezvous, the balcony scene (2.2), the atmosphere is so charged that the smallest gesture is loaded with significance. Juliet need not even speak in order to communicate to her beloved. 'She speaks, yet says nothing', comments Romeo, 'what of that? / Her eye discourses' (12–13). Transmuted into a purely visual emblem, a 'speaking picture', Juliet has become in herself the embodiment of pure poetry.[10] In the exchange that follows, language is distilled down to its most essential. 'I take thee at thy word' (49) is Romeo's response to Juliet's offer of love and she replies in kind: 'Dost thou love me? I know thou wilt say, "Ay", / And I will take thy word' (90–1). All vows and protestations of love can be reduced to the repetition of a single syllable. How different this is – thus substantiated by feeling and truth – from the earlier 'airy word' of the warring parties' empty provocations. By the end of the lovers' exchange, 'Three words' are sufficient to propose, accept, and arrange their hasty marriage (142).

It is during the balcony scene, of course, that Juliet famously meditates on the relation of words to meaning:

> 'Tis but thy name that is my enemy;
> Thou art thyself, though not a Montague.
> What's Montague? It is nor hand nor foot,
> Nor arm nor face, nor any other part
> Belonging to a man. O be some other name!
> What's in a name? That which we call a rose
> By any other word would smell as sweet
> (38–44)

Juliet resists nominalism – the argument that convention alone (and arbitrarily) links words to things. Against the potentially unrooted play of signifiers Juliet sets an altogether more conservative theory of language: one in which the inherent quality of a thing – its *quidditas* – articulates its true nature and not any arbitrarily imposed name. Inspired by her experience of love, Juliet adopts the position of Socrates who, in Plato's dialogue *Cratylus*, goes behind the shifting surface of language to the Forms in order to locate there the permanent and unchanging truth of things.[11]

Juliet's tendency to summarize, hone, and distil meaning down to some essential core surfaces again in 2.6, the scene in which she and Romeo are married at Friar Lawrence's cell. An ecstatic Romeo urges *copia*, encouraging her to 'blazon' forth their mutually 'heap'd' joy and 'Unfold' it to the air (26, 25, 28), but instead Juliet moves in the opposite direction. Rhetoric can be a surfeit. For her, a telescoping process makes the smallest unit better express the greatest experience. In place of expansiveness, therefore, Juliet's lapidary words argue rather for compression and conciseness as they strain towards epitome, *sententia*, and closure:

> Conceit, more rich in matter than in words,
> Brags of his substance, not of ornament;
> They are but beggars that can count their worth,
> But my true love is grown to such excess
> I cannot sum up sum of half my wealth.   (30–4)

Again, Juliet is adopting the conservative position that it is *materia* or substance which properly grounds human language. In a divinely governed universe where human words are guaranteed by a holy Logos, a distinct hierarchy of values comes into view. In the process of education, the 'knowl-edge of words comes earlier', as Erasmus admitted, 'but that of things is the more important'. And for Ben Jonson, too, there was no doubt about the proper ordering of priorities: 'Words, aboue action: matter, aboue words'.[12]

In *Romeo and Juliet* love is shown, through the miraculous effect it has on words, to be the agent of civilization. It promises to restore a debased language and with it a whole system of values. It is all the more tragic, there-fore, that this redemptive move towards meaning and order should founder. By a cruel irony of fate, the lovers' ability to concentrate meaning in a single word turns mockingly against them. After Romeo's murder of Tybalt and subsequent flight one word comes to sum up the whole awful situation: 'That "banishèd", that one word "banishèd", / Hath slain ten thousand Tybalts' (3.2.113–14). In the following scene, the word is spoken over and over again by the crazed Romeo with the fateful sonority of a tolling bell. In the face of tragedy language retreats into repetition and empty formulae, like the chorus of wails that goes up around the bed of the supposedly dead Juliet:

> LADY CAPULET Accurs'd, unhappy, wretched, hateful day! . . .
>
> NURSE O woe! O woeful, woeful, woeful day! . . .
>
> PARIS Beguiled, divorcèd, wrongèd, spited, slain! . . .
>
> CAPULET Despised, distressèd, hated, martyred, killed! . . .
>
> (4.5.43, 49, 55, 59)

After love's intensification of meaning it is as if language has been let loose again to be piled up indiscriminately in great catalogues of cliché.

It is the tragedy of Romeo and Juliet that their experience of love is, for all its redemptive capacity, not enough to save them. On the contrary, they remain victims of that same messy, prodigal world in which the play began – a world of illiterate servants and an inefficient postal system. It is significant that what first sets the play in motion is Romeo's reading of something that he is not supposed to read – the Capulets' guest-list – for what brings the tragedy round full circle is his failure to read something that is most definitely intended for his eyes: Friar Lawrence's explanatory letter. As in *King Lear*, tragedy is brought about by something as banal as a message not arriving in time. Given the demonstrable effect that love has had on their words, it is the more poignant that things 'not nice but full of charge, / Of dear import' like the Friar's missive should ultimately suffer the same fate as the emptiest of words (5.2.18–19). Love's great enrichment and refinement of language, its civilization of the forces of death, counts for nothing in the end. Only in the golden effigies, which are erected by the two grieving and belatedly reconciled families, can Romeo and Juliet ever approximate again to the speaking picture of love they experienced all too briefly in life.

Othello

Similar issues were preoccupying Shakespeare when, a decade or so later, he once more turned to love tragedy, this time with *Othello* (c. 1604). Again, love is portrayed as the great binding force, only here uniting not the warring elements within a single society but, more dramatically, two quite disparate cultures – the Moorish and the Venetian – symbolically encoded as black and white. And, once again, the vehicle of love's civilizing power is shown to be language. For Shakespeare makes it clear that Othello wins Desdemona's love, and indeed the ultimate acceptance of the Venetian state, through his words. We are first introduced to Othello as a great military general who is 'Horribly stuff'd with epithets of war' (1.1.14), a man who is, by his own self-deprecating account, rude in speech 'And little bless'd with the soft phrase of peace' (1.3.82). Yet Othello is most effective not in the field (where, in fact, we never see him) but in the gentler warfare of persuasive speech. Tamburlaine brings all down before him with a heady mixture of verbal and physical violence in Marlowe's play (1587), but Othello's best sword is in his words.

Accused by Brabantio of having made off with his daughter, Othello defends himself by telling the Senate the 'round unvarnish'd tale' (1.3.90) of all his dealings with Desdemona and, as he does so, he visibly captivates his listeners:

Her father loved me, oft invited me;
Still questioned me the story of my life
From year to year – the battles, sieges, fortunes,
That I have passed.
I ran it through, even from my boyish days
To th'very moment that he bade me tell it . . .
. . . These things to hear
Would Desdemona seriously incline;
But still the house affairs would draw her thence,
Which ever as she could with haste dispatch,
She'ld come again, and with a greedy ear
Devour up my discourse.   (1.3.128–33, 145–50)

If Othello's story is capable of mesmerizing the hardened heads of the Venetian Senate when, as here, retold at second hand, then how much the greater its unmediated effect upon the susceptible heart of Desdemona. It is a story which, as the impressed Duke comments, 'would win my daughter too' (1.3.170). Indeed, Othello's gift as a raconteur is akin to that of the poet who, in Sidney's phrase, 'cometh unto you, with a tale which holdeth children from play, and old men from the chimney corner'.[13] When seen as the understandable response to such a tale, Desdemona's choice is accepted as decisive and irreversible by all except Brabantio, the only character in the scene who closes his ears to Othello's rhetorical charms: 'But words are words; I never yet did hear / That the bruised heart was pierced through the ear' (1.3.216–17). Yet even this formidable father, who by Iago's calculation 'hath in his effect a voice potential / As double as the Duke's' (1.2.13–14), is successfully 'out-tongue[d]' by his opponent (19). It is Othello's conquering words that carry the day.

Othello is like the orator who, in countless Renaissance emblem and commonplace books, is depicted as leading his hearers with a golden chain: 'with his golden chaine / The Oratour so farre men's harts doth bind, / That no pace else their guided steps can find, / But as he them more short or slacke doth raine'.[14] And yet it is Othello's fate to become entangled, in turn, by just such a chain of another's devising and to be as tenderly 'led by th'nose / As asses are' (1.3.384–5). For, if Othello conquers Desdemona with the sheer irresistibility of his tale, so he falls victim to the sly suggestions and expert handling of Iago. A number of literary symmetries make it clear that Othello's miraculously effective words find their demonic counterpart in Iago, whose storytelling, though equally effective, works to wholly deadly effect. A brilliant raconteur himself, Iago catches Othello's ear with a skilful weaving of narrative cliché and readerly expectation. He presents the story of Desdemona's adultery with Cassio in the terms of a hackneyed city play whose plot is just waiting to happen: 'the knave is handsome, young, and hath all those requisites in him that folly and green minds look after. A pestilent complete knave; and the woman hath found him already' (2.1.231–5). Cassio's actions are presented by Iago as 'an index and obscure prologue to the history of lust and foul thoughts' (2.1.243–4) giving rise to a narrative logic which, in time, Othello's 'unbookish jealousy must conster' (4.1.99). Utterly taken in, Othello gazes on while Iago 'begins the story' (4.1.127), and he is so convinced by what he sees and hears that ultimately he too rewrites his wife: 'Was this fair paper, this most goodly book, / Made to write "whore" upon?' (4.2.70–1).

'That Cassio loves her, I do well believe't', Iago comments to himself; 'That she loves him, 'tis apt and of great credit' (2.1.266–7). The credibility of his tissue of lies rests, in other words, on the force not of truth but of probability and plausibility. Indeed, these are all that are required of the literary workman in order to evoke in his readers the most piteous response and emotional identification. In his essay *On the Composition of Comedies and Tragedies* (1543), the Italian poet Giraldi Cinthio discusses the traditional distinction, drawn from Aristotle, between comic and tragic plots. The comic is generally taken from 'actions that occur in the ordinary life of citizens' if not from contemporary events, while the tragic is generally drawn from the more public and well-known narratives of history. But, he goes on to say, it is just as possible for a poet to make up or 'feign' a tragic plot from his own imagination, provided he obeys the law of probability:

> it is in the power of the poet to move at his wish the tragic feelings by means of a tragedy of which he feigns the plot, if that plot is in conformity with natural habits and not remote from what can happen and often does happen.[15]

In essence, what Cinthio is doing here is describing the craft of Iago, who relies on the plausibility of Desdemona's liking for her own kind – 'Whereto we see in all things nature tends' (3.3.233) – in order to persuade Othello of her adulterous liaison with Cassio. Iago, that is to say, is merely putting into practice the literary advice of his own inventor, Cinthio also being, of course, the author of the novella which Shakespeare closely followed as the source for his play. And Othello's (in literary terms, quite proper) response to the tragedy that he's been told – 'O Iago, the pity of it, Iago!' (4.1.184–5) – shows just how effective Iago has been in being able to move tragic feelings in another at will; in being, that is to say, a perfect tragic poet.

In *Romeo and Juliet* the lovers fall victim to external circumstance, but there is nothing demonstrably wrong with their love in itself. On the contrary, its redemptive power is monumentalized in the golden statue which stands as a lesson for future generations. In *Othello*, however, Shakespeare deepens the tragic potential considerably. For here love is not merely a good in an evil world. It is shown to contain the seeds of evil within itself. Love's civilizing power is displayed in all its positive, creative effect in Othello's persuasive speech, but it also finds its diabolic double in Iago who operates the same persuasive speech to an utterly destructive end. The symmetry between the two lends a tragic irony to Othello's fate. As it is his propensity to love which makes him jealous, so it is his propensity to persuade others that, tragically, makes him all too persuadable himself. Renaissance humanists rested their case on the ability of rhetoric to make 'of wilde, sober: of cruel, gentle: of foles, wise: and of beastes, men'.[16] Yet Iago shows that all that rhetorical training could just as easily be turned in the opposite direction. The effect is to undermine confidence in a well-established and much-theorized educational practice. If civilization's principal tool can be used against itself in order to barbarize what has been refined, then what becomes of civilized values? The play plants a dark uncertainty at the heart of civilization itself, searchingly probing the slippery semantics of civility, liable to shift from a shared set of social values to civil war at a moment's notice.

'What meane you by that woord, Civile?', asks Stefano Guazzo in *La civile conversatione*, a courtesy-book translated by George Pettie and Bartholomew Young between 1580 and 1586. His interlocutor, one Annibale, replies as follows:

ANNIBALE If you meane to know my meaning of it, I must first aske if you know any citizen which liveth uncivilly?

GUAZZO Yes mary doe I, more then one.

ANNIBALE Now let me aske you on the contrarie, if you know any man of the countrey which liveth civilly?

GUAZZO Yea very many.

ANNIBALE You see then, that we give a large sense and signification to this woorde (civile) for that we would haue understoode, that to live civilly, is not sayde in respect of the citie, but of the quallities of the minde.[17]

Simply living in the city and being a denizen of its polite practices guarantees nothing. Civility is rather an inner virtue, an individual human quality that owes nothing to breeding or class (much scope for anti-court satire here). In Book VI of *The Faerie Queene* (1596), Spenser similarly extends the meaning of 'courtesy' beyond any narrow etymological derivation. 'Of Court it seemes, men Courtesie doe call', he rather sardonically writes, 'For that it there most vseth to abound', but in the course of Book VI it becomes apparent that true courtesy is to be found less in any social location than, as for Guazzo, 'deepe within the mynd'.[18]

In the concluding notes to his edition of Shakespeare's plays (1765), Samuel Johnson wrote of *Othello* that 'had the scene opened in Cyprus, and the preceding incidents been occasionally related, there had been little wanting to a drama of the most exact and scrupulous regularity'.[19] Shakespeare's decision to flout the classical unities by setting his first Act in Venice thus seems designed to dramatize the contrast between the two locations. In Shakespeare's day, the great trading city of Venice was a by-word for civilization and luxury, and the play opens with its citizens' comfortable assurance of that fact just about still intact. 'This is Venice!', cries Brabantio, called up in the middle of the night by the rowdiness of Iago and Roderigo: 'My house is not a grange' (1.1.106–7). It is only the gravity of the occasion – Desdemona's elopement with the Moor – which, Roderigo assures him, licenses their otherwise unwarrantable disturbance of the peace:

> Do not believe
> That, from the sense of all civility,
> I thus would play and trifle with your reverence.
> (1.1.129–31)

As the play progresses the parameters of the word 'civility' grow ever more extenuated and strained, and particularly after the scene has shifted to Cyprus. In contrast to the refinement of the city, Cyprus – the legendary birthplace of Aphrodite – is a wild, chaotic place, the more so as the island is, on the arrival of Othello and Desdemona and with the unlooked-for dispersal of the Turkish fleet, given over to revelry and carnival: 'It is Othello's pleasure ... [that] every man put himself into triumph; some to dance, some to make bonfires, each man to what sport and revels his addiction leads him' (2.2.1–5). Against this backdrop the mincing manners of an over-educated elite begin to look rather different. When Desdemona first arrives on the Cytherean shore she brings her city manners with her in the pleasantries and courtly *questioni d'amore* that she exchanges with Iago and Cassio. But in time this Venetian politesse and finger-kissing begin to have the thin and nervous feel of a foreign import. Indeed, it is precisely the free and easy manners of city living that Iago uses to entrap his victims: 'With as little a web as this will I ensnare as great a fly as Cassio. Ay, smile upon her, do; I will gyve thee in thine own courtship' (2.1.164–5). With its sense of menace, of love run to bestiality and madness, Cyprus has hints of Circe's isle, a nightmare version of the dream-like 'green world' to which the company traditionally repair in Shakespearean comedy.[20] In plays like *A Midsummer*

Night's Dream or *As You Like It*, the forest provides a foil to courtly manners and introduces the characters to their true feelings. But in *Othello* Cyprus distorts to the point of grotesqueness the norms of civil breeding such that it is Desdemona's very accomplishments and cultivated habits which finally indict her:

> OTHELLO So delicate with her needle! an admirable musician! O, she will sing
>   the savageness out of a bear. Of so high and plenteous wit and invention!
> IAGO She's the worse for all this.
> OTHELLO O, a thousand, a thousand times.   (4.1.177–81)

It is a sign of how far things have gone that, by the time Ludovico arrives in Cyprus in Act 4, Othello's violent behaviour towards his wife is, to the Venetian, frankly unrecognizable: 'this would not be believed in Venice' (4.1.232).

Translated to Cyprus where they are out of context and isolated from the supporting habitus of social and cultural assumptions, the civilized manners of Venice begin to look unnatural and strange.[21] Shakespeare's decision to visualize and thus dramatize the contrast not only emphasizes the juxtaposition between the two but drives home the dialectical nature of cultural self-definition. Notions of wildness, madness, Otherness and heresy are not moral absolutes but concepts which serve to confirm the value of their dialectical antitheses: civilization, rationality, identity, and orthodoxy. The self-esteem of a given group rests upon the security and unquestionability of such definitions, with the result that any unwanted libidinal desires or inadmissible aggressive urges classically get projected out upon the Other. 'In times of sociocultural stress', writes the cultural historian Hayden White, 'when the need for positive self-definition asserts itself but no compelling criterion of self-identification appears, it is always possible to say something like: "I may not know the precise content of my own felt humanity, but I am most certainly *not* like that." '[22]

In *Othello*, the first and most obvious target for such projection is, of course, Othello himself, the racial and cultural Other, Desdemona's passion for whom is designated by her fellow citizens as downright unnatural:

> BRABANTIO   A maiden, never bold;
> Of spirit so still and quiet that her motion
> Blush'd at herself; and she, in spite of nature,
> Of years, of country, credit, everything,
> To fall in love with what she feared to look on!
> It is a judgment maimed, and most imperfect,
> That will confess perfection so could err
> Against all rules of nature.   (1.3.94–101)

By a process of synecdoche, Othello's tales of the 'Anthropophagi, and men whose heads/Do grow beneath their shoulders' (1.3.142–3) cast an aura of the monstrous and the unknown over their teller and help the Venetians to locate the Other comfortably elsewhere in thrillingly distant and exotic lands. But as the play develops Shakespeare treats such projections with increasing scepticism. For, as the Venetians gradually discover to their cost, the Wild Man lurks not in his traditional haunts of the desert, the forest, or the wilderness but, far more disconcertingly, at home, right at the heart of civilization itself. The Venetian state is, in fact, less imperilled by the Other – the Turkish barbarian against whom Othello is engaged to fight, or indeed by the Moor himself – than it is by its own kind, a super-subtle Venetian whose evil is the more invidious for being homegrown. Iago is a perfect picture of that unsettling contradiction – the 'citizen which liueth vnciuilly' – who reveals civilization's claims to natural order and cultural superiority to be nothing but a sham.

In his essay 'On Cannibals' (1603), Montaigne writes that 'men call that barbarisme which is not common to them' and reports briefly on some of the more bizarre degustatory practices of primitive peoples as recounted by ancient and modern travellers. But he resists the occasion to prop his own culture's practices upon such projections. 'I am not sorie we note the barbarous horror of such an action, but grieved, that prying so narrowly into their faults we are so blinded in ours', he writes, for, turning his attention to the apparently civilized Europeans, Montaigne finds that they in fact exceed the cannibals 'in all kinde of barbarisme'.[23] Here, as throughout his sceptical philosophy, Montaigne's object is to force his own people to reconsider their unexamined assumptions and to recognize the degree to which their civilization hides a deeper, more horrifying barbarity. The savage exists in a state of nature which, in itself, is neither good nor bad. But for Montaigne it is infinitely preferable to civilization's *perversion* of nature – its attempt to naturalize its fictions as truths, its parochial categories as moral absolutes.

The most unsettling thing about Iago, therefore, is his unblushing separation of being from seeming. For him Venetian culture is but a whited sepulchre in which 'our country disposition' is not a natural gentility or courtesy but a merely seeming so: 'In Venice [women] do let God see the pranks/They dare not show their husbands', he urges (3.3.204–5). The charge of hypocrisy instantly undermines the conservative attempts of a Guazzo or a Spenser to locate the true source of civility 'deepe within the mynd', for it merely runs into the old Catch 22: the more natural, the more feigned. It is this that enables Iago cynically to treat civility as mere show – like the 'flag and sign of love' (1.1.155) he displays to the trusting Othello – and which makes it easy for him to accuse the suave Cassio of 'putting on the mere form of civil and humane seeming' (2.1.226). It is only a small step from this to insinuating that Othello's cultivated wife is equally capable of giving out 'such a seeming' (3.3.211). As a purely artificial construction which can be bent to self-advantage at will, civility loses at a stroke its pretensions to order, superiority, or goodness. To the extent that *Othello* scrutinizes the contradictions embedded at the heart of civilization, therefore, it shares in the larger question posed by Shakespeare's tragedies and history plays as a whole: what is it that makes a civilization or a nation state collapse in upon itself and descend from civil practice to civil war?

Antony and Cleopatra

The issue receives perhaps its grandest treatment in Shakespeare's next and last tragedy of love, *Antony and Cleopatra* (1606–7). For the civilization that is held up to scrutiny here is none less than that great repository of learning and (for the Renaissance in particular) model of civilized values – imperial Rome. The contrast between Venice and Cyprus in *Othello* expands to the wider political and geographical sweep of a play that tilts not once but continually between those two great historical symbols of cultural difference, Egypt and Rome. In this play, Rome is depicted as the home of austerity and *virtus* – the manly vigour that draws its strength from the self-assured and stable identity of the Roman self. The qualities of Rome are characterized, furthermore, by a linguistic propriety of which Octavia's 'holy, cold, and still conversation' is a typical example (2.6.120). When Lepidus endeavours to bring the disgruntled Caesar and Antony together in common cause against Pompey, he knows that the success of the meeting depends upon 'soft and gentle speech' all round (2.2.3). It is a Roman trait to try to put aside mutual recriminations and to contain conflict in diplomatic language: 'Touch you the sourest points with sweetest terms' (26). The guarding of the tongue is an exercise in self-control, one in which the two sides just about succeed – ''Tis noble spoken', 'Worthily spoken, Maecenas' (105, 109). When the plain-speaking Enobarbus bluntly cuts through the careful rhetoric, it is not the content but only 'The manner of his speech' to which Caesar objects (119). For the Romans, as for the Renaissance humanists who drew their cherished precepts from the handbooks of Roman rhetoric and oratory, the control of words was a first step in the control of the world.

By comparison with such staid and ponderous procedure, however, Egypt represents everything that is Other. Indeed, Rome defines its own reputation for due measure, order, proportion, and degree against the quality that it projects out most insistently upon Egypt – a country whose presiding genius is, as for Spenser's Bower of Bliss, Excess.²⁴ Egypt's great symbol and metonymic centrepiece, 'the o'erflowing Nilus' (1.2.46), metaphors the gush and flow that characterize the landscape, language, and everything else in Egypt. Egypt melts, stretches, bursts, swells, spills over – the dialectical antithesis of the political, sexual and rhetorical containment of Rome. To the critical eye of Rome any encounter with such difference can only be met with blank incomprehension. Antony's proper 'self' compromised by the perceived lust and luxury of the East, he can only be described as 'transform'd', as 'not Antony' (1.1.12, 59). The failure of one culture to define difference in terms more imaginative than simply what it is not was never so starkly indicated. Antony's dotage, like everything else Egyptian, 'O'erflows the measure' (2). A single blanket epithet makes do to characterize the culturally different, reducing its heterogeneity to the bland and partial statements of 'the common liar' (61), 'the general tongue' (1.2.101), or 'the world's report' (2.3.5).

The play obliges us, however, to redraw the parameters of civilization and to question Rome's self-appointed role as the great world-civilizing power. For it is not in Rome or in Octavia's cold bed that love flourishes, and love is, as in *Romeo and Juliet* and *Othello*, the principal agent of civilization, the creative force whose mission is to unite individuals, harmonize the group, and temper the forces of destruction. Love, of course, flourishes in Egypt where its effect, as in the other plays we have looked at, is a marvellous enrichment and expansiveness of human language and experience. For the besotted Antony, the experience of love redefines the contours of the civilized world and indeed totally redraws the map. For him, as for the lover in Donne's elegy 'To his Mistress Going to Bed', Cleopatra is his new empire, his new-found-land:

> Let Rome in Tiber melt, and the wide arch
> Of the ranged empire fall! Here is my space.
>
> (1.1.33–4)²⁵

The spirit of excess extends to human speech and has the natural effect of making hyperbole the common currency in Egypt. Here men do not search, as in Rome, for an etiolated *mot juste* but for words that overgo the limits of convention. 'We cannot call her winds and waters sighs and tears', remarks a jocular Enobarbus of Cleopatra, 'they are greater storms and tempests than almanacs can report' (1.2.144–5). The Romans naturally put such expansiveness down to an Egyptian excessiveness which has rubbed off on and bewitched their Antony, rather as Brabantio assumes that his daughter must have been seduced by magic and witchcraft as nothing else could explain her actions.

Egypt wonderfully expands the limits of human experience and leaves Rome looking increasingly fusty and hidebound. This move towards expansiveness and amplification finds one famous example in Enobarbus's description of the Nile-borne Cleopatra:

> The barge she sat in, like a burnish'd throne,
> Burnt on the water. The poop was beaten gold,
> Purple the sails, and so perfumed that
> The winds were love-sick with them; the oars were silver,
> Which to the tune of flutes kept stroke, and made
> The water which they beat to follow faster,
> As amorous of their strokes. For her own person,
> It beggared all description: she did lie
> In her pavilion – cloth of gold, of tissue –
> O'er-picturing that Venus where we see
> The fancy outwork nature.   (2.2.201–11)

Enobarbus is describing a privileged moment here – Antony's first sight of the Egyptian queen – and his words conjure the sheer visual impact of the scene which, like a great painting, captivates all who see it. Through the artfulness of her self-presentation, Cleopatra outdoes the famous painting of Venus by Apelles in which the painter's art was said to transcend nature. Art outdoes art. 'The *istoria* which merits both praise and admiration will be so agreeably and pleasantly attractive that it will capture the eye of whatever learned or unlearned person is looking at it and will move his soul', writes Leon Battista Alberti in his treatise *On Painting* (1435–6); 'that which first gives pleasure in the *istoria* comes from copiousness and variety of things'.[26] In the same way, Cleopatra's 'infinite variety' (2.2.246) captivates the gaze (and the soul of the gazer), drawing for its power on a subtle blending of the natural with the artificial. As Erasmus writes in *De Copia* (1512), one of the best-known Renaissance schoolbooks instructing youth in the arts of rhetorical embellishment and amplification, 'Nature above all delights in variety; in all this huge concourse of things, she has left nothing anywhere unpainted by her wonderful technique of variety.'[27] For Erasmus, *copia* properly used is the art of bending a great natural resource to one's own use, simply imitating the artfulness or 'painting' of nature itself in order to enhance one's own literary style. If taken to extremes, he concedes, *copia* can assume an excessiveness or 'Asian exuberance' (touches of Rome here) but at its best *copia* is, like the Nile itself, 'a golden river, with thoughts and words pouring out in rich abundance'.

It is the tendency of love to expand and fill all the available space. The sight of Cleopatra in her barge was so extraordinary, enthuses Enobarbus, that had nature not abhorred a vacuum the air itself had gone to gaze on her and 'made a gap in nature' (2.2.228). Cleopatra endures Antony's absence as an empty void, a 'great gap of time' (1.5.5), for where the beloved is the world is and where the beloved is not there is nothing: 'O, my oblivion is a very Antony' (1.3.91). Love's expansiveness does not only move centrifugally, however, pressing out to the limits of the known universe. It also works in the opposite direction, rolling the universe up into a ball and creating language and experience of high intensity. Indeed, the two tendencies are, as Erasmus noted, intimately related for 'who will speak more succinctly than the man who can readily and without hesitation pick out from a huge army of words, from the whole range of figures of speech, the feature that contributes most effectively to brevity?'[28] Here, therefore – as in *Romeo and Juliet* – love also sponsors a move towards epigram and closure. The largest is expressed by the smallest, the greatest by the least – or better still by silence. Antony cannot tell Cleopatra how much he loves her – 'There's beggary in the love that can be reckoned' (1.1.15) – exactly as Juliet refuses Romeo's invitation to blazon their love abroad: 'They are but beggars that can count their worth' (2.6.32). And, again as in *Romeo and Juliet*, *Antony and Cleopatra* demonstrates the same drift from verbal to visual, iconic representation being the most economic form of representation. The play opens with Demetrius and Philo describing Antony as 'the bellows and the fan / To cool a gipsy's lust' (1.1.8–9) to give way immediately to a visual picture of the same: *Enter Antony and Cleopatra . . . with eunuchs fanning her* (stage direction). The exhortations to 'Look', 'Take but good note', 'Behold and see' (10, 11, 13) remind us that the theatre is, before it is anything else, a 'place for seeing' (from θεατρον). In Enobarbus's famous speech, the royal barge that 'Burned on the water' (2.2.202) likewise becomes a word-picture, a visual paradox equivalent to Donne's epigram of the burning ship: 'They in the sea being burnt, they in the burnt ship drown'd'.[29] It is the same privileged vision of Cleopatra that we finally come to see for ourselves, moreover, when, staging her own death in the play's closing moments, she is 'again for Cydnus' (5.2.227), arrayed once more as Antony eventfully saw her for the first time.

Love thus enriches experience and refines and intensifies human language. As such, it is the world's great civilizing force, showing human society the best of which it is capable and forcing us to extend our definition and to reconsider what 'civilization' means. Yet, this being a tragedy, love does not triumph. In the end, love's expansiveness proves unsustainable and its redemptive power too weak for the forces of death. As in *Othello*, furthermore, love is not the innocent victim of circumstance or an uncaring world but, rather, is shown to be compromised, to be the vehicle of its own destruction. The surrounding world 'Shines o'er with civil swords' as Antony notes (1.3.45), but love is not enough to save it because it is not exempt from such internal struggles itself. Love's ability to civilize the world falls victim to its own civil wars, in other words, making battles rage not only around but within the individual and causing self-destruction all round.

Antony and Cleopatra is full of characters who figure the state of civil war within themselves. Octavia is the very picture of predicament. She first appears standing between Caesar and Antony (2.3), an icon of betweenness who becomes increasingly desperate as the parties it was hoped her marriage would bind together only split further apart:

> A more unhappy lady,
> If this division chance, ne'er stood between,
> Praying for both parts...
> ...no midway
> 'Twixt these extremes at all.
> (3.4.12–14, 19–20)

Enobarbus is another such emblem of dilemma, the once-loyal soldier who turns against Antony, sickened by the latter's apparent folly and indecisiveness at the battle of Actium, only to turn back to him again, pricked by remorse at his master's magnanimity. As with Octavia, however, there is no resolution for such divided loyalties, only a state of total impasse: 'I fight against thee? No, I will go seek / Some ditch wherein to die' (4.6.38–9).

The archetype of such self-destructiveness, of course, is Antony himself. In the course of the play Antony comes for many characters to stand as an emblem or summation of particular qualities. He is 'th'abstract of all faults' for the high-minded Caesar (1.4.9). His mere name – 'That magical word of war' (3.1.32) in which lay 'a moiety of the world' (5.1.19) – is enough to spell out a whole universe of ideas and values. Like the Egyptian crocodile which, as Antony jokes, 'is shaped...like itself' (2.7.38), Antony has no point of reference outside himself. He becomes his own metaphor – for Cleopatra, her 'man of men' (1.5.75) or 'Lord of lords' (4.8.16) – since the superlative can have no other point of comparison. Metaphor thus devolves upon itself to become mere tautology – an extreme example of the trend towards epitome or distillation that we have seen elsewhere in the play. Ultimately, however, such magnificent economy and self-reference implodes and collapses in upon itself. Cursing himself for losing at Actium by blindly following Cleopatra's fleeing boats, Antony's once-stable Roman identity breaks apart altogether: 'I have fled myself... My very hairs do mutiny' (3.11.7, 13). Caesar works such self-destructiveness to his own advantage, putting Antony's deserters in his own front line so that when Antony encounters his troops in battle he 'may seem to spend his fury / Upon himself' (4.6.9–10). In the end Antony comes to symbolize what Sidney styles the 'wretched state of man in self-division' and, like the chief characters in the *Arcadia*, he proves incapable of resolving this terrible internal conflict.[30] As with Enobarbus, suicide is the only way out, an end that provides both an economical and a logical conclusion to love's bitter civil wars:

> ANTONY Not Caesar's valour hath o'erthrown Antony,
> But Antony's hath triumphed on itself.
>
> CLEOPATRA So it should be, that none but Antony
> Should conquer Antony, but woe 'tis so! (4.15.14–17)

Antony and Cleopatra thus takes Shakespeare's tragedies of love to their final point of paradoxical resolution – a resolution in self-cancellation and death. Freud's 'struggle between Eros and Death' has been decisively called, and, where the civilizing forces of life and love collapse in upon themselves, woe is indeed the only properly tragic response that is left to us.

NOTES

1. Sigmund Freud, *Civilization and its Discontents* (1930), in *The Standard Edition of the Complete Psychological Works of Sigmund Freud*, ed. and trans. James Strachey, 24 vols. (London: The Hogarth Press, 1960), XXI. 122.
2. For example: 'I will be civil with the maids; I will cut off their heads' (1.1.22); 'Come, civil night, / Thou sober-suited matron all in black' (3.2.10–11); see also the punning exchange between Mercutio and Romeo on the meaning of 'courtesy', 2.4.50–7.
3. 'Wisdom is better than wealth, and a golden sentence worth a world of treasure', a typical humanist view as expressed in Thomas Lodge, *Rosalynde* (1590), ed. Donald Beecher (Ottawa: Dovehouse Editions, 1997), p. 100. For an alternative view of words as nothing but small change, contrast Thomas Nashe, *Christs Teares Over Jerusalem* (1594), in *The Works of Thomas Nashe*, ed. R. B. McKerrow, 5 vols. (Oxford: Blackwell, 1966), II. 184: 'Our English tongue of all languages most swarmeth with the single money of monasillables, which are the onely scandall of it. Bookes written in them and no other seeme like Shop-keepers boxes, that containe nothing else saue halfe-pence, three-farthings, and two-pences.'
4. See Edmund Spenser, *The Faerie Queene* (1590), ed. A. C. Hamilton (London: Longman, 1977), II.ix.51.
5. Ben Jonson, *Discoveries* (pub. 1640), in *Ben Jonson*, ed. C. H. Herford and Percy and Evelyn Simpson, 11 vols. (Oxford: Clarendon Press, 1925–52), VIII. 593.

6. Roger Ascham, *The Schoolmaster* (1570), ed. Lawrence V. Ryan (Charlottesville: University of Virginia Press, 1967), p. 115.

7. Sir Thomas Wilson, *The Arte of Rhetorique* (1553), ed. Thomas J. Derrick (New York: Garland, 1982), pp. 18–19.

8. Samuel Daniel, *Poems and A Defence of Ryme* (1603), ed. Arthur Colby Sprague (University of Chicago Press, 1930), p. 138.

9. Spenser, *Colin Clouts Come Home Againe* (1595), lines 781–2, in *The Yale Edition of the Shorter Poems of Edmund Spenser*, ed. William A. Oram *et al.* (New Haven: Yale University Press, 1989), p. 555.

10. The concept of poetry as a speaking picture – *ut pictura poesis* – derives from Horace's *Ars Poetica*, paragraph 361. See also Sir Philip Sidney, *An Apology for Poetry* (1595), ed. Geoffrey Shepherd (Manchester University Press, 1973), p. 101.

11. See Plato, *Cratylus*, in *Plato: Complete Works*, ed. John M. Cooper (Indianapolis: Hackett, 1997), pp. 101–56.

12. Desiderius Erasmus, *De rationi studii* (1512), in *Collected Works of Erasmus*, vol. XXIV, ed. Craig R. Thompson (University of Toronto Press, 1978), p. 666; Ben Jonson, *Cynthia's Revels* (1601), Prologue, line 20, in *Ben Jonson*, ed. Herford and Simpson, IV. 43.

13. Sidney, *Apology*, ed. Shepherd, p. 113.

14. Sidney, *Astrophil and Stella*, 58, in *The Poems of Sir Philip Sidney*, ed. W. A. Ringler (Oxford: Clarendon Press, 1962), pp. 193–4.

15. Giraldi Cinthio, *On the Composition of Comedies and Tragedies* (1543), selections reproduced in *Literary Criticism: Plato to Dryden*, ed. Allan H. Gilbert (New York: American Book Co., 1940), these quotations pp. 252–3.

16. Thomas Wilson, *Arte of Rhetorique*, p. 18.

17. Stefano Guazzo, *La civile conversatione*, translated by George Pettie and Bartholomew Young as *The Civile Conversation of M. Steeven Guazzo* (1580–6), ed. Charles Whibley, 2 vols. (London: Constable, 1925), I. 56.

18. Spenser, *The Faerie Queene* (1596), VI.i.1, VI. Pro. 5.

19. Samuel Johnson, *The Yale Edition of the Works of Samuel Johnson*, ed. Allen T. Hazen *et al.*, 16 vols. (New Haven: Yale University Press, 1958–90), VIII. 1048.

20. See Harry Berger, *Second World and Green World: Studies in Renaissance Fiction-Making* (Berkeley: University of California Press, 1988).

21. For a discussion of the social habitus, see Pierre Bourdieu, *Outline of a Theory of Practice*, trans. Richard Nice (Cambridge University Press, 1977).

22. Hayden White, 'The Forms of Wildness: Archaeology of an Idea', in *The Tropics of Discourse* (Baltimore, MD: Johns Hopkins University Press, 1978), pp. 150–82, this quotation p. 151.

23. Michel de Montaigne, *Essays*, translated by John Florio (1603), 3 vols. (London: Dent, 1910), I. 219, 223, 224.

24. Spenser, *The Faerie Queene*, II.xii.55–7.

25. See John Donne, Elegy XIX 'To his Mistress Going to Bed', lines 27–9: 'O my America! my new-found-land, / My kingdome, safeliest when with one man man'd, / My Myne of precious stones: My Emperie', in *The Complete English Poems of John Donne*, ed. C. A. Patrides (London: Dent, 1985), p. 184.

26. Leon Battista Alberti, *On Painting*, ed. and trans. John R. Spencer, rev. edn (Yale University Press: New Haven, 1966), p. 75.
27. Desiderius Erasmus, *On Copia of Words and Ideas*, in *Collected Works*, vol. XXIV, ed. Thompson, p. 302, the following two quotations pp. 301, 295.
28. *Ibid.*, p. 300.
29. Donne, 'A burnt ship', line 6, in *Complete English Poems*, ed. Patrides, p. 128.
30. Sir Philip Sidney, *The Countess of Pembroke's Arcadia (The Old Arcadia)*, ed. Jean Robertson (Oxford: Clarendon Press, 1973), p. 63.

11

COPPÉLIA KAHN

Shakespeare's classical tragedies

As twenty-first-century readers, when we approach the five tragedies that Shakespeare set in the Greco-Roman world – *Titus Andronicus*, *Julius Caesar*, *Antony and Cleopatra*, *Coriolanus*, and *Timon of Athens* – we must negotiate among several kinds of cultural and historical differences.[1] A striking moment in *Antony and Cleopatra* exemplifies the challenge these plays pose for us. In the wake of Antony's death and the victory of his arch-rival Octavius, Cleopatra imagines herself a captive in Rome, chief trophy amongst the victor's spoils:

> The quick comedians
> Extemporally will stage us and present
> Our Alexandrian revels; Antony
> Shall be brought drunken forth, and I shall see
> Some squeaking Cleopatra boy my greatness
> I'th'posture of a whore.   (5.2.215–20)

The Egyptian queen pictures this public display in the terms of Elizabethan theatre, her feminine role performed by a boy; strictly speaking, Shakespeare has created an anachronism. Her theatrical imagery also peers into the future, as it were, reminding us that this play has in fact been staged countless times since Shakespeare penned these lines. His play lives on in our own cultural present, in film and popular culture as well as onstage. The events on which it is based took place from 41 to 30 BC, and were fraught with political controversy that was debated in the Renaissance and is still argued over by scholars today. That controversy moulded the views of Antony and the Egyptian queen that came down to Shakespeare through his main source, Plutarch, who wrote nearly a century after Octavius won the empire from Antony. Various perspectives on Antony and Cleopatra criss-cross the centuries, then, none more objective than another. Thus it isn't possible to read directly back in time from Shakespeare to what 'really' happened in Rome, or forward from Shakespeare to 'modern' revisions. 'The classics' doesn't designate an apolitical realm of transhistorical values but rather, like any body of literature, a discourse always open to reinterpretation and even reconstruction, as critical tastes and historical understanding change through the centuries.

Inevitably we bring our own notions of 'the classics' to these plays, and Shakespeare – notwithstanding his own original perspective – gives us not the Romans we think we know, but rather 'the Elizabethan Romans'.[2] Yet because the Elizabethans carried on continuous reassessment of ancient heroes, events, and authors, no single classical tradition existed even then. Thus the category that inspires this essay, '*the* classical tragedies', is somewhat misleading, as is our term 'Greco-Roman'. To us, Greeks and Romans are closely linked, equally honoured, and knowable mainly through the work of erudite scholars. Quite differently, in Shakespeare's day Rome was a sort of cultural parent and ever-present model, and Greece a less familiar, often disparaged distant relative of Rome. We honour Greece for creating tragedy and epic, our most valued literary genres, but few if any links between English Renaissance tragedy and epic and the Greek originals have been demonstrated.

In Shakespeare's day, Rome took precedence over its predecessor Greece for several reasons. First, in English chronicle histories, the founding of Britain was connected to the founding of Rome through Brutus, the grandson of Aeneas, founder of Rome. Richard Grafton, writing in 1569, declares: 'When Brute...first entred this Island and named it Briteyne: there beginneth mine history of this Realme.'[3] In 55 BC, Julius Caesar had invaded Britain, and Roman troops occupied it for several centuries: legend had it that he had built the Tower of London. Indeed, the old Roman wall still defined the boundaries of the city of London, and Hadrian's wall in the north was a well-known landmark linking Britain's past to Rome's.

Second, in the humanistic culture of England, as of Europe generally, reading, writing, and speaking Latin was the key to privilege and authority, and Rome the model of civilization itself. Since the reign of Henry VIII (1509–47), a state-authorized curriculum of Latin authors had trained men, village parsons as well as princes, to govern England, while only well-connected and especially ambitious gentlewomen might, for their own pleasure, learn Latin from tutors at home. Progressing from Terence through Plautus, Virgil, Horace, Cicero, Caesar, and Sallust, generations of schoolboys translated back and forth from English to Latin, memorized passages, and acquired a *copia* (store) of rhetorical figures they could wield to defend any proposition, or flaunt to impress any patron or mistress. They wrote compositions on such themes as 'Vituperate Julius Caesar' or 'That...Cicero...should not accept the condition offered by Antony',[4] engaging in the clash of viewpoints that had shaped Roman history and its historians. As I will argue throughout this essay, Shakespeare brought these ambiguities and contradictions into his classical tragedies, so that 'the conflict of interpretation that the audience brings to the theater becomes part of the play'.[5]

Finally, the Latin curriculum shaped habits of reading and thought long after formal schooling. The ruling elite sought political and ethical models in Latin authors, extracting *sententiae* (mottoes) from them to copy down in their commonplace books, or writing marginalia in their Latin texts to work out analogies between the politics of republican Rome and of the English court. Elizabethans read the Latin historians in particular as a source of military strategy and models for government. William Fulbecke, for example, finds a homely moral for Englishmen in the fall of Rome, which in his eyes was due solely to ambition, and advises his countrymen to a 'humble estimation of ourselves'.[6] In the character of Fluellen, the Welsh captain in *Henry V* blindly devoted to 'the disciplines of the pristine wars of the Romans' (3.2.82–3), Shakespeare mocks infatuation with the ancients as models for the present. Near the end of Elizabeth's reign, the question of whether it was right to rebel against a tyrant was being discussed under the cover of whether Julius Caesar was a tyrant.

Though humanist educators promoted the study of Greek, and praised the ancient Greeks enthusiastically,[7] Greek was only introduced midway in the grammar school curriculum, and rather than studying Greek 'classics', students read the New Testament in Greek. Editions of Latin texts and translations of Latin texts into English far outnumbered those of Greek: even by 1640, for example, none of Aeschylus' tragedies had been translated, and only one of Aristophanes' comedies. Furthermore, a Roman and medieval tradition of denigrating the Greeks persisted in the Renaissance: 'merry Greeks' were held to be typically 'licentious, luxurious, frivolous, bibulous, venereal, insinuating, perfidious, and unscrupulous'.[8] This widespread cultural valorization of Latin over Greek, then, partly accounts for the fact that Shakespeare wrote four tragic dramas and a tragic poem (*The Rape of Lucrece*) based on Roman legend and history, and only one tragedy (which has often been called a satire) drawn from Greek materials, though he used Greek settings in other genres (Hanna, pp. 107–28). For all these reasons, then (in addition to its own artistic peculiarities), *Timon of Athens* stands apart from the four Roman tragedies, as it will to some extent in this essay.

Shakespeare probably learned his Latin (and possibly some Greek) in the local grammar school of Stratford-upon-Avon, beginning at about the age of seven. We don't know how long his formal training may have lasted, but we do know that he read Latin because he sometimes appropriates or echoes the wording of Latin authors, even when an English translation is available. Ever since Ben Jonson asserted, in the tribute he wrote for the 1623 Folio edition of Shakespeare's works, that the poet knew 'small Latine and lesse Greeke', scholars have tried to determine just how learned Shakespeare was. Whether he read his favourite Latin authors in the original or in translation, or whether he knew Greek at all, however, matters less than what he found in his reading and how he used what he found. Besides, in addition to a fair selection of translations, Shakespeare had access to the ancient world through contemporary abridgements, digests, anthologies, dictionaries, encyclopaedias, and handbooks that organized what the educated person should know about the Greeks and Romans: 'the classical presence was ubiquitous'.[9]

Just as important as what Shakespeare read about the ancient world, however, is what he saw and heard of it in his workplace, the great city of London. Royal entries and coronation pageants and the annual Lord Mayor's pageants, open to all, linked Rome to the political order of Britain. For example, on 24 November 1588, to celebrate the defeat of the Armada, Elizabeth imitated the ancient Romans by riding in triumph in a symbolic chariot and, on his accession to the throne, James was welcomed to London in 'imperial style', triumphal arches decked with Roman gods and Latin inscriptions proclaiming him 'England's Caesar'.

When Shakespeare began writing about Rome in the early 1590s, a tradition of plays drawing on Roman history and legend was already well established. Frequent onstage representations of the senate and the capitol, tribunes and triumphs, Caesar and Pompey in the theatre made Rome seem less strange. In fact, Rome in the theatre was as much assimilated to an English scene and an English sensibility as it was distanced to the antique past. This all too comfortable familiarity produced some jarring aesthetic disjunctions, though. For example, in Thomas Lodge's *The Wounds of Civil War* (1587), two 'burghers' with English names talk in comic *double-entendres* like Dogberry and Verges in Shakespeare's *Much Ado About Nothing*. In Thomas Heywood's *The Rape of Lucrece* (1609), a courtier turned balladeer who sings bawdy songs in a thoroughly English idiom rubs shoulders with the noble Romans of Livy's sombre narrative.

Because the public theatre had no established canon like the one on which the Latin curriculum was founded, playwrights picked up material for plays from every conceivable source. Roman history and legend competed with Italian novellas, medieval romances, and English histories as matter for the stage, and often combined with them in the same play. Here, Rome didn't command the priority it enjoyed in elite culture. Both the anonymous *Caesar's Revenge* (printed 1607) and Thomas Lodge's *Wounds* owe as much in structure and convention to the revenge play and the *de casibus* tragedy as they do to Roman history. Though many in the audience might have recognized the quotations, allusions, appropriations, and parodies of the ancients that could pop up in any play, many others knew little more than the names of a few famous classical 'worthies'. This popular milieu, eclectic and improvisational, freed Shakespeare to find his own perspective on the Greeks and the Romans. He could approach venerable figures of the ancient world in the opportunistic spirit of a popular playwright, a cultural entrepreneur hoping to make a profitable entertainment.

Even Plutarch's *Lives of the Noble Greeks and Romans*, 'Englished' by Thomas North in 1579, Shakespeare's major source for the Roman tragedies, offered no coherent account, or even a vague idea, of the course of Roman history. Writing near the end of the first century AD, Plutarch could assume that his readers knew the institutions, mores, political issues, and events of Roman history, and plunge into the circumstantial details of each biography without explicitly contextualizing it. Shakespeare, in contrast, had to evoke the workings of a republic or an empire and make them intelligible to the subjects of a monarchy. Succeeding brilliantly, he created credible playworlds by drawing not just on Plutarch's highly anecdotal and digressive narratives, but on any source that served his purposes.

Yet in contrast to the mingle-mangle of English and Roman styles in Heywood or Lodge, Shakespeare makes his Roman and Greek tragedies coherent and probing representations of the dilemmas and struggles of life in the city, the republic, or the empire. His famous anachronisms – clocks in *Julius Caesar* and billiards in *Antony and Cleopatra* – help dramatize the underlying logic of interests, ideologies, and personalities in those tragedies. The entertainments he produces are of a different order from those of Heywood or Lodge because he takes his ancient materials seriously: he makes Rome, or Athens, the testing-ground rather than the backdrop of heroic virtue. In other Roman plays, ethical or psychological questions arising from the heroes' actions are often subsumed into the overarching *de casibus* motif of Fortune's turning wheel. As Cassius declares of Caesar in the anonymous *Caesar's Revenge*, 'Thou placed art in top of fortunes wheele, / Her wheele must turne, thy glory must eclipse.'[10] In contrast, Shakespeare's hero turns that wheel himself. What he does brings about his fate, and his commitment to the ethical and political ideas of his community determines what he does.

As Timothy Hampton explains, 'The promotion of ancient images of virtue as patterns that aim to form or guide readers is a central feature of almost every major text in the Renaissance...The heroic or virtuous figure offers a model of excellence, an icon...[who] can be seen as a marked sign that bears the moral and historical authority of antiquity.' These exemplars were widely disseminated in the Renaissance, as a key motif in the humanistic programme of emulating the ancient world. The exemplar's name served as a sign that contained 'the entire history of the hero's deeds'[11]. Not only educated people but unlettered common folk could recognize the great exemplars from Greek and Roman history. 'Julius Caesar' or 'Pompey' signified a puissant conqueror who commanded vast foreign territories and enjoyed universal fame, only to be brought down by a fellow Roman who had been his ally; 'Lucrece' stood for a narrative of rape, revenge, and revolution that culminated in the founding of the republic. The heroes of three of Shakespeare's Roman tragedies – Brutus, Julius Caesar, Mark Antony – are renowned exemplars, and the fourth, Titus Andronicus, is modelled on exemplars of the early republic. The heroine of his tragic poem *The Rape of Lucrece* is an exemplar of chastity for women. Plutarch's *Lives of the Noble Greeks and Romans* was a treasury of such exemplars, which in Elizabethan and Jacobean England embodied an ethical image of Rome particularly: 'a set of virtues, thought of as characterizing Roman civilization – soldierly, severe, self-controlled, self-disciplined'.[12]

Because Rome was a patriarchal society, Romanness *per se* was closely linked to an ideology of masculinity. Though the Roman plays include vivid, complex female characters, they no less than the male characters are configured in terms of the overriding cultural ideal of *virtus*, a word for manliness or manly virtue that is derived from the Latin word for man, *vir*. In the fiercely martial Rome of *Coriolanus*, courage in battle is the essence of manliness; in *Julius Caesar*, it is shaped by the idea of the republic, in *Titus Andronicus*, by *pietas* – or devotion to family honour. Whatever its specific content, Roman manliness is characterized by service to the state: all Shakespeare's Roman heroes are first and foremost public men whose family ties and personal relations don't exist in what we would call a 'private' realm, but rather are conceived and pursued as part of the hero's public identity.

This compelling idea of Roman manliness is dramatized in three central motifs: emulation, wounds, and chastity. These motifs will be explained briefly here, to be fleshed out as each play is discussed. First, emulation: derived from the Latin *aemulari*, to rival, the word itself is defined in the *OED* as 'to copy or imitate with the object of equalling or excelling'. The cultural pattern it describes originated in Greek society as a one-on-one rivalry or *agon* through which a hero wins his name by pitting himself against his likeness or equal in contexts of courage and strength. Like Hector and Achilles in the *Iliad*, in the Roman plays pairs of evenly matched heroes act out a mixture of admiration, imitation, and domination that ends in the destruction of one rival and the triumph of the other. Second, wounds are a central, recurring image that is the sign both of *virtus* and of its instability. The Latin word for wound is *vulnus*, the root of 'vulnerability'. In an obvious sense, wounds image a bodily vulnerability that, in patriarchal cultures, is easily associated with women: they show that flesh can be penetrated and bleed, they make apertures in the body. But when Roman heroes, armed with 'soldierly, severe' traits of self-control and self-discipline, seek, endure, and surmount wounds, they demonstrate their manliness and their Romanness. Third, though women seem 'socially peripheral' to the patriarchal Roman state, they are actually 'symbolically central' to it, by means of their chastity.[13] Chastity isn't a freely willed practice or a trait natural to women; rather, it arises from their acculturation to patriarchal control over their reproductive power – their wombs. Through the national cult of Vesta, virgin goddess of the hearth, Rome made such control sacred and identified it with the very continuity of the state.

Titus Andronicus

Shakespeare was about thirty in 1594 when *Titus Andronicus* was published, but this sensational revenge tragedy is marked by the bravura of a younger poet who wants to show off both his knowledge of classical authors and his mastery of a crowd-pleasing popular genre. Weaving the Ovidian tale of Philomel into a Senecan revenge tragedy that culminates in a Thyestean banquet of parent eating child, seeding allusions to the *Aeneid* in nearly every scene, Shakespeare even seems to compete with his Latin predecessors, making the horrors of his source-tales more horrible: 'Not one rapist but two, not one murdered child but five, not one or two mutilated organs but six, not a one-course meal but a two.'[14] Yet a serious purpose underlies its sensationalism. Shakespeare generates his main action from versions of Roman *virtus* and *pietas*, making this play a serious critique of Roman ideology and institutions that resonates with contemporary English concerns. He fashions his hero's character along the lines of the great exemplars from the republic while placing him in a milieu of imperial decadence. The play insists on an antithesis between civilized Rome and the barbaric Goths, only to break it down: the real enemy lies within Rome, in its extreme, rigid conception of manly virtue, personified in Titus.

The play opens in high Roman fashion by staging two public ceremonies, an election and a funeral. A general returning victorious from a ten-year campaign against the Goths, Titus is declared the new emperor, but final rites for his two sons slain in battle take precedence over public office. His surname 'Pius' recalls the epithet describing Aeneas, founder of Rome. Titus's form of *pietas*, however, trips off the revenge mechanism that drives the play to its savage denouement. Deaf to the pleas of his prisoner Tamora, queen of the Goths, he insists on sacrificing her eldest son so that his own two sons can rest in peace. Ironically alluding to his surname, Tamora brands his action 'cruel irreligious piety' (1.1.130).

Once her son's limbs are 'lopp'd', Tamora becomes Titus's enemy, and once she conspires against his children, he becomes the injured, avenging father on the model of *The Spanish Tragedy*. The play can be seen as the story of Titus's transformation from pious Roman to revenge hero, a transformation he accomplishes by struggling through the tangled matrix of outrages that Tamora perpetrates. One crime spawns another, and the ultimate source of all is the offended, alienated mother who has escaped patriarchal control. As a *quid pro quo* for her murdered son, Tamora engineers the rape and mutilation of his daughter Lavinia, who then becomes the focus of action in the middle part of the tragedy, and the most shocking of its many images of bodily violation. Not only is she violated by the queen's two surviving sons: her tongue is cut out and her hands are cut off.

The audience is privy to the knowledge of Lavinia's rape, which leaves no outward mark. It is her all too obvious mutilations that capture the attention of her male kin, but hinder them from realizing that she has been raped. In a painful sequence of scenes (2.3, 3.1, 3.2, 4.1), first Titus's brother Marcus, then Titus and the remaining Andronici try to interpret Lavinia's signs, but project on to them their own mistaken meanings. Because we know Lavinia's hidden truth, however, these scenes ironically serve to dramatize the erasure of the female voice in the Roman patriarchy; to destabilize the language in which women are customarily figured as objects of exchange or vessels of reproduction; and to bring obliquely to light what has been censored.

Lavinia finally tells her story by rifling the pages of Ovid's *Metamorphoses*, one of the master texts of Latin culture, to cite the tale of Philomel. Then, in a gesture as ironic and ambiguous as that of the handmaiden, she takes her uncle's staff in her mouth, guides it with her stumps, and scratches the Latin word for rape and the names of her attackers in the earth (4.1). Thus she figures the double bind of women, who must either speak in the language of the fathers or improvise other means of communication in its interstices. Once Lavinia has made the rape known, the task of avenging it passes into the hands of her father, who is now positioned between the injured daughter and Tamora, the avenging mother, whose rampant evil (she has, meanwhile, given birth to Aaron's bastard child) he must contain. In terms of the play's gender politics, Titus repossesses the initiative illicitly seized by the mother, and re-establishes patriarchal control over her.

He does so in a clever, supremely fitting denouement typical of revenge tragedy. Tamora attacked his progeny by supervising the murder of his sons and the rape of his daughter; she raided his treasury and mocked the sign of his power, his daughter. Now he insults her womb (the word also means stomach), the site of her power, by making her 'swallow her own increase' (5.2.191). Then, citing as 'pattern, precedent, and lively warrant' Verginius's murder of his daughter in Livy's history of Rome, he kills Lavinia. Both murders are intended to assert the social and ideological centrality of the father's guardianship of his daughter's chastity. Thus despite the inconceivable wounds Titus has endured with heroic strength, he remains unchanged in his adherence to the central precepts underlying Roman patriarchy. What has changed, in the course of this daring, clever, and moving tragedy, is our awareness of the destructiveness inherent in the manly virtue it produces.

Julius Caesar

In Anglo-American culture, *Julius Caesar* more than any other literary work has created a lasting image of public duty, political idealism, ringing oratory, and patrician Stoicism as keynotes of the classical world. It is surely Shakespeare's most 'classical' tragedy. This popular image, however, is belied by the textual reality, for in fact it is an enigmatic play, representing the assassination of Caesar from shifting perspectives that frustrate any certain judgement of either the victim or his assassins. Cicero's statement, 'But men may construe things after their fashion, / Clean from the purpose of the things themselves' (1.3.34–5), better suggests how we experience the play, for though it poses many questions it provides no clear answers, leaving us to 'construe things' for ourselves. Was Caesar a tyrant who deserved to die, or a ruler whose greatness provoked the envy of lesser minds? Was Brutus 'the noblest Roman of them all', or a misguided idealist? How can we tell? By making the motives and the personalities of Caesar, Brutus, and Mark Antony so richly ambiguous, Shakespeare involves us in their political dilemma as if it were our own.

Because an extensive critical literature explores these questions concerning the play's main characters, this essay will focus instead on the conception of 'Rome' (mentioned thirty-two times in some form, more than in any other play): that, I suggest, from which both characters and action are generated. The Rome of *Julius Caesar* is specifically the republic, and it is the mysticized ideal of the republic that impels Brutus to lead the conspiracy against Caesar, that compels the conspirators' belief in their cause, that generates a discourse endowing them and Caesar as well with identity, agency, and manly virtue. Most of all it is the 'public' style of the play that makes its Rome a republic. The major scenes take the form of public debates. Even in private, characters speak formally, in lofty abstractions, and refer to themselves in the third person ('illeism'), as though they are spectators and audience of themselves as public figures.

This construction of the self as a public entity emanates from the patrician reverence for ancestry and public service so prominent in Roman social practice as in literature. In the words of Leo Braudy,

> the political history of Rome was clearly written in the genealogies of its great families for all to see. *Nobilis* in Latin originally means someone who is *known*. The upper class, the political class, was therefore by definition a class whose families were known for their public adherence to the public good...[15]

Yet, as Gary Miles remarks, 'It is...precisely the public dimension of his Romans' lives that is most problematic for Shakespeare', because he is at the same time deeply engaged in revealing 'the interior life of his characters'.[16] It isn't the predominance of the public realm, but rather the dilemma of how public and private are related to each other that is central to the play's conception of Rome. In the course of the conspiracy, the ethos of the republic demands that Brutus and his comrades separate their inner worlds from the public domain, by placing the public good above any personal consideration. It is this separation that constitutes them as Romans. More specifically, the republic makes them men, infuses them with manly virtue, because the public realm is associated with Roman 'firmness' and the private realm with 'the melting spirits of women'(2.1.122).

It is already evident from the play's first scene, however (and becomes even clearer as the roar of the crowd punctuates their conversation), that even though the *idea* of the republic governs patrician mentality, in actual practice the republic has already ceased to exist. The tribunes rebuke the plebs for transferring their allegiance from Pompey to Caesar – from one strong man to the next – not for transgressing against the republic. Allusions to Pompey run through the play to remind us that before Caesar, another charismatic leader bypassed Rome's 'noble bloods' to gain a plebeian power base. Though in person Caesar may fall short of the mystique he generates, like Pompey he knows how to use 'the tag-rag people', as Casca calls them, but for Brutus and Cassius they hardly exist (1.2.252). These patricians imagine themselves the ethical and political heartbeat of the republic, while in reality they have lost power to a constituency they despise. Thus the republic is for them, in the sense proposed by the post-Marxist philosopher Louis Althusser, an ideology, an imaginary conception of their actual relation to the Roman state.[17] As Sigurd Burckhardt argues, Brutus and the conspirators aren't guilty of treachery, nor is their conception of the republic 'right' or 'wrong': in a deeper sense than clocks or billiards, it is an anachronism.[18]

In another sense as well, the republic of *Julius Caesar* can be understood in terms of ideological contradiction. It is intricately bound up with the basically agonistic, highly competitive practices of the Roman ruling elite institutionalized in the sequence of electoral contests for state office known as the *cursus honorum*. At the top level, the level at which a Caesar or a Pompey wins or loses, the *cursus* is based on emulation, 'an unstable combination of identification and rivalry, love and hate'.[19] But how can emulation coexist with 'the general good'? Cassius and Brutus believe that all Romans are brothers, united by their shared belief in the republic. But emulation is equally Roman, as the shifting allegiances in the play suggest. Caesar and Pompey were allies before they were rivals, and Brutus first supported Pompey, then became Caesar's favourite when Pompey fell. Even Brutus and Cassius, friends and confederates profoundly united by shared ideals, quarrel bitterly at the end of the play. When Brutus, genuinely dedicated to the common good, ponders whether Caesar would be king, he imagines Caesar as climbing 'ambition's ladder', attaining 'the upmost round', and then 'scorning the base degrees by which he did ascend' (2.1.21–7). It is this vision of being trampled on by a rival that enables Brutus to 'fashion it thus' despite the admitted lack of evidence, to make the leap beyond proof and logic to kill Caesar.

Yet Brutus is at the same time reluctant to murder Caesar, and it is precisely his reluctance that gives rise to the second scene, a conversation with Portia on the eve of the assassination (2.1). The scene depends on our prior knowledge that, as she suspects, Brutus does have 'some sick offence within his mind'. Just before the conspirators arrived, in two brief soliloquies he admitted that his 'genius' (immortal spirit) and his 'mortal instruments' (his powers as a man) were at war as he contemplated 'the acting of a dreadful thing' – the assassination (2.1.61–9, 77–85). Then, in taking leadership of the conspiracy, he repressed his doubt and fear. But they return when Portia urges him to confide in her by declaring,

> Tell me your counsels, I will not disclose 'em.
> I have made strong proof of my constancy,
> Giving myself a voluntary wound
> Here, in the thigh: can I bear that with patience,
> And not my husband's secrets?   (2.1.298–302)

Women – untrained in reason, dwelling in the *domus* (household) and excluded from the forum, susceptible in the extreme to the affections – lack access to constancy: control over the affections, adherence to rationally grounded principles like those of the republic, firmness. It is men who are firm, and women who are 'melting spirits'. The constancy to which Portia lays claim through self-wounding can be traced to Stoic philosophy, well-known in England through translations of Boethius, Cicero, Seneca, and

Justus Lipsius, and a hallmark of Romanness as presented on the English stage. Not surprisingly, its leading postulates are framed in the same terms as the opposition of masculine to feminine: reason and opinion, soul and body, constancy and inconstancy.

For the sake of 'the general good' as the republican ethos defines it, individual moral scruples must be overcome. If such scruples are voiced by a woman, in the private sphere of the *domus*, all the more reason to disregard them (as Caesar also does, in the following scene). Portia's urgings allow Brutus's scruples to be feminized, privatized, and discarded as he embarks upon the conspiracy, but nonetheless, those urgings underpin his construction as a tragic hero who must embrace a man's duty and repress his 'feminine' fears. On the other hand, Portia's wound also denaturalizes constancy, suggesting that it can be learned, and isn't necessarily native to the male gender. Furthermore, the site of the wound, in her thigh, hints ambiguously at a genital wound, which psychoanalysis would take to be the wound of castration, signifying that as a woman, she lacks the phallus, symbol of power in patriarchal society. In the words of Madelon Sprengnether, 'she reveals the underlying paradox of the play, which equates manliness with injury, so that the sign of masculinity becomes the wound'.[20]

Mark Antony eulogizes Brutus as 'the noblest Roman of them all', because 'He only, in a general honest thought / And common good to all' murdered Caesar (5.5.68–72). Voicing the same cherished ideal of the republic that Brutus stated when he reasoned his way into the conspiracy, the vengeful and ambitious Mark Antony sees him as he saw himself. The triumvirate of which he is a member rules by fiat and terror. Yet he too affirms the republic as a government of and for 'the common good'. But perhaps it is more significant that he envisions one man only in that republic who triumphs – in virtue – over all the rest.

Antony and Cleopatra

Antony and Cleopatra, published in 1608 nine years after *Julius Caesar* was first performed, is Shakespeare's most daring and original classical tragedy. Actually, the play refuses to confine itself to a single genre: it is tragedy, comedy, history, and romance all at once. As a 'love tragedy', in Renaissance terms it is an oxymoron, and probably better classified as 'a tragic experience embedded in a comic structure' (Adelman, *Common Liar*, p. 52). Still, no generic category can explain its disjunction between realism and romance, personified in the hero and heroine, who are petty and grand by turns, who declaim and then squabble. Michael Neill identifies hyperbole (called 'the overreacher' by the Renaissance rhetorician George Puttenham) as the play's basic rhetorical and structural principle. Aiming high, this tragedy often tumbles into anticlimax, creating the 'perceived gap between expectation and performance' that is the leitmotiv of so much interpretation.[21]

Perhaps in reaction to this stylistic and generic hybridity, many have read the play in terms of binary oppositions under the general headings 'Rome' and 'Egypt'. War and love, public and private, duty and pleasure, reason and sensuality, male and female then make up the framework of the play's meaning.

From the beginning, however, when Octavius and Mark Antony became rivals for rule of the empire, the opposition of Rome to Egypt was politically motivated and crafted. Writers under Octavius's patronage who were later venerated as 'Augustan' – Virgil, Ovid, Horace – fused xenophobia with patriarchal ideology in order to demonize Cleopatra as Rome's most dangerous enemy, a foreigner and a woman whose power was fatally inflected by her sexuality. They made Cleopatra and Egypt the Other, at the same time portraying Antony as a traitor to Rome corrupted and alienated by his love for her. In this discourse, Octavius seemed the only true Roman fit to rule. This play, then, isn't only *about* two super-heroes competing for sole dominance over an empire; in a historical sense, the literary and historical materials on which it draws *constitute* part of that struggle. Shakespeare draws on Plutarch even more closely here than in *Julius Caesar*, and though Plutarch – a Greek writing more than a century after the events in question – makes Cleopatra more complex and ambiguous than his predecessors do, he too sees her as the cause of Antony's downfall.

Understandably fascinated by Cleopatra, generations of critics have focused on her, viewing the play primarily as a 'love tragedy'. But the contest for mastery between Antony and Octavius is at least as important as the love affair, and much of the continuity between this play and those before and after it resides in the agonistic relationship of two heroes. Despite the obvious contrasts of character between Antony and Octavius, they mirror each other in a blinding desire for *imperium*. Early in the play, when Antony asks the soothsayer, 'Whose fortunes shall rise higher, Caesar's or mine?', it is clear that Antony, like Brutus with Julius Caesar or Coriolanus with Aufidius, is locked into the Roman cultural pattern of emulation (2.3.15). For his part, eulogizing Antony at the end, Octavius Caesar admits, 'I have followed thee to this . . . We could not stall together / In the whole world' (5.1.36, 39–40). 'If thou dost play with him at any game', the Soothsayer warns Antony, 'thou art sure to lose,' explaining that Antony's 'high, unmatchable' guardian spirit will always be overpowered if Caesar is near (2.3.25–30). Significantly, the Soothsayer doesn't advise Antony to abandon Cleopatra but rather, to preserve his 'lustre' – his charisma, fame, authority – by keeping his distance from Caesar. Thus not only Antony's pleasure but also his advantage lies in the East, in Egypt. His genuine fascination with Cleopatra notwithstanding, she also serves as an alibi for gaining the distance from Caesar that can enable his 'unmatchable' spirit to triumph in the end.

Yet, however typically Roman Antony is in emulation, in another sense he fails to fit the mould. In his passion for Cleopatra, he 'o'erflows the measure', crosses the boundary between Rome and Other, and violates the cultural codes in which manly virtue is written. His passion for her shakes the foundations of that virtue and reveals its fragility in relation to the feminine Other, while his rivalry with Caesar enables him to shore up his masculine identity. Repeatedly, Cleopatra draws Antony to her, dividing him from Caesar and all that is Roman; repeatedly, he spins back into Caesar's orbit, to the familiar, fatal game of emulation. Thus his passion, rather than simply feminizing him in service to her lust as the Romans believe, actually enters into the dynamics of rivalry.

In the dizzying succession of defeats and victories, quarrels and reconciliations that follow Antony's defeat at Actium, he undergoes an experience of self-loss triggered not so much by defeat at Caesar's hands as by his sense of betrayal at Cleopatra's: not defeat *per se*, but what he perceives as domination by a woman, is what unmans Antony.[22] 'O, thy vile lady!', he cries to the eunuch who serves her, 'She has robbed me of my sword' (4.14.22–3). Defeated and believing Cleopatra dead, through suicide he seeks to regain his manly virtue and Roman identity. Almost invariably, critics call Antony's attempt to kill himself 'bungled' or 'botched', and consider it a theatrical and moral disaster. But on the English stage and in humanistic studies, suicide was a well-established marker of the Roman exemplar's dignity. Many were familiar with the deaths of Lucrece, Cato, and Brutus as signifying their rationality and free will. Moreover, the hero who died *sua manu* – by his own hand – robbed his rival of victory over him, avoided the shame of defeat, and retained his own name and honour untarnished. Though this secular rationale clashed with well-ingrained Christian prohibitions, still, because defence of one's honour was as central to the ethos of the ruling elite in England as it was to the Roman patricians, suicide served as a marker of nobility and commanded a certain respect. Finally, the prospect of being led in triumph as Caesar's captive, twice anticipated by both hero and heroine in four vivid descriptions of some length, and often referred to by others, makes suicide more urgent: it is Antony's last gesture in the contest that has defined him, the only means left to him of besting his rival.

Coriolanus

Gail Kern Paster astutely remarks that *Julius Caesar* and *Coriolanus* both 'enact a central urban paradox: the social mandate for heroic self-sacrifice collides with the heroic mandate for self-realization conceived in civic terms'.[23] With some qualifications, the same might be said of *Timon of Athens*. In all three tragedies, the city turns against heroes who seemingly embody its fundamental values, and in both *Coriolanus* and *Timon* the paradox is doubled when the hero in turn becomes the city's enemy and sets out to destroy it. Though this harsh, violent play has never enjoyed the popularity of other Shakespearean tragedies, in recent decades it has gained respect: feminist critics especially have unpacked the logic underlying its profound critique of Rome's militaristic ethos.[24] That critique focuses on the paradoxical position of mothers in patriarchy, for it is the hero's relationship to his mother, Volumnia, that accounts for both his greatness and his downfall.

In *Coriolanus*, Shakespeare follows Plutarch's biography in leaving the father's place vacant, thus focusing on Volumnia's power as a mother, which she gains by fusing her nurturance with the masculinist ideology of Rome. 'Thy valiantness was mine', she says to her son: 'thou suck'st it from me' (3.2.130). In this Rome of the early republic, 'Valour is the chiefest virtue' (2.2.78). Here Shakespeare plays on words by identifying valour as the essence or virtue of *virtus*.[25] Volumnia uses nursing as a metaphor for her role in forming her son's temperament and value system, but that role doesn't end when she sends him, still only 'a man-child', to war. Though he has become Rome's most honoured warrior, he remains 'bound to his mother'. He seeks his wounds obsessively, for two contradictory reasons: to please his mother and to assert his supremacy in valour – precisely as a defence against that emotional dependency on her, which in fact impels his hypermasculine immersion in blood and wounds. Furthermore, on a social and political level, the corollary of his valour is his unflinching contempt and blistering anger towards whatever he sees as deviation from his patrician warrior code, notably, the hungry, mercurial proletarian mob.

Coriolanus is Shakespeare's least inward hero: he has little if any self-knowledge, and only one soliloquy. Rather, through the play as a whole, Shakespeare makes the psychological and political dimensions of his tragedy deeply coherent through the fusion of emotionally resonant imagery with highly charged, often brutal action. For example, in the seven battle scenes (1.4–10) dramatizing Rome's siege against the city of Corioli, the hero re-enacts his dilemma of trying to be at once a man and his mother's boy. He enters the quasi-feminine enclosure of the city alone to fight an entire army, then emerges victorious, 'mantled', 'smeared', and 'masked' in blood (1.6.29,

69, 1.8.10). Despite his contempt for the cowardly soldiers who refuse to follow him, 'They all take him up in their arms' as he shouts, 'Make you a sword of me!' (1.6.75–6).

The play begins at a political turning point in the history of Rome: the creation of tribunes to represent the interests of the proletarians. Though the patricians retain political supremacy, the election ritual is designed to reflect the newly won power of the people: the candidate must don humble garb and show his wounds to them as proof that his service to the state makes him worthy of their votes. Coriolanus, nominated to stand as candidate for consul, cannot refuse the honour. This ritual demands of him, however, precisely what he cannot perform: he must beg the people for their votes and show his wounds to them. Because both wounds and people represent for him the hidden reality of his dependency on Volumnia, any social recognition he wins as man, warrior, or office-holder also reinscribes him as her nursling. He cannot force himself, despite her urgings, to dissemble his scorn for the mob, and so when he lashes out at them, he is banished from Rome. 'Like to a lonely dragon', Coriolanus stalks into exile – but immediately allies himself with Aufidius, his enemy rival, and vows to destroy Rome. In the bonding of the two warriors, Shakespeare represents Roman emulation with more explicitly erotic intensity than in any of the classical tragedies. When Aufidius embraces Coriolanus as a new-found ally, he confesses that ever since being defeated by him, he has 'Dreamt of encounters 'twixt thyself and me – / We have been down together in my sleep, / Unbuckling helms, fisting each other's throat – ' (4.5.120–3), and compares his joy to that of a bridegroom. Yet in the end his rivalry, less noble-minded than Coriolanus's, will lead him to devise the hero's death.

The play's tragic denouement stages a contradiction between the patrician warrior ethos Volumnia inculcated in Coriolanus and the kind of pity and tenderness she has, it seems, rooted out of him. On the one hand, to pursue his revenge would indeed be to 'stand as if a man were author of himself / And knew no other kin' (5.3.35–7), the most extreme denial of his bond to a matrix both social and emotional. It would also be completely congruent with the relentless, narrowly defined integrity she instilled in him in the name of valour. On the other hand, to relent as he finally does means to feel pity and love for the first time, to be more of a man and yet, paradoxically, less than ever his mother's son. He relents as she asks him to, but on grounds that she has never allowed him to recognize. And ironically, though she is hailed as the saviour of Rome, the power that the state invested in her as a mother also locked her son into the kind of manly virtue that turned him into its enemy. The mother who has lived only through her son survives, but he is sacrificed so that she and the state with which she is identified may live. Surely *Coriolanus* constitutes Shakespeare's most trenchant critique of Rome.

Timon of Athens

Three of the Roman plays are set in the city itself, and though *Antony and Cleopatra* ranges far and wide in locale, it consistently counters Egyptian sensuality with Roman measure. The Athens of *Timon of Athens*, in contrast, lacks monuments such as the capitol to signify that it is a seat of government, landmarks like the Tiber, or the carpenters and cobblers of *Julius Caesar*'s first scene to evoke daily urban life. When Timon turns his back on the city walls to exile himself, an archetype of the city as marker of civilization itself is invoked, rather than any specific sense of Athens as the city in which democracy began. Like the comedies and romances with Greek settings or sources (*The Comedy of Errors* or *Pericles*, for example), this play is ec-centric rather than centred in the polis: it moves outwards, beyond the wilderness in which Timon digs for roots, to 'the very hem o'th'sea' (5.4.66).

Similarly, its hero is eccentric, veering from boundless generosity to single-minded misanthropy, each stance absolute and uncompromising. His extremes give the play its distinctive bi-polar structure, the first three acts dramatizing Timon's mysteriously indiscriminate, obsessive giving that inevitably collapses when resources run out; the last two acts, his rejection of Athenian society and failed attempt to raze it to the ground. We are even more disengaged from Timon than from Coriolanus, because whether he demonstrates love or hatred for mankind, he is set apart: he has no family, holds no office, and is equally estranged from women and from politics. Though his alienation from society has been compared to Lear's, Timon's venomous diatribes take the form of a satirist's anatomizing catalogues rather than of cries from the heart.

Clues to the play's coherence reside both in the emotional resonances of its imagery and in the similarity of Timon's giving to Jacobean practices of patronage and credit finance.[26] In the first scene, a poet describes his depiction of the goddess Fortuna in a work he will present to Timon in hope of remuneration. A colossal, maternal presence, she first nurtures a crowd of beneficiaries, then singles out Timon for her favours while 'translating' his rivals to 'slaves and servants' (1.1.73–4). In the following scenes, Timon's bounty is similarly grandiose and magical: in his eyes, it needs no replenishment, it cannot be depleted, it has no limits. In the final movement of the poet's *paragone*, however, 'Fortune in her shift and change of mood / Spurns down her late beloved' (1.1.86–7). Similarly, Timon experiences the loss of his fortune (of which his steward Flavius often warns him) and of the friends gained through lavish gifts and hospitality (whose hypocrisy the cynic philosopher Apemantus frequently points out) as a sudden, brutal, and unmerited transformation of his world. Thus the play hints at the hero's infantile fantasy of identification with a maternal presence that ultimately betrays him.

Timon's peculiar generosity violates normal social exchange: by refusing any reciprocity, he makes everyone his inferior as well as his dependent. Yet he imagines that he presides over an idealized community of 'brothers':

> We are born to do benefits; and what better or properer can we call our own than the riches of our friends? O what a precious comfort 'tis to have so many like brothers commanding one another's fortunes.   (1.2.101–3)

In this speech, Timon portrays friendship as a bond that ambiguously entails helping, needing, and 'using' friends. Thus he conflates two registers of social exchange that actually conflict with each other: an ethos of disinterested friendship and reciprocity among peers, drawn from Cicero and Seneca, and the widespread practice of loaning money at interest known pejoratively as use or usury. Actually, Timon's 'friends' do make use of him. For example, a senator preparing to call in his loans when he sees the great man's credit failing refers to the gifts he gave Timon as investments: 'If I want gold, steal but a beggar's dog / And give it Timon – why, the dog coins gold' (2.1.5–6).[27]

It cannot be said, however, that the misanthrope of the play's second half commands more sympathy or credibility than the universal benefactor of its first half. Both his states of mind seem rooted in primitive fantasy rather than being rational responses to reality. The loyalty of his steward and the gratitude of his other servants belie his categorical denunciation of 'All feasts, societies, and throngs of men' (4.3.21). Yet the very extremes of his situation and his language lend themselves to pungent theatrical effects. When his friends refuse to loan him money, thus reducing him to destitution, Timon invites them to one last banquet, fills the covered dishes with warm water, and after delivering a caustic grace, intones, 'Uncover, dogs, and lap' (3.6.82). Upon leaving the city, he reverts to a primitive, pre-social existence supposedly free of Athenian corruption. Muttering 'Earth, yield me roots', he scratches the ground and in the play's boldest stroke, instead finds gold, the root of all evil (4.3.23–6). Neither these moments of mordant humour nor his last-act encounters with Alcibiades, who 'testifies to . . . a more complex sociopolitical world than the one we witness for most of the play', allow us to see Timon's descent into misanthropy as tragic rather than curious or perverse.[28] Nonetheless, a pathos that resonates with his betrayal by Fortuna clings to the imagery of his demise. Described four times and then shown on-stage, his tomb is located 'Upon the beached verge of the salt flood', where, he says to himself, 'the light foam of the sea may beat / Thy grave-stone daily' (5.1.215, 4.3.381–2). The quasi-maternal, rhythmic embrace of the sea suggests regression towards a primal state preceding the separation of self from world, a surrogate for the human bonds he never established in life.

NOTES

1. Parts of this essay have been adapted from my books *Man's Estate: Masculine Identity in Shakespeare* (Berkeley and Los Angeles: University of California Press, 1981) and *Roman Shakespeare: Warriors, Wounds, and Women* (London: Routledge, 1997).
2. T. J. B. Spencer, 'Shakespeare and the Elizabethan Romans', *Shakespeare Survey* 10 (1957), 27–38.
3. Richard Grafton, *A Chronicle At Large and Meere History of the Affayres of England and Kinges of the same* ... (London: 1569), p. 31.
4. T. W. Baldwin, *William Shakespere's Small Latine and Lesse Greeke*, 2 vols., (Urbana: University of Illinois Press, 1944), 1. 88, 89.
5. Janet Adelman, *The Common Liar: An Essay on Antony and Cleopatra* (New Haven: Yale University Press, 1973), p. 53.
6. William Fulbecke, *An Historical Collection of the Continuall Factions, Tumults, and Massacres of the Romans and Italians* ... (London: William Ponsonby, 1601), sig. A 2.
7. Sara Hanna, 'Shakespeare's Greek World: the Temptations of the Sea', in *Playing the Globe: Genre and Geography in Renaissance Drama*, ed. John Gillies and Virginia Mason Vaughan (Madison: Fairleigh Dickinson University Press, 1998), pp. 107–28.
8. T. J. B. Spencer, ' "Greeks" and "Merrygreeks": a Background to *Timon of Athens* and *Troilus and Cressida*', in *Essays on Shakespeare and Elizabethan Drama in Honor of Hardin Craig*, ed. Richard Hosley (Columbia: University of Missouri Press, 1962), pp. 223–33.
9. Robert S. Miola, *Shakespeare's Rome* (Cambridge University Press, 1983), p. 9.
10. Anon., *The Tragedie of Caesar and Pompey. Or Caesar's Revenge* ... (London: imprinted for Nathaniel Fosbrooke and John Wright, 1607).
11. Timothy Hampton, *Writing From History: The Rhetoric of Exemplarity in Renaissance Literature* (Ithaca: Cornell University Press, 1990), pp. 5, i, xi, 25.
12. G. K. Hunter, 'A Roman Thought: Renaissance Attitudes to History Exemplified in Shakespeare and Jonson', in *An English Miscellany: Presented to W. S. Mackie*, ed. B. S. Lee (Capetown and New York: Oxford University Press, 1977), p. 94.
13. Barbara Babcock, ed., *The Reversible World: Symbolic Inversion in Art and Society* (Ithaca: Cornell University Press, 1978), p. 32.
14. Leonard Barkan, *The Gods Made Flesh: Metamorphosis and the Pursuit of Paganism* (New Haven: Yale University Press, 1986), p. 244.
15. Leo Braudy, *The Frenzy of Renown: Fame and Its History* (New York: Oxford University Press, 1986), p. 59.
16. Gary B. Miles, 'How Roman are Shakespeare's "Romans"?', *Shakespeare Quarterly* 41.3 (Fall, 1989), 279.

17. Louis Althusser, 'Ideology and Ideological State Apparatuses', in *Lenin and Philosophy and Other Essays* (New York: Monthly Review Press, 1971), pp. 164–5.
18. Sigurd Burckhardt, 'How Not to Murder Caesar', *Shakespearean Meanings* (Princeton University Press, 1968), p. 9.
19. Wayne A. Rebhorn, 'The Crisis of the Aristocracy in *Julius Caesar*', *Renaissance Quarterly* 43.1 (Spring, 1990), 77.
20. Madelon Sprengnether, 'Annihilating Intimacy in *Coriolanus*', in *Women in the Middle Ages and the Renaissance*, ed. Mary Beth Rose (Syracuse University Press, 1986), p. 96.
21. Michael Neill, 'Introduction', *The Tragedy of Antony and Cleopatra* (Oxford University Press, 1994), p. 68.
22. Richard P. Wheeler, ' "Since First We Were Dissevered": Trust and Autonomy in Shakespearean Tragedy and Romance', in *Representing Shakespeare: New Psychoanalytic Essays*, ed. Murray Schwartz and Coppélia Kahn (Baltimore, MD: Johns Hopkins University Press, 1980), *passim*.
23. Gail Kern Paster, *The Idea of the City in the Age of Shakespeare* (Athens: University of Georgia Press, 1985), p. 58.
24. See Janet Adelman, ' "Anger is My Meat": Feeding and Dependency in *Coriolanus*', in *Representing Shakespeare*, ed. Schwartz and Kahn, pp. 129–49.
25. Phyllis Rackin, '*Coriolanus*: Shakespeare's Anatomy of *Virtus*', *Modern Language Studies* 13, 2 (1983), 68–79.
26. See Coppélia Kahn, ' "Magic of Bounty": *Timon of Athens*, Jacobean Patronage, and Maternal Power', *Shakespeare Quarterly* 38.1 (Spring 1987), 34–57.
27. As Louis Adrian Montrose has shown, in Shakespeare's England, on a scale comparable to Timon's, royal gift-giving was likewise 'a tacitly coercive and vitally interested process predicated on the fiction that it [was] free and disinterested' ('Gifts and Reasons: the Contexts of Peele's *Arraynement of Paris*', *ELH* 47 (1980), 433–61); see also Lawrence Stone, *The Crisis of the Aristocracy 1558–1641*, abridged edn (London: Oxford University Press, 1967).
28. Katharine Eisaman Maus, 'Introduction' to *The Life of Timon of Athens*, The Norton Shakespeare, gen. ed. Stephen Greenblatt (New York: W. W. Norton, 1997), p. 2250.

12

R. A. FOAKES

The critical reception of Shakespeare's tragedies

This chapter offers a sketch in broad strokes of some of the main trends in critical reaction to and theories about Shakespeare's tragedies since the late seventeenth century. By this time the culture of Shakespeare's age had come to seem crude and barbarous to educated Londoners, distanced as it was by the restoration of Charles II in 1660, the influence of French drama, the introduction of actresses playing female parts, and the restrictive licensing of only two indoor theatres that targeted moneyed patrons. The first critical writings on Shakespeare's works began to appear before the end of the century, though as an industry Shakespearean criticism developed during the eighteenth century, fostered by the spate of editions of the plays that followed that of Nicholas Rowe, published in 1709. For almost a century after Thomas Rymer's *A Short View of Tragedy* was published in 1693, editors and critics felt obliged to consider Shakespeare in relation to what were called the 'Rules of Art', rules derived from the French and from Horace, though often ascribed to Aristotle, especially the three unities of time, place, and action. Shakespeare was regarded as a prodigy, whose 'wild and extravagant' works possessed genius but lacked refinement, the 'Turn and Polishing of what the *French* call a *Bel Esprit*'.[1] Rymer, a learned but dogmatic polemicist for the 'ancients' (in the battle between ancients and moderns mocked by Swift in his satirical *Battle of the Books*, written 1697 and published in 1704), is chiefly notorious for calling *Othello* 'none other but a Bloody Farce'.[2] Writing about *Julius Caesar*, he condemned Shakespeare as a writer of tragedies: 'In Tragedy he appears quite out of his Element; his Brains are turn'd, he raves and rambles, without any coherence, any spark of reason, or any rule to controul him or set bounds to his phrenzy' (Vickers, 11. 58).

Among those who quickly responded by defending Shakespeare was John Dryden, who wrote in a letter to John Dennis in March 1694, 'Almost all the Faults which he [i.e., Rymer] has discover'd are truly there; yet who will read Mr. *Rymer*, or not read *Shakespeare*?' (Vickers, 11. 86). The intemperate comments of Rymer invited such contempt, but nevertheless some of the faults he discovered were allowed to be there, and subsequent assessments of the tragedies had to take notice of them. Dryden had earlier revised *Troilus and Cressida* (as a tragedy in which an innocent Cressida commits suicide) and rewritten *Antony and Cleopatra* (as *All for Love*) to suit the refinements of his age; in his essay on 'The Grounds of Criticism in Tragedy' published as a preface to the first of these (1679), he had already found fault with Shakespeare: 'the fury of his fancy often transported him beyond the bounds of judgment', and in his constant use of metaphor and imagery he smelled 'a little too strongly of the buskin' (Vickers, I. 263). In the Preface to his edition Rowe saw no point in dwelling on the 'faults' of 'a Man Excellent on most Occasions', and expressed a common assumption in considering him as 'a Man that liv'd in a State of almost universal License and Ignorance', who knew nothing of the rules of art. Rowe praised Shakespeare for raising terror, 'a proper Passion of Tragedy', rather than horror in the minds of the audience, in *Hamlet* and *Macbeth* especially;[3] but defences of the tragedies that began from acknowledging Shakespeare's failure to meet current refinements in drama encouraged a freedom in adapting and reworking his plays for the stage. John Dryden, the dominant literary figure of the age, led the way with his *All for Love* (1677), a revision of *Antony and Cleopatra* that observes the unities in an action which lacks Enobarbus, includes Cleopatra's children, and takes place in one day in Alexandria. Drastic adaptation was needed to contain the sprawling action of *Antony and Cleopatra* within the unities of time and place, but most reworkings preserved the basic structure of the plays. For example, the changes in William Davenant's adaptation of *Macbeth* (published 1674) consist mainly of genteel 'improvements' in the dialogue, a number of cuts, including the omission of the Porter's bawdy lines, and a considerable expansion of the parts of the Weird Sisters with songs and dances; this version held the stage until 1744, and was not finally supplanted until much later.[4]

The most well-known of such reworkings is Nahum Tate's adaptation of *King Lear* (1681) into a domestic drama with a happy ending. Tate's changes were in part politically motivated, as he gave prominence to Edmund and turned the play into a 'bastard's rebellion crushed and the legitimate monarch triumphantly restored'.[5] But his excisions, rewritings and alterations also suited the taste of the age. Among many changes he made were the omission of the Fool; the addition of a confidante, Arante, for Cordelia; and an ending in which Lear is rescued from attackers by Edgar and Albany, Lear gives Cordelia to Edgar as his bride, and the three old men, Lear, Gloucester, and Kent, who all remain alive, plan to withdraw to a 'cool cell' to meditate. Modified successively by George Colman (1768), David Garrick (1773), and Philip Kemble (1808), this adaptation remained the only version of the play performed on the London stage until 1838. During the early eighteenth century the tragedies were being staged at the same time as a new wave of plays by contemporary dramatists with titles like *The Mourning Bride* (William Congreve, 1697), *The Fair Penitent* (Nicholas Rowe, 1703), and *The Distrest Mother* (Ambrose Phillips, 1712), titles which indicate the orientation of tragedies towards women and sentiment. Shakespeare's tragedies were altered in part to emphasize virtuous heroines and appeal to women, so that in 1753, by which time a Shakespeare Ladies Club was well established in London, Joseph Warton felt it necessary to argue against 'the prevailing custom of describing only those distresses that are occasioned by the passion of love', which had led to *King Lear* being treated as a domestic tragedy.[6] Of the tragedies only *Othello*, which can be played as a domestic tragedy, and *Julius Caesar* escaped substantial alterations in performance during the late seventeenth and eighteenth centuries.

Early in the eighteenth century a gap opened between stage and study, between Shakespeare's plays as staged and the texts as we now know them. The first scholarly editions, beginning with that of Rowe in 1709, were published in six or eight volumes, often in a large format and designed for the libraries of wealthy patrons; but these editions by Rowe, Alexander Pope, Lewis Theobald, Sir Thomas Hanmer, and others, culminating in Dr Samuel Johnson's edition of 1765, did much to establish full texts of the plays and the authority of Shakespeare as the national poet and dramatist. At the same time, the influence of the Ladies Club exemplified a desire to promote the tastes of polite society, to demand decency, good manners, and propriety, aims not served by the crudities of Shakespeare's original texts. As the century wore on middle-class readers could take satisfaction in the availability of play texts as they were presented on the stage, notably by the publication in 1773–4 of John Bell's complete acting edition of the plays 'as *altered* and accommodated to the taste of an age more refined than that in which the Author lived and wrote'.[7] These were Shakespeare's plays as staged by leading actors such as David Garrick, who modified them so as to assert his own respectability and establish his authority as an actor.[8] For example, in his production of *Hamlet* (1772), he cut the funeral of Ophelia, and had Gertrude rush out at the end to die offstage, while Laertes and Horatio survive to join hands and 'calm the troubled land'. Garrick also restored some eloquent passages that had usually been cut, such as Polonius's advice to Laertes, while omitting Osric and the low humour of the gravediggers. The editor George Steevens was pleased by the 'lopping' of such excrescences, which he suggested might make a farce to be entitled 'The Grave-diggers; with the pleasant Humours of Osrick'.[9]

In general, however, the editors of Shakespeare continued to defend Shakespeare's 'beauties' while admitting faults. In his preface (1725) Pope had argued, 'To judge therefore of *Shakespeare* by *Aristotle's* rules, is like trying a man by the Laws of one country, who acted under those of another'. He blamed actors for most of the faults, especially for adding 'trifling and bombast passages' in the 1623 Folio (Nichol Smith, p. 53), and he 'degraded' to the foot of the page and printed in smaller type passages he judged to be 'excessively bad', while marking outstanding scenes with a star (Nichol Smith, pp. 51, 57). Pope's assessment marks a period when Shakespeare was becoming generally accepted as the national poet, and Pope may have been the first to compare the plays to majestic Gothic architecture as having greater variety and 'nobler apartments' than 'a neat Modern building', and as striking us with 'reverence' (Nichol Smith, p. 58). In the magisterial Preface to his edition in 1765 Dr Johnson sums up the paradoxes of his age in its attitude to Shakespeare. On the one hand, Shakespeare's plays offer instruction in 'civil and oeconomical prudence', they constitute 'the mirrour of life', and always 'make nature predominate over accident'; and Dr Johnson ably defends Shakespeare's neglect of the rules and unities. On the other hand, Shakespeare's faults cannot be excused even allowing for the barbarity of the age in which he lived; he 'sacrifices virtue to convenience, and is so much more careful to please than to instruct, that he seems to write without any moral purpose'. Johnson may have felt this to be especially true of the tragedies: 'In his tragick scenes there is always something wanting, but his comedy often surpasses expectation or desire' (Nichol Smith, pp. 107, 108, 114, 112). Dr Johnson sums up a conception of Shakespeare that has its roots in Rymer and Dryden, but by the time his edition appeared the plays had been modified on the stage, to conform to middle-class domestic virtues. Garrick especially made the plays and acting itself respectable and safe for viewers.

In the course of the eighteenth century Shakespeare's plays were reprinted in numerous editions, were established as the focus of the repertory on the London stages, and stimulated critical debate in the growing number of periodicals. Dr Johnson had observed '*Shakespeare* has no heroes; his scenes are occupied only by men' (Nichol Smith, p. 108), and the new critics, like Thomas Whately, in his essay on Richard III and Macbeth (1785), and William Richardson, who wrote on Macbeth and Hamlet in 1774, King Lear, Richard III, and Timon in 1784, analysed particular characters conceived as men in order to show them as representative of human nature or guided by a ruling passion.[10] As Shakespeare became the national poet, so what had been faults became virtues, for his plays exemplified freedom from rules imposed by the French, with whom the British were at war off and on for much of the period. It is against this background that the critical writings of the Romantics need to be understood. Shakespeare was at once elevated as a transcendent bard and domesticated as thoroughly English and familiar, as in David Garrick's birthday Ode written for the Stratford Jubilee in 1769, which is addressed to 'Avonian Willie, bard divine'. The effort to establish a correct text of the plays culminated in the massive scholarly edition of Edmond Malone in 1790, while at the same time the plays were made familiar and sanitized on the stage or abbreviated into farces and afterpieces, and were soon to be made available for reading in bowdlerized form in Thomas Bowdler's *Family Shakespeare* (1807),[11] and tamed into innocence and simplified prose in such collections as Charles and Mary Lamb's *Tales from Shakespeare* (1807).

Richardson was a professor of Humanity at Glasgow in Scotland from 1773 until he died in 1814, and in England the beginning of what might be considered professional criticism of Shakespeare was fostered by the founding of a number of so-called Institutions in London, the first being the Royal Institution (1799). These served to promote the general diffusion of science and literature by means of lectures and experiments for subscribers, many of whom had been denied access to the two universities of Oxford and Cambridge because they were nonconformist or Catholic in religion. His old friend Humphry Davy invited Samuel Taylor Coleridge to give a series on the principles of poetry at the Royal Institution in 1808. At least eight of these lectures were devoted to Shakespeare, and Coleridge went on to give, at other locations, six later courses of lectures devoted mainly to Shakespeare by 1819. During the second series, in 1811, Coleridge encountered the newly published lectures, given in Vienna, of A. W. Schlegel, the German critic whose approach was very much in tune with his own – hardly surprising, since Coleridge had read Kant, Lessing, Schiller, and Herder, and had studied in Germany. Schlegel helped him to formulate his concept of organic unity, which had great influence on later Shakespeare criticism. He allowed that of course there must be rules in poetry, but as a mechanical necessity; what gave Shakespeare's plays their individual life was their organic form, which 'is innate; it shapes as it develops itself from within, and the fullness of its perfection is one and the same with the perfection of its outward form'.[12] As against earlier critics like Dr Johnson, who said that Shakespeare holds a mirror up to manners and life, Coleridge argued that the dramatist's characters are not drawn from observation, but from meditation, and that the plays offer an imitation, not a copy or mirror-image, of life. The poet's mind is diffused throughout each play so that all is 'in keeping' (a term drawn from art criticism) and contributes to a sense of unity.

Charles Lamb's essay 'On the Tragedies of Shakespeare', in which he expressed his opinion that 'the plays of Shakespeare are less calculated for performance on a stage, than those of almost any other dramatist whatever',[13] has led to a misleading impression that the Romantics were hostile to the theatre. In fact Lamb's argument concerns performances he saw of *Richard III*, *King Lear*, and *Hamlet*, and the limitations inherent in the work of an actor who 'must be thinking all the time of his appearance' (Bate, p. 115), so that on the stage 'we see nothing but corporal infirmities and weakness, the impotence of rage; while we read it we see not Lear, but we are Lear, – we are in his mind, we are sustained by a grandeur which baffles the malice of daughters and storms' (Bate, p. 123). Lamb was also conscious of the difference between the play as acted, exclaiming at the absurdity of Tate's happy ending in *King Lear*, and as read. So it was understandable that emergent Romantic criticism should be primarily concerned with the plays as read. The method Coleridge developed in his later lectures was to deal at length with the opening scenes of a play in order to show 'the judgment with which Shakespeare always in his first scenes prepares, and yet how naturally, and with what a concealment of art, for the Catastrophe' (*LL* I. 559). In his close reading of texts he was a forerunner of modernist new critical approaches, and he invented the term 'practical criticism' (*LL* II. 34) popularized much later by I. A. Richards, who published his *Practical Criticism* in 1929. In his analysis of characters from within, so to speak, Coleridge pursued, as he said in 1808, a 'psychological' mode of reasoning (*LL* I. 253), a term he effectively introduced into criticism, i.e., drawing his concept of characters from internal evidence, and seeing them as created in Shakespeare's mind, not from observation of particular types or individuals. In this way he greatly influenced later psychological critics such as A. C. Bradley.

Coleridge lectured on a limited range of plays, and is best known for his commentary on *Hamlet* with its brilliant account of the character as inhibited from action by a habit of introspection, as 'called upon to act by every motive human and divine, but the great purpose of life is defeated by continually resolving to do, yet doing nothing but resolve', until he ends by becoming 'the victim of circumstances' (*LL* I. 390, 544). Like this one, other formulations by Coleridge have remained a challenge to interpreters of the tragedies ever since, notably his incisive account of Iago's 'passionless character, all *will* in intellect', whose soliloquies express 'the motive-hunting of motiveless Malignity' (*LL* II. 315). He dismissed the common stage treatment of the Weird Sisters as comic witches with broomsticks, and recognized their mysterious 'grotesqueness mingled with terror'; he also rejected the hitherto common idea of Lady Macbeth as a monster lacking any conscience, seeing her rather as showing 'constant effort' in the play to '*bully* conscience'

(*LL* 1. 532). His comments on *King Lear* show a subtle appreciation of Edmund as potentially admirable, and one whose circumstances, his bastardy, being sent abroad for education, and his humiliation by his father in the opening scene prevent his evil from 'passing into utter *monstrosity*' (*LL* 11. 326–7).

In this comment, made in 1819, Coleridge saw in Edmund an analogy with Napoleon, whose 'commanding genius' had been the topic of numerous newspaper essays by Coleridge. For him Shakespeare represented 'absolute genius', and by associating Napoleon with Macbeth or Edmund, he subjugated Napoleon imaginatively to Shakespeare as the national poet of England.[14] In a note on *Coriolanus*, Coleridge praised the 'philosophic impartiality in Shakespeare's politics',[15] whereas William Hazlitt, his younger contemporary, who remained a political radical all his life, took a quite different view in his *Characters of Shakespeare's Plays* (1817). For him Coriolanus was an appalling play, which offered the 'dramatic moral' that 'those who have little shall have less, and that those who have much shall take all that others have left';[16] at the same time, his introductory remarks to this essay, arguing that 'The language of poetry naturally falls in with the language of power' (Hazlitt, IV. 214), are very incisive, and may be usefully related to recent historicist approaches to Shakespeare. Hazlitt wrote on a much wider range of plays than Coleridge dealt with in his lectures, often in relation to the great actors of the period, as in his praise for Mrs Siddons as Lady Macbeth: 'she was tragedy personified' (IV. 189) in the sleepwalking scene. One play he did not want to see acted was *Hamlet*, in which he felt both Edmund Kean and Philip Kemble inadequate to the role of the prince; for him Hamlet's 'ruling passion is to think, not to act' (IV. 235), and, incapable of action, he is 'as little of the hero as a man can well be' (IV. 233). He expressed his scorn for the bowdlerized *Family Shakespeare*, and for the disgraceful alterations made in the Colley Cibber 'patch-work' of *Richard III* which was still being staged. He differs from Coleridge in arguing that Iago does not lack motives in his love of power, and shares Lamb's views, quoted at some length in his account of *King Lear*.

In rejecting the rules of art in his 1808 lectures, Coleridge dismissed the notion that Shakespeare's plays were written 'in obedience to Aristotle' (*LL* 1. 78). He did speak on the origins of Greek tragedy and the impact of the rise of Christianity in Lecture 2 of that series, but he did not consider the effect of tragedy, as Hazlitt did briefly in his essay on *Othello*, which begins, 'It has been said that tragedy purifies the affections by terror and pity', so creating a 'balance of the affections' (Hazlitt, IV. 200). It was left to A. C. Bradley at the end of the century to outline what he thought to be the 'substance' of Shakespearean tragedy in relation to Aristotle, but he was much more influenced by the ideas of George Wilhelm Friedrich Hegel (1770–1831). For Aristotle plot took precedence over character; character was formed by action, so that what the character chooses to do to achieve an end reveals a moral quality or habit. Hegel, whose philosophy was influential in England in the late nineteenth century, argued that tragedy has to do with a self-division 'involving conflict and waste', so that the tragic conflict 'is one not merely of good with evil, but more essentially, of good with good'.[17] The implications of this shift were enormous; where Aristotle had described the tragic hero as someone who suffers a change of fortune because of *hamartia*, an error of judgement, the Hegelian theory points rather to an inner struggle in the hero, 'whose virtues help to destroy him' through a 'weakness or defect' that is intertwined with what is good in him.[18] The idea of a 'tragic flaw' or 'fatal imperfection' (Bradley, p. 22) is implicit in much Romantic criticism, as in Coleridge's account of Hamlet. Its perspective is psychological, whereas Aristotle's concern is more with the structure of an action in which the hero's intentions are overthrown (peripeteia) and he undergoes a change from ignorance to knowledge (anagnorisis).

It should not surprise a reader therefore to find that Bradley refers to Coleridge nineteen times, to Hazlitt seven times, and to Aristotle only twice in the course of lectures in *Shakespearean Tragedy* on what he called the four 'principal tragedies', *Hamlet*, *Othello*, *King Lear*, and *Macbeth*. For Bradley tragedy lay not in 'the expulsion of evil: the tragedy is that it involves the waste of good' (Bradley, p. 37). In order to explain the struggle in the soul of the hero it was necessary to analyse his character, conceived in the Coleridgean manner as autonomous, and to show how 'strength and weakness should be so mingled in one soul'. So Bradley proceeds at once in his first lecture to the central question of Hamlet's character, the cause of his 'delay' in carrying out the Ghost's 'commission of Vengeance' (Bradley, p. 94). His analysis is fuller and more subtle than earlier accounts, and finds the immediate cause of Hamlet's inaction in melancholy induced by the moral shock of his mother's remarriage, working on a 'nature distinguished by that speculative genius on which the Schlegel–Coleridge theory lays stress' (Bradley, p. 127). Hence Hamlet's 'failure'. Hazlitt had said, 'It is *we* who are Hamlet' (Hazlitt, IV. 232), and through the nineteenth century the combination of what Anna Jameson called frailty and grandeur in him made Hamlet a central point of reference politically in Europe. The term 'Hamletism' was established by 1840, with reference usually to (a) the well-intentioned but ineffectual behaviour of characters in plays and novels (by writers such as Turgenev, Chekov, Thomas Mann, Jules Laforgue and D. H. Lawrence); or (b) to dithering intellectuals in European politics; or (c) the sensitive artist or intellectual who felt out of place in a philistine world. Hamlet haunted the consciousness of Europe and the idea of Hamletism was so potent in Germany that the Furness Variorum edition of the play, published after the Franco-Prussian war in 1877, was dedicated to the German people, 'whose recent history has proved once for all that Germany is not Hamlet'.

In Britain Hamlet came to be seen by many as failing in his duty to revenge, whether because he was incapacitated by melancholy or nauseated by his environment. The idea of 'duty', a word not found in the play, and perhaps connected with the needs of empire in the nineteenth and of wars in the twentieth century, has remained a rod with which conservative critics may chastise Hamlet as 'a man with a deed to do who conspicuously fails to do it'.[19] In larger terms Hamlet seemed to typify the very nature of Man as a fallen creature, representative of 'human weakness, the instability of human purpose, the subjection of humanity to fortune – all that we might call the aspect of failure in man'.[20] Hamlet could also be seen as a rebel, one who rejects the tainted values of his world and is crushed by it, as in Stalinist days in eastern Europe, when the play could be staged as a 'drama of political crime',[21] or in the context of the cold war and the atom bomb in Britain and America, when it was directed in 1965 by Peter Hall as a 'play about the problems of commitment in life and in politics'.[22] Hamlet is so various and so richly developed in the play that he could be extrapolated as a subject in his own right, endowed by Bradley with an 'unconscious', and reconstructed as embodying the qualities of the critic or of the age. The sensitivity and delicacy of Hamlet also encouraged the feminization of the character on stage by Edwin Booth and Henry Irving among others, and more than twenty actresses played the role during the nineteenth century, most famously Sarah Bernhardt.

If Hamlet thus acquired a special status, the other tragedies also were analysed by Bradley chiefly in terms of characters, often perceptively, as in his insight into Iago not in terms of his motives but as an artist, or his comments on Lady Macbeth's 'want of imagination' (Bradley, p. 373), or his insistence on the 'greatness of soul' of Lear, leading him to see the play in terms of redemption, anticipating *The Tempest*. Bradley's account of the tragedies built on a tradition of criticism established by the Romantics, and became a point of reference or departure for much later criticism, which was increasingly professionalized as Shakespeare figured centrally in literary studies in schools and colleges in the twentieth century. In their basic concern with character critics writing in this tradition gave little attention to theories of tragedy, though Bradley raised some important issues in his opening chapter. He argued, for instance, that accident as a fact of human life cannot be excluded from tragedy, as against Aristotle's rule of probability and necessity; and he insisted that however much characters might speak of God or the gods, 'The

Elizabethan drama was almost wholly secular' (Bradley, p. 25), so that if we have the sense of the hero as a doomed man, it is in relation to fate identified as a moral order (Bradley, p. 31). By the 1930s character criticism was under attack both from 'new critics' who argued that the plays should be treated as dramatic poems, and studied in terms of language and imagery, and from G. Wilson Knight, who rejected 'false and unduly ethical criticism' in favour of a concern with temporal and spatial patterns in each play conceived as a 'visionary whole'.[23] So he wrote perceptively on the central importance of style, of 'The *Othello* music' in this play, and on the contribution 'the demonic grin of the incongruous and absurd' (Knight, p. 175) makes to the pathos of *King Lear*.

Knight ended with a chapter called 'The Shakespearean Metaphysic', in which there is much reference to the spirit as opposed to actuality, and although he avoided an explicitly Christian reading of the tragedies, he may be linked with those who, after World War 1 and the withering of the possibility of heroism in wars of mass destruction, reclaimed the plays in Christian terms. Hamlet could be reconstructed as possessing a heroism that depended less upon 'acting or even knowing than upon *being*',[24] and seen as a Christian serving for God's scourge in an evil world. The murder of Duncan in *Macbeth* was interpreted as 'profoundly impregnated with the central tragedy of the Christian myth'.[25] A number of Christian readings of *King Lear* extended Bradley's suggestion that the play could be called 'The Redemption of King Lear', and after World War 2 the play was read in relation to the rejection of fascism and attempts to reconstruct a better society so that 'distribution should undo excess, / And each man have enough' (4.1.70). These redemptionist readings emphasized the sufferings of Lear as a good old man, and were given wide currency in Kenneth Muir's Arden edition (1952), which stressed the joy of reconciliation as 'the goal of Lear's pilgrimage' (p. lix), and in G. I. Duthie's New Cambridge edition of 1960, in which the play is said to be about the 'attainment of salvation' (p. xx).

The 1960s brought a marked shift in the interpretation of the tragedies, a shift related to the impact of the cold war, the rediscovery of the holocaust, the development of nuclear weapons, and the building of the Berlin Wall. A voice from eastern Europe had a tremendous impact, as Jan Kott reimagined the tragedies in bleaker terms. Hamlet becomes a disillusioned rebel, brutal and passionate (Kott, p. 52), *King Lear* is linked with the 'modern grotesque' of Samuel Beckett's *Endgame* as a play in which the gods are 'just as cruel as nature and history', and Macbeth embodies 'the "Auschwitz experience"' (Kott, p. 95). *Coriolanus* also was given prominence as a play that 'shows the eternal face of war and occupation' (Kott, p. 167). Jan Kott greatly influenced Peter Brook, whose production (1962) and subsequent film (1970) of *King*

Lear helped to establish this play as especially relevant to the cynicism of the late twentieth century, in showing the 'annihilation of faith in poetic justice, and annihilation of faith in divine justice within the confines of a grim pagan universe'.[26] Such a view informs Edward Bond's reworking of the play as *Lear* (1970), though in the same year Grigori Kozintsev's remarkable Russian film ended with a muted sense of affirmation as a close-up of Edgar is accompanied by the music of the Fool's pipe.

The desire for affirmation that shaped so many readings of *King Lear* was in the 1960s countered by an argument that 'all moral structures, whether of natural order or Christian redemption, are invalidated by the naked fact of experience'.[27] Neither of these ways of reading this play, like the shifting readings of the other tragedies, undermined the basic assumption of the tradition stemming from Coleridge and Bradley, that the plays reveal an organic unity, an assumption that surfaces in Wilson Knight's belief (1930) that 'we should first regard each play as a visionary unit bound to obey none but its own self-imposed laws' (p. 14), or Helen Gardner's concern to show 'the extraordinary unity of action, characterization, and language' in *King Lear* (1966).[28] Just how this unity is constituted remained a topic of debate. Patterns of poetic imagery or thematic patterns for a time offered an interesting method of finding coherence in the plays,[29] but were displaced by attempts to define the formal properties of the tragedies in other terms. The most challenging arguments have sought musical analogies for the structure of the plays, as constructed in scenic units, somewhat like 'movements' in classical music, or showing a 'meaningful orchestration of groups of scenes'.[30]

The 1980s brought another shift, to postmodernism, which is marked by a repudiation of the concept of organic unity as an aesthetic value, and indeed abandons any concern with aesthetics. Influenced by European theorists, notably Roland Barthes, Jacques Derrida, and Michel Foucault, critics have questioned such notions as authority, insisted on the instability of language and meaning, and claim that Shakespeare's plays are 'not intelligible by commonsensical notions of coherence, since they are constituted by historical contingencies of the stage, conventions, location, and audience'.[31] Deconstructionists argued that literature privileges the free play of language over meaning, so that language cannot be reduced to 'a series of unified, graspable, "readable" and authorially validated meanings'.[32] Such an approach liberated the critic to pursue verbal connections or their absence without any concern for the controls exerted by history, context, or interplay of characters. So, for instance, Jonathan Goldberg sees the *absence* of references to Dover in *King Lear*, 4.6, as establishing 'the place that *Dover* occupies in the text', while Margreta de Grazia reads the play in terms of one word, 'superflux', in an essay entitled 'The Ideology of Superfluous Things'.[33] The emphasis by these critics on a particular moment or idea or term has tended to produce essays rather than books, essays designed to demonstrate what, in speculating about transvestism in *Othello*, Peter Stallybrass called a 'dizzying indeterminacy'.[34]

At its best, deconstruction could free a critic to perceive the structure of Shakespeare's tragedies in a new way, as in Stephen Booth's essay on *King Lear* (1983). He argued that with the deaths of Edmund, Goneril, and Regan *King Lear* 'has formally concluded, while its substance is still in urgent progress', and that the climax of the story, the entry of Lear with Cordelia in his arms, 'comes after the *play* is over'.[35] In other words, he finds a pattern that seems to shape a formal order in the play, but the inconclusiveness of the ending points to a radical instability and 'a failure of form'. An alternative postmodernist approach, that of new historicism, has been more influential in relation to Shakespeare's tragedies. As the deconstructionist looks for discontinuities in a text, reading it against its overt meanings, so the new historicist seeks to track 'what can only be glimpsed, as it were, at the margins of the text',[36] reading a play against its overt ideological stance or claims for order. Stephen Greenblatt bases his readings on the idea that 'Shakespeare's plays are centrally, repeatedly concerned with the production and containment of subversion and disorder' (Greenblatt, *Shakespearean Negotiations*, p. 40). The drama is perceived as representing state power and simultaneously contesting that power. This perception is not based on a concern with history in any large sense, but characteristically makes use of an interesting anecdote or instance to gain leverage from the margins into a text, as in Greenblatt's application to *King Lear* of Samuel Harsnett's attack on exorcism, a work that supplied Shakespeare with a vocabulary he could give to Edgar playing the mad Poor Tom. Edgar's 'fraudulent, histrionic performance' reveals Shakespeare writing for the theatre as a 'fraudulent institution that never pretends to be anything but fraudulent'; so, paradoxically, in marking out its ceremonies as frauds, the play satisfies our need for them while undermining them and working 'to unsettle all official lines' (Greenblatt, *Shakespearean Negotiations*, p. 128). The use of the word 'official' here relates to the new historicist fascination with power and with the human subject as ideologically produced; so in what has often been considered a domestic drama, *Othello*, Greenblatt seeks to show 'that Shakespeare relentlessly *explores* the relations of power in a given culture'.[37]

In Britain cultural materialism, more Marxist and more overtly political, has also been centrally concerned with power, and with resistance to it. So for Jonathan Dollimore, whose book *Radical Tragedy* (1984, enlarged 1989) has been influential, *King Lear* is a play about 'power, property, and inheritance' as the 'material and ideological basis' of the society it depicts.[38] Dollimore was himself much influenced by the Marxist critic Raymond Williams, who, in his *Modern Tragedy* (1966), had rejected the humanist assumption of a 'permanent, universal, and essentially unchanging human nature';[39] he argued that tragedy should be 'seen as in different ways a response to a culture in conscious change and movement' (Williams, p. 62), and should be understood in a contingent relationship to 'changing conventions and institutions' (Williams, p. 46). Concepts such as 'evil' lose their transcendent status and refer merely to 'many kinds of disorder which corrode or destroy actual life' (Williams, p. 59). Where Williams thought of tragedy as historically opposed to revolution (Williams, pp. 63–5), Franco Moretti has sought to show that Elizabethan and Jacobean tragedy discredits the values of the monarchy and paves the way for revolution;[40] he headed a chapter on *Gorboduc* and *King Lear* 'Tragic Form as the Deconsecration of Sovereignty'. The formal properties of tragedies tend thus to be assimilated into political and ideological concerns.

This is true too for other significant developments in postmodern criticism of the tragedies. Feminist writers such as Catherine Belsey in her *The Subject of Tragedy* (1985) are concerned with the politics of gender and with what Elaine Showalter called 'the ideology of representation'.[41] They have contributed to our understanding of patriarchy and the representation of women in the tragedies, and they have had much to say on other tragedies besides the big four on which Bradley and many other critics concentrate. Already the variety of Shakespeare's early tragedies had been explored by N. S. Brooke in *Shakespeare's Early Tragedies* (1968); in it he disclaimed any desire to advance a theory of tragedy. The late tragedies have also received a lot of attention in the decades since World War 2, some of the best criticism relating especially to the concept of heroism or greatness in relation to characters like Antony and Coriolanus.[42] Feminist critics have explored other aspects of these early and late tragedies, as in Catherine Belsey's account of the body and desire in *Romeo and Juliet*, and Janet Adelman's fine analysis of identity in *Antony and Cleopatra* (*The Common Liar*, 1973). The feminist interest in gender and sexual relations connects with psychoanalytical thinking, and Adelman's seminal essay on the construction of masculinity in *Coriolanus* (1980) is reprinted with later comments on it, and a notable chapter on *King Lear*, in her important book, *Suffocating Mothers* (1992). *Titus Andronicus* has also been brought into focus in relation to the repression of women in the context of rape.[43] The vast body of postmodernist critical writing on Shakespeare can be sampled in various published collections of essays, the essay being perhaps the natural mode for criticism that denies the concept of the autonomous subject, rejects the idea of organic unity in a play, and looks within texts for discontinuities, fissures, and indeterminacy.[44]

Critical theories that have no interest in concepts of formal structure, of closure, or of coherence, and foreground instead 'contradictions within the text which transgress both its principles of construction and the intentions of its author' (Drakakis, p. 9) inevitably deconstruct Shakespeare's plays in pointing to what an earlier age would have called faults. Shakespeare may be perceived, for example, as patriarchal, as an orthodox reactionary in his culture, as devaluing the 'feminine principle' (Drakakis, p. 263), or as confirming the Machiavellian nature of royal power. In the eighteenth century Shakespeare was castigated for failing to observe the supposed classical rules and unities in constructing his plays. The cult of Shakespeare by the Romantics as an author almost above criticism led to Shakespeare's works becoming the focus for literary studies in schools and colleges by the end of the nineteenth century. In recent decades, however, the limitations of Shakespeare have again come under scrutiny, but in ideological rather than critical terms. It seems odd that in spite of the postmodern levelling of all literary works which, in the absence of any theory of value, become equally worthy of attention, the critical industry devoted to Shakespeare is greater than ever. Perhaps a new formal theory will emerge, either through a revival of wider interest in traditional theories of tragedy, such as A. D. Nuttall has sought to promote in his book *Why Does Tragedy Give Pleasure?* (1996).[45] Alternatively, it could be that new theories will be produced by a developing performance criticism that returns the plays from the study, where they are dismantled as ideological constructs, to the stage. In the theatre directors seek to achieve coherence in productions that challenge critics to find ways of relating performance and spectacle in the modern theatre to plays written centuries ago. However scrupulously a director aims to be faithful to the text, a production necessarily reflects the age in which it is staged. Some idea of the nature and potential of this approach can be gained from W. B. Worthen's book, *Shakespeare and the Authority of Performance* (1997).[46]

NOTES

1. *The Spectator*, 161 (3 September 1711).
2. See Brian Vickers, *Shakespeare: The Critical Heritage*, vol. II, 1693–1733 (London: Routledge, 1974), p. 54.
3. *Eighteenth-Century Essays on Shakespeare*, ed. D. Nichol Smith (Oxford: Clarendon Press, 1963), pp. 9, 15, 19.
4. See *Macbeth*, ed. A. R. Braunmuller (Cambridge University Press, 1997), pp. 61–2.

5. Michael Dobson, *The Making of the National Poet: Shakespeare, Adaptation and Authorship, 1660–1769* (Oxford: Clarendon Press, 1992), p. 81.

6. Warton, 'King Lear', in *The Adventurer*, 113 (4th December 1753). On the Shakespeare Ladies Club, see Dobson, *The Making of the National Poet*, pp. 93, 146–61. Dobson's book and Jean I. Marsden's *The Re-imagined Text: Shakespeare, Adaptation, and Eighteenth-Century Literary Theory* (Lexington: University Press of Kentucky, 1995) provide the best accounts of shifting attitudes to Shakespeare during the eighteenth century.

7. According to a review in the *Monthly Review* 50 (1774), 144; cited in Dobson, *The Making of the National Poet*, p. 209.

8. *Ibid.*, pp. 176–8.

9. See George C. D. Odell, *Shakespeare from Betterton to Irving* (New York: Scribner, 1920; rpt New York: Dover Publications, 1966), 1. 389.

10. Marsden, *The Re-imagined Text*, pp. 135–8. The best-known character analysis is Maurice Morgann's account of Falstaff (1777).

11. The first collection of twenty plays was published in Bath in 1807; a fuller collection of all the plays in ten volumes appeared in London in 1818. It seems Bowdler's sister, Henrietta, was the main creator of an edition designed, according to the preface, to remove 'everything that can raise a blush on the cheek of modesty'.

12. Citing a lecture of 1813, in Samuel Taylor Coleridge, *Lectures 1808–1819 On Literature*, ed. R. A. Foakes, The Collected Coleridge, 2 vols. (Princeton University Press and London: Routledge, 1987), 1. 53 (hereafter referred to as *LL*).

13. *The Romantics on Shakespeare*, ed. Jonathan Bate (London and New York: Penguin Books, 1992), p. 113.

14. See R. A. Foakes, 'Coleridge, Napoleon and Nationalism' in *Literature and Nationalism*, ed. Vincent Newey and Ann Thompson (Liverpool University Press, 1991), pp. 140–51.

15. *Coleridge's Criticism of Shakespeare*, ed. R. A. Foakes (London: Athlone Press, 1989), p. 177.

16. William Hazlitt, *Complete Works*, ed. P. P. Howe, 21 vols. (London and Toronto: J. M. Dent and Sons, 1930), IV. 216.

17. A. C. Bradley, 'Hegel's Theory of Tragedy', in *Oxford Lectures on Poetry* (London: Macmillan, 1909, rpt 1965), p. 86. Bradley does not mention Friedrich Nietzsche, whose *The Birth of Tragedy* (1872) has had surprisingly little influence on Shakespeare criticism.

18. A. C. Bradley, *Shakespearean Tragedy: Lectures on 'Hamlet', 'Othello', 'King Lear', and 'Macbeth'* (London: Macmillan, 1904; 2nd edn, 1905), p. 29.

19. *Hamlet* ed. Harold Jenkins (New Arden edn, London: Methuen, 1982), pp. 139–40.

20. Maynard Mack, 'The World of *Hamlet*', *Yale Review*, new series, 41 (1951–2), 515.

21. Jan Kott, *Shakespeare our Contemporary*, trans. Boleslaw Taborski (London: Methuen, 1964), p. 51.

22. See R. A. Foakes, *'Hamlet' versus 'Lear': Cultural Politics and Shakespeare's Art* (Cambridge University Press, 1993), p. 38.

23. G. Wilson Knight, *The Wheel of Fire* (Oxford University Press, 1930; 5th rev. edn, New York: Meridian Books, 1957), p. 11.

24. G. K. Hunter, 'The Heroism of Hamlet', in *Hamlet*, ed. J. R. Brown and Bernard Harris, Stratford-upon-Avon Studies, 5 (London: Arnold, 1963), p. 105.

25. Roy Walker, *The Time is Free* (London: Andrew Dakers, 1949), p. 55.

26. William R. Elton, *King Lear and the Gods* (San Marino, CA: Huntington Library, 1966), p. 334.

27. Nicholas Brooke, *King Lear*, Studies in English Literature (London: Arnold, 1963), pp. 59–60.

28. Cited in G. R. Hibbard, '*King Lear*: a Retrospect', *Shakespeare Survey* 33 (1980), 11.

29. For example, Caroline Spurgeon, *Shakespeare's Imagery and What it Tells Us* (Cambridge University Press, 1935); William Empson, *The Structure of Complex Words* (1951; 3rd edn, Totowa, NJ: Rowan and Littlefield, 1979); M. M. Mahood, *Shakespeare's Wordplay* (London: Methuen, 1957); Wolfgang Clemen, *Shakespeare's Dramatic Art* (London: Methuen, 1972).

30. Emrys Jones, *Scenic Form in Shakespeare* (Oxford: Clarendon Press, 1971); Mark Rose, *Shakespearean Design* (Cambridge, MA: Belknap Press of Harvard University Press, 1972); Jean E. Howard, *Shakespeare's Art of Orchestration* (Urbana: University of Illinois Press, 1984). In *Tragic Form in Shakespeare* (Princeton University Press, 1972), Ruth Nevo's idea that the development in the plays correlates with the five-act division of them in the First Folio gives too much weight to divisions that may be arbitrary, and have little to do with the author or the stage.

31. Susan Zimmerman (ed.), *Shakespeare's Tragedies*, New Casebooks (New York: St Martin's Press, 1998), p. 2. For a survey of trends in modernist and postmodern criticism, see Hugh Grady, *The Modernist Shakespeare* (Oxford: Clarendon Press, 1991).

32. Terence Hawkes, 'Shakespeare and New Critical Approaches', in *The Cambridge Companion to Shakespeare Studies*, ed. Stanley Wells (Cambridge University Press, 1986), p. 292.

33. Zimmerman, *Shakespeare's Tragedies*, pp. 157, 255–84.

34. *Ibid*, p. 206.

35. Stephen Booth, '*King Lear*', '*Macbeth*', *Indefinition, and Tragedy* (New Haven: Yale University Press, 1983), pp. 1–11.

36. Stephen Greenblatt, *Shakespearean Negotiations: The Circulation of Social Energy in Renaissance England* (Berkeley and Los Angeles: University of California Press, 1988), p. 4 (hereafter referred to as Greenblatt).

37. Stephen Greenblatt, *Renaissance Self-fashioning from More to Shakespeare* (Chicago University Press, 1980), p. 254.

38. For Dollimore, nature becomes an 'ideological concept' used to 'police disruptive elements', a far cry from J. F. Danby's vision of an essentially beneficent nature in his book on *King Lear*, *Shakespeare's Doctrine of Nature* (London: Faber and Faber, 1949).

39. Raymond Williams, *Modern Tragedy* (London: Chatto and Windus, 1966; rev. edn Verso, 1979), p. 45.

40. Franco Moretti, *Signs Taken for Wonders* (London: Verso, 1983), cited in *Shakespearean Tragedy*, ed. John Drakakis (London and New York: Longman, 1992), pp. 27, 45–84.

41. Elaine Showalter, 'Representing Ophelia: Women, Madness, and the Responsibilities of Feminist Criticism', in *Shakespeare and the Question of Theory*, ed. Patricia Parker and Geoffrey Hartman (London: Methuen, 1985), p. 94; see also *Shakespearean Tragedy*, ed. Drakakis, p. 292. Belsey's book (London and New York: Methuen, 1985) has little reference to Shakespeare, but influenced other critiques of liberal humanist readings of the plays.

42. See, for example, Eugene Waith, *The Herculean Hero in Marlowe, Chapman, Shakespeare and Dryden* (New York: Columbia University Press, 1962); Reuben Brower, *Hero and Saint: Shakespeare and the Graeco-Roman Heroic Tradition* (Oxford: Clarendon Press, 1971).

43. By Marion Wynne-Davies in ' "The swallowing womb": Consumer and Consuming Women in *Titus Andronicus*', in *The Matter of Difference: Materialist Feminist Criticism of Shakespeare*, ed. Valerie Wayne (Ithaca and London: Cornell University Press, 1991), pp. 129–51; see also Janet Adelman's *The Common Liar* (New Haven: Yale University Press, 1973) and *Suffocating Mothers: Fantasies of Maternal Origin in Shakespeare's Plays* (New York and London: Routledge, 1992).

44. Representative collections include *Shakespeare and the Question of Theory*; *Shakespearean Tragedy*, ed. Drakakis, which has a useful introduction by the editor touching on theories of tragedy; *Shakespearean Tragedy and Gender*, ed. Shirley Nelson Garner and Madelon Sprengnether (Bloomington: Indiana University Press, 1996); and *Shakespeare's Tragedies*, ed. Zimmerman. For a powerful critique of postmodernist critical theories in relation to the tragedies, see Brian Vickers, *Appropriating Shakespeare: Contemporary Critical Quarrels* (New Haven and London: Yale University Press, 1993).

45. Oxford: Clarendon Press, 1996; see also his *A New Mimesis* (London and New York: Methuen, 1983). These books include discussion of *King Lear*, *Julius Caesar*, *Coriolanus*, and *Othello*. See also Foakes, 'Hamlet' versus 'Lear'.

46. Cambridge University Press, 1997. See also *Shakespeare and the Sense of Performance*, ed. Marvin and Ruth Thompson (Newark, NJ: University of Delaware Press, 1990); Sidney Homan, *Shakespeare's Theater of Presence* (Lewisburg: University of Kentucky Press, 1986); Susan Bennett, *Performing Nostalgia: Shifting Shakespeare and the Contemporary Past* (London and New York: Routledge, 1996); Harry Berger Jr, 'Text against Performance: the Gloucester Family Romance', in *Shakespeare's Rough Magic: Essays in Honor of C. L. Barber*, ed. Peter Erickson and Coppélia Kahn (Newark, NJ: University of Delaware Press, 1985). The *Prefaces to Shakespeare* of Harley Granville-Barker, written in the late 1920s and 1930s, energized performance criticism and still repay reading.

13

BARBARA HODGDON

Antony and Cleopatra in the theatre

Speaking to himself – and heard by an offstage audience – Hamlet decides to have the visiting troupe of actors 'play something like the murder of my father': 'the play's the thing', he concludes, 'Wherein I'll catch the conscience of the king'. Hamlet imagines theatrical enactment as a persuasive intervention which will provoke his uncle to reveal his guilt. Implicitly, he also affirms that his words – and those of the already 'extant' play in the troupe's repertoire – will tell only part of the story and that the acted and felt play will be the 'real' thing. Real, and also material, for performance not only reimagines 'the play' but invites us to think concretely about how words – and silences – do theatrical work. How do particular actors' bodies, their physical and gestural languages, make meanings; how do theatrical set design, lighting, and costume discipline and enhance those bodies? How do particular spaces and stage images arrest attention, remain etched in memory? Tracing a range of performances of a play such as *Antony and Cleopatra* – once considered by literary critics to be, like *King Lear*, unperformable – opens a window on to a flexible, shape-shifting theatrical literacy and legacy, revealing how changes in theatrical spaces and fashions, in critical and cultural histories, have shaped and reshaped both the imaginative and material contours of Cleopatra's 'infinite variety' as well as those of the play.

> Here is the most spacious of the plays . . . Shakespeare's eyes swept no wider horizon.
>
> Harley Granville-Barker, *Preface to 'Antony and Cleopatra'* (1946)

As though taking Granville-Barker literally, both the Variorum (1990) and Arden 3 (1995) editions preface *Antony and Cleopatra* with maps of the Mediterranean world, c. 31 BC, inviting readers to situate the play within a specifically historical geography and a series of local habitations – Rome, Misenum, Toryne, Actium, Athens, Tarsus, the River Cydnus, Alexandria.

Figure 2 Herbert Beerbohm Tree's production of *Antony and Cleopatra* at His Majesty's
Theatre, London, December 1906. Antony's welcome in the marketplace.

Shakespeare's play names them all, takes the action on a virtual tour of the
ancient Near East which circles from Egypt to Rome, crossing and recrossing
the 'wide arch / Of the ranged Empire'. Ever since *Antony and Cleopatra* left
the open, non-illusionistic platform stage for which it was written, where
change of scene did not mean change of scenery and where locale was established by characters' lines ('Welcome to Rome') and actors' presences,
subsequent performances have struggled with (and against) the play's geographical restlessness, its sheer size, its evocative spaces. Among these,
Egypt – home to that 'great fairy' Cleopatra – offers the greatest theatrical
temptations.

Appropriating the then-current discourses of Egyptology and antiquarian-
ism for theatrical display, Herbert Beerbohm Tree's 1906 staging at London's
His Majesty's Theatre brought spectators face to face with the 'strange pervasive influence of Oriental luxury and vice' through palatial sets decorated
with gaudy gold, their walls bearing monstrous figures, their rooms filled
with silken canopies and cushioned divans (fig. 2). Giving 'bodily semblance'
to the play's 'inner meanings', Tree peopled his picture stage with dancing

girls, 'flamingoes' holding their outstretched phoenix-wings aloft, Nubians, incense bearers, dimpled Cupids, and hordes of court attendants. At the centre of the first stage spectacle, Constance Collier's Cleopatra (wearing one of six extravagant gowns) appeared in a clinging underdress of gold-spangled gauze, a jewelled girdle and breastplates, a flowing mantle of salmon-pink silk and a headdress with a golden disc, red flowers at the sides; at each ear hung jewelled medallions and chains of turquoise.[1] Filling the stage with imperial fantasies, Tree created a theatre of consumption where, like Antony, a Victorian Briton might '[pay] his heart/For what his eyes eat only'. By mid-century, Tree's spectacular dreams had travelled beyond their turn-of-the-century link to cinema's newly emergent art form and had deserted the theatre entirely, reappearing in glitzy film epics directed by Cecil B. De Mille (1934) and Joseph Mankiewicz (1963), both titled *Cleopatra* and and starring respectively Claudette Colbert and Elizabeth Taylor. Any traces of 'Shakespeare' had been reshaped as the story of everyman's fantasy sex object, the ultimate 'Egyptian dish'. However non-Shakespearean, Mankiewicz's film, in which Taylor and Richard Burton appeared to be reliving their own notorious romance, marks one shape for the theatrical enactment of *Antony and Cleopatra* – that of a world-shaking grand passion.

Yet by the late twentieth century the play, like Antony's crocodile, had transmigrated. Performed in chamber spaces as well as on expansive stages and no longer envisioned exclusively as a *Romeo and Juliet Redux* played out by middle-aged, over-the-hill lovers, the play's mixture of state tragedy and domestic comedy re-emerged as a brilliant study of political actors in which, as Michel Foucault writes, 'Pleasure and power do not cancel or turn back against one another; they seek out, overlap, and reinforce one another.'[2] Although many performances retained vestiges of Egyptian exotica and stage spectacle, the politics of design and theatrical enactment had also changed. By 1999, *Antony and Cleopatra* had become a modernist-inspired vision of two consummate actors' behaviours in which all traces of Britain's imperial acquisition – sphinxes, caryatids, palm-frond fans and ankhs – were stacked at the margins of the Royal Shakespeare Theatre's main stage. And in that same year, the play returned to its 'original' performance space, the (new) Globe Theatre on London's Bankside, where, as in its early modern performances, Cleopatra was played by a young man and 'Egypt' was simply another place on the stage.

Beginners, please

Consider, now, the first few seconds of three late twentieth-century performances. In 1987, Peter Hall opened the play with an 'overture' of wind and string instruments, bursts of laughter and a rustle of silk: resplendent in Renaissance-inspired robes, Judi Dench's Cleopatra swirled on to the Royal National Theatre's Olivier stage leading her Antony, Anthony Hopkins, mounted on the shoulders of a Mardian wearing a Minotaur-like bull's head and tethered with a rope. Michael Bogdanov's English Shakespeare Company (1998) began with reporters rushing on to a stage hung with clocks telling the time in Rome, Athens, Misenum, and Alexandria to file the latest Mediterranean sensation: 'Antony Red Hot in Alex'; 'Cleo Carves Another Notch in Her Bedpost'; 'High Jinxs in the Shadow of the Sphinx'. As the stage gradually filled with women lolling on cushions and khaki-clad soldiers, on came Cleopatra, riding a bicycle and pulling a slobber-drunk Antony behind it: dressed in tuxedos and bowler hats à la Charlie Chaplin, they played Beckett's Pozzo and Lucky to Miles Davis's trumpet riffs before, tumbling to the floor, they made a quick exit to return 'as themselves', Cleopatra now in a purple gown, Antony in safari jacket and sandals. Frances de la Tour and Alan Bates, Stephen Pimlott's famous pair (Royal Shakespeare Company 1999), were discovered at an Alexandrian cocktail party, Cleopatra reclining on a chaise, her legs apart, Antony's head buried between them.

Each opening throws the action into anamorphic perspective, inviting Hall's spectators to juggle Renaissance order with Egyptian excess, Bogdanov's to frame their viewing through tabloid headlines and vaudeville performance, Pimlott's to become voyeurs of a sexual intimacy to which Shakespeare only alludes. All signal the theatrical strategy of a play that, as Carol Rutter writes, 'builds on binaries that begin at the level of language and extend into performance and its reception'.[3] Each also re-envisions Shakespeare's framing device of soldiers' gossip in which embittered Philo complains to Demetrius of Antony's 'dotage' in a feminized Egypt where Rome's most famous general has 'become the bellows and the fan / To cool a gypsy's lust' (1.1.9–10). 'Look where they come!' he says, prefacing Folio's stage direction *Enter Antony, Cleopatra, her Ladies, the train, with Eunuchs fanning her*. That direction does not indicate *how* Antony is to enter – *before* Cleopatra or *with* her? separate from or part of her *train*? – but performances consistently use it to define their relationship. Whether he is playfully led, parodically mocked or steeped in decadence, each image shows Antony 'bound' as Cleopatra's follower or sexual servitor, appears to believe Philo's report, makes him oracle to debauchery. Beginning with gossip which sets 'Egyptian Antony' against 'Noble Roman', this relatively short scene maps out, with extreme economy, the territory that *Antony and Cleopatra* will explore: a territory that invites spectators to see double, to set the claims of pleasure and duty side by side, blending their politics, to invest in 'becomings' – above all, to watch performers' performances.

Celebrity gossip

Just as writing about performances depends upon what Joseph Roach identifies as two 'necessarily problematic' procedures, 'spectating and tattling',[4] *Antony and Cleopatra* is *about* looking and telling tales. Shakespeare's early modern audiences may have recognized, in such tale-telling, echoes of the erotic gossip surrounding Elizabeth I and her favourites, Robert Dudley, the Earl of Leicester, and his stepson, Robert Devereux, the Earl of Essex; they might also have recognized, in the figure of Octavius Caesar, their current ruler, James I, who configured his public image through Roman, Augustan iconography. Yet if such echoes did resonate in the play's first performances, that topicality cannot be reperformed – even though several stagings, among them a 1931 Shakespeare Memorial Theatre performance, have dressed Cleopatra in Elizabeth I's royal regalia. All that can be played, as with any reperformance, is present-day culture's preoccupation with a play's issues, and the engagement of *Antony and Cleopatra* with celebrity gossip is hardly unfamiliar to late twentieth-century spectators, whose knowledge of contemporary public figures derives from rumours and reports – some 'true', others patently false – that shape their opinions. Consistently, in this play, what spectators actually see plays beside what they are made to see through verse that encompasses a vaulting language of display. And it is not just the minor figures – those unnamed messengers (more than in any other play) – who arrive bringing news, telling stories which alternately embellish or deflate the reputations of figures who speak of each other in hyperbole and who, in performance, inhabit 'real' bodies that demystify the myths they construct. Report also works to read characters' performances; and in this play, identity depends on how those performances are received.[5] Caesar reads Antony through his past and present behaviours – the one 'masculine', dutiful, Roman; the other 'feminine', debased, Egyptian (1.4); Enobarbus lifts Cleopatra's barge performance to legend and (too late for them both) reads Antony as the sure loser (2.2, 3.13); second-hand, Cleopatra reads Octavia (3.3), dreams dead Antony as emperor (5.2). Trying to catch Cleopatra, Antony always misses her, snares only glimmers of her dazzling 'becomings'; likewise, Cleopatra cannot comprehend Antony's address to his servants ('What does he mean?' she asks Enobarbus (4.2)). Even the ending turns on fictions of performance: Mardian reports Cleopatra's supposed death to Antony (4.14); Cleopatra fears being upstaged by a 'quick comedian' who will 'boy [her] greatness/I' th' posture of a whore' (5.2).

On behalf of the play in the theatre

Antony and Cleopatra is one of many plays – *The Merchant of Venice*, the *Henry IV* plays, and *King Lear* among them – where Shakespeare bodies forth two places – Venice and Belmont, Westminster and the Boar's Head Tavern, court and heath – gives each cultural (and theatrical) significance that sets them in opposition and moves the action between them. Like *Merchant*, it embeds a tragic action in a comic structure; like *Lear*, it uses a 'time-lapse' strategy to synchronize its Egyptian and Roman actions. One way to configure it, as A. C. Bradley did, is as Antony's tragedy, interrupted (or marred) by Cleopatra's comic interludes, and to view her as becoming appropriately 'tragic' only by dying 'in the high Roman fashion'.[6] Yet the play it most resembles is *1 Henry IV*, not just with its constant moves between Westminster's court, marked by Lenten duty and royal obedience, and the carnivalesque tavern world, where Falstaff and his cronies drink up fleshly pleasures and indulge in civil disobedience, but also because, like Falstaff, Cleopatra is at the centre of events, the fulcrum on which history turns. Telling a story of imperial power politics, *Antony and Cleopatra* dramatizes its protagonists' histories through intimate encounters in which they are always accompanied by onstage spectators and sets these against an expansive public tapestry. It brings the 'triple pillars of the world' to a summit meeting, negotiates faction towards shaky peace achieved by political marriage, and conquers outside threats to the triumvirate. The play then discards both Lepidus and Pompey as the triangular relation between Cleopatra, Antony, and Caesar – warring over Antony's body – condenses into a long finale, where Antony, trying to emulate his reputed self, plays out his deflated heroism until the space in which he has to act shrinks – on the early modern stage, to the size of the inner stage or the balcony. Constantly see-sawing between Egypt and Rome, the political action drives forward, intercut with scenes in slow-paced Alexandria where Cleopatra and her women live in a 'what-shall-we-do-today?' world, playing theme-and-variations on Antony's domestic betrayals, waiting out his return.

How does the theatre realize this infinite variety? What space does the play occupy? How does a staged world convey these strands of action that interweave sexual and imperial politics? Scholars conjecture that Shakespeare's own theatre, privileging actors' 'personations', worked through economy and immediacy, one scene melting into the next, but even though modern practitioners adopt (and adapt) those techniques, most present-day stagings still bow to realist conventions which suppose that characters need to be *somewhere*. Translating words into material terms – sets, costumes, properties, lighting, and sound – theatre design evokes intellectual and emotional as well as political meanings: on the stages, *everything* has 'character'. In general, late twentieth-century designers strike a middle road between Shakespearean scarcity and the epic splendour inherited from Victorian pictorial stagings like Beerbohm Tree's. But however actors are surrounded, clothing sculpts their bodies, carving out cultural silhouettes that mark gender, class, and nationality; changing costume refashions social identity, signals different behaviours or 'selves'. Antony (often) wears 'Eastern' robes in Egypt but puts on armour, a toga or (in modern-dress stagings) a business suit in Rome; Cleopatra, following Antony's death, discards Egyptian veils for mourning black and puts off that for Isis' golden robes.

In 1953 at Stratford's Shakespeare Memorial Theatre, Glen Byam Shaw staged *Antony and Cleopatra* on a revolve – perhaps the ideal theatrical image for a play that travels rapidly over space and time; fixed in their seats, spectators literally followed the moves from one locale to the next. In 1972, Trevor Nunn, directing the play for a season called 'The Romans',

Figure 3 Trevor Nunn's 1972 production of *Antony and Cleopatra*, Shakespeare Memorial Theatre, with Richard Johnson as Antony, Janet Suzman as Cleopatra.

tested the Royal Shakespeare Theatre's newly installed hydraulic machinery. Rome's council table, backed by a huge map which made the triumvirate's project visible, rose from the stage floor, eclipsing Egypt's canopied langour; lighting shifted from hot Mediterranean sunshine, where Cleopatra lay on richly coloured cushions among blackened eunuchs and waiting women, to the cool whites of monotoned Roman austerity, etching sharp shadows in the bureaucrats' toga-ed figures, turning them into classical sculpture. Filmed for television, where editing took the place of the theatre's hydraulics, Nunn's staging shrank to the size of the boxed TV set, where bodies and faces became its primary landscape, revealing an intensely private 'hidden play'. Four years later, in 1978, Peter Brook re-envisioned expansiveness as intimacy on Stratford's main stage. His designer, Sally Jacobs, set the play within a semicircle of curved translucent panels, bounded at stage-side by movable trestles; cushions, low benches, and a few stools marked Egypt or Rome. Most scenes took place downstage of the curve, generating a claustrophobic sense of enclosure: the protagonists seemed to experience the emblematically staged battles that took place behind the panels as though they were half-real, the distant forerunners or results of their private encounters.

At times, design takes off from a particular image, as in Peter Hall's 1987 staging. Taking her inspiration from Veronese's painting of *Alexander and the Wife and Daughter of Darius* in London's National Gallery, Allison Chitty backed her set with a blood-red surround, against which broken columns and fragmented porticoes gestured towards the heroic perfection associated with Renaissance ideals. Its architecture emphasized Antony's own half-ruined promise; the environment stood in contrast to the rather stocky middle-aged couple (Dench and Hopkins) who inhabited it, living out an epic fantasy past the size of dreaming, seeking to live up to a reality and reputation greater than their human scale.[7] Determined to avoid sphinxes and snakes (until the ending appearance of a real snake nicknamed Keppel, after one of a team of vaudeville performers famous for a 'sand dance' called 'Doing the Egyptian'), she designed costumes in a palette of ambers, oranges, and deep reds that amplified the protagonists' identities as Renaissance semi-deities: Cleopatra wore 'laces' that *could* have been cut; Antony's leather armours grew rusty in the fading light. For Stephen Pimlott's 1999 staging, Yolanda Sonnabend's design deliberately downplayed any sense of location, hierarchy, or grandeur in favour of an image that stressed the lovers' self-obsessive behaviours, amplifying their performances as a 'show'. Backing the theatre's upstage walls, huge panelled mirrors reflected and magnified the performers – a perfect image for the ways in which historical (and theatrical) figures lead their lives under public scrutiny as well as for their own self-reflecting narcissism: when they see themselves reflected, they are seeing the world – and their audience, seated in the theatre, looking back.

Kissing away kingdoms and provinces

Although theatre historians conjecture that early modern performances were continuous, on today's stages (even at Shakespeare's Globe), a single interval break is standard theatrical practice. Where a performance places that interval offers another frame for looking, inviting spectators to connect one event with another, reinforcing structural rhymes and stressing a particular interpretive emphasis. In *Romeo and Juliet*, taking an interval after their mid-play marriage and opening the second half with the quarrels resulting in Mercutio's and Tybalt's deaths not only sets the lovers' marriage against their union in death but also marks a split between comedy and tragedy; moreover, by echoing the play's opening quarrel, events appear to repeat themselves, drawing the two halves together. Alternatively, breaking the play after the quarrel and opening the second half with Juliet's 'Gallop apace' soliloquy calls attention to public violence and the Prince's repeated attempts to restore order – a choice which embeds Romeo and Juliet's story within a wider civil context.

For *Antony and Cleopatra*, no such convenient choices emerge. Blurring conventional generic markers, the play ebbs and flows, Nile-like, resisting a visible shape, and any choice seems destined to blunt the contrast between scenes, retexturizing a sequence that looks as though it needs to be played consecutively. Perhaps the most tempting alternative is to put the interval after the bacchanal on Pompey's barge (2.7), closing the first half, as Nunn did, with rousing male camaraderie that widened the gulf between 'Egyptian Antony' and Caesar's Roman frigidity to presage further action. Such a choice can also make the point that Egypt is not a sink of debauchery; rather, it is the Romans who stage it as a brothel, body forth its drunken excess, banqueting, and revels in an all-male stag party where, although absent, Cleopatra seems just offstage or is proxied by the 'boy singer' – near-naked in 1990, swan-diving into the arms of the soldiers below him; travestied at Shakespeare's Globe in 1999. Unwilling to sacrifice juxtaposing the barge scene with the sight of Pacorus's corpse borne by Ventidius (3.1), Brook staged both scenes emblematically: as Zorba-like dance music faded away, Alan Howard's Antony caught hold of a sail and was hoisted aloft, stranded between heaven and earth; a similar image recurred at his death where, once again, his body was drawn up, this time by women. Then, directly downstage of him, Pacorus was killed, pairing bacchanal with butchery.

Choosing more spectacular means, John Caird (1992) turned Caesar's report of the lovers and their bastard children enthroned in the marketplace (3.6) into a hieratic tableau, prefiguring Cleopatra's reappearance as the Goddess Isis as she robes for death. Reminiscent of Beerbohm Tree, who had opened his third act by massing 145 people on the stage, all cheering Antony's ascent through the crowd to embrace Cleopatra, standing at the top of a long staircase, Caird's staging threw additional weight on to the play's hyperbole and overblown emotion by framing the action with rhyming images of Antony and Cleopatra silhouetted hand-in-hand at the back of the stage against a glowing azure sky – a *Gone with the Wind* romantic cliché that clarified his emphasis on grand passions. Bogdanov (1998) and Pimlott (1999) waited until after Antony's defeat at Actium (3.11), privileging the lovers' reunion with a centre-stage embrace accompanied by soft trumpets and a slow fade; the second half opened as Octavius, receiving Antony's schoolmaster, knew he would win (3.12). Also in 1999, the Globe closed the first half after Octavia returned 'a milkmaid to Rome', marking the shift from private politics to public warfare by opposing two women's bodies (3.6): as the second half opened, Cleopatra's squabbling with Enobarbus over her participation in the wars echoed her behaviour at the play's opening.

Whatever the choice, each in some way marks the difference between 'feminine' and 'masculine' performances, the one associated with comedy, the other with tragedy. Roughly speaking, performances reverse the terms of the title – or, perhaps more accurately, frame 'Antony' between two versions of 'Cleopatra'. In the opening acts, Cleopatra dominates: whether performing or reperforming herself for Antony, reminiscing with her women or playing out comic routines with the messenger, she is active, and, like the spoiled child or the diva, she needs an audience for her melodramatic performances. In 1972, Janet Suzman registered motion with her voice – one moment moody, the next commanding; so did Dench, whose Cleopatra generated a driving physical energy. Once she left her couch, de la Tour ranged over the stage, as though constant motion might divert Antony from 'Roman thoughts'. In 1999, Mark Rylance's Cleopatra immediately took command of the Globe's wide platform: staking out its territory like an animal, she marked every corner of it as hers alone, as though cancelling out any possibility that Roman puppets might replace her. By contrast, Antony has little to do: watching from the sidelines, he remains largely reactive until he returns to Rome. The last acts, however, reverse their positions. Once Antony moves back on to the warrior's stage to play out the last shreds of his generalship, Cleopatra, relegated to the margins, becomes a 'divided' character – another observer of his ruin who, after his death, chronicles his fame before, facing off against

Caesar, she becomes 'Roman Egyptian', collapsing both categories in her final performance.

During these final acts, any performance has to negotiate how to stage the actions which encompass the story of Caesar's wars against Antony. Bound to print conventions and literary structures such as act and scene divisions – modern texts divide Acts 3 and 4 into twenty-eight scenes, several only four to eleven lines long – editorial practice mangles any sense of precisely what sort of performance is indicated by this hurried action. Moreover, the Folio's stage directions are characteristically sparse, and no verbal scene painting indicates where characters are: they come and go, marking the back-and-forth swing from Antony to Caesar; one moment yielding to the next in a theatre of event designed as a series of dissolves in which focus rests, as in *Henry V*, not on the battles themselves but on what comes before and after them. In 1978, Brook brushed the wars across a deep rear stage where soldiers and messengers passed one another in shadowy pageantry behind the set's translucent panels. Actium was represented by the sounds of waves and the 'noises off' of trumpet alarums; as in a Jackson Pollock painting, huge splatters of blood dotted the panels. Reading Shakespeare's theatrical strategy as prefiguring cinematic montage, Hall (1987) staged it as a kaleidoscopic action: waves of soldiers, marked by coloured standards, passed each other in marching ranks, their shouts announcing victory or defeat from all corners of the Olivier's huge stage. Barrie Rutter, in 1995, set both armies side by side behind steel oil drums. 'Pounded out as percussion on the drums and punctuated by speech, the "war" emerged as a story told by a chorus...; the rout happened as Cleopatra dropped her drumsticks and ran, throwing the sound on the Egyptian side into a-rhythmia; after a horrible silence, Rome [struck up] a deafening triumphalist crescendo.'[8] At the Globe in 1999, competing armies marched through the groundlings' space, passed over the stage and out again, crossing one another's paths in each entrance and exit.

Performers: earning a place in the story

Antony and Cleopatra requires a huge cast: there are thirty-six named speaking parts plus entourages of messengers, soldiers, sentries, and servants (in the Globe's 1999 staging, sixteen actors doubled and redoubled roles). At its centre are two larger-than-life protagonists, historical celebrities with citational pasts who have been played (famously and infamously) by theatrical 'stars' whose own citational pasts double up their notorious identities. Derived from historical accounts, paintings, opera, and film as well as from past theatrical performances, all that cultural baggage burrs onto the roles, magnifying them in memory, opening them to spectators' own fantasy scenarios of power, gender, and erotic sensuality, so that, in some sense, theatrical culture always finds itself in the position of auditioning stand-ins for an 'original' that lies just outside representation, 'beggars all description'.[9] Above all, these two – together with Caesar – carry presence on to the stage. For, much like actors in the 'real' theatre of politics, they are performers: rarely if ever do they soliloquize; instead, spectators see the faces they put on for the world. In this as in any performance, much depends on what Bert States calls 'the DNA of character' in any given moment in theatrical culture;[10] consistently, their story is never theirs alone but is shaped and perceived in relation to current narratives of power and sexuality.

Late twentieth-century actors playing Octavius Caesar – the 'boy' emperor who will become Emperor Augustus – have pitched their performances to emulate the behaviours of contemporary executives. In 1972, Corin Redgrave's white-robed Octavius was a conservative obsessed with order: he looked and acted like a walking refrigerator, clipped his consonants so that each word fell like a chunk of ice. Desiring Cleopatra not for herself but for the power she represented, he pimped his sister (second-hand, through his associates) into a marriage that consolidated his position as 'sole sir o' th' world'; deeply homophobic, he shied violently away from Antony's touch, shrugged himself free of the drunken dance on Pompey's barge, a thin smile masking his self-disgust. Tim Piggott-Smith's Caesar (1987) was similar: a man of calculated passions, he delegated authority (and sheaves of paper) to a host of subalterns, delighted in playing on the flaws of lesser men. But whereas Redgrave cynically pawned off Octavia, Piggott-Smith adored and idolized her 'holy still disposition' as the single anchor to a family bond in a world from which family is notably absent, proxied by followers and servants. For both, the moment when they order Antony's 'revolted' soldiers to be placed in the vanguard of the Roman front-lines was a schoolboy's revenge calculated to show the playground's hero who was boss. More youthful than either Redgrave or Piggott-Smith, Jonathan Hyde (1978) respected Antony in the early scenes but turned against him after the bacchanal, hardening his determination to win at all odds. At the Globe (1999), Ben Walden was also a boy learning his statecraft and in awe of Antony: when Dercetus brought him Antony's sword (5.1), he moved away from his advisors and stood looking at it as though to catch his hero's aura. Also in 1999, Guy Henry's tall, spider-thin, priggish Caesar was more brutal – a triumph-hungry automaton, he was surrounded by a guard of clones, all, like him, dressed in sinister black leather.

Just as Caesar mediates state politics, Enobarbus acts as a go-between for personal (and sexual) politics: speaking brusquely to both Antony and

Cleopatra, he counters their self-inflating rhetoric. In 1978, Patrick Stewart turned his initial exchange with Antony about Fulvia's death (1.2) into a comic routine that exposed Antony's put-on piety and left them both laughing: 'I must with haste from hence', says Antony, not moving a muscle. Serving as an often-ironic Chorus, his medium is wry reason, not hyperbole, and yet it is he who delivers the play's most famous speech, 'The barge she sat in, like a burnished throne,/Burned in the water...' (2.2). In Tallulah Bankhead's 1937 staging, it opened the play, generating images of Cleopatra play-acting Venus on the River Cydnus which, as it turned out, was a hard act to follow. Stewart (1972) relished its lists, making his onstage audience Cleopatra's desirous captives as he turned her, in Linda Charnes's apt phrase, into 'a tourist attraction'.[11] Repeating the role in 1978, Stewart spoke to the offstage audience; now his tone was more ironically distanced, so that it became just another report, a traveller's tale designed to give auditors what they expected to hear. Older and more grizzled than Stewart, Michael Bryant (1987) began the speech clinically, one booted leg cocked up on the empty boardroom table, but as he gradually became engulfed by his own memories, he finished it deep in reverie. Whereas Bryant aped Antony's drinking and womanizing and shared his erotic dream, Pimlott's Enobarbus, Malcolm Storry (1999), admired Antony the soldier: a knowing, loyal observer, always at Antony's elbow, he anguished over the decision to desert him, and his confession of guilt, terrifying in its intensity, vividly expressed both his devotion and the catastrophic effect that Antony's infatuation with Cleopatra had on the lives of those who followed his 'wounded chance'. In 1998, Bogdanov's Enobarbus (John Labonowski) was the opposite of Tim Woodward's antiheroic Antony, a profligate Prince Hal on a *Long Day's Journey into Egypt* in which both stood at the centre of a homosocial, even homoerotic, staging that sidelined Cleopatra, demystifying her legendary status and robbing her of any political resonances, to look squarely at the men's relationships; Enobarbus's love for Antony made him a stand-in for a near-absent Cleopatra, and when he died, the play seemed over.

Calling Antony 'an absolute twerp', a 'stupid man' who becomes a 'middle-aged lap-dog', Laurence Olivier nonetheless acknowledged, 'It's still a great part.'[12] In 1906, Beerbohm Tree's Antony did appear stupid – little more than a stolid façade; and in 1999 at the Globe, Paul Shelley, wearing an unfortunate Jacobean hat, seemed far too lightweight for a role that begins with sensuality and near-emasculation and moves through honour, political opportunism, humility, sentimentality, self-serving bluster, and blatant misogyny to death, deified by Cleopatra's report (the twin to Enobarbus's description of her). Few Antonys have successfully externalized the polar conflict between lover and soldier. In 1972, Richard Johnson, the image of authority – bearded, sweaty, with a thick, growling voice – was a charmingly hesitant lover, a less convincing general; reprising Antony in 1992, he had an air of vanished glory, most apparent as he attacked Caesar for 'harping on what I am, not what he knew ... I was'. Hopkins (1987) played Cleopatra's passive partner, allowing her to seduce him because he believed himself invulnerable; patronizing to Lepidus, he played the politician and bon vivant, dancing an ironic *pas de deux* at the barge revels, but couldn't wait to get back to battle. His was a big performance – that of a man too dignified to reveal his deep despair to his followers – and his most telling moments came in the false gaiety with which he covered inner grief and, later, committed to death. Those were also key moments for Alan Bates, Pimlott's Antony, whose reputation as a star made him knowable to spectators just as, at the play's opening, Antony was a well-known hero. More restless and dishevelled than either Johnson or Hopkins, he caught the voluptuary Antony undone by passion, brilliantly ironized his self-loathing. Gently chiding Cleopatra's comic mistakings as she helps him to arm, he bid her farewell with tender passion and, as rose petals fluttered around him and his men, standing upstage of Cleopatra, her back to the audience, he was suddenly all soldier. Raising their swords, they all saluted Cleopatra before, in a silence that intensified her exclusion, the sound of their boots rang sharply on the stage as they turned to leave.

'Age cannot wither her, nor custom stale / Her infinite variety', says Enobarbus, summing up Cleopatra (2.2) in a phrase remarkably like Ben Jonson's praise of Shakespeare: 'not of an age, but for all time'. More than the others, Cleopatra reveals the play's engagement with a particular historical moment, feeds its cultural imaginaries of desire, elects to stress, in performance, particular facets from the clusters of descriptors the play names: 'gypsy', 'strumpet', 'slave', 'enchanting queen', 'royal wench', 'boggler', 'lass unparalleled'. Moreover, just as Antony 'becomes' his warrior-self when accompanied by his soldiers and loses that shape when they desert him, Charmian and Iras define Cleopatra's identity. In the early modern theatre, surrounding the 'boy actor' with other boys who played her 'girls' marked one way of defining 'him' as 'her'; similarly, today's 'real' girls form what Rutter calls a 'subversive triumvirate': 'their faces', she writes, 'are surfaces on which who she is becomes legible ... [They] continuously write Cleopatra's notices.'[13] Nineteenth-century Cleopatras were *femmes fatales*, a pattern which peaked with Elizabeth Taylor's cinematic siren (1963) but was already, in the theatre, outdated. Late twentieth-century Cleopatras establish other contours: performing her as a thoroughly modern woman, spiky rather than soft, intelligent and calculating rather than consumed by sexual passions, they explore sensuality as power. Often, Cleopatras have

Figure 4 Peter Brook's Shakespeare Memorial Theatre production of *Antony and Cleopatra*, 1978, with Glenda Jackson as Cleopatra, 5.2.

dressed themselves in images of female power, enhancing the character's historical resonance: Judi Dench (1987) was Veronese's Venus, Elizabeth I. Suzman (1972) played (brilliantly) in a range between innocence and toughness; changing from radiant queen to fearful woman, examining her wrinkles in a mirror, she could also theatricalize love. Egging on Antony's own performance ('You can do better'), she suddenly changed gears ('But that's not it') so that 'Oh, my oblivion is a very Antony, / And I am all forgotten' marked one of the few moments, until the end, where she escaped performance, revealing it as a mask for deep-felt emotion (1.3). Dench also turned emotional somersaults: giving orders one moment, cancelling them the next, she exposed the insecurities of a woman attempting to hold on to her man by any means. Different from both, Glenda Jackson, Brook's Cleopatra (1978),

Figure 5 The 1999 Shakespeare's Globe production of *Antony and Cleopatra* with Mark Rylance as Cleopatra.

dressed in flowing caftans, was a cool, rational queen who played power games on an equal standing with men (fig. 4). Sweeping hand movements and poses evoking Egyptian art gave her exotic distance in a staging which emptied the play of passion and of the 'Othering' fantasies it generates: only rarely did she and Antony touch one another. Like Jackson, Frances de la Tour (1999) did not look like – or play – the classic beauty. Tall and gangly, her blue-robed Cleopatra slithered and shimmied in perpetual motion, her arms cutting the air in whirling curves. She could spin on a dime: quickly ill and well again, she fell to the floor in a mock-faint and rose again like a jack-in-the-box mechanical figure, suddenly transformed into another 'self'. If her physical performance was uninhibited, her faultless comic timing nailed every mocking nuance with superb irony, catching, in her vocal delivery, the role's caustic humour and high intelligence as well as its aura of grand sluttishness.

De la Tour stressed Cleopatra's unpredictability and made her histrionics visible *as performances*. Mark Rylance's 1999 Cleopatra *was* the play, and what was on view caused critics to worry over whether the failure to 'do' gender 'right' interfered with spectators' theatrical experience (fig. 5). Such anxieties, of course, mark the wide gap of time between early modern theatrical culture and our own as well as the difficulties of attempting 'authentic' staging for the benefit of audiences made up of 'inauthentic' modern spectators attuned to keeping gender in place. Yet for those who could forget the body beneath the role (and even for those who could not), Rylance gave the most tantalizing physical performance of the season. Wearing a curly black wig that flowed over his shoulders and laced into low-cut period gowns that gave him a hint of cleavage, he spoke in a bright tenor, making no attempt to disguise his voice. In this staging, femininity was displayed externally through costume, as though clothes made the woman: Cleopatra wore a green-flowered skirt and 'gipsy' bodice for the opening (reminding at least one critic of a young Elizabeth Taylor); later, she put on cothurni (raised boots) to make herself taller than Octavia and produce the right air of majesty, and when Antony went to war, she donned an armoured breastplate and a helmet topped with flowers and feathers, as though emulating a dream Amazon, Greek Minerva or English Britannia. Playfully throwing cushions at Antony, she was by turns flirtatious and funny, temperamental and commanding – a teasing impersonation which, like de la Tour's, made Cleopatra's infinite capacity for self-dramatizing behaviours overt. Throughout, Rylance's performance seemed disarmingly instinctual – one moment stroking a messenger's hand, the next pulling a knife and hauling him around by his hair, then speaking 'I will not hurt him' like a child self-consciously claiming her innocence to a scolding parent. Reacting with swift wit to those around her, her restless energy gradually settled towards stillness until, at the end, losing the disguises that costume gave her, she appeared in a plain white penitent's gown, without her wig, revealing a bloodied, scarred scalp that made her look like a World War 2 collaborator or a Joan of Arc shaved for sacrifice. Suddenly, gender impersonation was dismantled; all that mattered was the acting.

Playing till doomsday

Death and dying occupy one-fifth of the action of *Antony and Cleopatra*, which stages six deaths, each different. How does each take place? Whose bodies matter, and how? Two deaths – those of Enobarbus (4.9) and Iras (5.2) – deny realistic representation: how are they made performance-persuasive? Enobarbus dies first – mysteriously; even the soldiers who take up his body assume that he may recover. His death measures the distance between a culture in which it was thought possible to die of a broken heart and one in which autopsies dissect bodies, fixated on causes; here, only his language pictures his anguish and grief. Patrick Stewart, Nunn's and Brook's Enobarbus, simply collapsed; Malcolm Storry, Pimlott's Enobarbus, pounded his bare chest ritualistically, all affect faded from his face, and, as in Asian mime performances of death, he walked slowly offstage. Like Enobarbus, Iras dies suddenly but is given no language, only a farewell kiss before she slips to the floor. Like Enobarbus's comrades, Cleopatra cannot read her body ('Have I the aspic in my lips?' (5.2.287)), and Iras ends her role by anticipating her mistress's death and, like her, becoming a stage property, a theatrical artifact. At the last – in a coda that fulfils the Soothsayer's prophecy ('You shall outlive the lady whom you serve' (1.2.30)) – Charmian also proxies Cleopatra, and her final words ('Ah, soldier' (5.2.322)) suggest that, again like her mistress, she longs for her own 'Antony' (perhaps one of the many men she had earlier wished to seduce). In this patterning and repatterning, both protagonists are linked to their loyal followers; in addition, the manner of each death distinguishes between women's bodies, which remain intact, and those of Eros and Antony – broken, ruptured, mangled. In Nunn's staging, Eros cut his throat; as Alan Howard, Brook's Antony, sat cross-legged, his arms outstretched, waiting for the blow, his Eros committed hara kiri. Most performances sustain tension in these moments, invite empathy, even tears – and then tragedy dissolves into travesty, death into farce.

Antony's messy, botched suicide seems designed to contrast with Cleopatra's seemingly effortless and painless death, where nothing interrupts the final icon she becomes and where all focus rests on her sensations and fantasized imaginings. However staged, everything about Antony's protracted dying makes him look ridiculous: the stage direction – *They heave Antony aloft to Cleopatra* – suggests a physical performance that was meant to raise laughs as well as a body. Yet many recent stagings, attempting to sustain the idea of Antony as 'tragic hero', have deliberately tried to avoid laughter at this point – another mark of the gap between early modern and twentieth-century performance – often by relying on emblematic means. In 1978, Cleopatra and her women swathed Antony in long scarves to draw him up the slope of Brook's steeply raked stage (fig. 6). Pimlott borrowed the idea in 1999 (theatre always raids itself) but stylized it further: Antony sat in an upstage chair while downstage, Cleopatra and her women pulled at invisible ropes, moving themselves towards him and, finally, surrounding him. In 1992, Caird reversed things, using the theatre's hydraulics to lower Cleopatra to Antony on the main stage; after his death, Roman soldiers descended from the flies on ropes, their invasion punctuated by offstage drum-rolls that often obscured her speeches. All of these stagings have the advantage of keeping actors safe even as they translate Shakespeare's directions for 'heav[ing] Antony aloft'.

Peter Hall came closest to that 'original' staging by lifting Hopkins's Antony in a huge net on to the set's upper level, where the women waited. Confined to a space that seemed too small to hold them, the lovers played out the 'death' of their grand romance, not on the main stage but at its margins, revealing the extent to which their world had shrunk.

Some scholars conjecture that a description of this scene as it was staged at the Globe survives in Samuel Daniel's *Tragedie of Cleopatra* (1607). In Daniel's play, Cleopatra 'draws [Antony] up in rowles of taffatie' – presumably thrown down from the upper stage or from a window. Further on, the passage tells how Charmian and Iras 'tugged at the pulley' and indicates two pauses (whether accidental or designed) in the lifting – 'the frame stood still, the body at a stay', and 'then again / It [came] to stay' – while Antony hung, 'showring out his blood / On th' under-lookers'.[14] As though bringing this description to life, the 1999 Globe staging used a pulley and suspended Antony in a sling, where he swung, a clumsy, awkward weight which exposed the theatre's machinery *as* machinery and caused a rupture in the action. Yet the difficulty of pure 'doing' engaged spectators' visceral attention as they willed Antony's body up. Although Cleopatra's 'How heavy weighs my lord!' drew outright laughter, the applause that followed Antony's successful 'raising'

Figure 6 Peter Brook's Shakespeare Memorial Theatre production of *Antony and Cleopatra*, 1978. Hauling Antony to the monument, 4.16. Glenda Jackson as Cleopatra, Alan Howard as Antony.

celebrated what had seemed, at least momentarily, a collaborative effort between actors and audience members. Whatever this staging demonstrated about the difficulties of the Globe's architecture, it certainly erased any idea of the 'boy actors' as anything other than muscular adolescents.

The potential laughter raised by the spectacle of Antony's death disappears from the play once Cleopatra's myth-making recreates him as another 'self', then turns herself (again pretending) into Caesar's abject subject and determines her own end. But it does not dissipate entirely. As though replaying Cleopatra's own comic routines, the Clown who brings the asp-basket delays her last, supreme performance, speaks of women's lying, and indulges in sexual puns. Richard Griffiths's red-nosed Clown (1978) waggled his shoes, miming asp-movement, and took a series of false exits which further deferred any sense that what was to come might be significant – or even tragic. At the Globe, Michael Rudko sat on Cleopatra's throne, chattering away, momentarily usurping the space where, in the next few moments, she would become wife, mother, goddess. Claiming the seat, and the right to ascend it, Rylance's Cleopatra, oddly Christ-like, kissed the Clown's feet before he left. Although literary critics regularly pick out Cleopatra's lines on how 'some squeaking Cleopatra [will] boy [her] greatness / I'th'posture of a whore' as the moment when her performance risks self-exposure, the ones that stood out at the Globe were 'My resolution's placed, and I have nothing / Of woman in me' (5.2).

Whereas Antony takes off his armour ('bruised pieces go'), Cleopatra, having revealed (and recostumed) herself as 'no more but e'en a woman' after Antony's death, now dresses up, staging herself as spectacle; then, further delaying and deferring her final moments of performance, she keeps talking. Suzman and Dench, transformed into golden idols, sat on (burnished) thrones; taking the asp from its basket, Dench laughed with pleasure at 'the worm', her last practical joke on Caesar. Jackson knelt upright, a shrine-like presence, and her voice measured words into a final whisper; when the lights went down, an after-image of her face remained, silhouetted against blackness. In 1998, Helen Mirren dropped the rough smock she had put on after Antony's death and for a moment stood naked before putting on royalty; like Dench, she welcomed the asp's bite as erotic fulfilment. Uniquely, de la Tour prepared for death quietly by staging a silent ritual. Having discarded her silk shift and her wig, she appeared in a monkish brown robe, a hairnet covering her head (fig. 7). Flanked by Charmian and Iras, she spread sand over a small carpet lit by candles, bathed her hands and her women's faces and necks; taking up a mirror, she painted her face, outlining her eyes with a kohl stick, applying lipstick and powder. Like *Madam Butterfly*'s brilliant impersonator or an Egyptian Norma Desmond preparing for her close-up,

Figure 7 Stephen Pimlott's 1999 production of *Antony and Cleopatra*, Shakespeare Memorial Theatre, with Frances de la Tour as Cleopatra, 5.2.

she staked out rights to her own performance, a consummate actor to the last. Then, after her women had shown her 'like a queen' in her 'best attires' and the last words had been spoken, she discarded her garments like a second skin and walked off, sometimes exposing one or both breasts and in some performances leaving the stage completely naked, her body exceeding costume.[15]

How Caesars respond to Cleopatra's death reads her performance into memory. Corin Redgrave (1972) was aloof, clinical; Jonathan Pryce (1978) gave crisp orders for burial and then, exiting, looked backward. Most often, Caesar's words – 'she looks like sleep, / As she would catch another Antony / In her strong toil of grace' (5.2.340–2) – gloss the image of Cleopatra as icon, stilled into a piece of performance art. The Folio's final stage direction, however, reads *Exeunt Omnes*. In Shakespeare's theatre, it was designed to clear the stage, making way for the jig which often followed performances or, in later years, for an afterpiece, often a comic interlude. To my knowledge, no present-day performance obeys it, yet Pimlott's staging, with its absent bodies, perhaps came closest. Following Cleopatra's and Charmian's deaths, the set's mirrored panels were flown out, revealing the plain brick wall of the theatre. Carried aloft in a chair to the rasp of military trumpets, blaring out his triumph, Caesar descends a long ramp to the tiny downstage mat to find only the fig basket, candles and Cleopatra's 'tires' – the theatrical leftovers of her performance. She herself has left the stage, if not the building, for she will return to take a curtain call – with Antony – a move that repositions them both as variable, contingent and open to further re-enactment. Although Caesar speaks of '*their* story', as though it were his to tell, Pimlott's staging denied him what Shakespeare's *Antony and Cleopatra* seems to afford him: the opportunity to put Cleopatra's body to his own political use, to write its history as his own.

Coda

On 22 October 2000, London's *Sunday Times* carried a front-page story about the British Museum's recent authentication of Cleopatra's signature on a scrap of papyrus that had lain for more than a century in a Berlin museum. It was not, as fantasy might desire, one of those letters Shakespeare's Cleopatra sends so fast, but a document granting one of Antony's powerful commanders a lucrative tax-break for his import–export business – evidence, perhaps, of her attempt to influence leading Romans in the struggle with Octavius Caesar. Written in Greek, it reads *genestho*: 'So be it' – an appropriate gloss for the performers who have sought to embody the elusive legacy of a powerful Egyptian queen.

NOTES

1. Barbara Hodgdon, 'Doing the Egyptian', *The Shakespeare Trade: Performances and Appropriations* (Philadelphia: University of Pennsylvania Press, 1998), pp. 81–94.
2. Michel Foucault, *The History of Sexuality*, vol. 1, trans. Robert Hurley (New York: Pantheon Books, 1978), p. 48.
3. Carol Chillington Rutter, '*Antony and Cleopatra*' in Performance, Arden*Online*, 1999. I am deeply indebted throughout to Rutter's fine introduction; at the time of writing, Arden's subscription-only website is no longer active. For details of performances, I also rely on my own viewing notes and on the press reviews of Royal Shakespeare Company stagings in *Theatre Records*, filed by year, at the Shakespeare Centre Library. See also Richard Madelaine, *Antony and Cleopatra*, Shakespeare in Production (Cambridge University Press, 1998).
4. Joseph Roach, *Cities of the Dead: Circum-Atlantic Performance* (New York: Columbia University Press, 1996), p. 3.
5. For a brilliant reading of this aspect of the play, see Linda Charnes, *Notorious Identity: Materializing the Subject in Shakespeare's Plays* (Cambridge, MA: Harvard University Press, 1993), pp. 103–47.
6. A. C. Bradley, 'Shakespeare's *Antony and Cleopatra*', 1906; rpt in *Oxford Lectures on Poetry* (London: Macmillan, 1965), pp. 279–308.
7. On Hall's staging, see Tirzah Lowen, *Peter Hall Directs 'Antony and Cleopatra'* (London: Methuen, 1990).

8. Rutter, '*Antony and Cleopatra*'.

9. Roach, *Cities of the Dead*, pp. 3–4.

10. Bert O. States, 'The Phenomenological Attitude', in *Critical Theory and Performance*, ed. Janelle G. Reinelt and Joseph R. Roach (Ann Arbor: University of Michigan Press, 1992), p. 374.

11. Charnes, *Notorious Identity*, p. 121.

12. Laurence Olivier, *On Acting* (New York: Simon and Schuster, 1986), pp. 162, 164.

13. Rutter, '*Antony and Cleopatra*'. See also Rutter, *Enter the Body: Women and Representation on Shakespeare's Stage* (London: Routledge, 2001), pp. 57–103.

14. Cited in Margaret Lamb, '*Antony and Cleopatra' on the English Stage* (London: Associated University Presses, 1980), p. 183.

15. Russell Jackson, 'Shakespeare at Stratford-upon-Avon: Summer and Winter, 1999–2000', *Shakespeare Quarterly* 51.2 (2000), 222.

Adelman, Janet, *Suffocating Mothers: Fantasies of Maternal Origin in Shakespeare's Plays, 'Hamlet' to 'The Tempest'* (New York and London: Routledge, 1992).
  The Common Liar: An Essay on 'Antony and Cleopatra' (New Haven: Yale University Press, 1973).
Allen, Michael J. B., and Kenneth Muir, eds., *Shakespeare's Plays in Quarto: A Facsimile Edition of Copies Primarily from the Henry E. Huntington Library* (Berkeley and Los Angeles: University of California Press, 1981).
Anderson, Linda Marie, *A Kind of Wild Justice: Revenge in Shakespeare's Comedies* (Newark: University of Delaware Press, 1987).
Andrews, Michael Cameron, '*Hamlet*: Revenge and the Critical Mirror', *English Literary Renaissance* 8 (1978): 9–23.
Axton, Marie, *The Queen's Two Bodies: Drama and the Elizabethan Succession* (London, 1977).
Ayres, Philip J., 'Degrees of Heresy: Justified Revenge and Elizabethan Narratives', *Studies in Philology* 69 (1972): 461–74.
Baldwin, T. W., *William Shakespere's Small Latine and Lesse Greeke*, 2 vols. (Urbana: University of Illinois Press, 1944).
Bate, Jonathan, ed., *The Romantics on Shakespeare* (London and New York: Penguin Books, 1992).
Bayley, John, *The Characters of Love* (London: Constable, 1960).
Belsey, Catherine, *Shakespeare and the Loss of Eden: The Construction of Family Values in Early Modern Culture* (London: Macmillan, 1999; New Brunswick, NJ: Rutgers University Press, 2000).
  The Subject of Tragedy: Identity and Difference in Renaissance Drama (London and New York: Routledge, 1985).
  'Tragedy, Justice and the Subject', *1642: Literature and Power in the Seventeenth Century*, ed. Francis Barker (Essex, 1981), pp. 166–86.
Bennett, Susan, *Performing Nostalgia: Shifting Shakespeare and the Contemporary Past* (London and New York: Routledge, 1996).
Bentley, Gerald Eades, *The Profession of Dramatist in Shakespeare's Time* (Princeton University Press, 1971).
Berger, Harry, Jr, 'Text against Performance: the Gloucester Family Romance', *Shakespeare's Rough Magic: Essays in Honor of C. L. Barber*, ed. Peter Erickson and Coppélia Kahn (Newark, NJ: University of Delaware Press, 1985).

Bevington, David, *Tudor Drama and Politics* (Cambridge, MA: Harvard University Press, 1968).

Blayney, Peter W. M., *The First Folio of Shakespeare* (Washington, DC: The Folger Shakespeare Library, 1991).

Booth, Stephen, *'King Lear', 'Macbeth', Indefinition, and Tragedy* (New Haven: Yale University Press, 1983).

Bowers, Fredson, *Elizabethan Revenge Tragedy, 1587–1642* (Princeton University Press, 1940).

Bradbrook, Muriel, *Themes and Conventions in Elizabethan Tragedy* (Cambridge University Press, 1960).

Braden, Gordon, *Renaissance Tragedy and the Senecan Tradition: Anger's Privilege* (New Haven and London: Yale University Press, 1985).

Bradley, A. C., *Oxford Lectures on Poetry* (London: Macmillan, (1909) rpt 1962).
  Shakespearean Tragedy: Lectures on 'Hamlet', 'Othello', 'King Lear', and 'Macbeth' (London: Macmillan, 1904; 2nd edn, 1905).

Brodwin, Leonora, *Elizabethan Love Tragedy, 1587–1625* (London and New York University Presses, 1971).

Broude, Ronald, 'Revenge and Revenge Tragedy in Renaissance England', *Renaissance Quarterly* 28 (1975): 38–58.

Brower, Reuben, *Hero and Saint: Shakespeare and the Graeco-Roman Heroic Tradition* (Oxford: Clarendon Press, 1971).

Burckhardt, Sigurd, 'How not to Murder Caesar', *Shakespearean Meanings* (Princeton University Press, 1968), p. 9.

Callaghan, Dympna, *Women and Gender in Renaissance Tragedy* (Atlantic Highlands, NJ: Harvester Wheatsheaf, 1989).

Campbell, Lily B., 'Theories of Revenge in Renaissance England', *Modern Philology* 28 (1931): 281–96.
  Shakespeare's Tragic Heroes: Slaves of Passion (Cambridge University Press, 1930).

Cavell, Stanley, *Disowning Knowledge in Six Plays of Shakespeare* (Cambridge University Press, 1987).

Chambers, E. K., *William Shakespeare: A Study of Facts and Problems*, 2 vols. (Oxford: Clarendon Press, 1930).

Charnes, Linda, *Notorious Identity: Materializing the Subject in Shakespeare's Plays* (Cambridge, MA: Harvard University Press, 1993).

Clemen, Wolfgang, *Shakespeare's Dramatic Art* (London: Methuen, 1972).

Coghill, Nevill, *Shakespeare's Professional Skills* (Cambridge University Press, 1964).

Cole, Susan, *The Absent One: Mourning Ritual, Tragedy, and the Performance of Ambivalence* (University Park: Pennsylvania State University Press, 1985).

Collinson, Patrick, *The Religion of Protestants: The Church in English Society, 1559–1625* (Oxford University Press, 1982).

Cox, John D., *Shakespeare and the Dramaturgy of Power* (Princeton University Press, 1989).

Crockett, Bryan, *The Play of Paradox: Stage and Sermon in Renaissance England* (Philadelphia: University of Pennsylvania Press, 1996).

Davies, Horton, *Worship and Theology in England from Cranmer to Hooker 1534–1603*, 5 vols. (Princeton University Press, 1970).

De Grazia, Margreta, *Shakespeare Verbatim: The Reproduction of Authenticity and the 1790 Apparatus* (Oxford: Clarendon Press, 1991).

Dickey, Franklin M., *Not Wisely But Too Well: Shakespeare's Love Tragedies* (San Marino, CA: Huntington Library, 1957).

Diehl, Huston, *Staging Reform, Reforming the Stage: Protestantism and Popular Theater in Early Modern Drama* (Ithaca, NY: Cornell University Press, 1997).

Dillon, Janette, 'Is There a Performance in this Text?', *Shakespeare Quarterly* 45 (1994): 74–86.

Dobson, Michael, *The Making of the National Poet: Shakespeare, Adaptation and Authorship, 1660–1769* (Oxford: Clarendon Press, 1992).

Dollimore, Jonathan, *Radical Tragedy: Religion, Ideology and Power in the Drama of Shakespeare and his Contemporaries* (Brighton: Harvester Press, 1984).

Doran, Madeleine, 'History and Tragedy', *Endeavors of Art: A Study of Form in Elizabethan Drama* (Madison, WI: University of Wisconsin Press, 1954).

Drakakis, John, ed., *Shakespearean Tragedy* (London: Longman, 1992).

Duffy, Eamon, *The Stripping of the Altars: Traditional Religion in England, c. 1400–1580* (New Haven: Yale University Press, 1992).

Elias, Norbert, *The Civilizing Process*, trans. Edmund Jephcott, 2 vols. (Oxford: Blackwell, 1982).

Ellis-Fermor, Una, 'The Equilibrium of Tragedy', *The Frontiers of Drama* (London: Methuen, 1948).

Elton, William R., *King Lear and the Gods* (San Marino, CA: Huntington Library, 1966).

Esler, Anthony, *The Aspiring Mind of the Elizabethan Younger Generation* (Durham, NC: University of North Carolina Press, 1966).

Fitz, Linda T., 'Egyptian Queens and Male Reviewers: Sexist Attitudes in *Antony and Cleopatra* Criticism', *Shakespeare Quarterly* 28 (1977): 217–316.

Foakes, R. A., '*Hamlet' Versus 'Lear': Cultural Politics and Shakespeare's Art* (Cambridge University Press, 1993).

Fowler, Alistair, *Kinds of Literature: An Introduction to the Theory of Genres and Modes* (Oxford: Clarendon Press, 1982).

Frye, Northrop, *Anatomy of Criticism* (London: Penguin, 1957).

Frye, Roland Mushat, *Shakespeare: The Art of the Dramatist* (London: Allen and Unwin, 1982).

Gardiner, Helen, *Shakespeare and Religion* (London: Faber, 1971).

Garner, Shirley Nelson, and Madelon Sprengnether, eds., *Shakespearean Tragedy and Gender* (Bloomington: Indiana University Press, 1996).

Gillies, John, *Shakespeare and the Geography of Difference* (Cambridge University Press, 1994).

Girard, René, *Violence and the Sacred*, trans. Patrick Gregory (Baltimore, MD: Johns Hopkins University Press, 1977).

Goldberg, Jonathan, *James I and the Politics of Literature: Jonson, Shakespeare, Donne and Their Contemporaries* (Baltimore: Johns Hopkins University Press, 1983).

Grady, Hugh, *The Modernist Shakespeare* (Oxford: Clarendon Press, 1991).

Graham, Kenneth J. E., *The Performance of Conviction: Plainness and Rhetoric in the Early English Renaissance* (Ithaca, NY: Cornell University Press, 1994).

Green, Douglas E., 'Interpreting "Her Martyr'd Signs": Gender and Tragedy in *Titus Andronicus*', *Shakespeare Quarterly* 40 (1989): 317–26.

Greenblatt, Stephen, *Shakespearean Negotiations: The Circulation of Social Energy in Renaissance England* (Berkeley: University of California Press, 1988).
   Renaissance Self-Fashioning from More to Shakespeare (Chicago University Press, 1980).
Greg, W. W., *The Shakespeare First Folio: Its Bibliographical and Textual History* (Oxford: Clarendon Press, 1955).
   The Editorial Problem in Shakespeare, 3rd edn (Oxford: Clarendon Press, 1954).
Griswold, Wendy, *Renaissance Revivals: City Comedy and Revenge Tragedy in the London Theatre, 1576–1980* (University of Chicago Press, 1986).
Gurr, Andrew, *The Shakespearean Stage*, 3rd edn (Cambridge University Press, 1992).
Hall, Kim F., *Things of Darkness: Economies of Race and Gender in Early Modern England* (Ithaca, NY: Cornell University Press, 1995).
Hallett, Charles, and Elaine S. Hallett, *The Revenger's Madness: A Study of Revenge Tragedy Motifs* (Lincoln: University of Nebraska Press, 1980).
Hanna, Sara, 'Shakespeare's Greek World: the Temptations of the Sea', *Playing the Globe: Genre and Geography in Renaissance Drama*, ed. John Gillies and Virginia Mason Vaughan (Madison: Fairleigh Dickinson University Press, 1998), pp. 107–28.
Harbage, Alfred, *Twentieth-Century Views of Shakespeare's Tragedies* (Englewood Cliffs, NJ: Prentice-Hall, 1964).
   Hegel on Tragedy, ed. Anne and Henry Paolucci (New York: Harper and Row, 1975).
Henn, T. R., *The Harvest of Tragedy* (London: Methuen, 1956).
Hibbard, G. R., '*King Lear*: a Retrospect', *Shakespeare Survey* 33 (1980): 1–12.
Hillman, David, 'Visceral Knowledge: Shakespeare, Skepticism, and the Interior of the Early Modern Body', *The Body in Parts: Fantasies of Corporeality in Early Modern England*, ed. David Hillman and Carla Mazzio (New York and London: Routledge, 1997), pp. 81–105.
Hinman, Charlton, *The Printing and Proof-Reading of the First Folio of Shakespeare*, 2 vols. (Oxford: Clarendon Press, 1963).
Hinman, Charlton, ed., *The Norton Facsimile: The First Folio of Shakespeare*, 2nd edn, intro. by Peter W. M. Blayney (New York: W. W. Norton, 1996).
Hodgdon, Barbara, 'Doing the Egyptian', *The Shakespeare Trade: Performances and Appropriations* (Philadelphia: University of Pennsylvania Press, 1998), pp. 81–94.
Homan, Sidney, *Shakespeare's Theater of Presence* (Lewisburg: University of Kentucky Press, 1986).
Honigmann, E. A. J., *The Stability of Shakespeare's Text* (London: Edward Arnold, 1965).
Howard, Jean E., *Shakespeare's Art of Orchestration* (Urbana: University of Illinois Press, 1984).
Hunter, G. K., 'The Heroism of Hamlet', *Hamlet*, ed. J. R. Brown and Bernard Harris (Stratford-upon-Avon Studies, 5; London: Arnold, 1963).
Hunter, Robert Grams, *Shakespeare and the Comedy of Forgiveness* (New York: Columbia University Press, 1965).
Ioppolo, Grace, *Revising Shakespeare* (Cambridge, MA: Harvard University Press, 1991).

Jacoby, Susan, *Wild Justice: The Evolution of Revenge* (New York: Harper & Row, 1983).

Jones, Emrys, *Scenic Form in Shakespeare* (Oxford: Clarendon Press, 1971).

Jones, Ernest, *Hamlet and Oedipus*, rev. edn (New York: Doubleday, 1949, 1954).

Jones, John, *On Aristotle and Greek Tragedy* (Stanford University Press, 1962).

Jowett, John, 'After Oxford: Recent Developments in Textual Studies', *The Shakespearean International Yearbook*, ed. W. R. Elton and John M. Mucciolo (Aldershot: Ashgate, 1999), pp. 65–86.

Kahn, Coppélia, ' "Magic of Bounty": *Timon of Athens*, Jacobean Patronage, and Maternal Power', *Shakespeare Quarterly* 38, 1 (Spring 1987): 34–57.

Kastan, David Scott, ' "His Semblable Is His Mirror": Hamlet and the Imitation of Revenge', *Shakespeare Studies* 19 (1987): 111–24.

Shakespeare and the Shapes of Time (Hanover, NH: University Press of New England, 1982).

Kerrigan, John, *Revenge Tragedy: Aeschylus to Armageddon* (New York: Oxford University Press, 1996).

Keyishian, Harry, *The Shapes of Revenge: Victimization, Vengeance, and Vindictiveness in Shakespeare* (New Jersey: Humanities Press, 1995).

King, John N., *Tudor Royal Iconography* (Princeton University Press, 1989).

Kirsch, Arthur C., *The Passions of Shakespeare's Tragic Heroes* (Charlottesville: University Press of Virginia, 1990).

Kyd, Thomas, *The Spanish Tragedy*, ed. Philip Edwards (London: Methuen, 1959).

Lamb, Margaret, *Antony and Cleopatra on the English Stage* (London: Associated University Presses, 1980).

Leech, Clifford, *Tragedy* (London: Methuen, 1969).

Leggatt, Alexander, *Shakespeare's Political Drama: The History Plays and the Roman Plays* (London: Routledge, 1988).

Lever, J. W., *The Tragedy of State* (London, 1971).

Levin, Harry, *The Overreacher* (Cambridge, MA: Harvard University Press, 1952).

Limon, Jerzy, 'Revenge Tragedy, or, A Decayed Form – A Review Essay', *Southern Humanities Review* 16 (1982): 257–67.

Loomba, Ania, 'Shakespeare and Cultural Difference', *Alternative Shakespeares* 2, ed. Terence Hawkes (London: Routledge, 1996).

Lucas, F. L., *Tragedy in Relation to Aristotle's Poetics* (London: Hogarth Press, 1927).

Mack, Maynard, 'The World of *Hamlet*', *Yale Review*, new series, 41 (1951–2): 515.

Maguire, Laurie E., *Shakespearean Suspect Texts* (Cambridge University Press, 1996).

Mahood, M. M., *Shakespeare's Wordplay* (London: Methuen, 1957).

Marsden, Jean I., *The Re-imagined Text: Shakespeare, Adaptation, and Eighteenth-Century Literary Theory* (Lexington: University Press of Kentucky, 1995).

Marshall, Cynthia, 'Man of Steel Done Got the Blues: Melancholic Subversion of Presence in *Antony and Cleopatra*', *Shakespeare Quarterly* 44 (1993): 385–408.

Mason, H. A., *Shakespeare's Tragedies of Love* (London: Chatto and Windus, 1970).

Maus, Katharine Eisaman, *Inwardness and Theater in the English Renaissance* (Chicago and London: University of Chicago Press, 1995).

McAlindon, T., 'Cultural Materialism and the Ethics of Reading: or, the Radicalizing of Jacobean Tragedy', *The Modern Language Review* 90 (1995): 830–46.

'Tragedy, *King Lear*, and the Politics of the Heart', *Shakespeare Survey* 44 (1992): 85–90.

Shakespeare's Tragic Cosmos (Cambridge University Press, 1991).

McEachern, Claire, *The Poetics of English Nationhood, 1590–1612* (Cambridge University Press, 1996).

McEachern, Claire and Debora Shuger, eds., *Religion and Culture in Renaissance England* (Cambridge University Press, 1997).

McElroy, Bernard, *Shakespeare's Mature Tragedies* (Princeton University Press, 1973).

Mehl, Dieter, *Shakespeare's Tragedies: An Introduction* (Cambridge University Press, 1986).

Mercer, Peter, *Hamlet and the Acting of Revenge* (University of Iowa Press).

Miles, Gary B., 'How Roman are Shakespeare's "Romans"?', *Shakespeare Quarterly* 41, 3 (Fall, 1989): 257–83.

Miola, Robert S., *Shakespeare and Classical Tragedy: the Influence of Seneca* (Oxford: Clarendon Press, 1992).

Shakespeare's Rome (Cambridge University Press, 1983).

Montrose, Louis, *The Purpose of Playing: Shakespeare and the Cultural Politics of the Elizabethan Theatre* (Chicago University Press, 1996).

Muir, Kenneth, *Shakespeare's Tragic Sequence* (London: Methuen, 1972).

Nevo, Ruth, *Tragic Form in Shakespeare* (Princeton University Press, 1972).

Newman, Karen, 'Cultural Capital's Gold Standard: Shakespeare and the Critical Apostrophe in Renaissance Studies', *Discontinuities: New Essays in Renaissance Literature and Criticism*, ed. Viviana Comensoli and Paul Stevens (University of Toronto Press, 1998), pp. 96–113.

Nietzsche, Friedrich, *'The Birth of Tragedy' and 'The Genealogy of Morals'*, trans. Francis Golffing (New York: Doubleday, 1956).

Orgel, Stephen, 'Nobody's Perfect: or, Why Did the English Stage Take Boys for Women?', *South Atlantic Quarterly* 88 (1989): 7–29.

'The Authentic Shakespeare', *Representations* 21 (1988): 1–25.

Orgel, Stephen, and Sean Keilen, eds., *Shakespeare and the Editorial Tradition* (New York: Garland, 1999).

Ozment, Steven, *When Fathers Ruled: Family Life in Reformation Europe* (Cambridge, MA: Harvard University Press, 1983).

The Age of Reform 1250–1550 (New Haven: Yale University Press, 1980).

Parker, Kenneth, *William Shakespeare: Antony and Cleopatra* (Tavistock: Northcote House, 2000).

Parker, Patricia and Geoffrey Hartman, eds., *Shakespeare and the Question of Theory* (London: Methuen, 1985).

Paster, Gail Kern, *The Idea of the City in the Age of Shakespeare* (Athens: University of Georgia Press, 1985).

Patterson, Annabel, *Shakespeare and the Popular Voice* (Oxford University Press, 1989).

Prosser, Eleanor, *Hamlet and Revenge*, 2nd edn (Stanford University Press, 1971).

Puttenham, George, *The Arte of English Poesie* (1589), ed. G. D. Willcock and A. Walker (Cambridge University Press, 1936).

Rabkin, Norman, *Shakespeare and the Common Understanding* (New York: Free Press, 1967).

Rackin, Phyllis, 'Shakespeare's Boy Cleopatra, the Decorum of Nature, and the Golden World of Poetry', *PMLA* 87 (1972): 201–12.

Rebhorn, Wayne A., 'The Crisis of the Aristocracy in *Julius Caesar*', *Renaissance Quarterly* 43, 1 (Spring, 1990): 75–111.

Richards, I. A., *Principles of Literary Criticism* (London: Routledge, 1926).

Rose, Mark, *Shakespearean Design* (Cambridge, MA: Belknap Press of Harvard University Press, 1972).

Rosenmeyer, Thomas G., *Senecan Drama and Stoic Cosmology* (Berkeley, Los Angeles, and London: University of California Press, 1989).

Rossiter, A. P., *Angel with Horns: Fifteen Lectures on Shakespeare* (London: Hutchinson, 1961).

Rozett, Martha Tuck, *The Doctrine of Election and the Emergence of Elizabethan Tragedy* (Princeton University Press, 1984).

Rutter, Carol Chillington, *Enter the Body: Women and Representation on Shakespeare's Stage* (London: Routledge, 2001).

Schoenfeldt, Michael C., *Bodies and Selves in Early Modern England: Physiology and Inwardness in Spenser, Shakespeare, Herbert, and Milton* (Cambridge University Press, 1999).

Schwartz, Murray and Coppélia Kahn, eds., *Representing Shakespeare: New Psychoanalytic Essays* (Baltimore: Johns Hopkins University Press, 1980).

Seneca, *Four Tragedies and 'Octavia'*, trans. E. F. Watling (London: Penguin, 1966).

Shuger, Debora, *Habits of Thought in the English Renaissance: Religion, Politics, and the Dominant Culture* (Berkeley: University of California Press, 1990).

Sibly, John, 'The Duty of Revenge in Tudor and Stuart Drama', *Review of English Literature* 8 (1967): 46–54.

Sidney, Sir Philip, *An Apology for Poetry* (1595), ed. Geoffrey Shepherd (London: Nelson, 1965).

Siegel, Paul N., ' "Hamlet, Revenge": The Uses and Abuses of Historical Criticism', *Shakespeare Survey* 45 (1993): 15–26.

Siemon, James R., *Shakespearean Iconoclasm* (Berkeley: University of California Press, 1985).

Simpson, Percy, 'The Theme of Revenge in Elizabethan Tragedy', *Proceedings of the British Academy* 21 (London: Humphrey Milford, 1935).

Singh, Jyotsna, 'Renaissance Antitheatricality, Antifeminism, and Shakespeare's *Antony and Cleopatra*', *Renaissance Drama* 20 (1989): 99–121.

Smith, Bruce. *Shakespeare and Masculinity* (Oxford University Press, 2000).

Homosexual Desire in Shakespeare's England: A Cultural Poetics (University of Chicago Press, 1991).

Spencer, T. J. B., ' "Greeks" and "Merrygreeks": a Background to *Timon of Athens* and *Troilus and Cressida*', *Essays on Shakespeare and Elizabethan Drama in Honor of Hardin Craig*, ed. Richard Hosley (Columbia: University of Missouri Press, 1962), pp. 223–33.

'Shakespeare and the Elizabethan Romans', *Shakespeare Survey* 10 (1957): 27–38.

Spurgeon, Caroline, *Shakespeare's Imagery and What it Tells Us* (1935; rpt Boston: Beacon Hill Press, 1958).

Szonyi, György E., and Rowland Wymer, eds., *The Iconography of Power: Ideas and Images of Rulership on the English Renaissance Stage* (Szeged: JATE Press, 2000).

Taylor, Gary, and Michael Warren, eds., *The Division of the Kingdoms* (Oxford: Clarendon Press, 1983).

Thompson, Marvin, and Ruth Thompson, eds., *Shakespeare and the Sense of Performance* (Newark: University of Delaware Press, 1990).

Urkowitz, Steven, *Shakespeare's Revision of 'King Lear'* (Princeton University Press, 1980).

Vickers, Brian, *Appropriating Shakespeare: Contemporary Critical Quarrels* (New Haven and London: Yale University Press, 1993).

Shakespeare: The Critical Heritage, 6 vols. (London: Routledge, 1974).

Waith, Eugene M., *Ideas of Greatness: Heroic Drama in England* (London: Hutchinson, 1971).

Watson, Robert N., *Shakespeare and the Hazards of Ambition* (Cambridge, MA: Harvard University Press, 1984).

Wayne, Valerie, ed., *The Matter of Difference: Materialist Feminist Criticism of Shakespeare* (Ithaca, NY, and London: Cornell University Press, 1991).

Wells, Robin Headlam, *Shakespeare, Politics and the State* (Basingstoke: Macmillan, 1986).

Wells, Stanley, *Re-Editing Shakespeare for the Modern Reader* (Oxford: Clarendon Press, 1984).

Wells, Stanley, ed., *The Cambridge Companion to Shakespeare Studies* (Cambridge University Press, 1986).

Werstine, Paul, 'A Century of "Bad" Shakespeare Quartos', *Shakespeare Quarterly* 50 (1999): 310–33.

'Narratives about Printed Shakespeare Texts: "Foul Papers" and "Bad" Quartos', *Shakespeare Quarterly* 41 (1990): 67–86.

Wheeler, Richard P., *Shakespeare's Development and the Problem Comedies: Turn and Counter-Turn* (Berkeley: University of California Press, 1981).

White, Paul, *Theatre and Reformation* (Cambridge University Press, 1993).

Williams, Raymond, *Modern Tragedy* (London: Chatto and Windus, 1966).

Wright, George T., *Shakespeare's Metrical Art* (Berkeley and Los Angeles: University of California Press, 1988).

INDEX

CAMBRIDGE COMPANIONS TO LITERATURE